Grouchy's Waterloo

Grouchy's Waterloo

The Battles of Ligny and Wavre

ANDREW W. FIELD

Pen & Sword
MILITARY

First published in Great Britain in 2017 by
Pen and Sword Military
an imprint of
Pen and Sword Books Ltd
47 Church Street
Barnsley
South Yorkshire S70 2AS

Copyright © Andrew W. Field, 2017

ISBN 978 147385 652 3

The right of Andrew W. Field to be identified as the author
of this work has been asserted by him in accordance
with the Copyright, Designs and Patents Act 1988.

A CIP record for this book is available from the British Library

All rights reserved. No part of this book may be reproduced or
transmitted in any form or by any means, electronic or
mechanical including photocopying,
recording, or by any information storage and retrieval system
without permission from the Publisher in writing.

Printed and bound in Malta
by Gutenberg Press Ltd

Typeset in Ehrhardt by Chic Graphics

Pen & Sword Books Ltd incorporates the imprints of
Pen & Sword Archaeology, Atlas, Aviation, Battleground, Discovery,
Family History, History, Maritime, Military, Naval, Politics, Railways,
Select, Social History, Transport, True Crime, Claymore Press,
Frontline Books, Leo Cooper, Praetorian Press, Remember When,
Seaforth Publishing and Wharncliffe.

For a complete list of Pen and Sword titles please contact
Pen and Sword Books Limited
47 Church Street, Barnsley, South Yorkshire, S70 2AS, England
E-mail: enquiries@pen-and-sword.co.uk
Website: www.pen-and-sword.co.uk

Contents

List of Maps..vi
List of Plates..vii

Introduction 1
Chapter 1   Preliminaries 7
Chapter 2   14 June 21
Chapter 3   Morning, 15 June 32
Chapter 4   Afternoon, 15 June...46
Chapter 5   The Night of 15/16 June 57
Chapter 6   Morning, 16 June 68
Chapter 7   Prelude to Ligny 87
Chapter 8   The Battle of Ligny..98
Chapter 9   The Night of 16/17 June 148
Chapter 10   Morning, 17 June 162
Chapter 11   Afternoon, 17 June...179
Chapter 12   The Night of 17/18 June 190
Chapter 13   Morning, 18 June 198
Chapter 14   Afternoon, 18 June: The Battle of Wavre 215
Chapter 15   The Night of 18/19 June 235
Chapter 16   Morning, 19 June 240
Chapter 17   Analysis and Conclusion 253

Orders of Battle...278
Notes 295
Select Bibliography..311
Index 315

List of Maps

Map 1: Campaign map 13
Map 2: Morning, 15 June 34
Map 3: Afternoon, 15 June 49
Map 4: Morning, 16 June 70
Map 5: Morning, 16 June (2). 82
Map 6: St. Amand..100
Map 7: Pajol and Namur 164
Map 8: Afternoon, 17 June 182
Map 9: Morning, 18 June 201
Map 10: Morning, 18 June (2) 210
Map 11: Wavre, 18 and 19 June 228

List of Plates

Colour
The Combat at Gilly.
The Battle of Ligny, 16 June 1815: Initial Deployment.
The Battle of Ligny.
The Battle of Wavre, 18 and 18 June 1816.
The Battle of Wavre.

Black & White
The Emperor Napoleon.
Marshal Grouchy.
Marshal Soult.
General Vandamme.
General Gérard.
General Pajol.
General Exelmans.
General d'Erlon.
General Girard.
General Letort.
General Bourmont.
General Subervie.
General Domon.
General Habert.
General Berthzène.
General Vichery.
Field Marshal Blücher.
General von Thielemann.
A modern photo of the Naveau mill.
The farm d'en Haut today.
The farm of d'en Bas.
The farm at Walhain where Grouchy famously ate his strawberries.
The Dyle river.
The farm of la Bourse.
A print of the battle of Ligny.
An old print of the Bridge of Christ at Wavre.
An old map (1769) of the town of Wavre.

Ask one hundred Frenchmen; who was Grouchy?
At least sixty would reply, 'A general who betrayed Napoleon at Waterloo.'
Why? Because in France, any lost game, political or military, requires one or more traitors and a scapegoat.
>	Commandant Henry Lachouque, *Le Secret de Waterloo*.

It is obvious that Providence had condemned us and that it had chosen Marshal Grouchy to punish us!
>	M.A. Thiers, *Waterloo*.

The loss of the battle first lies mainly of the great lethargy of Grouchy and his failure to execute my orders.
I would have won that battle without the imbecility of Grouchy.
>	Napoleon to Barry O'Meara on St Helena.

Introduction

This book is not specifically about the battle of Waterloo, perhaps the most written-about battle in history. It is about some of the other actors and actions of the Waterloo campaign which led to Napoleon's devastating defeat at that battle.

The book continues my planned series covering the whole of the Waterloo campaign written primarily from the French perspective with the aim of balancing the overwhelming number of Anglo-centric accounts. This edition complements my two previous volumes, *Waterloo, The French Perspective* and *Prelude to Waterloo; Quatre Bras*. All three books draw heavily on French documents, official reports, primarily eyewitness accounts and memoirs of French soldiers and officers, many of which have not been previously available in English. The aim has not just been to give an account of the campaign through the eyes of the French military, but also to analyse the performance of the key French commanders.

My book on Quatre Bras looked at Marshal Ney's performance in detail and analysed to what extent Napoleon's criticisms of him were justified. It also explored the extent to which Napoleon himself was to blame. In this book, I will look at the performance of Marshal Grouchy and the army's right wing that he commanded, by following its marches and actions. Having been sent by Napoleon to pursue the Prussian army, defeated by the emperor at the battle of Ligny, Grouchy's actions and decisions have been the subject of intense scrutiny by French military historians and critics ever since.

This book is not primarily a critical analysis of Grouchy's part in the campaign. My main aim has been to provide as accurate a picture of what actually happened as possible, basing my narrative on the accounts of those who were there. First-hand accounts must always be treated with some suspicion as there are many reasons why they may not be wholly accurate; a personal grudge against one or other of the major participants, a faulty memory for those that wrote later in life, a need to enhance a personal reputation, jingoism or to support the position of another. Certainly many, if not all, writers in this drama are guilty of one or more of these 'crimes'. Despite this health warning, the accounts do agree on much detail and start to contradict each other only where the main controversies arise. I have tried to keep the more detailed discussion on these key controversies to a chapter at the end of the book so as not to interrupt the flow of the narrative too much.

Although it is common knowledge that Grouchy did not fight at Waterloo, it is to his newest marshal that Napoleon attributes his defeat by his failure to arrive on that battlefield and to swing the action back in his favour. In exile, Napoleon is quoted as saying, 'I would have won that battle without the imbecility of Grouchy'.[1] It is for this reason that French history condemns Grouchy and blames him for the emperor's downfall, largely influenced by Napoleon's own accounts of the campaign. Whether Grouchy truly deserves this blame is what motivated him and his descendants to write prolifically in his defence. Regrettably, although Napoleon's integrity in his own accounts of the campaign has been challenged by many historians, Grouchy's accounts proved to be less than wholly consistent at best, and dishonest at worst, and this has seriously undermined his case. Even Charras, who wrote an anti-Bonaparte analysis of the campaign, commented, 'He [Grouchy] has not always been very exact, or very sincere.'[2]

The scale of France's humiliation, and Napoleon's in particular, has inevitably been the topic of many books and polarised French popular opinion into two distinct groups; those anti-Bonapartists who exclusively blamed Napoleon for the defeat and those many supporters of Napoleon who were prepared to blame anyone but him for the catastrophe. The restoration of the Bourbon monarchy after Napoleon's second abdication inevitably generated a climate which did not encourage the publication of memoirs and accounts of the campaign by those who took part in it. Ironically, therefore, it was Napoleon, unrestrained by this reticence in his exile on St Helena, who was first[3] to give a French account through the publication in 1818 of *The Campaign of 1815*.[4] This book, written by General Gourgaud, Napoleon's senior *officier d'ordonnance* during the campaign, is widely accepted to have been either dictated by Napoleon or (more likely) based on the conversations these two had during their exile on St Helena. The reaction to this book was predictable, not least because Napoleon blames his two key lieutenants during the campaign, Grouchy and Ney, for the defeat.

Grouchy and his family were certainly prolific writers on this campaign. Their aim was to try and restore a reputation that had been tarnished by the two accounts dictated by Napoleon in exile on St Helena and subsequent writings of other historians and critics, based on those accounts. Napoleon's criticism had clearly cut deeply, and this criticism was repeated in the many accounts by the emperor's admirers and apologists that followed. Thus many officers that fought in the campaign were quick to take up Napoleon's criticism of Grouchy (and Ney) and to weave them into their own works. Thus the image of Grouchy being responsible for the defeat was reinforced.

As Gourgaud's account was one of the earliest of those published, it was perhaps inevitable that this should serve as the starting point for many that followed it. It is not therefore surprising that Grouchy was quick to respond; his *Observations sur la Relation de la Campagne de 1815* appeared in 1818, despite not having access to his personal papers and correspondence due to his exile in the United States. These papers included the *Registre d'ordre et de correspondance du major-général* (Register of Orders and Correspondence of the *major-général*, as the army chief-of-staff was known) that had remained in his possession at the end of the campaign. Without these references it is perhaps forgivable that a number of errors crept into his works, but these were seized on by his critics to undermine his arguments. Unfortunately, his dependability as a witness was further significantly weakened when he consistently denied that he had received any written orders from Napoleon in regards to his pursuit, only for a copy to later emerge which contained details that further undermined his veracity. A full study of his writings reveals seemingly small, but significant, amendments that appear to have been made solely to reinforce his position.

Grouchy's writings were supplemented by those of his son, who authored a summary of his father's activities from 16 to 19 June 1815 that was published in 1864,[5] and by his grandson, who published five volumes of his grandfather's memoirs in 1873–4 which featured this campaign in detail and sought to further refute the accusations made against him. These in fact were not Grouchy's memoirs at all, but the publication of much of his correspondence, interspersed by a narrative of events written by his grandson. The fifth volume of Grouchy's memoirs, in particular, directly challenged accounts and accusations made in a number of later publications, as well as those directly influenced by Napoleon himself.

However, Napoleon was not the only one to blame others for his own shortcomings; Grouchy himself, although clearly stung by the emperor's criticism, did not shrink from using the same tactics. He shifted the blame for some of the criticisms levelled against him on his own two key subordinates, Generals Vandamme and Gérard, writing in *Observations*,

> . . . the manifest dissatisfaction that had developed in this general officer [Vandamme], as well as in General Gérard, their mutual jealousies of the command that had been entrusted to me, the tardy and incomplete obedience of them both and their pretensions that shook my constant and boundless patience and forbearance that was so little appreciated by them since it made them weak, overwhelming me with bitterness and disgust and effectively threatening the success of my operations.[6]

It is almost certainly true that both Vandamme and Gérard believed that they should have been made marshals for this campaign, and both displayed some anger at not being awarded the honour for the hard fighting of their corps at the battle of Ligny. Gérard had certainly been identified by Napoleon as a future marshal,[7] but we cannot be sure whether the emperor held the same opinion of Vandamme. Although this general had a reputation as a hard fighter, he also had a track record as a very difficult subordinate, had insulted Napoleon's brother Jérôme on many occasions under his command in 1809 and had a less well-earned, but firm, reputation as a plunderer. But nor were these two otherwise highly-regarded generals the only ones who fell foul of Grouchy's pen; other subordinates, corps and divisional commanders, also came in for more or less criticism.

My aim with this book has been not to get drawn deeply into the controversy surrounding Grouchy's performance during the campaign, but to present an interpretation as close to the truth as can be established based on the evidence that is available. Many books have been written on the conspiracy theories and accusations of treason and incompetence that surround this campaign. I therefore leave this mainly to others listed in the bibliography, although I do raise a number of them in the last chapter for those who are interested.

Napoleon is credited with two accounts of the Waterloo campaign, although it seems he only authored one. The first to be published was *The Campaign of 1815 or, a Narrative of the Military Operations which took place in France and Belgium during the Hundred Days*,[8] which we have already mentioned. The other account is accepted as having been dictated by Napoleon to another of his fellow exiles, General Bertrand, and published as part of Napoleon's memoirs.[9] These two accounts were written without reference to any documents or correspondence and we must assume they were dictated from memory. It is therefore not surprising that they contain a number of verifiable errors. His detractors, both contemporary and modern, have also been quick to accuse him of selective memory and out-and-out lies, recorded to protect his own reputation and deflect criticism onto others, primarily Ney and Grouchy. It is fair to say that in relation to the actions of Grouchy, Napoleon's memoirs cannot be depended on as a true and balanced record of events.

Neither Soult nor Vandamme wrote accounts of the campaign and thus we do not have their vital perspectives which might give more clarity to events. We do have copies of at least some of Soult's despatches, but it is clear that not all correspondence from Imperial Headquarters was included in the *Registre*. Vandamme's correspondence is available, but the account published with his correspondence appears to be written by another. A number of Vandamme's officers did write accounts, however, which help to explain his actions and describe the exploits of his troops.

Gérard initially decided not to get drawn into the very public spats that followed Napoleon's accounts and Ney's and Grouchy's challenges. However, as the various accounts, accusations, challenges and 'remarks' were published, so some of his old staff officers encouraged him to make his own contribution and demanded he defend not just his own reputation, but also that of his troops. Gérard did not publish an account of the campaign, but rather, like Ney's son who wrote in his father's defence, he published two pamphlets challenging the various charges that Grouchy levelled against him and his corps. *Quelques Documens sur la Bataille de Waterloo, Propres à Éclairer la Question Portée devant le Public par M. le Marquis de Grouchy* (published in 1829) and *Dernières Observations sur les Opérations de l'Aile Droite de l'Armée Francaise a la Bataille de Waterloo en*

Response à M. le Marquis de Grouchy (published in 1830) specifically addressed the charges laid against IV Corps and its commander by Grouchy, but also attempted to justify the value of his celebrated advice to 'march to the sound of the guns'. In these short pamphlets (fifty-nine and sixty-three pages respectively), Gérard also published testimony from a number of his staff and key commanders in support of his defence. These have been incorporated into my own narrative where appropriate, but like many accounts of the campaign, we must remember that many of them were written specifically to support one clique or the other and will inevitably be somewhat biased.

Much of this 'evidence' almost inevitably contradicts each other and the whole contributes to a tangled web of claim and counter-claim that leads to the conclusion that we shall probably never get to the whole truth. The best that we can do is to judge each piece of evidence on its merits, corroborate it where possible, judge the motivations of the witness or author and try to apply what is often called inherent military probability, to try and interpret where the balance of the evidence lies. Importantly too, we should follow Clausewitz's advice, in using the benefit of hindsight to analyse what went wrong, rather than to criticise;

> We need not point out here that, with battle plans and all sorts of retrospective accounts in front of us, and with the events behind us, it is very easy to discover the actual causes of failure and, after thoroughly considering all the complexities of events, to highlight those things that can be deemed mistakes. But all of this cannot be done so easily at the time of action. The conduct of war is like movement in a resistant medium, in which uncommon qualities are required to achieve even mediocre results. It is for this reason that in war, more than in any other area, critical analysis exists only to discover the truth, not to sit in judgement.[10]

I have endeavoured, as far as possible, to tell the story of the campaign through the eyes (or more accurately the pens) of those who took part in it with the exaggeration, inconsistencies and errors that this inevitably introduces. What analysis there is, is my own, but I have also tried to present the accounts of both sides of any argument, so that readers can make up their own minds. Having said that, in keeping with my books on the other aspects and battles of this campaign, I have unapologetically offered a strictly French perspective of the campaign, as others, many from the British/Hanoverian/Netherlands perspective, and Peter Hofschröer's from the Prussian perspective, have already covered the detail from these other nations' accounts.

The truth is that most, if not all accounts of this campaign are a complex and contradictory web of lies, misinformation, vindictiveness, deceit, jealousy and treachery, designed to support one or other of the many individual and national agendas that were in play.

Notes

Although I covered the opening of the campaign in my Quatre Bras book, albeit with the emphasis on the left wing of the army, I have felt compelled to cover it again with the emphasis on the right wing. D'Erlon's appearance and disappearance at Ligny was also covered. As I cannot assume that everyone has read my previous offerings there is inevitably a small amount of repetition and I apologise in advance for this.

Finally, we should identify some rules that I have applied to my narrative that should clarify some points which might otherwise cause confusion. All French first-hand accounts use 'league' and '*toise*' as units of distance. A league is a very old measure of distance and was defined as how far you could march in an hour. This of course has many variations that can be built into it, and the more modern equivalent often varied from country to country. In France the distance varied from century to century; some sources give it as close to five kilometres, but in modern parlance it is generally taken as four kilometres. A *toise*, used for much smaller distances, was just under two metres until 1812, when it was rounded up to exactly two metres.

In most armies of the Napoleonic Wars, divisions of different nations were loosely of the same size and composition; two to six or so battalions formed into two or three brigades, with an attached battery or two of artillery. However, in the Prussian army, there were no brigades of the same type as the ones in a French division, for example, and a divisional-sized formation consisted of a number of regiments, each generally of three or four battalions, and a battery of artillery, although it was not unusual to also have a cavalry regiment under command. This Prussian organisation was called a brigade. Thus throughout this book a Prussian brigade should be considered as roughly the same size as a French or British division.

Throughout the empire, a French divisional commander's rank was *général de division*, and a brigade commander, *général de brigade*. After the first restoration of the monarchy in 1815, these ranks were changed to *lieutenant-général* and *maréchal de camp* respectively. On Napoleon's return in 1815, given the short time available to re-organise the army, it was decided to retain these new ranks rather than to return to the previous, more familiar ones.

To avoid any confusion between infantry and cavalry corps, I have used roman numerals, I, II etc, for army corps and the traditional 1st, 2nd etc, for cavalry corps.

In the many accounts of this campaign, there are many different spellings of the same place name. Some are very similar, but some can be quite different. In order to avoid confusion, I have spelled place names consistently throughout the book, to the point of changing the spelling in quoted first-hand accounts to avoid this possible confusion. To the purists among you, I apologise profusely, but feel this is the right thing to do, particularly when readers face the need to find place names on maps. I have tried really hard to ensure that any place that appears in the narrative also appears on a map; I know that there is nothing more frustrating when reading about a place that does not so appear. I apologise if one or two have escaped.

Chapter 1

Preliminaries

Napoleon's Return from Exile
After his defeat in 1814, Napoleon had abdicated as emperor of the French and was exiled by the allied powers to the island of Elba in the Mediterranean. Less than a year later, the impact of his escape and landing, with just a thousand men, sent shockwaves throughout the whole of Europe. Already sick of the unsympathetic reign of their new king, much of the population and virtually all of the army flocked to welcome him. Having landed on 1 March 1815, less than three weeks later he marched into the Tuileries in triumph as Louis XVIII fled north to the Netherlands.

Grouchy Rallies to the Emperor
Whilst the junior officers and soldiers of the army were enthusiastic about Napoleon's return, the same was not true of the senior officers. Many were sick of war and had welcomed the opportunity to enjoy the rewards of their long and arduous service in peace. Most had hurried to swear their allegiance to Louis after Napoleon's abdication and had retained their positions and wealth. Napoleon's return presented them with an uncomfortable dilemma; many of them had retained their love of and devotion to the emperor, many of them believed in the republic and empire, but aside from their comfortable, privileged lives, they had all sworn allegiance to the king, and to break such an oath was unconscionable. Whilst some could not countenance such an action, others had become Royalist in their sentiments and yet others were not prepared to try their chances once more against the whole of Europe.

Those whose natural instinct and loyalty lay with Napoleon, and those who had been frustrated in their hopes for an enlightened reign from Louis, used his flight from France as releasing them from their oath. Other marshals and generals, although not prepared to flee with the king, but equally suspicious of Napoleon's ambition, felt compelled to serve as a patriotic duty; to protect France from a second foreign invasion. Most of them did so reluctantly.

During the 1814 campaign in France, Grouchy had served with distinction as the commander-in-chief of Napoleon's cavalry. His tenure in command came to an abrupt end when he was wounded during the bloody battle of Craonne on 7 March 1814; it was his fourteenth wound. The wound forced him to relinquish his post and he had not recovered before Napoleon's abdication and the return of Louis XVIII. Accepting the new reality, Grouchy swore allegiance to his new sovereign and, believing the promises that had been made to respect the ranks, titles and privileges of Napoleon's most senior officers, he resigned himself to loyally serve his new master. In May 1814, Grouchy travelled to Paris to swear his loyalty to Louis. However, on leaving the Tuileries, Grouchy was approached by the Duke de Berry and told that he was to lose his post as Inspector-General of the mounted *chasseurs*, the *colonel-général*, and that he, the Duke de Berry, was to replace him.

Grouchy immediately wrote to the king protesting the loss of this privileged post:

> Sire, His Royal Highness the Duke de Berry, announced to me this morning as I left Your Majesty, that he was taking my place as the *colonel-général* of *chasseurs*, and that I was to fill instead, the secondary post as first inspector of this arm. I humbly ask you, Sire, to respect the proclamations you have made on this subject. It has been five years since I was named as *colonel-général* on the battlefield of Wagram. I am one of the most senior commanders of the army. Your Majesty, by your declaration of the 2nd March, put before the whole of France, committed yourself not to deprive any officer of his rank, his titles or his honours. You are too just, Sire, to strip me, without cause, of a reward for life, honourably acquired, and to wish that by demoting me a rank, that I should now be placed second in an arm at the head of which I have been for such a long time.
>
> In the ancient military organisation of France, Sire, gentlemen have always been employed as *colonel-générals*: M. de Coigny, that of the dragoons, M. de Béthune of the cavalry. The declaration of Your Majesty gives me the right to think that I am only to be deprived of my position by a promotion to fill a more important function, that my services and the confidence of the army gives me the hope of entitling me. If, Sire, to the contrary, the new military organisation assigns me an inferior post to the one that I occupy at the moment, it only remains to me to protest such a position and to challenge it. I would be profoundly disappointed by such a need; but at least by this I would not have given up that noble pride that distinguishes the French soldier and the consolation of carrying into my retirement the esteem of Your Majesty and the regrets of my companions in arms.[1]

It is hard to believe that Grouchy hoped that a letter such as this would get the decision reversed and it could have been no surprise that the reply refused to do this and banished him from Paris, exiling him to one of his estates. Grouchy complied with the order, but protested it as unjust, feeling he was being punished as much for having betrayed his Royalist roots by supporting and fighting for the Revolution, as for this most recent indiscretion.

Grouchy's exile did not last long. Without wishing to speculate as to the motivations of the king or Minister of War Dupont, Grouchy was reinstated as an active lieutenant-general in the army and made first inspector-general of the *chasseurs* and lancers, effective from 19 July. He was later awarded the Order of Saint-Louis. On Napoleon's escape from exile in 1815, Grouchy, despite the feeling of injustice he felt from the previous year, but bound by his oath of loyalty to the king, reported to the Duke of Berry to put himself at his disposal. However, he was reproached for having reported so tardily and told that he would not be employed. Hurt by this rejection, he then went to see the *Comte* d'Artois, who, whilst trying to smooth things over, offered Grouchy no employment.

As Napoleon swept north unchecked, Grouchy remained unemployed in Paris and was still in residence when Napoleon entered the Tuileries. Grouchy did not present himself there, but his absence was soon noticed by the emperor, who called for him. Napoleon demanded to know if Grouchy was prepared to serve him again, pointing out that Louis' flight released him from his oath of loyalty. Grouchy claims to have replied, 'I have always thought, although I passionately wished for your return, it was important for the tranquillity of France and to yourself that you were placed on the imperial throne by the wishes of the French people, and without the intervention of the army, upon which otherwise Your Majesty would have to have relied, not least also on all your old lieutenants.'[2] Grouchy recalled that the emperor laughed at this reply.

Napoleon's return was not universally welcomed and there were a number of insurrections in the most royalist parts of France. There were risings in the Vendée, at Bordeaux and also in the Midi, the latter organised by the *Duc* d'Angoulême. Although none of them posed a significant military threat, with the whole of Europe slowly organising itself, Napoleon needed to deal with them before major hostilities broke out. On 30 March, as Angoulême appeared to be gaining ground on the local imperial forces, Napoleon directed that Grouchy should take the senior command in that area, and mobilised sufficient forces to deal with the threat. Napoleon did not want Angoulême harmed and hoped to exchange him for his wife, Marie-Louise, and his son, who were held by the Austrians.

Grouchy was not keen on the mission he had been entrusted with, but led a swift and decisive campaign which quickly overwhelmed the meagre forces the duke commanded. On 7 April at Montpellier, the small Royalist army, facing being completely surrounded, either declared for Napoleon or capitulated; Angoulême himself was allowed to escape. Marseille submitted soon after.

The most dependable of Angoulême's regular regiments was the 10th *de ligne*. After the campaign ended, Napoleon had the 10th marched to Paris: including them in one of his regular reviews, the emperor approached the regiment and said to it,

> 'Soldiers of the 10th, I am not content with you; you have fought against your emperor. We are about to go on campaign, you will march with the advance guard and without cartridges.'
> The regiment responded with enthusiasm, '*Vive l'empereur*! We will fight with the bayonet!'[3]

The 10th were to become part of Lobau's VI Corps during the Waterloo campaign, and although they did not get the opportunity to provide the advance guard, they fought bravely at Waterloo against the Prussians.

Having concluded this short campaign entirely to the satisfaction of Napoleon, in a letter from the Minister of War, dated 19 April, Grouchy learnt of his promotion to the marshalate:

> *Monsieur le comte*, I have the honour to inform you that, by a decree of the 17th of this month, the Emperor has nominated you as Marshal of France.
> I am pleased to have to transmit this great testimony of His Majesty's satisfaction for the services which have marked your military career and the proofs you have constantly given of your complete devotion to his person.[4]

Many of Napoleon's own officers, and many historians since, have questioned whether Grouchy had truly earned his baton and whether this short campaign, involving comparatively few troops on either side, truly merited such approbation. Marshal Marmont wrote in his memoirs,

> Grouchy is the worst officer to put at the head of an army. He lacks neither bravery nor some talent for the handling of troops; but he lacks resolution and is incapable of seizing an advantage: this is the worst thing in war.[5]

However, the truth is that by 1815, Grouchy was one of the most senior *général de division* in the army. Indeed, he came from the same generation as many of the very first of Napoleon's marshals, having fought in the early campaigns in the Vendée, Ireland, and Italy, and with Moreau in Germany. Many have speculated that Grouchy only missed the baton in the first nominations because he was viewed as being in the Moreau faction opposed to Napoleon. However, having joined the *Grande Armée* under the emperor's eye, he excelled in the 1805 Austrian campaign, in the pursuit after Jena, at Eylau and at Friedland. Although he had little opportunity to shine during a brief, if exciting, tour in Spain in 1808, he played a prominent part in Italy at the battles of the Piave and at Raab. After again fighting at Wagram he took temporary retirement before being recalled as commander of a cavalry corps for the Russian campaign. Involved in much fighting during the invasion, at Borodino he had his horse killed under him and was wounded. He recovered in time to take part in the retreat which saw the disintegration of the French cavalry, and he finished the campaign commanding the *bataillon sacré* made up of unattached officers that provided Napoleon's escort. Broken by his experience in Russia, he requested retirement. This was accepted in April 1813, but he had little opportunity to enjoy his retirement; he was again recalled to lead the cavalry in 1814. He once more showed his capabilities at the head of the cavalry during this campaign, particularly at Vauchamps, and at Craonne where he was wounded and forced to withdraw from the army.

It is wrong to claim he had no experience commanding infantry or combined-arms forces; however, it is certainly true that his greatest achievements were always at the head of cavalry. His career was certainly not unblemished, but this is true of nearly all the marshals. Napoleon knew well his value as the leader of large formations of cavalry and it is clear from the letter he wrote to Grouchy on making him a marshal, that it was certainly not because of the short and undemanding campaign in the Midi that he decided to promote him,

> My cousin, I write to you to let you know my satisfaction of the services that you have rendered to me, the attachment you have always shown to me and to *la patrie*, as well as with the fine manoeuvres, the talents and courage that you have displayed in all circumstances, and notably at Friedland, at Wagram and in the plains of Champagne [in 1814]. These have all convinced me to nominate you Marshal of France.[6]

Whilst Grouchy had been campaigning in the Midi, Napoleon was organising the army for the inevitable war against the European coalition that was forming against him. Menaced with invasion on all fronts, he created a *corps d'observation des Alpes*, numbered VII Corps, and planned to give the command to his new marshal.

The Situation in June 1815
Even by the time Napoleon entered the Tuileries on 20 March, he had already been declared an outlaw by the Congress of Vienna and it soon became clear that he could not avoid war against the major powers of Europe. By the Treaty of Chaumont, the allies each pledged to put an army of 150,000 men into the field until he was crushed. His desperate attempts to avoid conflict were rebuffed and Napoleon quickly realised he would have to fight. Having placated the liberal bourgeoisie and secured his political position with the *Acte Additionel*, the emperor turned his mind to rebuilding the army.

The *Armée du Nord* (Army of the North) that Napoleon led into Belgium in June 1815 has often been described as one of the finest he ever commanded. Whilst it is true that it was not filled by newly-raised and partially-trained conscripts as the army had been in 1813 and 1814, most of the true veterans of Napoleon's greatest campaigns lay dead around the many battlefields of central Europe and the wastes of Russia. The so-called veterans of 1815 were still very young men, the survivors of his last two campaigns, both of which had ended in defeat. However, it was an extremely enthusiastic army, dedicated to their iconic leader and desperate to avenge their previous defeats. But it also suffered from some significant flaws which were to manifest themselves in the coming campaign; these flaws were not in its organisation, its numerical strength, its courage or *élan*, but in fundamental defects in its leadership, cohesion, spirit and discipline.[7] The raising, strength and organisation of the *Armée du Nord* has been described in detail many times and readers are directed to the plethora of fine books that cover this subject, some of which are included in the bibliography.

The *Armée du Nord* consisted of about 124,000 men organised as follows; I Corps (20,731 men under Drouet d'Erlon), II Corps (25,179 men under Reille), III Corps (18,105 men under Vandamme), IV Corps (15,404 men under Gérard) and VI Corps (10,821 men under Lobau), the Cavalry Reserve (13,144 men under Grouchy) and the Imperial Guard (20,755 men under Drouot). The army had 370 pieces of artillery. This powerful army faced Wellington's Anglo-Dutch army of 93,000 and Blücher's Prussian army of 117,000.

Orders for the concentration were issued early in June. Napoleon planned to move up from Beaumont and Philippeville, cross the Belgian border and then the River Sambre in the vicinity of Charleroi. The concentration took place in the greatest secrecy to try and ensure that the allies got as little warning as possible. By the 14th, all were in position and although the allies had got word of the French movements, the information was insufficiently detailed to justify ordering their own concentration and neither was expecting to be attacked. Napoleon had already stolen a march on his enemies.

Given the very real internal and external threats that he faced, Napoleon felt he had little option but to take the initiative and attack his enemies before they could concentrate all their forces against him. French military culture has always emphasised the offensive and Napoleon's military genius was based on seizing the initiative and bringing his enemy's army to decisive battle. Whilst the combined armies of Wellington and Blücher would almost certainly overwhelm him, the need to supply them demanded they were spread across relatively large areas, offering him the opportunity to defeat each in detail before they had the time to concentrate. What was more, the British lines of communication ran towards Ostend, Antwerp and the sea, whilst those of the Prussians ran towards Liège, Maastricht and Prussia, in opposite directions to each other. Through Gourgaud's account of the campaign, Napoleon expressed his plan thus:

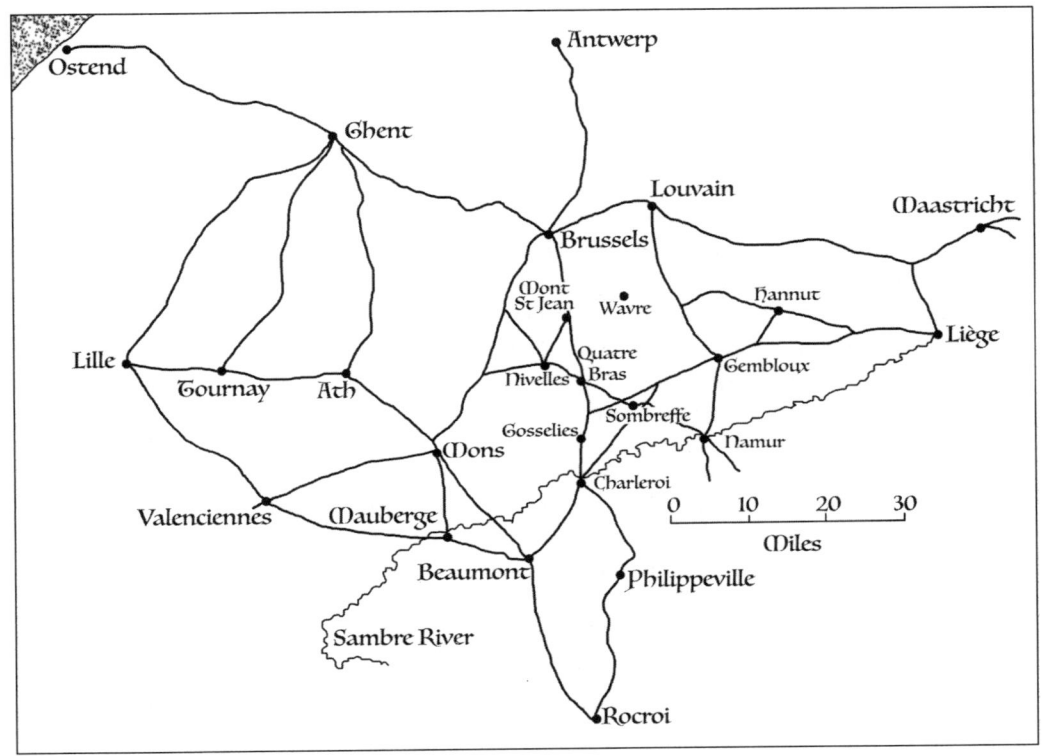

Campaign Map

The Prussian army, having intimation of the enemy's intentions eight or ten hours before the English, would accordingly be first concentrated. Hopes were even entertained of attacking the Prussians before their four corps were united, or of obliging them to fall back in the direction of Liège and the Rhine, which was the line of their operations; and by thus separating them from the English, to create an opportunity for new operations.

In these calculations, the characters of the enemy's commanders were much to be considered. The hussar habits of Marshal Blücher, his activity and decided character, formed a strong contrast to the cautious disposition, the deliberate and methodical manner of the Duke of Wellington. Thus it was easy to predict that the Prussian army would be first concentrated, and also that it would evince decision and promptitude in hastening to the aid of its ally. If Blücher had had only two battalions ready to act, he would have employed them in support of the English army; but there was reason to believe, that Wellington, unless his whole army was prepared for action, would not attack the French to assist Blücher. All these considerations rendered it desirable, that the attack should be commenced against the Prussian army; it necessarily followed, that it would be first concentrated, which was in reality the fact.[8]

Napoleon's aim was undoubtedly to destroy each of these armies in succession, force them away from each other along their lines of communication and then to occupy Brussels. He hoped that such a blow would dissolve the coalition and might even bring peace; after all, the emperor of Austria was his father-in-law and the interest of distant Russia was largely theoretical. To concentrate such an army, he could only cover the rest of his frontiers with very weak detachments, albeit with the grand title of 'army'. These bodies, too feeble to resist a determined enemy, were designed to impose upon and delay them, buying him time to achieve his key victories in Belgium.

There is no doubt that if Napoleon had succeeded in destroying these two armies, the morale of the allies would have been seriously affected. After their defeat, Napoleon could have turned with part of his army against the next developing threat with a huge moral advantage. It could certainly be argued that the determination of the allies would have been shaken to the point where they were prepared to make an accommodation with France, but at worst it would still buy the emperor considerable time; the time he needed to secure his position. And it is certainly true to say that a great victory would have galvanised the majority of France behind him.

Thus, Napoleon's march into the Kingdom of the Netherlands was not aimed primarily at capturing Brussels, as many allied leaders and commanders thought, but to engineer a confrontation with Wellington or Blücher in such a way as to give him the greatest chance of destroying their armies one after the other. The capture of Brussels was almost irrelevant if the allied armies remained intact. His march on the capital of the Netherlands, therefore, was almost the bait that he used to force the allies into battle.

Napoleon had four lines of operation from which to choose. He could concentrate at Valenciennes and advance on Brussels via Mons, destroying Wellington before the Prussians could move to his support. He could concentrate at Maubeuge and move on Brussels through Charleroi, striking at the junction between the two allies and defeating them separately. On the right he could descend the Meuse towards Namur and fall on the Prussians, cutting their lines of communication; or he could sweep even further east, threatening their lines of communication and hoping to draw the Prussians away from Wellington. Wellington clearly feared the first of these options, but Napoleon felt that such a move would merely push the British commander into the arms of the Prussians and risk him having to fight them concentrated. Napoleon chose to fall on the central point, conveniently marked by the main Charleroi to Brussels *chaussée* (main road), hoping to destroy Blücher before Wellington could come to his support.

Whilst the concentration was not as faultless as many French historians suggest, it was still a remarkable achievement. Whilst the allies knew that the French army was assembling in the north, its strike did come as something of a surprise and Wellington in particular, unsure if the advance on Charleroi was a deception, refused to nominate his own concentration point until he was sure, thus prompting Wellington's comment on the 15th that Napoleon had stolen a march on him. Although Blücher was able to concentrate quicker than Wellington, even he was unable to ensure his whole army was concentrated in time for the first battle.

Allied Plans
On 3 May, Wellington and Blücher met at Thirlemont to discuss their strategy to defeat Napoleon. At this time they were both building up their forces with a view to an offensive into France in concert with the other allied armies, probably in July. However, given that this process was still far from complete, and complicated by the mutiny of the Saxon forces that were under Prussian command, their first thoughts were on how to counter a French offensive launched to try and catch them unprepared.

Wellington was certainly a great commander, but he was very much a politicised and politically astute general. He therefore saw his priorities as the need to protect the capital of the Kingdom of the Netherlands, Brussels, and to protect the exiled French king, Louis XVIII, who was in Ghent. His conviction was that the French would attack via Mons, and this was based on the premise that Napoleon's priority was the capture of Brussels.

As Napoleon had three distinct options for advancing on Brussels through the Anglo-Dutch deployment area, Wellington would be unable to cover all of them in sufficient strength. His plan therefore saw his army concentrating well back from the frontier so that he could then deploy it to the threatened route, allowing the French to advance virtually unopposed until this was complete and giving the Prussians time to march to his assistance. Wellington was therefore trading space, giving up Netherlands' territory, for the time required to concentrate his army and receive support.

Blücher faced a slightly less complicated problem; whilst he needed to protect his communications with Prussia, he also had to maintain his communications with Wellington. His plan was therefore to concentrate forward, around Fleurus and Sombreffe, and to fight a battle there, in order to protect his line of communications to the east, or to march west and support Wellington along the main road from Namur towards Nivelles that passed through Sombreffe.

By the time of Thirlemont, therefore, both commanders already had their own plans in place, although they were diametrically opposed; Wellington concentrating in depth and Blücher forward. But the priority now was to agree a plan that saw them co-ordinating their efforts with a view to concentrating an overwhelming force against Napoleon. The intelligence they had available at that time hinted that any French offensive would be focussed on western Belgium rather than the Meuse valley, suggesting that Wellington's forces would be engaged first. Thus, although at their meeting at Thirlemont the principle of mutual support was agreed, their expectation was that Napoleon would advance against Wellington.

By the end of May, both allied armies were complete and ready to start the campaign. As no threat had developed, when Blücher made an official visit to the Netherlands between 28 and 30 May, all the talk was of an allied offensive into France; all thoughts of co-ordinating defensive arrangements had been forgotten and the dichotomy between forward and rearward concentrations was no longer an issue. Just a few days before Napoleon launched his offensive, Blücher had written to his wife, 'We shall soon enter France. We might remain here another year, for Bonaparte will never attack us.'[9]

Marshal Grouchy joins the *Armée du Nord*
Grouchy did not remain at the head of VII Corps for long. As Napoleon organised the *Armée du Nord*, he was recalled and appointed commander of all the cavalry. In early June, he received his letters of service from Marshal Davout (the Prince of Eckmühl), who had been appointed as Napoleon's minister of war:

> The Minister of War to Grouchy. Paris, 3 June 1815
> *Monsieur le maréchal*, I have the honour to inform Your Excellency that the Emperor has nominated you as commander-in-chief of the cavalry, for which he is to give orders for its new organisation.
> I attach the letter that the minister has written on this subject to Your Excellency and which contains its letters of service as well as the states of this new organisation of the cavalry in personnel and in troops.
> I will have the honour to inform Your Excellency tomorrow the arrangements that I have ordered for the execution of the Emperor's intentions; His Majesty orders, M. *le maréchal*, that you leave on the 5th at the latest, to move to Laon, to organise there, and to pass in review, all your regiments, to put them in a state to enter campaign, to write to the depots for them to hasten to increase the war squadrons, to assure yourself that all the men are armed and to issue them with cartridges.[10]

No doubt pleased with this new appointment, Grouchy moved without delay to his new post. He was soon involved in the many day-to-day issues of command:

> *Le duc de Dalmatie* to Grouchy. Paris, 5 June 1815
> *Monsieur le maréchal*, the Emperor wishes to dispense with the distinctions established by the last government and which could cause brawls between

the troops, as has already happened in a number of units. He has decided that the white aiguillettes given last year to the first regiments of each arm of cavalry are no longer to be worn. But His Majesty's intention is that this measure should be executed with consideration and that it should be initiated, as far as possible, by the units themselves.

I request, *Monsieur le maréchal*, that you take all the necessary measures to ensure His Majesty's wishes are complied with and, in giving your instructions in this regard to the generals under your orders, to recommend to them to use as much consideration as they find amenable.[11]

Perhaps more concerning for the new commander of the cavalry was the state of some of his command,

> Grouchy to the *major-général* Beaumont, 14 June 1815, 2pm.
> I hasten to warn you that the men of the train of the artillery batteries attached to the 4th and 5th Divisions forming the 1st Cavalry Corps are in a deplorable situation, as to clothing and personnel.
>
> These men are, for the most part, children. They have no overcoats, few good garments and no boots. If the cold and rainy weather continues, they will fall sick in bivouacs or will desert. I have been informed that several have already disappeared.
>
> I have the honour to request, M. *le maréchal*, for you to do what you can to change the train soldiers of these two batteries, or at least to have them given clothing. This is all the more necessary as these are precisely the batteries attached to 1st Cavalry Corps which is the only one composed of light cavalry destined to provide the advance guard, which should at least be well looked after.
>
> There are no infantry caissons attached to the batteries of 1st Cavalry Corps. It is indispensable that some are sent without delay and I request you to give the order.
>
> Although the general commanding the artillery of 1st Cavalry Corps has written to General Ruty with the same aim as I do in writing this letter to you, I have thought it necessary to also speak to you because of the importance.[12]

The *Armée du Nord* Concentrates

On the morning of 12 June, Napoleon left Paris and slept at Laon. Arriving at that town in the evening, the emperor asked to see Grouchy. The first question that was put to the marshal was to find out if the cavalry was on the Sambre and what cantonments they occupied so that they could leave to cross the river. By this time, Grouchy had been in Laon for eight days, but had received no orders from Soult. Consequently, the cavalry remained around the town where they had been since the beginning of the month. Napoleon was surprised and very annoyed; he believed that the orders that had been despatched several days before would have arrived and been acted upon. He told the marshal to immediately send off all the staff officers he had available to carry the order to all the cavalry regiments to get them moving.

That these orders were sent is almost certain; they were found perfectly copied into the register of correspondence of the *major-général*. This failure in the sending of orders relative to the assembly of the cavalry is only one of many seemingly inexplicable failures in the transmission of orders during this campaign. As we shall see, later in the campaign Napoleon sometimes wrote personally to his key commanders to ensure that they received their orders. This was something that Napoleon had rarely done prior to this campaign and must be considered a lack of confidence in his own headquarters and Soult's competence in particular.

As a result of this latest mix-up, several cavalry regiments had to make journeys of fifteen and twenty leagues to reach the frontier in time. Thus, on 15 and 16 June, on their entry on campaign, men and horses were very tired.

On 13 June, Grouchy, like the other senior commanders of the army, received the following order dated from Avesnes on the same day:

> ORDER OF THE DAY. Position of the army for the 14th.
> The Imperial Headquarters is at Beaumont. The infantry of the Imperial Guard is to be bivouacked a quarter of a league in front of Beaumont, and to form three lines; the Young Guard, then the *Chasseurs*, and then the Grenadiers. The Duke of Treviso [Mortier][13] will reconnoitre the site of this camp: he will ensure that everything is in its place; artillery, trains, baggage, etc.
>
> The First Regiment of Foot Grenadiers is to proceed to Beaumont.
>
> The cavalry of the Imperial Guard will be posted in the rear of Beaumont; but the furthest corps must be within a league of that city.
>
> II Corps will take position at l'Aire, that is to say, as near as possible to the frontier without crossing it. The four divisions of this army corps will assemble and bivouac on two or four lines; the headquarters in the centre; the cavalry in advance, guarding all the approaches, also without passing the frontier, but ensuring it is respected by the enemy's partisans, who might seem inclined to cross it.
>
> The bivouacs are to be so placed that their fires may not be seen by the enemy: generals must prevent troops straying from the camp; and must ensure that each man is provided with fifty cartridges, four days allowance of bread, and half a pound of rice; that the artillery and trains are in good condition; and they must be placed in order of battle. Thus II Corps will be in readiness at three in the morning of the 15th to march on Charleroi, should it receive orders to that effect, and it may arrive there before nine o'clock.

I Corps will take position at Solre-sur-Sambre and bivouac in several lines in a similar way to II Corps and take care that its bivouac fires are concealed from the enemy and that no one is allowed to wander from the camp; its generals will satisfy themselves about the condition and supply of the ammunition and food carried by the troops, and that the artillery and ambulances are placed in their order of battle. I Corps must likewise hold itself in readiness to follow the movement of II Corps at three o'clock on the morning of the 15th; thus, on the day after tomorrow, these two corps may manoeuvre in the same direction and co-operate with each other.

Tomorrow III Corps will take a position a league in advance of Beaumont, as near as possible to the frontier, without, however, crossing it or allowing it to be violated by any party of the enemy. General Vandamme will keep everyone at his post and will give orders for concealing the fires so that the enemy may not observe them. His corps must also conform with the regulations prescribed to II Corps with respect to the ammunition, provisions, artillery, and trains, and must hold itself in readiness to march at three o'clock on the morning of the 15th.

VI Corps will proceed in advance of Beaumont, and bivouac on two lines, at the distance of a quarter of a league from III Corps. *Comte de* Lobau is to choose the ground, observing the general arrangements prescribed by the present order.

Marshal Grouchy will move the 1st, 2nd, 3rd and 4th Cavalry Corps beyond Beaumont, and establish them in bivouac between that town and Walcourt, causing the frontier to be respected, prohibiting anyone from crossing it or suffering themselves to be seen and taking measures to prevent the fires from being observed by the enemy; he will hold himself in readiness to march on Charleroi, at three o'clock in the morning of the 15th, in case he should receive orders to do so, and to form the advance guard of the army.

He must direct the generals to ensure that all the cavalry troops have been provided with cartridges, that their arms are in good condition, and that they have each four days allowance of bread and half a pound of rice as has been ordered. The bridge equipages are to be bivouacked behind VI Corps, and in front of the infantry of the Imperial Guard. The central park of artillery will halt in the rear of Beaumont.

The Army of the Moselle [Gérard's IV Corps] will take position tomorrow in front of Philippeville. Count Gérard will arrange it so that it may be in readiness to march the day after tomorrow, the 15th, at three in the morning, to join III Corps and support its movement on Charleroi according to the new order which will be given to him. But General Gérard must carefully guard his right flank and the head of his advance along all the roads from Charleroi and Namur.

If the Army of the Moselle has any pontoons in its train, General Gérard must keep them as far in advance as possible so that they can be employed if the need arises.

The *sapeurs* [engineers] and the means of transport that the generals have collected will march at the head of the columns.

The *sapeurs* of the Imperial Guard, the *marins* [the Sailors of the Guard generally served as engineers alongside the guard *sapeurs*] and the reserve *sapeurs* are to march after VI Corps and at the head of the Guard.

All the corps must march in close order. In the movement on Charleroi, advantage must be made of all the routes to overwhelm any enemy forces that may be inclined to attack the army or manoeuvre against it.

Only the Grand Headquarters will be at Beaumont. No other must be established there and the town must be free from all obstructions. The old regulations respecting the headquarters and equipages, the order of march and the policing of carriages and baggage, the laundresses and suttling women, must be enforced. A general order will be issued to that effect; but in the meanwhile, the generals commanding the army corps must make the necessary arrangements and the Provost-Marshal must ensure that these regulations are executed.

The Emperor commands that all the arrangements contained in the present order shall be kept secret by the generals.

> By order of the Emperor,
> The Marshal of the Empire,
> *Major Général, Duc de Dalmatie*[14]

All was set for the concentration of the army, but in the nights of the 13th and 14th the Prussian advance posts noticed the fires of the two great bivouac areas close to Beaumont and Solre-sur-Sambre. The Prussian army knew that Napoleon had arrived with the army, that the villages on the frontier were strongly occupied and finally that it was most likely that the French attack would be launched against them first.

Chapter 2

14 June

Grouchy's cavalry did not seem to be having a particularly happy opening to the campaign. After the need to force march forward to their concentration areas, they were now living in bivouacs. Grouchy's commanders were soon writing to him complaining of their lot; Grouchy had sympathy, but little power to change things:

> Grouchy to Kellerman. Bossus, 14 June
> ... Like you, I know that bivouacs, in such bad weather, are bad for the cavalry, but I also know that it is not for me to modify the orders that I have received. I must have them executed although distressing and I am restricted to pointing out their unfortunate effects ... [1]

On the same day, the army received the movement order below, that has been held up as a model of its type for its detail and its clarity.

> ORDER OF MOVEMENT Beaumont, 14 June 1815
> Tomorrow, the 15th, at half past two in the morning, General Vandamme's division of light cavalry [commanded by General Domon] will mount their horses and advance along the Charleroi road: it will send out patrols in all directions to scour the country, and to capture the enemy's advanced posts; each patrol must consist of at least fifty men. Before the division moves, General Vandamme will see that it is provided with cartridges.
> At the same hour, Lieutenant General Pajol must assemble the 1st Cavalry Corps and follow the movement of General Domon's division which will be under General Pajol's command. The divisions of the 1st Cavalry Corps are not to supply any detachments; they will be found by the 3rd Division [Domon]. General Domon will leave his battery of artillery to march after the first battalion of III Corps of infantry. Lieutenant General Vandamme will give it the necessary orders.
> Lieutenant General Vandamme will order the reveille to be beaten at half past two in the morning; at three he will march with his army corps in the direction of Charleroi. The whole of his baggage and followers must be

posted in the rear and must not commence their march until VI Corps and the Imperial Guard shall have passed. They will be under command of the Commissary General, who will unite them to the baggage of VI Corps and the Imperial Guard, and of the Grand Headquarters, and will give orders for their movement.

Each division of III Army Corps will have along with it its battery and trains: every other vehicle found in the ranks will be burnt.

Count Lobau will cause the reveille to be beaten at half past three o'clock, and he will order VI Army Corps to march at four, to follow and support General Vandamme's movement. He will direct the troops, artillery, trains and baggage to observe the same order of march that is prescribed to III Corps.

The baggage of VI Corps will be united with that of III Corps, under the orders of the Commissary General, as has been stated.

The Young Guard will beat the reveille at half past four, and will begin to march at five; it will follow the movement of VI Corps on the Charleroi road.

The Foot *Chasseurs* of the Guard will beat the reveille at five o'clock and will begin to march at half past five, to follow the movement of the Young Guard.

The Foot Grenadiers of the Guard will beat the reveille at half past five, and will march at six, to follow the movement of the Foot *Chasseurs*. The order of march for the artillery, trains and baggage, prescribed for III Corps must be observed by the Imperial Guard.

The baggage of the Guard will be united to that of III and VI Army Corps, under the orders of the Commissary General, who will direct the movement of the whole.

At half past five in the morning, Marshal Grouchy will cause that corps of cavalry of the three which is nearest the road to mount and follow the movement on Charleroi. The two other corps will depart successively at the interval of one hour after each other; but Marshal Grouchy will be careful to make the cavalry march on the lateral roads, whilst the column of infantry will proceed along the principal road, to avoid confusion, and likewise that his cavalry maintain better order than it otherwise would. He will direct the whole of the baggage to remain behind, parked and collected, until the Commissary General shall give orders for its advance.

Count Reille will cause the reveille to be beaten at half past two in the morning, and order II Corps to march at three on the bridge at Marchienne-au-Pont, and will make arrangements for its reaching that place before nine in the morning. He must station guards on all the bridges over the Sambre, to prevent anyone from passing them. The posts will be relieved by I Corps, but he must endeavour to anticipate the enemy on these bridges, to prevent their demolition, especially the bridge of Marchienne, to enable him to cross it, and which, should it be damaged, he must immediately have repaired.

At Thuin and Marchienne, as well as at all the villages on this road, Count Reille must interrogate the inhabitants respecting the positions and strength of the hostile armies. He must also take possession of and examine the letters in the post offices and forward to the emperor such information as he obtains.

Count d'Erlon will put I Corps in march at three in the morning and will also direct it on Charleroi, following the movement of II Corps, the left of which it will gain as soon as possible to support it if necessary. He will keep a brigade of cavalry in the rear to cover himself and to maintain, by small detachments, his communication with Maubeuge. He will send patrols beyond that place in the direction of Mons and Binche, as far as the frontier, to obtain information on the enemy and to report anything they learn. These parties must be careful neither to compromise themselves, nor to cross the frontier.

Count d'Erlon will occupy Thuin with a division; and should the bridge of that town be destroyed he must immediately repair it. He must likewise plan and construct a bridgehead on the left bank. This division will also be responsible for the bridge at the Abbey at Aulne and Count d'Erlon must ensure a bridgehead is also constructed at this place.

The order of march prescribed to III Corps for the artillery, trains and baggage will be observed by I and II Corps, the baggage of which will be united and will march on the left of I Corps under the orders of the most senior Commissary General.

IV Corps [the Army of the Moselle] has received orders to take position on this day in advance of Philippeville: if its movement is complete and the divisions that compose this army corps are concentrated, Lieutenant General Gérard will put them in march at three o'clock tomorrow morning and direct them on Charleroi. He must be careful to maintain alignment with III Corps, with whom he will maintain communication, in order to arrive before Charleroi nearly at the same time; but General Gérard must clear his right and will scour all the approaches leading to Namur. He will march in close order of battle, leaving at Philippeville all the baggage and followers so that his army corps will be better able to manoeuvre.

General Gérard will order the 14th Division of cavalry, which will arrive today at Philippeville, to follow the movement of his army corps on Charleroi where that division will join the 4th Cavalry Corps.

Lieutenant Generals Reille, Vandamme and Gérard will communicate with each other using patrols and ensure they arrive before Charleroi at about the same time and concentrated. If possible, they will attach Flemish speaking officers to their advanced guards so that they may interrogate the local population and thus gain information; but these officers must be careful only to give out that they command patrols and do not mention the Grand Army in their rear.

Lieutenant Generals Reille, Vandamme and Gérard will direct all the *sapeurs* of their army corps (having along with them materials for repairing the bridges) to march after the first regiment of light infantry and will direct the engineer officers to repair the bad routes, to open lateral communications and to throw bridges over those streams which the infantry cannot conveniently ford.

The *marins* and *sapeurs* of the Guard and *sapeurs* of the reserve, will follow the lead regiment of III Corps: Lieutenant Generals Rogniat and Haxo will be at their head. They will take along with them only two or three wagons: the remainder of the park of engineers will march on the left of III Corps. If the enemy is encountered these troops are not to be engaged, but Generals Rogniat and Haxo will employ them in the works for crossing rivers, the construction of bridgeheads, repairing roads and openings etc.

The cavalry of the Guard will follow the movement on Charleroi and set out at eight o'clock.

The Emperor will accompany the advanced guard on the Charleroi road. The Lieutenant Generals will be careful to send His Majesty frequent reports respecting their movements and the information they may obtain; they are aware that His Majesty's intention is to pass the Sambre before noon and to cross the army to the left bank of that river.

The bridge equipages will be divided into two sections; the first section will be divided into three parts, each consisting of five pontoons and five advanced guard boats to throw three bridges across the Sambre; to each of these subdivisions a company of *pontonniers* [bridging troops] will be attached; the first section will march in the train of the park of engineers after III Corps. The second section will remain with the reserve park of artillery with the baggage column; it will have along with it the fourth company of *pontonniers*.

The Emperor's equipages and the baggage of Imperial Headquarters will be collected and put in march at ten o'clock. As soon as they have passed, the Commissary General will direct the equipage of the Imperial Guard and III and VI Corps to depart: at the same time he will order the column of equipages of the reserve of the cavalry to march, and to follow the direction which the cavalry has taken. The trains of the army will follow the headquarters and march at the head of the baggage; but on no account should this baggage, the reserve parks of the artillery, or the second section of the bridge equipages advance within three leagues [about eight miles] of the army, without an order from the *major-général* or pass the Sambre without orders to that effect.

The Commissary General will form divisions of this baggage and appoint officers to command them so that he may detach from them what may afterwards be required at headquarters or for the service of the officers.

The *Intendant General* will unite to this column of equipages the whole of the baggage and transports of the administration to which he will assign a place in the column. The wagons which may be delayed will take the left and must not quit the rank in which they are placed except by order of the Quarter Master General.

The Emperor orders that all the equipage wagons which may be found in the columns of the infantry, cavalry or artillery shall be burnt, as well as the wagons of the equipage column which may quit their rank and disrupt their march without the express permission of the Quarter Master General.

For this purpose a detachment of fifty gendarmes shall be placed at the disposal of the Quarter Master General who, as well as the officers of the gendarmerie and the gendarmes, is responsible for the execution of these arrangements on which the success of the campaign may depend.

By order of the Emperor,
The Marshal of the Empire, *Major Général*
Duc de Dalmatie[2]

This order finally got the army into its final concentration areas prior to the launch of the offensive into Belgium. Essentially, Napoleon planned to advance in three columns; the left, consisting of Reille's II Corps and d'Erlon's I Corps, would guard the army's left flank and cross the Sambre at Marchienne-au-Pont. The centre, consisting of most of Grouchy's cavalry, Vandamme's III Corps, the Imperial Guard and Lobau's VI Corps, would cross at Charleroi. The right column, consisting of Gérard's IV Corps and Delort's cavalry division (the 14th Division of Milhaud's 4th Reserve Cavalry Corps) would guard the right flank and also cross at Charleroi. Sensibly, the baggage would move under strict control to avoid it interfering with the combat formations.

For Grouchy, this meant that the 1st Cavalry Corps, reinforced by Vandamme's cavalry division, would provide the army's advance guard; Exelmans' corps of dragoons would follow on in order to be able to support them; Milhaud's cuirassiers, heavy battlefield cavalry, would take no part in the advance and remain further back. Besides the general movement order for the 15th, Grouchy also received the letter below from the *major-général* giving him more detailed guidance:

Beaumont, 14 June 1815.
I send you, *Monsieur le maréchal*, the movement order for tomorrow, that the emperor has given; conform to the instructions that are in this order.

Several roads lead to Charleroi from Beaumont; that of the right passes through Bossu, Fleurieux, Vogénes and Yves, where it joins the main road from Philippeville to Charleroi. It is this road that you are to take, in order to not get in the way of the other columns, but make sure it is well known beforehand and regulate your movement so that you are always level with the column on the left, at the head of which General Pajol is to march.

I have warned General Gérard of the direction you are taking, whose corps is formed up in front of Philippeville and which is also to move on Charleroi from the same direction.

I must warn you that I have been informed that a force of 6,000 Prussian infantry is established at Jumignon. If this is true, the emperor wants this force to be taken; you should manoeuvre accordingly. I have written with the same direction to Generals Vandamme and Gérard.

Send me an officer as soon as you have started your march and at every hour during the movement.[3]

On the same day, 14 June, Grouchy wrote to the emperor, Soult and General Pajol, the following letters. To the Emperor:

Sire, I have the honour to send to Your Majesty the letter by which General Pajol has furnished me with various information on the enemy and on the movements that he presumes will be made on Mons. I also attach to these lines the report from a lieutenant of customs whom I had sent to the other side of the border. This person had previously served in the *chasseurs* of the Guard. His zeal and devotion could perhaps be of use. I have sent him with this despatch, thinking that he could perform well any missions that Your Majesty may wish to give him.[4]

To Marshal Soult as *major-général*:

I have the honour to inform you that the 1st Cavalry Corps has bivouacked at Valcourt, the 2nd at Bossu and the 3rd and 4th on the edge of the Gayolle wood.

I send you one of my officers from Bossu where I have established my headquarters, to receive your orders for tomorrow.

In a couple of hours I will send you a report that I await from one of the customs men of this part of the frontier, who has promised to inform us of what is happening opposite us. The word that we will attack them tomorrow, the 15th, has been common here for several days.[5]

To General Pajol:

General, please start your march today, the 14th, so that you will arrive, with your corps concentrated, at the village of Bossu.

You are to make a halt there of one hour and to receive new orders on the final location for where the 1st Cavalry Corps will bivouac this evening.

You are to be sure that all the men of your army corps are provided with cartridges; that their arms are in a good state and that four days of bread and a half-pound of rice that they are to be issued have been received.

In your march to bring you to the initial position of Bossu, you are to ensure that no one leaves the column or crosses the frontier. When you have established your bivouac for the night, that I will inform you of at Bossu, it is necessary that you position your fires so that they cannot be seen by the enemy. This means they should be hidden by woods and copses that I designate. I will be there with your army corps at midday at the latest.[6]

These letters give a good feel for the routine correspondence that was required to get an army in position and poised to launch an offensive. This same correspondence would have been going on at all levels of command and the number of *aides de camp* and *officiers d'ordonnance* riding to and fro delivering it must have been bewildering. In a time of far-from-perfect maps, it is perhaps not surprising that some couriers got lost and some messages went undelivered.

As Grouchy's troops were providing the advance guard on the following morning, the 15th, his orders to General Pajol needed to lay down the co-ordination required.

My dear General, please have your *corps d'armée* mounted at 2.30am to unite with Domon's division, that will come under your orders. You will form the advance guard of the army that moves on Charleroi.

Domon's division will be on the left of General Soult [son of the marshal], on the side of Castillon.

Attached is a copy of the movement order. Marching with the three other cavalry corps by a different direction to the one that you will follow, it is with General Vandamme that you are to act. You will receive immediate orders from either General Vandamme or the emperor himself, who is marching with the advance guard.

I am ordered to move on Charleroi, passing by Bossu, Fleurieux and Yves, where I am told I will find the main road from Philippeville to Charleroi.

As I am ordered to march with the left column, at the head of which you will be, you are to take care to keep in communications with me by sending frequent patrols.[7]

It was standard procedure to screen an advance with light cavalry and it was just this sort of duty that a light cavalry corps, such as that of Pajol, was designed for. Their job was to scout the countryside, locate the enemy outposts and to collect information from the local inhabitants. By destroying or pushing back enemy patrols and outposts, the aim was to deny information to the enemy commanders so that they remained unsure of where the main blow would fall. It was therefore a very important task and one that required a thorough and skilful approach. Luckily for Napoleon, Pajol was an officer of the highest calibre. In his memoirs, General Pajol lays down the composition of his corps, and the attached light cavalry division of General Domon.

General Pajol was to clear the route of the centre column, following as far as Jamignon and Bommerée, the valley of the river Heure and the tracks on the two sides of this valley. To fulfil this mission, he deployed his two divisions (Soult and Subervie) of his army corps (the 1st Cavalry Corps) and Domon's [light cavalry] division of Vandamme's corps.

This is the composition of the 1st Cavalry Corps on the 9th June:

4th Cavalry Division (Lieutenant General Baron Soult)

1st Brigade (General Clary)
Three squadrons of the 1st Hussar (General Clary), 471 men and 510 horses.
Three squadrons of the 4th Hussars (Colonel Blot), 304 men and 335 horses.

2nd Brigade (General Baron Ameil)
Three squadrons of the 5th Hussars (Colonel Baron Liégeard), 417 men and 481 horses.

1st Company of the 1st Horse Artillery Regiment.

5th Cavalry Division (General Subervie)

1st Brigade (General Colbert [brother of General Colbert of the Guard Lancers])
Three squadrons of the 1st Line Lancers (Colonel Jacquinot [brother of General Jacquinot]), 428 men and 508 horses.
Three squadrons of the 2nd Line Lancers (Colonel Sourd), 427 men and 479 horses.

2nd Brigade (General Merlin)
Three squadrons of the 11th *Chasseurs à Cheval* (Colonel Baron Nicolas), 484 men and 535 horses.

3rd Company of the 1st Horse Artillery Regiment.
Thus the 1st Cavalry Corps had an effective strength of eighteen squadrons

(2,531 men and 2,848 horses), eight 6-pounder cannons and four 24-pounder howitzers.

The composition of Domon's cavalry division (the 3rd) on the 1st June was:

1st Brigade (General Domanget)
Three squadrons of the 4th *Chasseurs à Cheval*, 308 men and 388 horses.
Three squadrons of the 9th *Chasseurs à Cheval*, 387 men and 416 horses.

2nd Brigade (General Vinot)
Three squadrons of the 12th *Chasseurs à Cheval*, 268 men and 293 horses.

4th Company of the 2nd Horse Artillery regiment.[8]

In all, Pajol's command totalled about 3,500 cavalry and artillerymen. If he required infantry support, he would have to wait for the following infantry formation, III Corps, to come forward. Now he had his orders, Pajol forwarded them to each of his three divisional commanders and allocated them each a separate route to follow. Once these orders had been sent off, and despite the need not to alert the Prussian outposts, Pajol sensibly sent patrols forward down the routes he would need to follow early the next morning. Given that even in modern times 'time spent on reconnaissance is never wasted', Pajol's memoirs record:

> On his own side, Pajol had happily had the foresight to gather information immediately after receiving the movement order. He learnt that it was necessary for the movement of artillery and even for the passage of cavalry, to have the tracks repaired, principally in the wood of Saint-Naubert, where they were cut by trenches, *abatis* and *trous de loup* ['wolf holes']. This work took place during the whole night. At daybreak they were only just practicable.[9]

Hubert-Francois Biot served as the senior *aide de camp* of General Pajol; he tells a similar story and adds:

> In this town [Bossu], close to the frontier, there was a division of customs men. The lieutenant and his men were at our disposal and were even to serve as guides. Well! Not a single one of them had thought of warning us of the impracticality of the tracks. One can see how poorly the emperor was seconded.[10]

For Milhaud's heavy cavalry, who were to follow far behind the advance light cavalry and infantry corps, the orders were far simpler.

> Grouchy to General Milhaud, from Bossu:
>
> Have your army corps mounted at 4.30am, to be at Bossu at 5.30 and to be there a little earlier yourself to receive your movement orders. Order your corps to get rid of all baggage and all impedimenta. Send the emperor's proclamation to the army to be read at the head of the corps before starting off.[11]

Without anticipating a significant event of the morning of the next day, the 15th, it is worth paying a quick visit to General Bourmont's 14th Infantry Division of Gérard's IV Corps. At this time, *Maréchal de Camp* Hulot commanded the first brigade of this division. In his report to his corps commander after the campaign had closed, he wrote:

> On the 14th June 1815, the IV Army Corps (called the Army of the Moselle), was assembled on the glacis of Philippeville, from where Lieutenant General Count Gérard, who was the commander, gave orders for the destination for all the divisions. The 3rd [within the corps, but officially the 14th in the army] commanded by General Count Bourmont, sent the 2nd Brigade, under the orders of *Maréchal de Camp* Toussaint, to *** [blank in the original with 'Walcourt' suggested in brackets]. General Bourmont established his headquarters at Florenne.
>
> I received his orders to establish the troops of my brigade [the 1st] on a war footing. Hostilities had not yet broken out. He ordered that arms should be loaded and proper guards should be posted etc. The lieutenant general conducted a reconnaissance. At 11pm I left him. A little after midnight, I received a letter which contained the last orders addressed to him by the corps commander. This letter warned me that before departing in the morning, I was to ensure that Count Gérard's orders were executed and everything was taken care of, to make all the arrangements that he would have taken himself and to report back.[12]

Hulot implies nothing unusual in receiving a letter from his divisional commander directing him to effectively take command of the division the next morning; however, many historians speculate that this suggests he had some prior warning of what was to happen in the early hours of the 15th. The whole army settled down in its bivouacs, no doubt wondering what momentous events the following day would bring.

Blücher Orders the Concentration of the Prussian Army

Both Wellington and Blücher had an effective network of spies inside France and also in some key positions within the French government. Although much of the information they were receiving was contradictory, they had a good idea that the

French army was concentrating on the Belgian border and even that Napoleon had recently moved to join it. So although hostilities had not yet broken out, they understood that they were imminent. Wellington, who believed that Napoleon would advance on Brussels through Mons, was reluctant to believe that the news of the French concentrating south of Charleroi was their main effort and was not prepared to order his own concentration until Napoleon's intentions were clear. Blücher could afford to be more decisive; late in the evening of the 14th he ordered the concentration of the Prussian army in the vicinity of Sombreffe, covered by General Zieten's I Corps. This meant relatively short marches for the II and III Corps, but was a much greater distance to cover for General Bülow's IV Corps that was deployed around Liège. Unfortunately for the Prussians, a succession of orders sent to Bülow failed to generate a sense of urgency into the march of IV Corps, which was to have serious repercussions less than forty-eight hours later.

Chapter 3

Morning, 15 June

Many of Napoleon's units, once they were formed up ready to march, had his address to the army read out to them.

> Soldiers! This is the anniversary of Marengo and of Friedland, which twice decided the fortunes of Europe. But then, as after Austerlitz, and as after Wagram, we were too generous; we believed the protestations and the oaths of the kings whom we had left on their thrones. Now, however, they have formed a League to overthrow the sacred rights of France. They have decided on the most unjust aggressions. Let us therefore march to meet them, for are not we and they still the same men?
>
> Soldiers! At Jena, the Prussians, so arrogant today, were three to one against you; at Montmirail you were one to six. As for the English, let those who have been their prisoners tell the tale of the miseries and tortures they suffered whilst cooped up on their prison hulks!
>
> Saxons, Belgians, Hanoverians, the forces of the Rhine Confederation, groan at being compelled to assist the cause of the kings who are enemies of justice and of the rights of the people. They know full well that this coalition will be insatiable. After having swallowed 12,000,000 Poles, 12,000,000 Italians, 1,000,000 Saxons, 6,000,000 Belgians, it will devour the second-tier States of Germany. Madmen! A moment of good fortune has made them blind. The oppression and humiliation of France are beyond their powers, if they cross her frontiers it will be but to find their graves.
>
> Soldiers! We shall be called upon to make forced marches, to fight battles, and to face dangers; but, with perseverance, victory will be ours; the rights, the honour, the happiness of our country will be regained.
>
> For every Frenchman who has a heart, the time has come to conquer or to die![1]

Despite the dark, chill damp of the early morning, it seemed to be well received; General Berthezène of III Corps later wrote,

The army did not need this stimulus. Its enthusiasm was at its height; its confidence and love for its chief was boundless and its impatience for the fight is impossible to describe.[2]

Despite the potentially dramatic fault-lines within the *Armée du Nord*, even the most experienced of Napoleon's commanders seem to have been swept along by the enthusiasm and almost fanatical devotion of the soldiers for their emperor; General Guyot, commander of the heavy cavalry of the Imperial Guard, surely one of the most respected battlefield commanders in the army, wrote in his diary,

15 June, at Charleroi (ten leagues) – The whole army is concentrated on this point at the orders of the emperor. The spirit amongst the troops is of the highest; I do not think that France has had so many experienced soldiers at one time; the order to march could not have been more detailed.[3]

The Prussian Forces
The first Prussian forces the French would meet were those of the 1st and 2nd Brigades of General Zieten's I Corps (it should be remembered that in the Prussian army a brigade was the equivalent of a British or French division) and some of the Cavalry Reserve. Steinmetz's 1st Brigade was centred on Fontaine-l'Evêque, covering the crossings at Lobbes, Thuin and the abbey at Aulne. Pirch II's 2nd Brigade, centred on Charleroi, covered the bridges at that place, Marchienne-au-Pont to the west and Châtelet to the east. Despite the efforts that the French troops had gone to in order to shield their bivouac fires from the Prussian outposts, the light was reflected off the low clouds and when the French crossed the frontier on the morning of the 15th, the Prussian outposts were formed up and under arms.

The Prussian II, III and IV Corps were now moving to concentrate around Sombreffe as they had been ordered. Whilst II and III Corps were already approaching, IV Corps was still some way away, the orders it was receiving failing to give a true sense of the urgency of the situation.

The Left Column
Reille's II Corps started off at 3am as laid down in Napoleon's movement order. Its objectives were the four bridges over the river Sambre at Lobbes, Thuin, l'abbaye d'Aulne and Marchienne-au-Pont. Of these, only the last was of real importance as the first three had poor access to major roads and the ground and routes were generally unsuitable for cavalry and particularly for artillery. Reille's advance was led by Bachelu's division supported by Piré's cavalry. These were followed by the division of Prince Jérôme and then Foy. Not long after starting their advance, they came into contact with Prussian forces at Thuin. After a short struggle the Prussians were pushed out of the town and the bridge secured. A

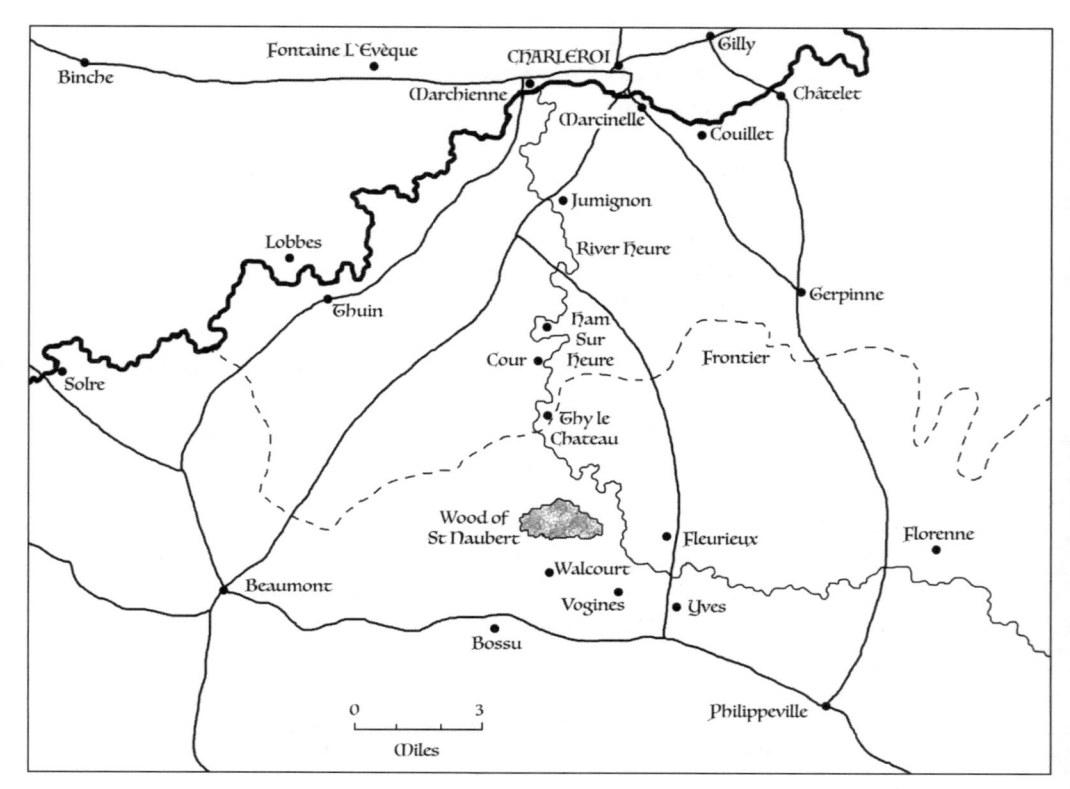

Morning, 15th June

second advance post at Lobbes was also quickly disposed of; the Prussian forces were too weak to much delay the French advance.

At about 7am, the Prussians attempted to fall back on Montigny where there were two squadrons of the 1st West Prussian Dragoons, who covered their retreat after this village was also taken by Bachelu's men. Unfortunately for the landwehr battalion, the dragoons were overwhelmed by a sudden attack by Piré's troopers and the battalion was almost destroyed before it could reach Marchienne. The bridge at abbaye d'Alnes fell to Reille's troops between 8 and 9am.

Once General Zieten was convinced that the whole of the French army was on the march he sent couriers to both Blücher and Wellington, warning them of events and sent orders to his two forward brigades; the 1st (Steinmetz) was to retire via Courcelles to a position to the rear of Gosselies on the road to Brussels, and the 2nd was to protect the bridges at Marchienne, Charleroi and Châtelet to cover the flank of the 1st Brigade and hold up the French on the line of the Sambre. His 3rd and 4th Brigades were to move to Fleurus, close to the army's concentration point of Sombreffe.

Although the bridges at Lobbes, Thuin and abbaye d'Alne were quickly taken, Reille's main objective was to capture the strategically-important bridge at Marchienne, as it was this that would allow the whole corps to cross and continue its advance on Brussels. Whilst Bachelu busied himself with the pursuit of the Prussians along the river, Foy's division took the lead towards Marchienne. Reille had reached this bridge without too much delay, but now he failed to push home his advantage. The bridge here was defended by the 2nd Battalion of the 6th Prussian Regiment, belonging to the 2nd Brigade. They had two guns in support and had barricaded, but not destroyed, the bridge. Instead of attempting a *coup de main* against a well-organised but nervous defence, Reille waited until most of his forces had struggled along the poor roads to join him and his first two attempts on the bridge were repulsed.

Reille was not ready to attack Marchienne again until around midday. This attack met with success and Foy's acting chief of staff, Lemonnier-Delafosse, recorded, 'the bridge was crossed by our skirmishers at the charge, supported by a deep column of infantry and the enemy started his retreat'.[4] However, most of the Prussian defenders had withdrawn in compliance with their orders and the small rearguard defended the bridge without determination. By this time the central column had seized the bridge at Charleroi over an hour before and Napoleon himself had crossed there. Although Reille could now start to get his corps across the river, this was to be a long and painful process. Not only was there a single, narrow bridge, approached by equally narrow streets, but he was still waiting for all his detachments covering the other captured crossings to be relieved by I Corps and to rejoin him.

The Centre Column
Pajol's cavalry, providing the advance guard in the centre, had indeed started their advance on time. Unfortunately, the same was not true of Vandamme's III Corps that was to follow them in support. Lobau's VI Corps was to follow Vandamme's troops and set off as ordered at 4am. However, they had not travelled far before they were forced to halt. *Adjutant-commandant* Janin of the VI Corps headquarters explained the problem,

> VI Corps, camped to the left and some distance from III Corps, conforming to the orders that it had received, had started its march at 4am on the 15th, heading towards this last, whose movement it was to follow. When it met it, it had to stop because they had still not left their positions. This halt had lasted more than an hour when the commander of VI Corps, fearing that the thick mist would dissipate and expose the march of III Corps, sent me off to inform him of the departure of their last troops. Arriving at their camp

> I found them as quiet as if they were planning to stay there; the soldiers were cleaning their arms, adjusting or repairing their equipment and I surprised their officers in announcing to them that the army was assembled and pressing their left, waiting for them to leave so that they could continue their march having been unfortunately held up by their inaction. I continued to wait for a long time and, wanting to understand the delay, I was going to General Vandamme's headquarters when I met a general officer who, when I informed him of my concerns, told me that the orders sent to General Vandamme in the night had not arrived, because a senior officer who, *alone* [his emphasis], was carrying them, had suffered a fall from his horse and having broken his thigh, was unable to complete his mission. At the same moment, General Rogniat, who marched at the head of the grand park, also approached and received, I think, the same information.[5]

General Rogniat, whose own column of engineers was to have followed the first regiment of Vandamme's corps, also started his own move on time and found himself confronted with the III Corps troops still in their bivouacs. Tracking down Vandamme, there was a strong exchange of words, the III Corps commander claiming he had not received any movement orders. Vandamme, had taken lodgings in Beaumont on the 14th, but was told to leave and move closer to his corps on the arrival of Imperial Headquarters. Soult had sent only a single officer to Vandamme with the army's movement order and this officer searched in vain for Vandamme's new headquarters. In his account above, Janin informs us that the movement orders were not delivered because the staff officer that was carrying them had an accident. However, one of Vandamme's own divisional commanders, General Berthezène, gives us a more likely explanation:

> The truth is that it did not leave its position until 8am, instead of leaving at 3am, as it had been ordered. General Vandamme, who commanded this corps, had been forced to give up his quarters the day before to Imperial Headquarters. In a mood, he had gone to lodge in the countryside without letting anyone know where he was, so that the movement orders did not reach him . . .[6]

Despite his anger, Vandamme immediately took the necessary steps to get his corps on the move, but it needed time to get 17,000 men up, formed and moving. Despite his determination, this unfortunate incident put III Corps well behind schedule. We have seen that Berthezène claims his division, at least, did not move off until 8 o'clock; however, Berthezène's division was the last in the corps and Captain Gerbet of the 37th *de ligne*, with no axe to grind, reports his division, Lefol's, set off on their march about 6am.[7] Lieutenant Lefol, who was one of his father's *aides de camp*, confirms this:

Instead of leaving at 3am, we did not start our march until 6, as a result of which we only arrived at Charleroi at 3pm . . . A misunderstanding by General Vandamme was the cause of this failure of which the emperor reproached him at precisely the moment when we passed before them. I heard these words from Napoleon to Vandamme, 'General, the hold up of your corps in this situation is a fatality . . .'. Vandamme appeared to take this remark very badly, replying to the emperor in an excessively aggressive manner, but, as we had already passed them, I cannot know the result of this encounter.[8]

Unaware of the problems with III Corps, the Imperial Guard also started its march on time, but, using a different route, were not held up by their inactivity. Thus, Pajol's cavalry was not followed by III Corps as planned, but by the Imperial Guard, with Napoleon himself at their head. VI Corps however, were forced to wait for Vandamme to get on his way before moving off themselves. In truth, Vandamme marched his corps hard, despite the difficult country and poor roads, but a large proportion of the army suffered a long delay and this ensured that Napoleon's timetable was immediately undermined.

Grouchy's main interest lay with Pajol's advance guard to the centre column. This general had his corps mounted and ready to move at 2.30am. His route followed the valley of the river Heure as far as Jumignon and Bommerée, and the tracks on both sides of this valley. Less than two leagues from their bivouacs they encountered the Prussian outposts which were centred on Ham-sur-Heure. These outposts were not surprised; a drummer from the Imperial Guard had presented himself to the outposts the previous night and warned them of the coming storm. Grouchy himself travelled with Exelmans' dragoon division.

Using secondary routes, each division of Pajol's light cavalry advanced on a slightly different axis. Some of these were extremely difficult, but this avoided any mix-ups and confusion. Pajol himself marched at the head of Soult's division where he was well placed to communicate with the emperor to his left, Gérard to his right, and Vandamme following up behind. The divisions on each flank were also ordered to maintain communications with the formations on their flanks. Warned of the Prussian post at Ham-sur-Heure, Pajol's deployment approached this position from left, right and centre, and in this way he hoped to capture it as he had been instructed by Marshal Soult's order of the night before.

The first contact with Prussian outposts and weak patrols was made near Cour-sur-Heure; these withdrew quickly as Pajol advanced and it was at Ham-sur-Heure, where Pajol had been warned there was a force of up to 6,000, that they faced their first serious opposition, albeit not the strong force he had been warned of. Arriving towards 6am, he found the route barricaded and defended by two companies of the fusilier battalion of the 28th Regiment. A vigorous charge was sufficient to compel them to retreat, leaving a hundred prisoners in French hands.

Chef d'escadron Biot, one of Pajol's *aides de camp*, had been attached to Subervie's division to lead its advance. Going ahead of the foremost troops into Thy-le-Château, Biot found Napoleon there with his escort conducting his own reconnaissance. The emperor, learning of Vandamme's late start, had taken the *sapeurs* and *marins* of the Guard, as well as part of the Young Guard, and taken a lateral route to the left. Napoleon wanted to interrogate the *burgmestre* (mayor), and Biot was ordered to find him. However, he returned with a young man who he had spoken to already, feeling he would have the information the emperor was seeking. Napoleon recognised the man, who was called Duhaut, and said:

'Have you not served in the Gardes d'Honneur?'
'Yes, Sire.'
'And what do you do now?' replied the emperor.
'I am married Sire.'
'Ah, Ah! You have done well; would you like to serve again?' The young man hesitated, but before he could properly answer, Napoleon pressed him and he was made a lieutenant in the cavalry. Biot, who recorded this story, comments, 'He was probably killed for I did not hear of him again'![9]

Pajol approached Jamignon at 7am, where he met the emperor accompanied by the four service squadrons (a squadron from each of the Imperial Guard cavalry regiments that provided the emperor's escort). No Prussians were found at this place and Soult's division continued its march towards Bommerée where he met Domon's division. These two divisions continued their march side by side. Cannon fire was heard to the west; this was from Reille's engagements. Pajol's advance took him up onto the high ground overlooking the river valley of the Sambre and where he had a good view of the surrounding area. Let's pick up in Pajol's memoirs,

> On coming up onto the plateau, Pajol was able to see the movements of II Corps whose success did not seem in doubt. Examining what was happening not far away, the general noticed that, in the direction of Mont-sur-Marchienne, small Prussian detachments were assembling around the farm of la Tombe. He sent the 4th *Chasseurs* there from Domon's division, and had them supported by the 9th. Struck by a lively fire, our cavalrymen attempted to corner them in the farm. But Pajol, understanding the situation, sent one of his howitzers to this point. The two or three hundred men surrounded in the farm surrendered. This was all that remained of the battalion that was broken at Ham-sur-Heure and the small outposts from the surrounding area.
>
> This incident had held up the whole of Domon's division. Soult's column continued to advance. At 8.30am, it arrived before Marcinelle. General Pajol

attempted a *coup-de-main*, but it did not succeed. Numerous skirmishers, hidden behind the hedges and walls of the gardens and in the first houses of the village, repulsed the hussars with a lively fire. Some men were wounded and one killed in Pajol's escort. It was necessary to give up trying to force a way through with cavalry alone and to await Vandamme's infantry which could not be far behind. Whilst awaiting III Corps, Pajol sent General Ameil to try and find a ford in the direction of Couillet, in order to try to turn Marcinelle by the left bank of the Sambre. None was found so further attacks had to be suspended. However, Domon's division rejoined Subervie and they went on to exit the Hublembue woods. If Vandamme had appeared, Charleroi would have been in French possession at 9am.[10]

Now the full effects of Vandamme's delay were beginning to be felt. Luckily, the *sapeurs* and *marins* of the Imperial Guard, led by Generals Haxo and Rogniat, arrived at Jumignon just as Napoleon learnt of Pajol's dilemma and he sent them forward. Arriving with Pajol at 10.30am, he immediately ordered them to attack Marcinelle. Despite their relative numerical weakness, the *élan* of their attack was irresistible and the Prussians fell back into Charleroi and prepared to defend the barricade and palisade that blocked the bridge over the Sambre. However, the French quickly followed up their advantage and the *sapeurs* and *marins* stormed over the bridge, followed by Soult's cavalry with Pajol at its head.

Captain Aubry of the 12th *Chasseurs* claimed the honour of being the first across the bridge and into the town,

> Two days later [15th June] we entered Charleroi, the 12th *Chasseurs* forming the extreme advance guard. It was my squadron who was first into the town; there were only a few enemy there. We had with us a company of *pontonniers* to re-establish the bridge over the Sambre. They behaved very well and we made prisoner there a battalion of light infantry which had formed the Prussian rearguard, without giving them enough time to destroy the bridge, with which the emperor was very satisfied.[11]

As Captain Aubry testifies, no attempt had been made by the Prussians to destroy the bridge and by 11.30am, Charleroi and its precious bridge, were in French hands.

Whilst Pajol's troopers and elements of the Guard were pushing back the Prussian advance posts and seizing the bridge at Charleroi, Vandamme's troops were closing the gap between them. His lead elements approached the bridge at midday[12] but it still took a long time for the whole corps to defile across the bridge and pass through the narrow streets of the town.

In contrast to the lukewarm reception even Napoleon himself had received at Beaumont, which was in France, there was a warmer welcome in Belgium. Despite being anti-Bonapartist in his account of the campaign, *Chirurgien-major* Bourgeois of the cuirassiers noted that after crossing the border,

> The whole of the army was now in the territory of Belgium, in the midst of the new subjects of the Kingdom of the Netherlands, who welcomed us with acclamations, as their deliverers, and asserted that they only waited for our arrival to rise *en masse* in favour of our cause . . . The inhabitants themselves were thunderstruck at our sudden arrival, as they thought we were fully employed in securing our own frontiers from invasion. They generally spoke very ill of the Prussians whom they represented as very extortionate and who daily mistreated them.[13]

Surprisingly, the Prussians abandoned Charleroi without a determined resistance and without destroying the bridge. Given that Zieten's job was to impose delay on the French to cover the concentration of the army, this seems inexplicable. The possibility that they may have wanted to use it in a counter-offensive is a possibility, but it is more likely that measures for its destruction were overlooked. The fact that the Prussians were to fight a delaying action at Gilly does not suggest that Zieten felt he had already bought enough time; a longer delay might just have allowed Bülow to arrive for the coming battle and allowed Wellington's army more time to concentrate. Furthermore, no attempt had been made to destroy the other crossings the French were to use at Marchienne or Châtelet.

Having abandoned the defensible line of the Sambre, most of the Prussians fell back through the suburb of Gilly, east towards Fleurus, beyond which the rest of the army was concentrating. However, some continued north, along the Brussels road towards Gosselies. Pajol, informed of this, sent General Clary with the 1st Hussars along that road whilst he went with Soult's other two regiments towards Gilly, followed by the divisions of Domon and Subervie.

It was a little after 11.30am when the emperor arrived north of Charleroi and approved Pajol's dispositions. Finding General Clary rather weak on the road to Gosselies, he had him supported by the guard *chasseurs* and lancers commanded by Lefebvre-Desnouëttes. Napoleon then ordered Pajol to continue to push the Prussians back towards Namur; but to stop and await Vandamme's infantry if the enemy stopped in a strong defensive position. Pajol galloped towards Gilly to take command of the move.

Towards midday, Marshal Grouchy arrived at Charleroi with Exelmans' dragoons (2nd Cavalry Corps), at the head of which he had left Boussu at 5.30am. The emperor sent him, with the dragoons, along the road to Gilly to support Pajol.

The Right Column
Of the whole army, Gérard's IV Corps was to start its march furthest from Charleroi and was therefore not expected to be involved in any fighting that day.

The corps was to have concentrated forward of Philippeville and then set off at 3am, regulating its move with that of III Corps to its left and followed by Delort's 14th Cavalry Division of the 4th Reserve Cavalry Corps (Milhaud). One of Gérard's main tasks was to protect the right flank of the advance, covering the approaches from Namur. The concentration areas of both the Prussian II and III Corps were in this direction. Gérard had been ordered to cross the Sambre at Charleroi.

However, not all Gérard's troops had reached Philippeville on the 14th and these required time to close up. Thus IV Corps was late forming up and did not gather on the heights of Florenne, their assembly area, until 7am. Gérard's movement orders did not leave his headquarters in Philippeville until 2am, only an hour before the troops were due to move out!

But these holdups were overshadowed by a far more significant event. First let us hear from Colonel Rumigny, one of Gérard's *aides de camp*:

> In the evening of the 14th, the movement order arrived from Imperial Headquarters. I was ordered to take it to Bourmont's division cantoned around Florenne and I left at 2am. I went at the full gallop, when two *chasseurs à cheval* approached me from the direction of the advance posts, signalling me to stop. 'General Bourmont has deserted,' they shouted to me from afar.
>
> 'Wretches!' I said to them, drawing my sabre, 'Silence, it is impossible.'
>
> 'We swear to you!'[14]
>
> Stunned by this news, of which they gave all the details, I ordered them to go to the headquarters at Philippeville, and to tell only the chief of staff, Colonel Saint-Rémy, what had happened and to advise him that I was continuing to Florenne. I arrived at this place a few moments later. On entering I was surrounded by soldiers shouting, 'We are betrayed, down with the traitors!'
>
> These shouts were directed at all the officers, including myself. I was aware of the danger of these menaces, but I put myself in the middle of them saying, 'Bourmont has left you because he is not worthy of commanding you. I carry the orders to march, *mes enfants*, take up your arms.' I took the orders to General Vichery, I encouraged the men and tried to put faith in their hearts . . .
>
> The news of the desertion had spread, but I don't know how. Arriving at Florenne, I found all in rumour. The division had the order to cross the Sambre at 8am. We were before the bridge when General Gérard joined us. He made a lively speech, passionate in stigmatising Bourmont and, in the middle of shouts of rage from the soldiers, he enlisted them to observe the strictest discipline. After a thousand oaths to follow him anywhere, the division recommenced its march and we crossed the Sambre to the sound of gunfire that we could hear in front of us.[15]

General Bourmont was a noted Royalist (he had once been imprisoned for being complicit in an attempt on Napoleon's life!), but one that had fought under Napoleon and had proven his combat ability the previous year in his successful defence of Nogent-sur-Seine which had seen him promoted to *général de division*. In 1815, Napoleon had only reluctantly agreed to give him a command after being urged to do so by Ney and Gérard who had both sworn to answer for him. It was a decision all three of them were to regret.

Maréchal de Camp Hulot was the senior brigade commander in the division and we have already seen how he had at least a suspicion that Bourmont was considering such a move. He gives us more detail on what happened.

> The troops took up arms at 4am on the 15th. At 5.30am one of my *aides de camp* informed me that M. de Bourmont and all the officers of his headquarters were already mounted; I paid no attention to this. Towards *** hours, two orderlies came to find me from the divisional commander, to be at my orders; I asked them where they had left him and they replied that it was close to the advance posts.
>
> Half an hour later, the *brigadier* [corporal] orderly with four *chasseurs*, brought me two letters from M. de Bourmont addressed to General Gérard. This *brigadier* had been ordered by the divisional commander to inform me that he was going to join King Louis XVIII and to request me to promptly send these two letters to the corps commander. I did not lose a minute in informing him of this incident. I then immediately left to join the colonels of the 9th and 111th Regiments [the two regiments of his own brigade] and ordered them to get their troops under arms and into their ranks. I hastened to go to announce to the two regiments the situation myself and determined to maintain their confidence, which will forever remain in my memory. As I received the order to march from the corps commander, I immediately set the brigade off to reassemble with the rest of the corps on the road to Charleroi, and to send off the orders to the rest of the division . . . There was not a single deserter in the division . . . Never, perhaps, had officers and soldiers displayed a more unanimous and energetic devotion.[16]

It may be of interest to see what Bourmont and his chief of staff, Colonel Clouet, wrote in their letters to General Gérard that Hulot mentions.

Florenne, 15th June 1815

My General,

If anything in the world could have enabled me, in the actual circumstances, to determine me to serve the emperor, it would have been your example and my attachment to you, for I love you and honour you sincerely. It is impossible for me to fight for a government which punishes my parents and all the landowners of my province.

I do not want to contribute to the establishment of a bloody despot in France who would destroy my country and that this despotism would be the result of any success we might attain.

I will not be seen in the ranks of foreigners: they will not get from me any information that might harm the French army, composed of men that I love and to whom I will never cease to take a lively interest, but I will try to defend the Frenchmen who have been punished, to drive away from *la patrie* the system of confiscations without losing from view the conservation of national independence.

I would have given my resignation and gone home if I thought I would have been allowed to do it; this does not appear likely in the current circumstances and I therefore have to ensure my liberty in other ways, in order not to lose all options of trying to re-establish a better order of things in France.

I suffer a profound grief of the idea of the anger that my departure will cause you; I would risk my life a hundred times to avoid this, but I cannot give up the hope of again being useful to my country.

Always, and whatever happens, I will retain for you the most sincere attachment and highest respect.

Lieutenant-général comte de Bourmont[17]

Colonel Clouet had written,

My General,
The motives that determined the departure of M. de Bourmont are also mine, and it was essential that they were powerful for me to resolve to leave an army full of my friends and commanded by a chief [Gérard, not Napoleon!] whose noble character and great talents have inspired together boundless respect, attachment and confidence.

My friends will tell you, my general, what a high price taking this course has cost me. I need that inner conviction that I am doing this for the good of my country, in order to be able to abandon all that which I find in serving under your orders.

I am with the most intense distress and profound respect.

Colonel Clouet[18]

Bourmont had deserted accompanied by Colonel Clouet,[19] Captains Doudigne and de Frélon (*aides de camp*), *Chef d'escadron* Villouty and Captain Sourdat (*officiers adjoints de l'état-major*). The impact on the division, IV Corps and the army is hard to gauge and the arguments over its true effect raged on for many years. We have seen above that Hulot was adamant that the incident merely galvanised the troops of the division, though later in the campaign Grouchy felt the discipline of the corps suffered and that the desertion 'rendered the movement of this corps slow and without precision'.[20] To this charge, Gérard responded,

> It is not true that there was any indication of the slightest disorder in the troops I commanded. Neither is it true that the desertion of General Bourmont and some officers of his headquarters had a poor influence on the morale of the troops; on the contrary, they only displayed more enthusiasm.[21]

Gérard goes on to say that the performance of the corps at the battle of Ligny proves that the spirit of his men was excellent, and as we shall see, it is certainly true that they performed heroically at that battle. However, many others had a different view, particularly those who wished to portray the eventual defeat of Napoleon as due to treason and betrayal rather than military failings or incompetence. Colonel Zenowicz, a Polish officer who was attached to Imperial Headquarters and who we will meet again later, wrote of its wider impact:

> This desertion, on the day of combat, greatly affected the morale of the army; not so much by its importance in itself, as by other desertions that it seemed to anticipate. The reputation of General Bourmont was well-established amongst both his seniors and equals; all, or nearly all, had confidence in his loyalty and in his talents; his desertion produced amongst these an immense effect, a sadness and anxiety. For the soldiers, who did not know how to hide their thoughts, they were so demoralised they saw traitors everywhere; they distrusted all their commanders. Long experience showed that the most certain means of beating an army, of paralysing its actions, was to affect its morale; the people behind Bourmont's desertion knew this truth and profited from it. In their view, our soldiers said that General Bourmont did not pass to the enemy solely for the satisfaction of treason, but as much to be useful, to warn them of the movements of the French army, to inform them of all the details of the campaign plan, to give away to the enemy the plans ordered the day before their desertion and to thus ruin in advance all the arrangements, all the plans of the emperor.[22]

Let's give the last word on this incident to *Adjutant-commandant* Etienne-Fulgence Janin who served on the headquarters staff of Lobau's VI Corps,

> The desertion of a few individuals, whatever their ranks, was only one more of those ordinary events, which was of no significance because we knew they were likely and it is to give them an over-exaggerated importance on

their supposed decisive influence on the success of the campaign. The results were not as terrible as one is led to believe; in fact to the contrary, since on the 15th June, at the moment when the French army penetrated into the enemy's cantonments, inexplicably, they had still not concentrated their troops.[23]

By the time the initial fallout of this event was over, there was no hope of IV Corps crossing the Sambre at 8am as Gérard's orders prescribed; the best that could be hoped for was to march hard and try to make up as much time as possible. Indeed, Janin wrote:

> He [Gérard] sent with the greatest speed, the order to cross the defile which split his corps into two parts, and which was executed in my presence with a precision and rapidity that was remarkable.[24]

Napoleon's hopes of having a major part of his force across the Sambre by midday had been frustrated by a series of mistakes, mishaps and treachery. However, despite the criticisms of military historians and critics, none of these can really be placed at Napoleon's feet, and given the inevitable friction of military operations things could certainly have been worse. Having successfully captured the Sambre bridges intact, it was now imperative that he should exploit the opportunities that this presented him with.

Chapter 4

Afternoon, 15 June

The Prussians
Zieten's I Corps was withdrawing east across the front of the French advance, leaving its southern flank vulnerable. Identifying that the main road to Brussels from Charleroi was a likely French axis, he had sent his 3rd Brigade (von Jagöw) to occupy Gosselies, through which this road passed. The 6th Uhlans, commanded by the former partisan leader Colonel Lützow, was also there having been left by the commander of the Reserve Cavalry to maintain contact with Zieten's men.

Pirch II's 2nd Brigade withdrew from Charleroi to the east, concentrating around the village of Gilly. Here he deployed his brigade covering the various roads that the French might take to advance on Fleurus to threaten the main Prussian concentration in the area of Sombreffe.

The French Left Column
On the northern edge of Charleroi was a major road junction, with main roads leading towards Mons, Brussels and Namur. As we have heard, Pajol had despatched General Clary with his 1st Hussars along the Brussels road that ran due north; these soon ran into determined resistance at Gosselies from von Jagow's brigade and after receiving a bloody nose, drew back and awaited reinforcements. Informed of this check by Colonel Gourgaud and concerned about the left flank of the advance towards Fleurus, Napoleon sent Gourgaud to Reille to hurry his advance and to vigorously attack the Prussian force occupying Gosselies. He then sent Lefebvre-Desnoëttes, with his two light cavalry regiments of the Guard and two batteries, up this road to establish a block half way between the two towns; he later reinforced them with a regiment of Duhesme's Young Guard.

When Reille finally arrived at Gosselies, he deployed his artillery and opened fire. Pushing forward the 2nd *léger*, he took possession of the town. However, as soon as he tried to continue up the Brussels road he was strongly counter-attacked and pushed back into the houses by Zieten's troops who were being forced to bypass Gosselies to the north. Reille sent Piré's cavalry round the Moncaux wood to cut off the road to Brussels, but the Prussian troops had been able to continue their withdrawal towards Fleurus.

Having despatched Grouchy to pursue the Prussian rearguard towards Fleurus, Napoleon took up position at the junction to the north of Charleroi. Whilst sitting on a chair outside the Belle-Vue inn and watching the troops file past, he was finally joined by Marshal Ney whom the emperor had summoned very late to the army. Napoleon had decided to split his army into two wings and a reserve. The emperor would command the latter, consisting of VI Corps, the 4th Reserve Cavalry Corps and the Imperial Guard; Ney would command the left wing consisting of I and II Corps and the 3rd Reserve Cavalry Corps; and Grouchy would command the right wing consisting of III and IV Corps and the 1st and 2nd Cavalry Corps. Ney was to march his wing up the Brussels road and occupy the strategically important crossroads of Quatre Bras and sooner or later meet Wellington who would no doubt be advancing down that road. Grouchy would continue in pursuit of the Prussian rearguard towards Fleurus and Sombreffe in the area of which the emperor expected Blücher's army to be concentrating. Napoleon would support one or the other with the reserve as the situation dictated. Each wing would be strong enough to hold its own against one of the allied armies, whilst the other wing, reinforced by the reserve, would defeat the other.

Leaving Napoleon, Ney immediately moved forward to join his command, meeting Reille as he was entering Gosselies. With this town in his hands, the road to Brussels was now open and there were still four hours of daylight left. He pushed forward Lefebvre-Desnouëttes's Guard cavalry as an advance guard towards Frasnes and led Bachelu's and Piré's divisions forward to Mellet. Girard's division of II Corps was sent in pursuit of the Prussians that had been driven from Gosselies towards the east, whilst Foy and Prince Jérôme's divisions remained around Gosselies.

The Centre Column and the Combat at Gilly
Having finally reached Charleroi at 3pm, Vandamme's troops had to file across the bridge and through the narrow, congested streets of the town. Other than the Guard, which Napoleon would be very loath to commit so early in the campaign, his was the first infantry formation to pass through Charleroi heading towards the east. Lefol's division led the march and the young Lieutenant Lefol recalls,

> After passing through Charleroi, we saw 150 to 200 disarmed Prussians that our soldiers looked at with interest. They were some of the prisoners made during the day by the 1st Hussars, commanded I think by General Clary, whose bravery had brought about this result.[1]

Having despatched the 1st Hussars towards Brussels, the remainder of Pajol's corps was directed along the main road towards Gilly and Sombreffe, towards which most of the Prussian defenders of Charleroi had retreated. Still awaiting the arrival of Vandamme, Napoleon also sent forward the division of the Young Guard, less the regiment sent up the Brussels road, to support him. General Ameil, with the 5th Hussars, acted as the advance guard, but had not gone far when he came under fire from the Prussian rearguard around Gilly. Biot, one of Pajol's *aides de camp* wrote,

> The 1st Hussars moved through the suburb of Gosselies; the rest of the cavalry followed the suburb of Gilly. This is bordered on each side, along its entire length, with an uninterrupted line of houses; it thus formed a very dangerous defile for cavalry.
>
> We profited from the first suitable location to form closed column by regiment. Then General Ameil with the 5th Hussars was sent on reconnaissance to the exit of the suburb. There he was saluted by volleys of musketry and artillery fire; the enemy occupied a plateau under the fire of which the main road passed.[2]

Pajol's memoirs describe his actions and the Prussian position:

> At first, Pajol pushed his scouts onto the different points of this position. The resistance that they encountered left him in no doubt that the enemy was determined to defend themselves there. Conforming to the emperor's orders, Pajol stopped his troops and awaited some infantry. However, he did not cease to harass his enemies and skirmished along the whole line.
>
> A little before 1pm, Grouchy appeared with Exelmans' dragoons. He conducted his own reconnaissance of the enemy position and took command of the situation. He then had Pajol's regiments massed on either side of the Namur road and took Exelmans' cavalry to the right, in the direction of Châtelet. Not wanting to carry out an attack without infantry, he simply skirmished with the Prussian advance posts whilst awaiting the arrival of III Corps.
>
> Pirch II profited from this time to complete his deployment and established his men a little to the rear of the junction of the roads to Fleurus via Campinaire and Namur, by Lambusart. His first line, composed of four battalions, stretched from the abbey of Soleilmont to close to Chatelineau, parallel to the road which ran between these two points; the battalion on the right held the Soleilmont abbey and was covered by *abatis* on the Fleurus road and as far as the Lobbes wood. The three other battalions deployed along the line and in front of the Trichehéve wood, extending to the south of the Namur road. To their left, a regiment of dragoons observed the exits of Chatelineau and Châtelet. Finally their artillery was distributed along the Fleurus road and on the slopes, firing down onto the road exiting Gilly. In the second line, Pirch II had established three battalions astride the Namur road and at the entry to the Rondechamp wood; they occupied all the space between le chêne de Vescourt and the village of Rondechamp.[3]

Colonel Count de Bloqueville, who was one of Grouchy's *aides de camp*, later recounted the events in the run-up to the combat.

> When the marshal had passed through Charleroi, he moved at the gallop along the road from Charleroi to Fleurus as far as the village of Gilly, where he saw a body of Prussians in position. Followed by a single *aide de camp*, he got as close as possible to the enemy who appeared to be about 20,000 strong. Then, protected by several clumps of trees which were spread along the edges of the small river which ran along a valley which separated the Prussians from Gilly, he explored the banks and returned to Gilly from

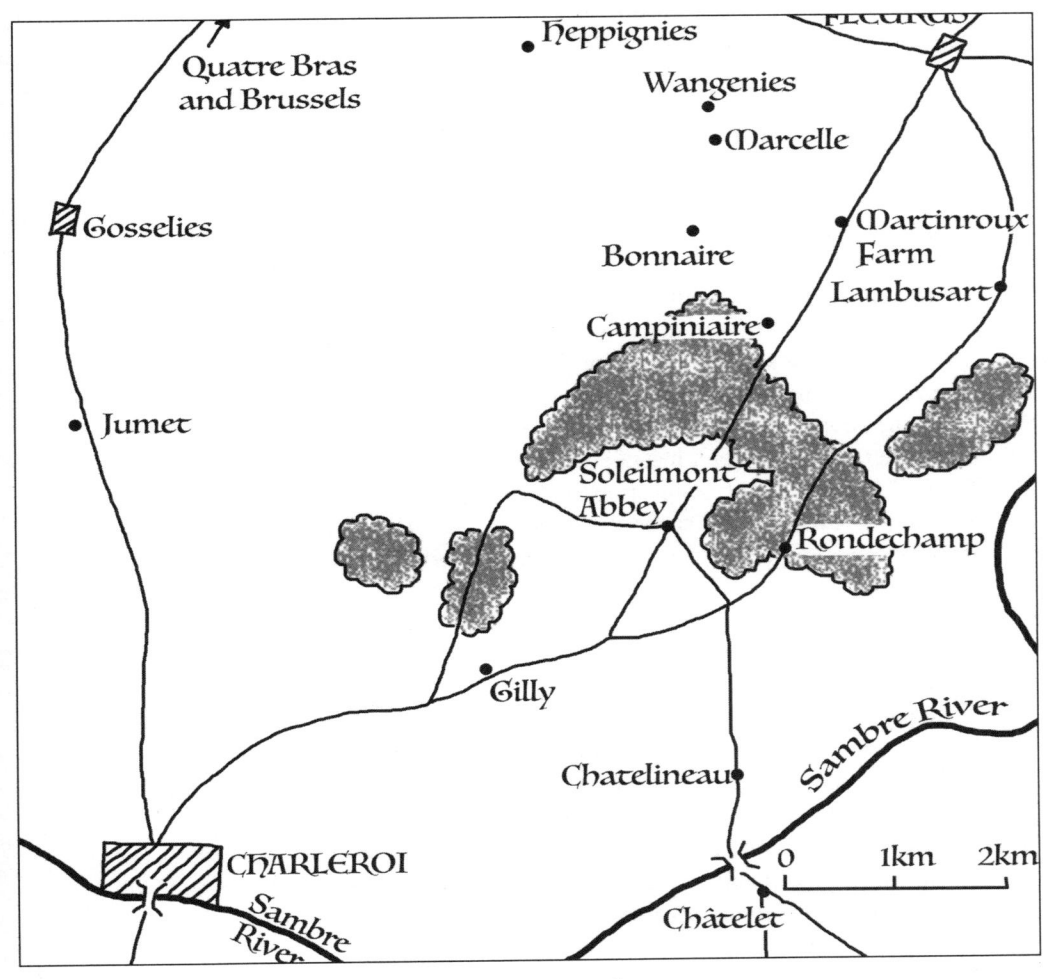

Afternoon, 15th June

where he sent his *aide de camp* Pont-Bellanger to the emperor to request permission to attack the Prussians and to request him to send some reinforcements, notably infantry, in order to carry out this attack.

Whilst waiting for a response from Napoleon, the marshal led General Exelmans' dragoons round to the right as far as a mill where the horses would be able to cross the small river. From where they could cross, the marshal, profiting from the lay of the ground which did not allow the enemy to observe the movement of the dragoons, placed them so that they would be able, at the first signal, to outflank the Prussian left and charge their flank.[4]

Whilst Grouchy conducted his reconnaissance, others were taking sensible precautions against a Prussian counter-attack. *Chef d'escadron* Biot tells us,

During our reconnaissance, a company of *sapeurs* was rushed to fortify the houses of the Gilly suburb that we were occupying. Infantry were deployed there as it arrived in order to resist the enemy in case they attempted to retake the suburb and throw us back on the bridge that our infantry and artillery continued to cross.[5]

The emperor was obviously not impressed when he received Pont-Bellanger's report; he no doubt felt that Grouchy should not have awaited orders, but immediately attacked Zieten and pushed on to Fleurus as he had been previously directed. He immediately set off for Gilly, annoyed at the holdup and determined to get the advance re-started. Before he left, he ordered Soult to write to Gérard to cross the river at Châtelet instead of Charleroi. This would have two advantages; firstly it would avoid congestion in Charleroi which was already holding up Vandamme's march, and secondly, it would bring IV Corps onto the flank of the Prussian position; if he arrived early enough the Prussian rearguard might well be destroyed.

Letter from the *major-général* to Gérard 15 June, 3.30pm
M. *le comte* Gérard, the emperor charges me to order you to move yourself and your corps to Châtelet where you are to cross the Sambre and advance following the road to Fleurus, the direction that the emperor is following at this moment with part of the army with the aim of attacking an enemy corps that has stopped in front of the wood of Lambusart. If this corps is still in position after you have crossed the Sambre, you are also to attack it. Let me know your positions and inform me if the 14th Cavalry division is with you; if so, you are to advance with it.[6]

Napoleon arrived at Gilly at about 4.30pm and met up with Grouchy. His irritation is clear in his memoirs:

The corps of Vandamme and Grouchy were both at Gilly. Misled by false reports they wasted two hours without moving, in the belief that 200,000 Prussians were behind the woods and in front of Fleurus. I made a personal reconnaissance of the enemy and, judging that these woods were only occupied by two divisions of Zieten's corps, consisting of between 18,000 and 20,000 men I forthwith gave the order to move forward.[7]

In fact, all Vandamme's troops were not yet fully up and Napoleon moved back to hasten their march. To the emperor's frustration, the combat did not start until 6pm. Joining the troops as they prepared to launch their attack, Napoleon came across the 37th *de ligne*, one of whose officers reported,

> . . . our divisions were massed on the plateau of Charleroi, where they waited for a time. Suddenly the emperor appeared on his horse in the middle of our columns. He addressed some words to the officer closest to him,
> 'What regiment?'
> 'Sire, the 37th'
> 'Ah! Gauthier's regiment? Your soldiers have poor greatcoats'
> 'The Prussians have new ones'
> 'They are there, go and take them!'[8]

Pirch II's brigade actually only consisted of a total of around 6,500 men in three regiments each of three battalions (the 6th and 28th Infantry Regiments and the 2nd Westphalian Landwehr), some cavalry from the corps cavalry reserve and an artillery battery. They had imposed on Grouchy and delayed his advance for several hours.

Some of Vandamme's corps were committed as soon as they came forward. Lieutenant Lefol wrote, 'Continuing our march, we encountered the enemy towards 6pm, and after taking part in a bloody combat where we lost many men . . . '[9] Pajol reported something similar: 'The head of III Corps arrived in front of Pirch II's positions towards 3pm. Vandamme attacked them immediately, but was unsuccessful.'[10]

It appears that Vandamme, perhaps sensing the emperor's frustration, launched Lefol's division in a premature attack. Then, realising that a single division was insufficient for the task, was forced to wait until his whole corps came up. Pajol again:

> He [Vandamme] was forced to wait for his whole corps to get forward and to combine his attacks with cavalry. Grouchy and Vandamme adopted the following deployment. Three infantry columns of infantry marched, one towards the Trichehève wood and the abbey of Soleilmont; another against the Prussian centre, following the Lambusart road; and the third against the Prussian left, turning Gilly. Exelmans' dragoons went towards the

Chatelineau mill to cross the stream at a ford and throw themselves, thanks to the cover of the ground which hid them from view, into the rear left of the Prussian position. Pajol's cavalry marched to the left of Vandamme's columns along the Fleurus road.

Informed of these deployments and of the attack which was about to be launched against Pirch II, Napoleon left Ney, to whom he had just given his orders and command of the left wing, and moved in all haste to Gilly. He arrived there towards 4.30pm. The attack was initiated by a violent artillery barrage aimed at the Prussian batteries. The infantry columns were then ordered forward.[11]

This time, faced by a co-ordinated all-arms attack by superior forces, and with his flank threatened by Gérard, Pirch II chose this moment to order the retreat before they became decisively engaged. Thus it seems, Vandamme's corps advanced but did not come into contact with the Prussians. General Berthezène reported: 'The III Corps, having found the enemy had withdrawn, continued its march towards Fleurus and took position on the road a little in the rear of this small town.'[12] We cannot be sure who provided the three columns that Pajol speaks of; some accounts mention that one of them was made up of a regiment of the Young Guard and the others from Vandamme's corps. Clearly, the whole of III Corps were not involved.

Napoleon, seeing that the Prussian infantry were escaping, hastened Vandamme's advance, but he must have realised that infantry would not catch the retreating Prussians. He therefore turned to his *aide-de-camp* and former commander of the Guard Dragoons, General Letort, and ordered him to take the four service squadrons and to wipe out the Prussian battalions as they moved towards the entry to the woods behind them. At the same moment, Pajol launched his cavalry on Soleilmont to seize the defile into the wood of Fleurus and Exelmans' dragoons swept onto the Prussian left from their covered position, scattering a small Prussian infantry force and forcing back the cavalry that was covering this flank. In his report on the action, Exelmans wrote to Grouchy:

I have the honour to inform Your Excellency that in the affair that took place yesterday under your eyes, General Vincent's brigade had two officers and twenty dragoons wounded and seven killed. The brigade did its duty perfectly. Led by the brave General Vincent who combines a rare and great experience, firmness and sang-froid, I pray Your Excellency to ask the emperor for him to be made a higher grade in the *legion d'honneur*.

Colonel Briqueville (of the 20th) behaved very well, also the commander of the 1st Squadron; as this officer is very senior, I ask for the rank of major for him. [He then goes on to list the men he wants promoted/decorated, including 'Grenadier Pissé (of the 20th Dragoons) who made twenty-seven prisoners.'][13]

The Prussian battalion positioned close to the Trichehève wood threw themselves into the trees. The two battalions to its left formed into square and marched towards the woods, stopping now and then to stand against Letort's charges, supported by the Prussian cavalry. Letort moved forward to demand the square's surrender; the battalions were from Berg, an old German state ally of the French, and perhaps he thought they may be prepared to change sides. However, the response was a shot that knocked him from his saddle. He died later in Charleroi.

One square became disordered, was broken, sabred and mostly destroyed (this was the fusilier battalion of the 28th), but the other managed to reach the safety of the Rondechamp wood, from which the three reserve battalions had already set off towards Lambusart. The right-hand battalion of the first line finally found protection behind the *abatis* that protected the Fleurus road and escaped into the wood, where it broke down into skirmishers and heavily engaged Pajol's cavalry which was marching on the direct road from Gilly to Fleurus. Despite having imposed considerable delay on the French, Pirch II's regiments suffered badly during this action. The fusiliers of the 28th lost 13 officers and 614 men; the fusilier battalion of the 6th lost a total of 216 killed wounded and missing.[14]

The firing in the woods continued for a long time. The battered battalions of Pirch II's brigade succeeded in reaching Lambusart where they were covered by Jagow's 3rd Brigade, which had been in position there since 4pm. Despite the difficulties of the tracks and the enemy skirmish fire, Pajol's regiments, after having taken a great number of prisoners, exited from the Fleurus woods sometime around 6.30pm, at about the same time as Exelmans' dragoons left the Trichehève wood. At the sight of these two cavalry corps, Jagow and Pirch II retired from Lambusart to Fleurus. Satisfied with the results of the action at this point, Napoleon left with the Imperial Guard cavalry and returned to Charleroi where he could update himself on Ney's situation and where he intended to pass the night.

In line with the emperor's intentions and instructions, Grouchy left the corps of Pajol and Exelmans to continue the pursuit of the Prussians in the direction of Fleurus. Pajol, who was then marching with Subervie's division on the direct route to Fleurus, passed close to the farm of Martinroux and launched Domon's division to his left towards Wangenies along the Bonnaire road, whilst he advanced Soult's division on his right towards Lambusart.

Biot described the difficulty of the ground for cavalry:

The road that we took to Lambusart is an elevated track, very narrow and bordered by woods on both sides. The enemy had made *abatis* out of trees across the road to slow our march as much as possible, for we were very close. His artillery sent us several balls from time to time, but to which we did not reply. An *aide de camp* to General Soult had his arm ripped off.[15]

The scouts of these three divisions harassed the enemy rearguards but without being able to make any great impression on them. It required infantry to really interfere with the Prussian retreat. Pajol resolved to await Vandamme, who only reached the exits of the woods towards 7.30pm.

Grouchy had ordered Vandamme to continue to advance on Fleurus to support Pajol's and Exelmans' corps, but Vandamme, whose soldiers had been marching and fighting hard for more than twelve hours, refused, saying his men were exhausted. Grouchy was furious, but Vandamme had not been informed that he had been put under his command and that he should obey the marshal's orders as commander of the right wing. He ordered his troops to bivouac. Lieutenant Lefol records: 'Our division went into bivouac in a small wood between Charleroi and Fleurus, which had been previously occupied by the Prussians.'[16]

Without infantry support, Pajol and Exelmans had to pull up their divisions. Domon stopped between Bonnaire and Marselle, almost reaching Wangenies; that of Subervie to the right and left of the Fleurus road, a little to the rear of Martinroux farm; that of Soult before Lambusart, with Exelmans' dragoons to their rear and right. At 8pm, all the infantry and cavalry were installed in their bivouacs. Pajol's advance posts were hardly half a league from Fleurus. Grouchy's headquarters were established at Campinaire, with Pajol's at Lambusart. In his report dated from this last village at 10pm, Pajol informed Grouchy of the locations occupied by his troops and expressed the regret that they had not been supported by Vandamme's infantry so that they could have attacked Fleurus.

The Right Column
After the inevitable delays following Bourmont's desertion and the need to close the corps up before starting their march, Gérard's IV Corps was further delayed by the poor state of the roads. We have already heard that in order to avoid congestion in Charleroi and to threaten the flank of Pirch II's brigade at Gilly, the corps had been ordered by Napoleon to cross the Sambre at Châtelet, a small town about five kilometres to the east. This would still offer good routes heading towards Fleurus. A staff officer reported, 'Happily, no effort, no steps, had been made to destroy the bridge, which was not even defended.'[17] The small garrison had withdrawn when the Prussian rearguard had made their stand at Gilly and so the first of Gérard's troops were able to file across unhindered. Only one division, Hulot's, got across the river before night, so they had no opportunity to get involved in the action at Gilly. Hulot wrote in his report,

> The corps was put in march on the road to Charleroi, the 3rd Division in the lead. No enemy were encountered. In the area of Châtelet, it turned to the right and crossed the Sambre. The 3rd Division moved beyond the town and bivouacked with a body of dragoons in the outer orchards of a large village that I think was Chatelineau.[18]

The village was indeed Chatelineau, and there they spent the night. The rest of the corps bivouacked around Châtelet on the other bank of the Sambre. Although they had done nothing except march throughout the day, they were close to joining the rest of the right wing and were well placed to take part in the operations planned for the 16th.

Vandamme's Refusal to obey Grouchy's Orders
Grouchy was outraged by Vandamme's refusal to continue the advance after the action at Gilly despite being ordered to do so. He put forward his case in one of his later writings:

> General Vandamme formally refused to obey the order that was carried to him towards 6pm on 15 June by *aide de camp* Bella on behalf of Marshal Grouchy. Instead of taking position with his infantry he was ordered to descend the heights in the rear of Fleurus and to co-operate in the attack on this town where General Zieten, pursued from the village of Gilly by French cavalry, had rallied the Prussians that had arrived there in the course of the day and from where the marshal had only cavalry available to expel them. This disobedience from General Vandamme resulted in the Prussians remaining masters of Fleurus throughout the night and that orders to occupy Sombreffe, which had come from the emperor, could not be executed.
>
> The serious culpability of General Vandamme's conduct on 15 June, weighs heavily on this general officer . . .[19]

He was not long in expressing his displeasure to the emperor; Captain Bella later wrote to Grouchy:

> You then sent your *aide de camp* Pontbellanger to Charleroi to inform the emperor of General Vandamme's conduct and of the impossibility of your being able to achieve his aims and of completing this first success that you would have achieved if you had been better seconded.
>
> You then had General Vandamme informed that the emperor had placed him under your command and that you were surprised by the premature attack that he had conducted without your direction [at Gilly]. You added that you would put yourself at the head of the dragoons and take the Prussian left wing in the flank; that he with his infantry should approach from the front with the support of Pajol's cavalry.
>
> These simultaneous attacks, in which two battalions of the Young Guard took a part led by General Labedoyere, were very successful. The enemy cavalry was thrown back, several infantry squares broken and sabred, and General Zieten's corps pursued through the wood until close to Fleurus,

where he rallied several bodies of Prussian forces which had concentrated there during the morning.

General Vandamme, who followed your movement, having arrived on the edge of the wood which dominated the plain of Fleurus, instead of joining you, took position there with his corps. Not able to pursue the Prussians into Fleurus with just your cavalry, you sent me to carry the order to him to immediately come and second you in the attack on Fleurus, from where the emperor had requested you to chase the Prussians, as well as from Sombreffe, and even to push reconnaissances as far as Gembloux. General Vandamme positively refused to execute this order that I gave him, alleging the extreme fatigue of his troops and adding that he would follow your movement, but would not fight this day.[20]

Even Pajol was drawn into the controversy, writing in his report on the action,

I would have occupied Fleurus if General Vandamme had been prepared to send me, or support me with, some infantry; but it appeared that this general did everything that is contrary to war, for he neglected to occupy Lambusart and the head of the wood of Gilly at Fleurus which were the two principal points in the front that we occupied.[21]

Despite this outpouring of disgust, it is only fair to say in Vandamme's defence that having been put under Grouchy's command by Napoleon, Soult, the *major-général*, must take some of the blame, as he had failed to inform Vandamme of the new command arrangements. However, one must still wonder why Vandamme felt he had the option of disobeying a superior officer, a marshal of France no less, and in the presence of the enemy.

The Day Ends
In his memoirs, Grouchy described how the day ended.

A regiment of Brandenburg Dragoons, sent by General Zieten, stopped the progress of the French army, allowing the Prussian brigade to reach Lambusart, between Fleurus and Gilly, the former being occupied by another brigade. General Roeder (cavalry division of I Prussian Corps) moved there with three regiments and a battery. At his approach, Grouchy's cavalry deployed in line and a lively cannonade ended the day of the 15th.[22]

Chapter 5

The Night of 15/16 June

After a long day of forced marches and fighting, the coming of night saw the exhausted troops establishing themselves in their bivouacs. Whilst the soldiers rested, cleaned their weapons and prepared their meals, the commanders and their staffs had much work to do before they had a chance to rest. *Chef d'escadron* Biot, *aide de camp* to Pajol, wrote:

> Finally, night arrived. The enemy took position at a cannon's range from Lambusart. The night was quiet; the enemy profited from this by continuing his retreat and taking position on the heights called the 'mill of Bussy'.[1]

In a letter to the marshal, Captain Bella, one of Grouchy's *aides de camp*, also wrote:

> Night having fallen before Pontbellanger had returned from Charleroi, you had Exelmans' corps bivouac in the corn a cannon's range from Fleurus. You yourself went to the village of Lambusart, where you drafted the report on the affair which had taken place during the day and you sent it to the emperor . . .[2]

The recriminations and anger surrounding Vandamme's refusal to advance further were still raging. Colonel Gourgaud, Napoleon's senior *officier d'ordonnance*, recalled:

> I found these generals [Grouchy and Vandamme] beyond the forest [of Lambusart]; the enemy was defending the exit with a dozen guns, but night arriving, they retired on Fleurus, where they had strong masses. Grouchy asked Vandamme for a battalion to occupy the village in front of his cavalry; Vandamme refused. I also asked him, as well as Exelmans, but he refused again. Finally, Exelmans got very angry and Vandamme agreed to give him a battalion.[3]

Once all movement had finished, the senior officers began to prepare the reports to send in to the headquarters that sat above them in the chain of command. Orders for the next day also needed to be sent out. The first requirement, was to report on the events of the day. Grouchy wrote to Napoleon:

> At the village of Campinaire, 15 June, 10pm.
>
> Sire, I have the honour to inform you that the cavalry corps of General Exelmans, which I had ordered to outflank the left wing of General Zieten, who was in position beyond the village of Gilly covered by a deep ravine and a muddy stream, crossed the obstacles and overthrew the Prussian cavalry, broke several squares and made a good number of prisoners. The enemy cavalry having rallied, and protected by the fire of its infantry which had reformed on the edge of the Lambusart wood, attempted to renew its advance, but it was repulsed in disorder on the track which went through the wood, and was pursued afar by the dragoons, of which some companies dismounted and continued the pursuit of the enemy infantry to the edge of the Ransart wood, thus giving time for General Vandamme's corps to arrive.
>
> General Pajol, at the head of 1st Cavalry Corps, chased the enemy on the direct route from Gilly to Fleurus, making a good number of prisoners and was no less distinguished than General Exelmans who I cannot praise enough to Your Majesty.
>
> It is to the shouts of '*Vive l'empereur!*', and with a true enthusiasm that the troops have attacked the enemy.[4]

In this letter we see the traditional, but now unusual, role of dragoons dismounting to act as infantry.

Grouchy also received the reports from his subordinate commanders, such as this one from Pajol.

> Lambusart, 15 June 1815, 10pm.
>
> I have the honour to inform you that I took position this evening with the 1st Cavalry Corps; a division at Lambusart and the second astride the road to Fleurus, in front of the junction which is behind the 'tree of brother Henry' [this is a tree marked on contemporary maps on a prominent junction between Lambusart and Campinière] and Campinière.
>
> . . .
>
> My troops were perfectly led today. I captured Charleroi, I was the first to cross the Sambre and supported alone, for four hours, all the efforts of the enemy; this needs rewards for those who were most distinguished, the kindness of His Majesty that I request you will demand for them. I will have the honour to put their names in your hands tomorrow.[5]

Much later in the night, Grouchy, despite now formally commander of the right wing, reported as if he was still commander-in-chief of the cavalry:

> Grouchy to Soult, Campinière, 16 June 1815, 3am.
> I request that you inform the emperor that the four cavalry corps are deployed in the following manner;
> The corps of General Exelmans [the 2nd] has one of his divisions at Lambusarc and the second on the route from Gilly to Fleurus, ahead of the junction at Campinière.
> General Pajol's corps [the 1st] has one of his divisions at Lambusart and the other ahead of the Rondchamp defile.
> Count Valmy [Kellerman], commanding the 3rd Cavalry Corps has not informed me of his location, but I presume that he has rallied his second division [Kellerman's corps had been put under Ney's command and would not have reported their position to Grouchy].
> The 4th Corps [Milhaud] is to be found next to Charleroi and the point where I had the Prussian infantry squares charged.
> I still have no reports of the losses suffered by the 1st and 2nd Cavalry Corps during the day; I have asked for them and I will send them to you when they are received.
> The total number of prisoners made by the cavalry yesterday is between 8 and 900 men.
> Grouchy
>
> PS. The 1st Hussars that are part of 1st Cavalry Corps has been detached on your orders and I would be grateful if you could send them back to Soult's division if it is possible.[6]

That Grouchy would report in this way seems rather strange; he really should have reported the locations, as commander of the right wing, of the corps of Vandamme and Gérard, as well as the 1st and 2nd Cavalry Corps which were under his command. That he did may stem from Napoleon's order which laid down that he would take direct command when he was present, but as the emperor had retired to Charleroi relatively early, it would seem natural for Grouchy to have reported just the locations of each of the corps under his own command.

Not everyone was able to settle down when it got dark. General Girard's division, that it will be remembered actually belonged to Reille's II Corps but had been ordered by Reille to follow the retreating Prussians (and thereby protect the flank of the corps), appears to have received orders from Napoleon which would keep it detached from its own corps and ultimately commit it to the battle that was to be fought the following day at Ligny. One of its officers reported:

We followed the enemy on the Brussels road, leaving Charleroi to our left. We made a halt in a village where we thought we would pass the night, but at 6pm General Girard had the brigade take up arms. He put himself at the head of the regiment and we marched on Fleurus by a back road, across the plains covered in crops which prevented us from seeing far. To our right we heard a fusillade and cannonade on the main road from Fleurus to Charleroi [this was the action at Gilly].

We arrived at a deserted hamlet [probably Wangenies] at 11pm where two Prussian cavalrymen were stopped. We were only half a league from Fleurus. We took position without lighting any fires because we could hear a considerable mass of Prussian troops very close to our left which, like us, were heading for Fleurus.

We passed the night standing to.[7]

Review of the Events of the 15th

Wellington first received news of Napoleon's offensive from the Prince of Orange sometime around 3pm, but the first formal report was received about 5pm. Although the report said that the attack was coming via Charleroi, Wellington continued to harbour the concern that this was merely a feint and that the real attack would come in the area of Mons. Consequently, at 7pm orders were prepared for the divisions to assemble and be ready to march as soon as an appropriate destination could be confirmed. The last of these orders were not despatched until 10pm and even at this time Wellington was unaware of the skirmish at Frasnes.

Luckily for Wellington, General Constant-Rebeque, the I Corps chief-of-staff, better informed of the situation by being much closer to the front, recommended the 2nd Netherlands Division, commanded by General Perponcher-Sedlnitzky, to concentrate at Quatre Bras. Shortly after this order was despatched, the movement orders arrived from Brussels directing that division to concentrate at Nivelles: the decision was taken to ignore these orders.

What Wellington did not realise is that through this hesitation and the withdrawal of Zieten's corps to the east, a ten-kilometre hole had opened up between his own left and the Prussian right, and that the main Charleroi to Brussels main road was virtually unprotected. It was only at 10pm, with Wellington at the Duchess of Richmond's famous ball, that he was finally convinced that the main French attack was coming from Charleroi and gave orders for the army's concentration to be on Nivelles, with Brunswick and Nassau troops to march to Quatre Bras.

At this time Quatre Bras was occupied by just Colonel Prince Bernard of Saxe-Weimar's brigade of 4,700 men and two batteries (sixteen guns) of Perponcher's 2nd Netherlands Division. If the Prince of Orange and his staff had ensured the concentration of his forces in strict accordance with their orders, then on the evening of the 15th, and even during the morning of the 16th, Ney would have been able to occupy Quatre Bras completely unopposed.

Although Zieten's delaying action bought vital time for the concentration of both Wellington's and Blücher's armies, it cannot be considered entirely successful; neither of the two allied commanders were able to fully concentrate their troops before the first battles, yet considerable further delay could surely have been imposed on the French advance by destroying the bridges over the Sambre. No doubt Napoleon was surprised that no efforts had been made to do this and the careful placing of his bridging units in the order of march display his expectation that he would have to re-establish them. In his famous *Waterloo Lectures*, British historian Colonel Charles Chesney wrote, 'No satisfactory explanation has ever been given of the reasons of his [Zieten's] allowing the bridges, which were left on his flanks as he quitted Charleroi, to fall into the enemy's hands un-mined and without resistance.'[8]

If the allies had wanted to buy time to cover their concentration, it would appear to have been a very wise precaution and certainly seems to have been a serious oversight. But not only had the bridges not been destroyed, it is also surprising that all three (Marchienne, Charleroi and Châtelet) fell cheaply, with little attempt at a determined defence. A well-planned, well-prepared and resolute defence of such narrow defiles should have gone a long way to countering the considerable superiority in numbers that the French otherwise enjoyed. Given the importance of speed for the emperor, if he had had to spend two or more hours erecting bridges before the main body of his army had been able to cross, on top of the time he actually lost, it would have had a significant impact on the following days.

The most serious outcome of the day for Blücher was the progress of IV Corps. Having originally been ordered to move to Hannut, in the late morning of the 15th Blücher had written to Bülow to march towards Gembloux at dawn the following morning. Blücher calculated that IV Corps would join him on the afternoon of the 16th. Unfortunately, both sets of orders that had now been sent to Bülow had arrived late and Bülow had also misunderstood where the whole army was concentrating, thinking he had more time than he actually did. The result was that he arrived late at Hannut, and consequently his march on Gembloux was also delayed. Late in the evening of the 15th Blücher realised that IV Corps would not be able to join him the next day and if he fought, he would have to do so without 30,000 men, a quarter of his army.[9]

In his orders for the 15th, Napoleon had directed that he wanted all the *Armée du Nord* across the Sambre 'before noon'. In this he had failed; the division of heavy cavalry of the Guard, half of Grouchy's cavalry reserve, an infantry division and cavalry brigade of I Corps and most of Gérard's corps had not managed this. Indeed, many of these troops had not done so by the end of the day and bivouacked to the south of the Sambre. Whether or not he was entirely sincere in his memoirs, Napoleon wrote that he was content with the achievements during the 15th:

> All my manoeuvres had succeeded as I wished; I could now take the initiative of attacking the enemy armies, one by one. Their only chance of avoiding this misfortune, the worst of all, was to yield ground and rally on Brussels or beyond.[10]

Ney had failed to occupy the vital crossroads at Quatre Bras as Napoleon stated in his memoirs that he had ordered. However, controversy still surrounds whether Ney actually received such an order; he claims he did not. As this was examined in detail in my book *Prelude to Waterloo: Quatre Bras*, I shall not re-visit this argument. Suffice to say that the light cavalry of the Guard had pressed a reconnaissance to the crossroads and its commander (Lefebvre-Desnoëttes) reported back to Ney that he believed it was unoccupied. No doubt Ney presumed he would be able to occupy it without opposition the following morning.

In many histories, Napoleon is criticised for not ensuring that the two strategically-important points of Quatre Bras and Sombreffe were in French possession on the 15th. This would have denied the key means of communication between the forces of Wellington and Blücher. Control of this road would then have denied them any chance of combining forces and allowed Napoleon to destroy them sequentially. Even General Pajol seems to have been of this school, as he wrote:

> If, on the evening of the 15th, Vandamme had at least gained Fleurus, he would have seriously threatened the Prussian concentration and Blücher would not have been able to have managed the concentration of his army around Sombreffe so easily. Marshal Grouchy had realised this because, as soon as Vandamme had refused to continue his march towards Fleurus and Sombreffe, he had sent one of his *aides-de-camp*, M. Pontbellanger, to the emperor to inform him of what had happened. This officer returned during the night when all the troops were in their bivouacs and announced to the marshal that orders would soon be given on the movements to be conducted the next day and that that at the same time orders would inform the army of its new organisation. The commanders of the corps of the right wing, thus informed that command of them had been conferred on Grouchy, still did not fully recognise his authority.[11]

Pajol is correct in stating that if the French had pushed on, they would have disrupted Blücher's concentration, but this ignores the fact that Napoleon wanted to engage the Prussians, not encourage them to withdraw. What's more, if Napoleon held Sombreffe and Quatre Bras, the two allies would have been forced to withdraw north and concentrate close to Brussels. This would mean neither of the two allied armies was likely to stand and fight, denying the emperor the opportunity that he sought; a decisive battle with one or other of them. Napoleon rightly predicted that

Blücher would therefore fight his battle south of the Namur to Nivelles road in order to maintain his communications with Wellington, just as he wanted.

On the evening of the 15th, therefore, Napoleon was quite content that Grouchy had not threatened Sombreffe as the emperor had no intention of him doing so. This is why Pontbellenger was not sent back with orders; the next day would be early enough. It is only in his orders of the following morning that he specifically names Sombreffe as a target for Grouchy and even then he could not be sure that Blücher would stand and fight. On the right wing he was intently focussed on bringing the Prussians to battle and he wanted to do nothing that might induce them to withdraw because they felt they had lost their communications with Wellington. The emperor later wrote:

> The Emperor's intention was that his advance guard should occupy Fleurus, keeping his troops concealed behind the wood near this city; he took good care not to let his army be seen, *and, above all, not to occupy Sombreffe* [my emphasis]. This would of itself have caused the failure of all his manoeuvres; for then, Marshal Blücher would have been obliged to make Wavre the place for the concentration of his army, the battle of Ligny would not have taken place, and the Prussian army would not have been obliged to give battle [as it did] in its then not fully concentrated condition, and not supported by the English army.[12]

It is likely that Napoleon would have been more reassured if Ney had already secured Quatre Bras and all his army had been north of the Sambre, but in the circumstances these could be put right early the next morning. Napoleon, like all generals, knew that his plans would not always go exactly as he would hope as the enemy's reactions could not be second-guessed with certainty. Nothing had happened that currently threatened to undermine his plans to destroy one of the two allied armies before they could concentrate; all remained on track. He was confident that he would beat the Prussians the next day if they chose to risk a battle, believing that as there were none, or only a few, of Wellington's troops at Quatre Bras, the duke's army was still not concentrated and would be unable to join his ally if Marshal Ney secured Quatre Bras first thing in the morning and held it with his whole force.

One of Napoleon's secretaries, Fleury de Chaboulon, also identified another positive born out of the day's achievements:

> This day, although not as important in its outcome, since it only cost the enemy five guns and 3,000 men killed or prisoners, produced the best effects in the army. The sciatica of Marshal Mortier and General Bourmont's treason had given rise to a feeling of uncertainty and fear which were entirely dissipated by the favourable outcome of this first combat.[13]

After leaving Gilly, Napoleon returned to Charleroi, where his headquarters had been established in the château Puissant.[14] Sergeant Mauduit served in the prestigious 1st Regiment of Foot Grenadiers of the Imperial Guard and wrote a lively account of the campaign. He described the scene at the château:

> Our battalion, having established itself in the courtyard of the Imperial Headquarters, occupied ourselves with preparing our food for the morning meal and for that evening, for we had been on the march or in position for nearly eighteen hours, without being able to take off our marmites [cooking pots], and everything suggested that it would be the same tomorrow. Thus each took his measures to procure rations and to get a few hours rest before marching on the enemy who awaited us and looked to take his revenge for the losses of the day.
>
> Every moment, the *officiers d'ordonnance*, the *aides de camp*, the headquarter staff officers entered and left the courtyard of the improvised palace, and in their hurry, they often knocked over several rows of our arms stacks causing our old grenadiers to grumble as they had a soft spot for their loyal travelling companions; for these muskets had served them so often as a mirror of the days of festivity, a support and last hope in days of fatigue or of combat.
>
> However, no one slept at the *quartier-général*. The day before a great battle is never a day of rest; time is precious for there can be no confusion, no error. The hope of *la patrie* can sometimes depend on a poorly delivered order or a word badly written; as we would soon be given the most painful confirmation.[15]

Napoleon dined in the same room that had been occupied by General Zieten that morning and then, knowing that his subordinates' reports could not be expected until midnight at the earliest and having been up since before 2am, Napoleon now took the opportunity to get some rest. His secretary wrote to Joseph, the emperor's brother,

> *Monseigneur*, it is 9pm. The Emperor, who has been mounted since three o'clock this morning, has returned overwhelmed by fatigue. He has thrown himself onto his bed for a few hours rest. He is to remount at midnight. His Majesty was not able to write to Your Highness and directed me to send you the following: 'The army forced the Sambre close to Charleroi and has deployed advance guards halfway between Charleroi and Namur and Charleroi to Brussels. We have taken 1,500 prisoners and captured six cannon. Four Prussian regiments have been wiped out. The emperor has lost few men, but he has suffered one loss that is very painful; it is his *aide de camp*, General Letort, who was killed on the plateau of Fleurus

commanding a cavalry charge. The enthusiasm of the inhabitants of Charleroi and all the countryside that we have crossed cannot be described. These are the same sentiments as in Bourgogne.' The Emperor wishes, *Monseigneur*, that you pass this news to the ministers and use it elsewhere as you see fit.

It is possible that tomorrow there will be a very important engagement.
First Secretary of the Cabinet,

Baron Fain[16]

Whilst Napoleon rested, Soult prepared a report summarising the operations of the day that was sent back to Paris and published in the *Moniteur* on the 18th.

On the 14th, the army was deployed as follows:

Imperial Headquarters at Beaumont.
I Corps, commanded by General d'Erlon was at Solre, on the Sambre.
II Corps, commanded by General Reille, was at Ham-sur-Heure.
III Corps, commanded by General Vandamme, was to the right of Beaumont.
IV Corps, commanded by General Gérard, had arrived at Philippeville.

On the 15th, at 3am, General Reille attacked the enemy and moved on Marcienne-au-Pont. He had a number of engagements in which his cavalry charged a Prussian battalion and took 300 prisoners.

At 1am the emperor was at Jamioulx-sur-Heure.[17]

General Domon's light cavalry division cut up two Prussian battalions and took 400 prisoners.

General Pajol entered Charleroi at midday. The *sapeurs* and *marins* of the Guard were with the advance guard to repair the bridges; they were the first to enter the town. General Clary with the 1st Hussars moved towards Gosselies on the main road to Brussels, and General Pajol moved on Gilly, on the Namur road.

At 3pm, General Vandamme approached Gilly with his corps.

Marshal Grouchy arrived there with General Exelmans' cavalry.

The enemy occupied a position to the left of Fleurus. At 5pm the emperor ordered the attack. The position was turned and taken. The four Service Squadrons of the Guard, commanded by General Letort, *aide de camp* to the emperor, broke three squares; the 26th, 27th and 28th Prussian Regiments were routed. Our squadrons sabred 4 or 500 men and took 1,500 prisoners.

During this time, General Reille crossed the Sambre at Marchienne-au-Pont and moved on Gosselies with the divisions of Prince Jérôme and General Bachelu. Attacking the enemy he made 250 prisoners and pursued them on the road to Brussels.

> This day has cost the enemy five guns and 2,000 men, of which 1,000 are prisoners. Our loss is ten men killed and eighty wounded, most from the Service Squadrons who made the charges and three squadrons of the 20th Dragoons, who charged a square with the greatest determination. Our loss, whilst small in number, has been painful to the emperor for the serious wound to General Letort, his *aide de camp*, when charging at the head of the Service Squadrons. This officer is of the greatest distinction. He was struck by a ball in the stomach, and the surgeon fears that the wound will be mortal.
> We have found several stores at Charleroi. The joy of the Belgians is difficult to describe. There are villages that have celebrated with dances in front of their liberators and their happiness is heartfelt.
> The names of the most distinguished officers and soldiers will be included in the report of General Headquarters.
> The emperor has given command of the Left Wing to the Prince *de la Moskowa*, whose headquarters this evening is at Quatre Bras on the road to Brussels.
> The *Duc de Travise* [Mortier], who the emperor had made commander of the Young Guard, has remained in Beaumont as he is sick with sciatica and is bedridden.
> IV Corps commanded by General Gérard is arriving this evening at Châtelet. General Gérard has made known that Lieutenant General Bourmont, Colonel Clouet and *chef d'escadron* Villoutreys have deserted to the enemy. The *major-général* has ordered that these deserters are to be immediately charged according to the law.
> Nothing can describe the good spirit and enthusiasm of the army. It regards this desertion of a small number of traitors as a happy event which is out in the open.[18]

This report is broadly accurate and further reflects the fact that Napoleon was generally satisfied with the day's achievements. Soult does not mention Lobau's VI Corps, whose *sous-chef* of the headquarters reported:

> On the 15th, for whatever reason, the columns of the right and centre were still only a league, at most, beyond Charleroi; VI Corps bivouacked more than a league to the rear, not having been able, in any case, to arrive there before night.[19]

On the night of the 15th Gourgaud gives the position of the French army as follows:

> Headquarters at Charleroi.
> The Left Wing of the army; headquarters at Gosselies.

Vanguard at Frasnes.

General Reille's corps stationed between Gosselies and Frasnes, but with one division (Girard's) at Wangenies in the direction of Fleurus.

General d'Erlon's corps was between Marchiennes and Jumet.

The centre, consisting of Vandamme's corps and Grouchy's reserves of cavalry lined the woods opposite Fleurus.

General Gérard's corps, forming the right wing, had passed the Sambre and was in front of Châtelet.

The Imperial Guard was echeloned between Fleurus and Charleroi. VI Corps was in front of the latter town. Kellerman's corps of cuirassiers, with the great park of artillery was on the left bank of the Sambre, behind Charleroi.[20]

What is interesting in these two letters is the fact that Soult reports Ney as occupying Quatre Bras, whilst Gourgaud more accurately has his leading formations still at Frasnes.

The day seems to have gone relatively smoothly for Napoleon and no doubt he fell quickly into a deep sleep. However, during the march, not all was going so well. His provost-marshal, General Radet, was preparing a report for him on what he had seen or had had reported to him.

> Report to Marshal Soult, *major-général*,
>
> The marauding and disorder has returned to the army; the Guard sets the example. I passed yesterday at the rear of the head of the column of the army to assure myself of the execution of the order of the 14th. I had sent back more than a hundred wagons of baggage belonging to general headquarters, the Guard and the different army corps, which were moving in the columns; they were then sent to where they should have been.
>
> I have had chased and returned many stragglers who were using force to procure food and drink. I have had pillaging of grain and forage from several farms stopped that the artillery and equipages took in disorder.
>
> I have had several mounted artillery detachments rejoin their units, amongst others a detachment of the Guard which had turned back to forage without an officer at their head, nor a necessary order or written requisition.
>
> I have been obliged to leave guards in each village to maintain order there until the column has passed; tonight they have brought back up the equipages of the headquarters which were parked at Marcinville, behind Charleroi; they reported to me that they had caught several soldiers red-handed with illegal loot, but they were met with force and anger, insulted and treated poorly by the regiments on the march so that it was impossible for the gendarmes to even establish the numbers of their units.[21]

Chapter 6

Morning, 16 June

The French army was up at first light on the morning of the 16th. Pajol's light cavalry provided the advance guard and he reports that they were in the saddle at 3am.[1] At this time they had received no new orders and consequently Pajol continued to push towards Sombreffe.

Captain Gerbet of the 37th *de ligne*, captured the mood of the army on this morning:

> The next day, 16 June, the troops, well rested, having eaten, were ready to march at daybreak, but at 10 o'clock they had still done nothing!
>
> Although surprised by this waiting around, they generated confidence in the combinations of the emperor and in their execution.
>
> The troops were impatient to come to grips with the Prussians.[2]

Young Lieutenant Lefol was acting as the *aide de camp* of his father who commanded the 8th Division in Vandamme's corps; he too seemed oblivious to the carnage that was to come: 'The next morning, the 16th June, the weather was magnificent; a hot sun announced a burning day . . . Our soldiers made their soup. . .[3]

The rumour of General Bourmont's desertion was beginning to spread throughout the army. Jean-Baptiste d'Héralde was the *chirurgien-major* to the 12th *léger*, part of Girard's division of II Corps:

> At 9.30 . . . a lieutenant general of the emperor's household came to General Girard. The two generals spoke together. He told me that the emperor was in Fleurus with part of his guard and his cavalry, that Count Lobau was due to arrive there, that Vandamme was coming into line. He also told us that General Letort, commander of the Guard Dragoons, had been mortally wounded the previous day.
>
> General Girard, told him that we were too slow in attacking and that the enemy would have taken position.
>
> 'My dear general,' this general said to him, 'if we have not attacked

earlier, it is because there are some fears. You know that General Bourmont passed over to the enemy yesterday with several officers of his headquarters. Bourmont, the protégé of Ney! It is this that really concerns the emperor on account of this marshal, of whom we are wary; his army corps had been very far from where he had been ordered yesterday evening! Our *officiers d'ordonnance* had been active all night; several have been lost. You see that we cannot attack until we are sure that we can communicate with him and that there is nothing to fear from our left!'

'F**k!' General Girard replied, 'if we are wary of Ney, we should shoot him and replace him with a corporal!'

This conversation between two lieutenant generals surprised me. After a while, this general disappeared.[4]

Many accounts of this campaign accuse senior officers of betraying Napoleon, but this is the only one that seems to implicate Ney so directly. For all Napoleon's subsequent criticisms of Ney, none suggest the emperor believed he was guilty of treason.

Napoleon Plans His Next Move
As we have heard, on the evening of the 15th, Napoleon had retired to Charleroi for the night and had fallen exhausted into bed at 9pm. However, he was up again at midnight and, once appraised of the situations of Grouchy and Ney, he could then formulate his plans and issue his orders for the coming day.

It was now clear that the Prussian advance guard was withdrawing north-east, across the front of the Anglo-Dutch concentration areas, heading towards Fleurus and Sombreffe. A small force from Wellington's army had been encountered by Ney at Frasnes, but this had appeared to withdraw to the north. No British troops had been encountered, suggesting that Wellington had not yet concentrated his army. The Prussian withdrawal had also opened up the main road towards Brussels, although Napoleon would have expected Wellington's troops to meet him on this road. However, the two allied armies had clearly not joined each other and this left the emperor relatively confident that he still had the opportunity to beat them one after the other.

From the varied information he had received, and from the direction of retirement of the Prussian advance guard, Napoleon concluded that their army was seeking to assemble on the Namur to Nivelles road, as it was by this route that the two allied armies would communicate. Having pushed his advance troops almost as far as Fleurus on the 15th, Napoleon believed Sombreffe was the most likely point for this concentration. However, there was currently no evidence to suggest that the Prussians were preparing for battle, so Napoleon wanted to push them further away from their allies, down their lines of communication towards either Namur or Liège. He could then turn on Wellington and beat him, confident in the

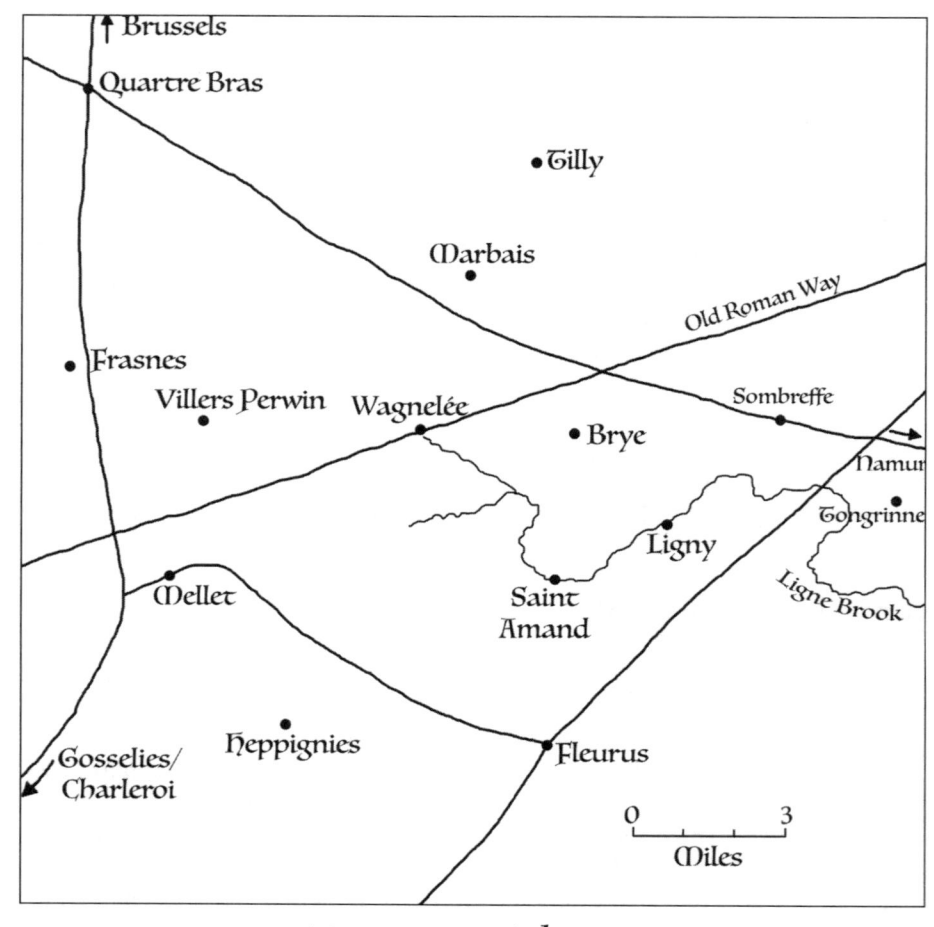

Morning, 16th June

thought that the Prussians would be in no position to assist him. If the Prussians did concentrate to fight, then so much the better, as it was clear that Wellington would be incapable of intervening in time.

Napoleon now finalised his plans; the Prussians clearly offered him the best opportunity for striking a significant blow; he would accompany Grouchy and the right wing which would advance against the Prussians, pushing them away to the east. If they stood, he would attack and destroy them. In the meantime, Ney and the left wing would occupy Quatre Bras, either defending the crossroads against an advancing Wellington, or to march some troops down the Nivelles to Namur road to support Napoleon against the Prussians. If the Prussians withdrew before him, then Napoleon would join Ney with the reserve (the Guard and VI Corps) and would then march on Brussels which the emperor believed he could reach at 7am on 17 June.

Napoleon dictated his orders to the *major-général*, who would then fill in the detail, write each of them out in full and then have them copied. This whole process must inevitably have taken some time and before they were ready to be sent out the emperor heard from the commander of the right wing. Like the good cavalry commander he was, Grouchy had been up at first light to go and visit his vedettes. General Pajol later wrote,

> Outposts of Subervie's division, which were beyond the Martinroux farm, soon reported that in the rear of Sombreffe there were numerous Prussian troops marching along the Nivelles to Namur road. It was Pirch I's II Corps which was coming from Mazy and Namur. Marshal Grouchy, who at this moment was visiting Pajol's and Domon's bivouacs, having also noticed this, moved quickly in the direction of Wangenies to get a better view. He encountered General Girard who had been watching these columns for a long time, which were heading towards Brye, Saint-Amand and Ligny.[5]

Immediately, Grouchy wrote to warn Napoleon,

> In bivouac close to Fleurus, 16 June 1815, 5am.
>
> Sire,
>
> Whilst touring my advance-posts, I noticed strong enemy columns moving towards Brye, Saint-Amand and the surrounding villages; they appeared to come by the Namur road.
>
> General Girard, whose infantry division is placed on my left, occupies a plateau higher than those occupied by troops under my command, has come to confirm to me the continuous arrival of Prussian forces since dawn.
>
> I thus do not waste a second in sending to Your Majesty this important and positive information. At this moment I am concentrating my troops to conduct the movement that you have ordered towards Sombreffe.
>
> Marshal Grouchy[6]

We have already seen how General Girard had been sent by his corps commander to follow the Prussian troops that had withdrawn from Gosselies the day before; he was thus positioned between the two wings of the army and clearly in a good position to observe the Prussian movements. Although not under Grouchy's orders, he sensibly judged that he needed to share what he was seeing with the commander of the right wing. An hour after his first letter, Grouchy wrote again to the emperor,

16th June 1815, 6am.

Sire,

I have just been informed by General Girard that the enemy continues to move in force, by Sombreffe, onto the heights that surround the mill of Brye. I hasten to send to Your Majesty this new information, confirming that which I informed you of an hour ago

Marshal Grouchy.[7]

Grouchy's reports clearly suggested that the Prussians were concentrating a large force in the area of Brye and Saint-Amand; perhaps they were preparing to make a stand after all. Although this was just what Napoleon wanted, it was still too early be sure of Prussian strengths and intentions. He therefore discounted this prospect for the time being whilst awaiting further information and reiterated the orders he had dictated to Soult by writing his own letters to each of his wing commanders.

Despite the repetition, it is worth considering the whole contents of both orders to Grouchy; not least for the subtle, if important, emphasis that Napoleon puts in his own letter. First, let us look at Soult's order.

Charleroi, 16th June 1815

M. le Maréchal

The Emperor orders that you are to march with the 1st, 2nd and 4th Cavalry Corps and that you are to move in the direction of Sombreffe, where you are to take position. I have also ordered Lieutenant General Vandamme, commanding the III Infantry Corps, and Lieutenant General Gérard commanding the IV Infantry Corps, and warned these two generals that they are under your orders and that they are to immediately send officers to you to inform you of their current march and to take your orders. However, I have told them that since His Majesty is present, they may receive orders directly from him, and that they are to continue to send me the routine reports and states that they would normally send me.

I have also warned General Gérard that in his movements on Sombreffe, he is to move with the town of Fleurus to his left, in order to prevent it getting blocked up. So, you are to give him the direction of his march, as well as the need to remain close to support the III Corps and be prepared to contribute to an attack on Sombreffe if the enemy offers resistance.

You are also to give appropriate orders to Lieutenant General Count Vandamme.

I have the honour to warn you that the Count of Valmy has received the order to move to Gosselies where, with the 3rd Cavalry Corps, he will come under the orders of the Prince of the Moskowa [Marshal Ney].

The 1st Regiment of Hussars will return to 1st Cavalry Corps during the day. I will take the Emperor's orders on this subject. I have the honour to inform you that Marshal Ney has received the order to move with I and II Corps, and the 3rd Cavalry Corps, to the road junction called the 'Trois Bras' [Quatre Bras] on the Brussels road and that he is to detach a strong force to Marbais to link with you at Sombreffe and to support your operations if there is a need.

Immediately that you are the master of Sombreffe, you must send an advance guard to Gembloux and reconnoitre in all directions from Sombreffe, particularly the main road to Namur, as well as establishing your communications with Marshal Ney.

The Imperial Guard is moving to Fleurus.

Marshal Duke of Dalmatia

It is worthy of note that in this letter, after the problem Grouchy had experienced with Vandamme refusing to obey his orders the previous day, Soult informs Grouchy that he has officially informed Vandamme and Gérard that they are now both under his command. Whilst this should have put the matter to bed, unfortunately for Grouchy, it was only the beginning of the uneasy relationship that he endured with these two competent, yet unruly subordinates.

Napoleon wrote to both Ney and Grouchy; in each letter he displays a more informal, yet direct, style. To Grouchy:

Charleroi, 16 June 1815

My Cousin,

I send you La Bédoyère, my *aide de camp*, to give you this letter. The *major-général* has informed you of my intentions, but as his officers are badly mounted, my *aide de camp* will probably arrive earlier. My intention is that, as the commander of the Right Wing, you are to take command of III Corps commanded by General Vandamme, IV Corps commanded by General Gérard, the cavalry corps of Generals Pajol, Milhaud and Exelmans, which together are not far from 50,000 men. You are to move with this Right Wing on Sombreffe. Have the corps of Generals Pajol, Milhaud, Exelmans and Vandamme follow on without halting, to continue the movement on Sombreffe. IV Corps, which is at Chatelineau, has received a direct order to move to Sombreffe without passing through Fleurus. This is important because I am moving my general headquarters to Fleurus and it is necessary to avoid hold-ups. Send one of your officers to General Gérard to make him aware of your movements and to establish his own. My intention is that all these generals are directly under your command; they will only take orders directly from me when I am present. I will be in Fleurus between 10 and 11 o'clock. I will then move on to Sombreffe, leaving my Guard, infantry and cavalry, at Fleurus. I will only take it to Sombreffe if this is necessary. If the enemy is at Sombreffe, I want to attack them, I want also to attack them at Gembloux and to take this position. My intention being, after having taken these two positions, to leave tonight and operate with my Left Wing commanded by Marshal Ney against the English. Thus do not lose a moment, because the quicker I achieve this, the better it will be for my future operations. I presume you are at Fleurus; stay in communications with General Gérard in order that he can help you attack Sombreffe if it is necessary. Girard's division is moving to Fleurus; do not employ it unless absolutely necessary, because it has had to march throughout the night. Also, leave my Young Guard and all its artillery at Fleurus. Count Valmy [Kellerman], with his two cuirassier divisions, is marching on the road to Brussels. He has linked in with Marshal Ney to be involved with this evening's operations on the left wing. As I have said to you, I will be at Fleurus between 10 and 11am. Send me news of everything you have learnt; ensure that the road to Fleurus is clear.

All the information I have is that the Prussians are not able to oppose us with more than 40,000 men.

Napoleon

In his letter to Ney, Napoleon clearly believed that the marshal would occupy Quatre Bras without a fight and directs his deployment with a view to drawing on some of his troops to aid him against the Prussians if they offered battle, and if not, to march with him on Brussels:

Charleroi, 8am, 16 June

My Cousin,

My *aide de camp*, General Flahaut, is directed to deliver this letter to you. The *major-général* should have given you orders, but you will receive mine first because my officers travel faster than his. You will receive the operation orders for the day, but I wish to write to you in detail because it is of the highest importance.

I am sending Marshal Grouchy with III and IV Infantry Corps to Sombreffe. I am taking my guard to Fleurus and I shall be there myself before midday. I shall attack the enemy there if I encounter them and clear the road as far as Gembloux. There, according to circumstances, I shall decide on my course, perhaps at three in the afternoon, perhaps this evening. My intention is that, immediately after I have made up my mind, you will be ready to march on Brussels: I will support you with the Guard which will be at Fleurus or Sombreffe, and I shall expect you to arrive at Brussels tomorrow morning. You will march this evening if I make up my mind early enough for you to be informed of it today, and to accomplish three or four leagues this evening and to be at Brussels at seven o'clock tomorrow morning.

You should dispose your troops in the following manner: the first division two leagues in advance of Quatre Bras, if there is no hindrance; six divisions of infantry about Quatre Bras, and one division at Marbais, so that I may draw them to me at Sombreffe if I want them . . .

From these letters we can see how Napoleon's mind was working. Grouchy was to continue his advance against the Prussians who, at the moment Napoleon dictated his orders, had shown no inclination to stand and fight; indeed, Napoleon estimated them at no more than 40,000, clearly not the whole of the Prussian army. Although Grouchy had informed him that they seemed to be concentrating before the emperor wrote his two letters, this still did not necessarily mean they were planning to fight a battle. If the Prussians did not stand, Grouchy was to capture Sombreffe, which would cut Blücher's communications with Wellington, and then Gembloux, which stood on the direct road between Namur and Brussels. If Blücher gave up this point it would suggest that he was withdrawing down his line of communications back to Prussia, as he would have had a very long and roundabout journey to join Wellington. If Napoleon then left a force at Gembloux, this would serve as a flank guard against any subsequent Prussian advance, giving him time to join Ney and either destroy Wellington or march on Brussels. If Blücher planned to fight, then so much the better; he would join Grouchy with his reserve and defeat the Prussians, whilst Ney, at Quatre Bras, held off Wellington.

With all his orders sent out, Napoleon prepared to leave Charleroi and join Grouchy at Fleurus to see for himself what the Prussian were doing; it was between nine and ten in the morning. Just as he was about to leave, a lancer officer sent by Ney arrived at headquarters to warn the emperor that there was a force massing at Quatre Bras. For Napoleon, this was the first intimation that Quatre Bras was still occupied by the allies and that Ney would probably have to fight for its possession. The emperor clearly wanted this vital crossroads in French hands and had Soult send the following message to Marshal Ney:

Charleroi, 16 June 1815

Monsieur le Maréchal, an officer of lancers has just informed the emperor that the enemy has appeared in force near Quatre Bras. Concentrate the corps of Counts Reille and d'Erlon and that of Count Valmy, who is just marching to join you. With these forces you must engage and destroy all enemy forces that present themselves. Blücher was at Namur yesterday and it is unlikely that he has sent any troops towards Quatre Bras. Thus you will only have to deal with the forces coming from Brussels.

Marshal Grouchy is moving on Sombreffe as I informed you, and the emperor is going to Fleurus. You should address future reports to His Majesty there.

Major-général
Duc de Dalmatie

Whatever uncertainly or lack of clarity there may be in previous orders Ney had received about seizing Quatre Bras, this order cannot be so criticised. It clearly tells Ney to concentrate his forces and to 'destroy' the enemy forces at the crossroads.

The Allies
During the evening of the 14th, Blücher had ordered the concentration of his army near Sombreffe with I Corps providing the delaying force that would give them the time required. Due to the mix-up that we have already examined, Bülow's IV Corps was unable to reach this point before the battle that was to be fought later that day. By midday on the 16th, Blücher had succeeded in concentrating his three available corps around Ligny. Throughout the morning he had remained ignorant of Wellington's location or intentions and therefore must have realised that the duke would be unlikely to be able to support him with a substantial part of his army. However, despite these considerable drawbacks, his naturally aggressive nature and hatred of the French seem to have ruled his thinking.

Sometime between 1.30 and 2am that morning, in a back room at the Duchess of Richmond's ball in Brussels, Wellington had uttered the famous words, 'Napoleon has humbugged me by God, he has gained twenty-four hours' march on me.' Finally convinced that the French attack through Charleroi was Napoleon's main effort, Wellington ordered his own concentration over twenty-four hours later than his ally. The first British troops left Brussels at 4am and most of the Brunswick corps at 6am. After a short rest, Wellington himself left at 7.30am.

By the time he left the Belgian capital, almost the whole of the 2nd (Netherlands) Division, 6,500 men and sixteen guns, were concentrated around Quatre Bras. Although there was a little skirmishing with French cavalry, at this time there was no evidence to suggest that there was any significant build-up of French forces to their south.

This initial skirmishing and the subsequent patrols that were sent out seems to have finally woken Ney to the possibility that Quatre Bras was occupied. Consequently, he sent an officer from the Guard lancers to warn Napoleon that this was the case, although other than the despatch of this message, the developing situation seems to have done nothing to spur Ney into any sort of further, more positive, action. Admittedly, he had not yet received his orders from the emperor, but crucially, had not felt the need to use the time to properly concentrate his troops so that whatever Napoleon's decision, he would be well balanced and ready to react to whatever was expected of him.

Wellington had originally expected to concentrate his troops well back from the frontier and then march forward as an army, but Napoleon's offensive through Charleroi was forcing him to concentrate forward and this held the prospect of his troops arriving at the front piecemeal. The duke arrived at Quatre Bras at 10am. Having listened to the Prince of Orange's report and endorsing his deployment, Wellington rode forward onto the Balcan plateau where he could look down on Frasnes. Despite the reports of French deserters that a large French force was present, there was little evidence to suggest this. With nothing of interest happening to his front and still to be convinced that a major French force was going to march on Quatre Bras, Wellington decided to ride the twelve or so kilometres to meet Blücher near Ligny. From Quatre Bras this was a simple journey straight down the road that led towards Namur and would allow the two commanders an opportunity to discuss their mutual support. Ordering the Prince of Orange to hold on until reinforcements arrived if he should be attacked, he set off.

The French Advance
The 16th had started with the Prussians still in possession of Fleurus. Having conducted his first reconnaissances, Grouchy now needed to continue to push the Prussian rearguard back. General Pajol takes up the story:

> Pajol's corps set off towards 9.30am and headed for Fleurus; Subervie's division advancing directly from the Martinroux farm and Soult's by the track from Lambusart. Exelmans's dragoons followed this last division whilst Vandamme's infantry marched behind Subervie. Towards 10am, Pajol occupied Fleurus as this town had been evacuated by the Prussians some time before. It continued to advance beyond the town on the road that led to Point-du-Jour. Hardly had it been committed, than its scouts reported the presence of Prussian cavalry. This cavalry belonged to Zieten and had remained on the right bank of the Ligny stream to observe Fleurus.
> Pajol ordered Subervie to threaten it; it did not wait to be attacked and retired on the banks of the stream both sides of Ligny. Pajol hastened its retreat with his artillery.[8]

Grouchy was controlling the French advance; his memoirs record that:

> Between 11 o'clock and midday, the French light troops had pushed back the cavalry of the Prussian I Corps and occupied Fleurus. The cannonade forced the 6th Uhlans to retire to the left of the Brandenburg Dragoons. When Grouchy's columns of cavalry moved on the right, General Roeder crossed over the stream.[9]

Behind the cavalry screen the whole of the right wing and reserve were in motion; a number of memoirs mention moving forward about 10 o'clock. Sergeant Mauduit's regiment had protected Napoleon's headquarters in Charleroi and their march forward took them over the scene of the fighting the day before:

At 9am we were marching to Fleurus, drummers and musicians in the lead. Our uniform was that for combat; greatcoat, trousers, bearskins without ornamentation. However, it had been the case for the guard to wear best uniform, for it would soon have a role deserving of it; it was to fix to our colours a well contested victory. But it is in paintings alone that we always fought in best uniforms, or even in ball uniforms, which borders on, we have to say, poetic licence.

The sky was clear, like the sky of Marengo, which we would celebrate, in a way, the anniversary. The sun shone and promised us a hot day . . .

Arriving at the village of Gilly where the first houses met the main road to Fleurus, we left our unit to cast a dismal look over the area of the previous day's fighting. The dead still waited there for their military graves; the ****, these ravens that follow the armies, had not had the time to fall on their prey and our brothers in arms, whose hearts had been so ardent, had hardly been there for twelve hours, were still lying there. About three hundred had been struck down.

Several of our own also slept the eternal sleep close to the square, broken and sabred by them. We shook hands with a *maréchal-des-logis*, our comrade of the Guard; dead on the field of honour! For all of them we left a sigh of regret and rejoined our company in the middle of the wood through which, with a little confusion, the army passed; for this road was the only route open in the middle of the forest and all the corps marched together in this defile.

An oppressive dust enveloped us like a thick cloud; it even made our breathing difficult and made our entry into the immense and fertile plain that nature had seemed to have destined to be the enclosed field of central Europe, for the battle of Ligny was to be the third since that of 1690 of Marshal Luxembourg.

All the infantry of the Old Guard formed in closed columns by division of fifty files, each company alone forming a division, because of their strength and then took position to the right of the main road and, as always, with the left ahead.

The four regiments of the Young Guard also formed in close columns, but on the left of the main road and level with us.

There we stacked our arms to leave time for all the corps to form up in their place of battle.[10]

With the Prussians being pushed back, Napoleon could now move forward and see the situation for himself. Colonel Petiet served as *adjutant-commandant* in Imperial Headquarters under Marshal Soult during the campaign.

The emperor gave me the order to instruct Marshal Soult to go to Marshal Grouchy to reconnoitre the position and to make the necessary arrangements for the attack. Napoleon followed these two marshals closely. All three of them climbed a narrow ladder up to a mill which dominated the countryside . . . The emperor watched the enemy's movements through his telescope and shouted, 'They will be taken *en flagrant délit.*'[11]

Having met up with Marshal Grouchy, Napoleon had moved to several elevated points to reconnoitre the Prussian movements and positions, accompanied by several of his generals. Grouchy reports that the emperor was convinced that Blücher did not expect to be attacked before the following day, not believing that the Prussian commander would fight before he was able to complete the concentration of his whole army and to receive support from of Wellington.[12]

The mill that Petiet mentions was the mill of Naveau; Napoleon used this as his main observation post as both armies manoeuvred into position. There he was joined by General Gérard; Petiet describes this interesting encounter:

Several generals and colonels accompanied the emperor and the two marshals (I was amongst those officers who had remained at the foot of the mill). I held my horse by the bridle and spoke in a low voice with Colonel Michal, who was on foot like me, when General Count Gérard, and not Marshal Ney as has been reported by some historians, came to take Napoleon's orders.

'*Eh bien*, Gérard,' shouted Napoleon from the height of the mill, 'you said you would answer for Bourmont with your head; you see what he has done.'

'Sire, General Bourmont has fought under my eyes with honour; he has shed his blood in Your Majesty's cause; I have always believed him to be irreproachable and devoted.'

'Bah!' said the emperor, 'those who are white will never become a tricolour and a tricolour will never become a white.'[13]

Given that most of the Prussian movements over the previous thirty-six hours or so had been to the east, towards their lines of communications, it would be reasonable to have expected the Prussians to orientate their line of battle facing to the west. However, it soon became clear that they were forming up facing to the south, which would require the French, who were following them eastwards, to wheel to the north.

Maréchal de Camp Berton commanded the 2nd Dragoon Brigade of Chastel's 10th Division that formed part of Exelmans' 2nd Cavalry Corps. He describes the Prussian deployment:

The French general [Napoleon], moving against the Prussian army on the morning of the 16th, expected to find it deployed to cover its line of communications on Namur; but having met it to his great astonishment, in a different order, he was satisfied, since this deployment allowed him to concentrate his forces to give himself the advantage of maintaining a simple line of operations, against the double lines of the enemy who was still far from being able to put all his forces in action at the same point. He quickly realised that the Prussians were established in a defensive line with the English army, that they considered as the secondary base of their operations and that they were not the same; his [the Prussian] columns arrived from several different directions.[14]

It now began to dawn on the French commanders that Blücher's position was designed to maintain his communications with Wellington rather than their lines of communications to the east and north-east; even Captain Gerbet understood this:

> ... at 10am, the right wing destined to attack the Prussian army, left the position where it had passed the night to move onto the Fleurus plain ... From there, we could see the Prussian army which occupied all the heights in front of us. Its front extended across the front of the Namur to Nivelles road and covered the communications between the enemy armies.[15]

If Blücher was relying on support from Wellington, the main road from Namur to Nivelles was the principal line that it was important for the two allied armies to conserve, as it was the only significant road that offered good communications between their two armies. North of this line, there were only narrow dirt roads which passed through difficult country, cut by the river Dyle and covered in woods and many other defiles. The Dyle had a deep and steep-sided valley and was a serious obstacle, as Grouchy later discovered. Heavy rain would turn the secondary roads into quagmires which would deteriorate quickly under the passage of large numbers of troops. The allies therefore needed to hold Quatre Bras and Sombreffe if they were to keep open their communications with each other, and particularly if they planned to move to each other's direct support. From Quatre Bras to Sombreffe is twelve kilometres. The next line of good communications between them would otherwise have been close to Brussels.

It was therefore this requirement that determined Blücher's deployment; an orientation that faced south. If he was merely protecting his lines of communication back towards Prussia, this orientation, given the direction of the French advance, would have demanded a deployment facing south-west. The orientation of his defensive line, and the fact that his right wing was 'in the air', should have served as a clear sign to Napoleon that he was expecting direct support from Wellington and not protecting his lines of communication; an important point that would have inevitably have interfered with a plan for some of Ney's troops to march down the same road onto the right rear of the Prussians. The unusual orientation of the Prussian position forced Napoleon into a change of face: he wrote in his memoirs, 'I ordered a change of front facing Fleurus, with the right in advance.'[16]

Let us return to Sergeant Mauduit's description of the move forward of the Guard from Charleroi:

> It was already 10am and not a musket shot had yet announced the presence of the enemy. The skirmishers however, met in the town of Fleurus; finally, a cannon shot was fired; the smoke rose quickly above an avenue of poplars; I thought, 'It is the first of the day!' It was met by a general shout of joyous acclaim! It was thought to be the signal for battle; that the whole line, from Sombreffe to Saint-Amand, would open up at the same time! But no, this was only the first shots of the advance guard.
>
> Nevertheless, the *grénadière* was beaten and in five minutes all the Young and Old Guard is on the march, formed in a single, deep column of twenty-four battalions, of which sixteen are of the Old Guard; what an imposing sight!
>
> We marched right on Fleurus, always across the fields, without respect for the good crop of wheat, for it was close to five *pieds* high. We only had a quarter of a league to go. Arriving at the entrance to this large town, the head of the column went to the left, crossing the main road in order to leave it free for the artillery that was still moving down it.
>
> There, we made a new halt, but it was short. Our second movement took us through Fleurus; all its inhabitants lined the hedges on both sides of the main road that we followed. All watched us with a mix of concern and sympathy.
>
> On our exit from Fleurus, to the left, we suddenly heard enthusiastic shouts of '*Vive l'empereur!*' They were from the first wounded of our advance guard, which had been bandaged or had amputations in an orchard and who still had enough strength and energy to salute their emperor who was mounted at the head of our regiment. All got up or were helped up to render what might be their last homage. What touching witness of affection and respect this salute of mutilated soldiers in such a solemn moment.[17]

With the Prussian army clearly deploying for battle, the French army marched forward into its designated positions. For the younger officers and soldiers, the whole spectacle and the coming battle clearly made a big impression:

> All was calm in this large and fertile plain which was before us, and which our infantry regiments, cavalry and artillery pieces trampled underfoot. In no time, the rich harvest of which this ground was covered, disappeared as

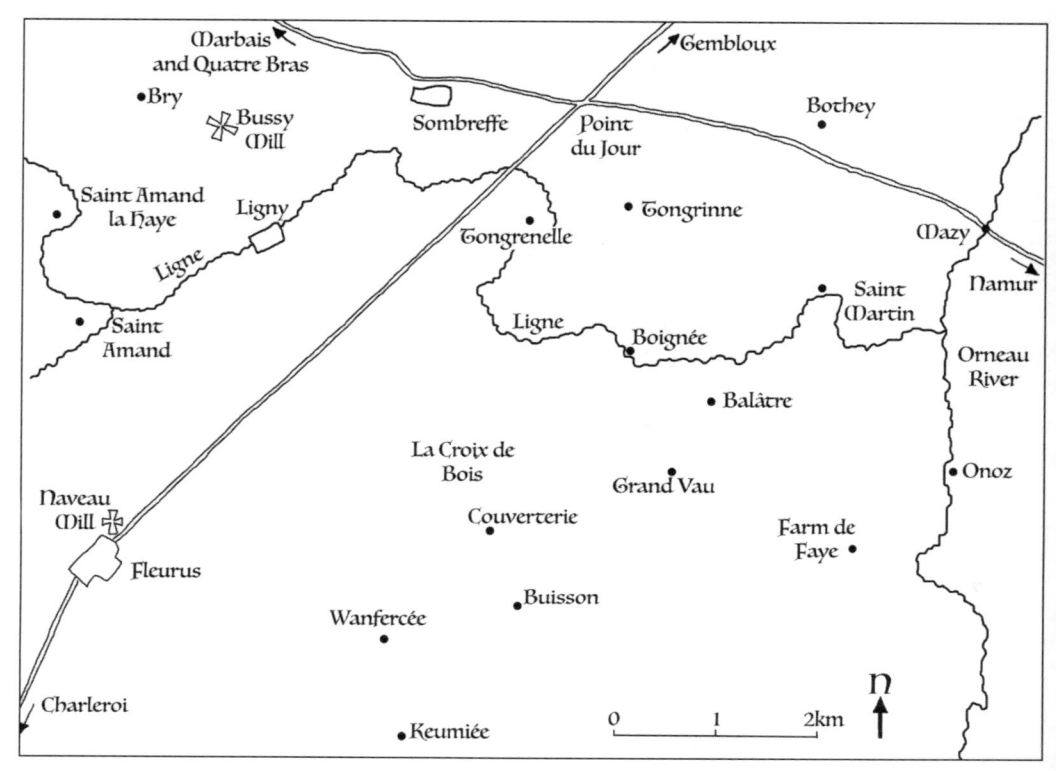

Morning, 16th June (2)

if by a spell. It was difficult to come to terms with the fact that 170,000 men were about to come together to dispute this ground with such fury that for a long time there was nothing to compare with it, and five hours later, of this number of 170,000 men, about 38,000 were dead, mutilated or put *hors de combat*. This calm, which resembled that which precedes a storm, had something to seize and make the heart beat faster. We saw in front of us on the ridge, between Saint-Amand and Ligny, the enemy army make its deployment like us: strong columns of Prussian infantry and cavalry formed an amphitheatre with murderous batteries placed in front of and between their masses, and I confess, this solemn moment, precursor of all our disasters, had a bad impression on me from the moment we came into contact.[18]

With the whole of the Guard, supported by Milhaud's cuirassiers, in reserve around the mill of Naveau, Vandamme's III Corps deployed opposite the village of Saint-Amand. To his left, opposite Saint-Amand-la-Haye, Napoleon deployed Girard's infantry division, deciding to keep this formation detached from the rest of its corps which was under command of Marshal Ney. Securing the extreme left wing was Domon's light cavalry division, which was part of III Corps. Pajol's and Exelmans' cavalry corps occupied the right, leaving the army's centre, opposite the village of Ligny, waiting to be occupied by Gérard's IV Corps. Lobau's VI Corps was still marching forward from Charleroi, having spent the night south of the Sambre.

Many military commentators have criticised Napoleon for not attacking the Prussian position earlier, before the Prussians were properly in position. Whilst there is no doubt that this would indeed have increased the chances of a great victory, such criticism is based on all the advantages of hindsight. The truth is that it was not until late morning that Napoleon could be sure the Prussians were prepared to accept battle and perhaps more importantly, the whole army was still not concentrated. One of Grouchy's *aides de camp*, Captain Bella, recalls the marshal's frustration at the perceived slow march forward of General Gérard's IV Corps:

> Having descended from the mill, Napoleon asked you where the IV Corps was. You replied that it had still not appeared, without doubt because Count Gérard had received the order to move off late. The emperor appeared to be very annoyed and you yourself, as well as a number of other officers, seeing the number of Prussians increasing every minute, regretted that we could not attack immediately.[19]

Indeed, in one of his many writings on the campaign, Grouchy wrote:

> However, the battle of Ligny only started at 3pm. One can only use as an excuse that the IV Corps only took its place in line towards one o'clock. But, since it was as Châtelet the day before, it could have reached the battlefield four or five hours earlier.[20]

In defence of the conduct of both himself and his corps in response to Grouchy's criticism, Gérard gave his reasons for the hold-up of his march:

> The IV Corps only arrived in line at 1 o'clock on the 16th because it had not received an order to be there before. It was only at 9.30am that the movement order was received by me. I personally went immediately to set the troops off on their march; thus not a minute was lost. On this occasion, I recall that on the morning of the 16th, General Exelmans came to see me at Châtelet. His troops were camped close to mine. Both of us had been warned to be ready to march at 2am. I showed him how I was again without

a movement order. I added that I foresaw that these delays which, in my view it was only by rapid movements that we would bring us into the middle of the enemy's cantonments almost without them knowing, that we could hope for great results, since it was clear that at this point, the enemy were much more numerous than us.[21]

It will be remembered that General Hulot had taken command of Bourmont's 14th Division after this latter's desertion the day before. Hulot describes their arrival:

> The next day, the 16th, the IV Corps assembled about 10 o'clock and moved by Lambusart to the windmill situated to the right of Fleurus. The 3rd Division was at the head of the column. After a very long rest, the whole corps was on the march and moved to the left to be in front of Fleurus. During this march I received the order from the corps commander to provide a battalion to move quickly to a clump of trees towards Tongrinne, an officer from the headquarters was to lead it there. The 50th Regiment was closest to me when I received this order and Colonel Lavigne was detached to the area indicated with his first battalion which he commanded himself throughout the day.[22]

Waiting for his troops to move into position and no doubt clear on his orders given to him by Napoleon himself, General Gérard took advantage of the time to make a reconnaissance. The story of what happened next comes from his *aide de camp*, Colonel Rumigny:

> General Gérard began his march on the right of Ligny village, when the Prussians assembled their forces and he observed the road to Namur, waiting for his infantry to arrive.
>
> A little later, he moved forward with his headquarters staff until he found himself in the presence of a squadron of Prussian lancers preceded by some skirmishers. The *chasseurs* of the general's escort started a skirmish fire whilst the general continued to advance at our head without concern that he had no immediate support.
>
> Colonel de Carignan, with the 6th Hussars, was behind, hidden by some high ground. Suddenly, the Prussian officer launched his squadron at the gallop and gave us what we call in war, a 'push'.
>
> The general and his escort faced up to the approach of the enemy squadron, which knocked down eight or ten of our *chasseurs*.
>
> The general and his chief of the headquarters, wanting to get down into a hollow lane, fell with their horses and found themselves without an escape. A Prussian lancer, galloping along the sunken lane, gave five or six lunges

with his lance at Saint-Rémy, who was luckily in front of the general. We arrived and the Prussian wisely retired, leaving his two adversaries on the ground.

General Saint-Rémy was left with some light wounds and General Gérard with some minor bruising to the arm.

I had gone to call forward some cavalry. It arrived at the trot and crushed the Prussian squadron in its turn, which retired on Ligny.[23]

It appears that the cavalry that Rumigny led to rescue General Gérard was from the 12th *Chasseurs*, as Captain Aubry of that regiment wrote in his memoirs:

The next day was the battle of Fleurus, a big and bloody battle where my squadron alone charged Prussian lancers who had approached too close to us and where I saved General Gérard whose *aide de camp* was Commandant Coffe.[24]

As the army re-orientated itself facing north, Grouchy's cavalry continued its push to the east. Pajol's deployment is described in his memoirs:

It was then about 11am. Vandamme had left Fleurus and had deployed a little beyond it on the road towards Saint-Amand. Exelmans' dragoons established themselves in the rear of Pajol's corps of which the two divisions occupied the space between le Gros-Buisson and the Faye farm. At this moment, Prussian troops appeared at Tongrinne, Tongrenelle, Boignée and Balâtre. Their skirmishers moved onto the plain of Fleurus. In order to push them back, Pajol moved Soult's division forward and to the right towards the farms of Keumiée and Couverterie, to close off the valley of Grand-Vau, and to support him on this side with Subervie's division, who he sent a little beyond the crossroads of the routes from Fleurus to Onoz, to Balâtre and to Boignée, and from Wanfercée to Ligny. Grouchy filled the gap to the right and left of the Fleurus to Point-du-Jour road with Exelmans' dragoons which advanced until they were level with Pajol. Exelmans' scouts pushed beyond the Tamines road, preventing the enemy advance guard to advance out of Tongrenelle, whilst those of Pajol launched beyond the Onoz road, holding back the Prussians who had occupied Boignée and Balâtre . . .

Exelmans' cavalry established itself beyond the Tamines road, to the left and right of the road from Fleurus to Boignée. Pajol's took position in front of the road from Fleurus to Onoz, from the tree of la Croix-du-Bois to beyond the Grand Vau farm, facing Biognée and Balâtre . . .[25]

Napoleon was now just waiting for IV Corps to come up and take its position opposite the village of Ligny before he could begin the battle. Captain Putigny of the 33rd *de ligne*, took the opportunity to prepare his company for the coming battle: '. . . calling the *cantinière* I treated them to a barrel of *eau-de-vie* [a poor-quality brandy] before the battle.'[26]

Sergeant Mauduit clearly identified the feeling of the thousands of men, already standing in their initial positions, just waiting for the great battle to begin, 'Everyone breathed in the calm . . . this calm resembled that which always precedes a storm.'[27]

Chapter 7

Prelude to Ligny

Wellington's Meeting with Blücher
Having left Quatre Bras towards 1pm, unconvinced that there was any genuine threat to the crossroads or up the Brussels road, Wellington joined Blücher on the heights of Brye. En route, Wellington had said to his Prussian liaison officer Müffling, 'If, as seems likely, the division of the enemy's forces posted at Frasnes, opposite Quatre Bras, is inconsiderable, and only intended to mask the English army, I can employ my whole strength in support of the Field Marshal [Blücher], and will gladly execute all his wishes in regard to joint operations.'[1] No doubt pleased to see his ally, Blücher climbed with Wellington up the mill of Bussy from which there was a commanding view of the plain surrounding Fleurus and the gathering French forces. From here they could see not only a very large French force assembling, but also, with their telescopes, they could see Napoleon himself, surrounded by a numerous staff. They quickly, but erroneously, concluded that the whole French army was concentrating before them. Given that Blücher knew that he would not be joined by Bülow's IV Corps, the discussion quickly turned to the likelihood of Wellington marching to support his allies, supposing that he had only a small French force in front of him at Quatre Bras.

Wellington's preference was to brush aside the force in front of him and march on Gosselies, thus threatening the French left rear and their lines of communication. This gave him a role that maintained his own independence of command and freedom of action. However, Gneisenau, Blücher's chief-of-staff, was unconvinced of Wellington's dependability, and therefore argued for the Anglo-Dutch army to march straight down the road from Quatre Bras and in behind the Prussian right. This would commit Wellington at the earliest opportunity and by bringing them into reserve they could then be available for use wherever they were required. Wellington, like any capable independent commander, opposed this option, as he foresaw his men being drip-fed into battle and anticipated losing centralised command of them. Although there was no doubt a lively discussion, no agreement was reached and Wellington reportedly ended the discussion with the words, 'Very well! I will come, if I am not attacked myself.'

The fact that Blücher continued to concentrate his army suggests he was determined to fight even without Bülow or Wellington. However, as we shall see, his deployment left his right wing 'in the air', that is, not anchored on a strong feature that would prevent it being outflanked, and this seems to imply that he was expecting Wellington to come in on this flank. Although the various accounts of this meeting are somewhat contradictory,[2] it is fair to conclude that whatever was actually said, Blücher believed he could rely on some help from his ally. Whether Wellington deliberately misled his allies has been hotly debated in recent years. At 2pm Wellington left the Prussian commander-in-chief to return to Quatre Bras.

Napoleon's Plans
In his orders to Ney, Napoleon had explained that he was planning to attack and drive the Prussians past Gembloux; this would push them away from Wellington, allowing time for him to rejoin Ney and march on Brussels. He also directed how Ney should deploy his troops around Quatre Bras, including a division at Marbais, only about four kilometres from Ligny and on the right rear of the Prussian army, adding, 'so that I may draw them to me at Sombreffe if I want them . . .'. This is the first intimation that Napoleon gives that he might want Ney's help in the coming operations, although at the time he wrote this, he was far from believing Blücher was planning to stand and fight.

As the morning progressed, Napoleon was surprised and no doubt rather angered, not to have heard the sound of artillery fire from the direction of Quatre Bras. Having been informed that there was an enemy force there and having then ordered Ney to destroy them and seize the vital crossroads, the lack of firing suggested this attack was not yet under way. Napoleon himself wrote another order to Ney,

> *Monsieur le Prince de la Moskowa*, I am surprised at your great delay in executing my orders – there is no more time to waste. Attack everything in front of you with the greatest impetuosity. The fate of France is in your hands.
>
> Napoleon[3]

It was now increasingly evident that Blücher was indeed planning to make a stand. As Wellington and Blücher met at the Bussy windmill, Napoleon's reconnaissance revealed that the Prussian right was vulnerable; the very flank beyond which Ney had been ordered to deploy. At two o'clock, it was clear that there was going to be a major battle at Ligny; it was now that Napoleon finally developed his idea of fixing the Prussian army in place by a strong frontal attack, and then enveloping their right wing by drawing troops from Marshal Ney, who he expected to have occupied the vital crossroads of Quatre Bras and to have deployed his troops as he had directed in the orders he had sent that morning.

To his immense frustration, Napoleon was not able to open the battle of Ligny as early as he had hoped. Gérard's IV Corps had still not come up and the emperor would not be able to start his attack until towards three o'clock. Napoleon now further developed the idea of drawing some of Ney's troops down the Nivelles to Namur *chausée* and straight onto the right rear of the Prussian army, enveloping its entire right wing. Consequently, just as the battle at Quatre Bras was starting, Napoleon had Soult write to Ney,

> 'In front of Fleurus', 16 June, 2pm.
> Marshal! The emperor has directed me to inform you that the enemy has gathered a body of troops between Sombreffe and Bry, and that at two thirty Marshal Grouchy will attack it with III and IV Army Corps. His Majesty's intent is that you should attack all that is in front of you, and that, after having vigorously pushed it back, you should advance towards us to assist in enveloping the force I have just mentioned. If this force has already been beaten, His Majesty will manoeuvre towards you to speed up your operation in turn. Immediately inform the emperor of your dispositions and what is happening to your front.
> *Major Général, Maréchal de l'empire, Duc de Dalmatie*[4]

This message should certainly have reached Ney by 3.30pm, just as he was about to launch his main attack. This was the first time that Ney had been ordered to actually send a force towards the emperor; in the orders he had received in the morning he had been directed to place a division at Marbais so they could be called on to support the emperor, but at that time Napoleon did not envisage fighting a major battle against the Prussians. Soult had also failed to make it clear that the Prussian force they faced was almost the entire Prussian army and had given this co-operation only secondary importance by placing it after the capture of Quatre Bras. This lack of clarity was to have serious repercussions.

The Battlefield
The battlefield of Ligny was large in comparison to Waterloo, stretching about eight kilometres from one end to the other. It was bisected east to west by the Ligne brook, also known as the Ligny brook, which was narrow and shallow to the west, but became deeper and slightly wider as it ran east and where the banks became deeper and steeper. Not an obstacle to infantry, it certainly was to artillery and difficult for cavalry. The banks of the brook were lined with trees providing defending forces with good cover. To the south of the brook where the French were destined to deploy, the ground was gently rolling and very open with no cover. This plain was dominated by the high ground which rose north from the Ligne. The slope was of medium steepness, providing a dominating height but not one of difficult ascent, although the slope was more challenging between Sombreffe and Bâlatre to the east. On top of the high ground and dominating the ground all around

it, was the village of Brye, forming a bastion on the heights well placed as a final refuge or defence. Five hundred metres forward of this village was the farm and mill of Bussy, which marked the highest point of the ridge. From this high ground, the Prussians could observe every French regiment and every French move on the plain below. It offered good fields of fire to the Prussian artillery, but Prussian troops crossing this open ground to drop down to the Ligne were very exposed to the powerful French artillery. However, in their initial deployment, much of the Prussian force, and its main reserves were hidden on the reverse slope.

In the west, a series of villages lay astride the brook as it ran south-east. From the west these were Wagneleé, which essentially formed the extreme Prussian right, then Saint-Amand-le-Hameau, Saint-Amand-le-Haye and then Saint-Amand itself. These villages formed an almost continuous ribbon of houses and hedges along the stream and a strong defensive line. Saint-Amand-le-Haye, with its large fortified farm and château, was particularly strong. From Saint-Amand, the Ligne changed course towards the east, passing through the middle of the village of Ligny and on the French side of the larger village of Sombreffe. Just to the west of Ligny village was the château de la Tour which, although in a state of disrepair, provided a powerful strongpoint for its defenders. Along this stretch of the brook there were areas of marshy ground which made the approach to the brook difficult. From Sombreffe, the biggest of the villages, the Ligne flowed south-east, so that along its length on the battlefield it showed a lazy S. Along this last stretch, the brook meandered somewhat, flowing across the villages of Tongrenelle, Tongrinne, Boignée and finally Balâtre, which effectively formed the extreme left of the Prussian line. The junction of the main roads from Charleroi to Gembloux, and Nivelle to Namur (via Quatre Bras) at Point du Jour was another key high point which provided good observation across the eastern side of the battlefield, in much the same way as the Bussy mill did to the west.

Behind the Prussian position, running roughly east to west, was the main *chausée* that ran from Namur to Nivelle. This road touched the rear (north) of Sombreffe, and it was important because it ran directly from the Ligny battlefield to Quatre Bras, and it was along this road that Blücher was expecting Wellington's army to march to his support and down which Napoleon was planning to draw some of Ney's troops onto the rear of the Prussians. Only three kilometres along this road from the Bussy mill, from which Blücher directed the battle, lay the village of Marbais where, as has been said, Napoleon had ordered Ney to place one of his divisions after having occupied Quatre Bras.

As a number of French eyewitnesses testify, the Prussian army occupied a strong position. Sergeant Mauduit described it thus:

> This position was good and well chosen, for these villages in front of the Prussian army offered marvellous shelter for their troops and the artillery on the semi-circular high ground which was between them commanded the

whole battlefield, whilst to the rear, on the hillside, surmounted by the mill of Bussy, formed a strong '*point d'appui*' [literally, 'a point of support'] in case of disaster.

The situation of the villages of Ligny and Saint-Amand, in low ground, but bristling with natural obstacles, was very favourable for defence; and if the hilly terrain, like an amphitheatre, from there as far as the farm of Bussy [next to the mill of the same name], proved to have the disadvantage for the Prussians of having no cover, from the bottom to the top and exposing them to the fire of our artillery, from that side also, the Prussian battalions had the advantage of plunging fire over us and finally, Blücher could easily see all our movements as well as all our stationary masses; for from Fleurus to Ligny and Saint-Amand, there was hardly a fold in the ground to hide our troops . . . the mill of Bussy was also high above the plain that we occupied . . .

The name of Saint-Amand belonged to a commune composed of three villages; Saint-Amand, properly called, is the part situated entirely on the right [the French side] of the brook towards Fleurus; Saint-Amand-la-Haye is the part between Saint-Amand and Wagneleé, and le Hameau de Saint-Amand covers, by its position, the interval between these two villages. The houses of Saint-Amand, like those of a great number of Belgian villages, are detached from each other, sit in the centre of gardens and orchards, called pastures, and which are covered by many fruit trees or high trees. In 1815, most of the trees around Saint-Amand made it look like a thick wood. Our troops were not even able to see the church and the houses that surrounded it, placed right on the edge of the Ligny side. The trees which formed this thick cover were nearly all cut down in 1818 and 1819, which has now changed the look of Saint-Amand.

Throughout its length, Ligny is cut into two halves by the brook, with each half cut into two by the main road that runs through it. This road has lateral tracks leading from it, most of which lead into sunken, muddy lanes. Those on the Prussian side were very narrow and hardly allowed passage by files; on the French side, to the contrary, they were able to penetrate by half sections of twelve files as far as the part where the same road suddenly shrinks.

The cemetery of Ligny, surrounded by a low wall, is on the right [French] bank of the stream, as well as an old château at the entry to the village on the side of Saint-Amand [west]. The Ligne stream, into which two others flow, has, not far from Saint-Amand, a deep course with steep banks; it needed to be crossed by bridges, the banks being too steep.

From Sombreffe they become steeper still, principally at Tongrinne and dominate alternatively. Beyond this place, the position is cut by thick hedges and ravines.[5]

General Berthezène also describes the ground in front of his division as:

> Naturally strong. [The villages were] composed of isolated farms surrounded by gardens and thick hedges, and very spread out. A marshy stream ran across the whole position, defended besides by many hedges and sunken lanes and by the hamlets of Longpré[6] and [Saint-Amand] La Haye, which almost touched the village of Saint-Amand and that of Brye. This stream, a little wider before Ligny, was very narrow at Saint-Amand. These different villages and hamlets were occupied by considerable forces and supported by large reserves, placed close to the Bussy mill, from where they could easily move on any point that was attacked which they dominated. The various accidents of the ground were well suited to the deployment of artillery, and very strong batteries could be seen at the quarries, next to Ligny.[7]

Blücher's Dispositions (See colour plates)
Clausewitz tells us that Blücher's original plan was to concentrate his army at Sombreffe and then to attack Napoleon's flank as he advanced up the main road to Brussels. Once again, this presumes that Napoleon's main effort was the capture of that city rather than the destruction of the two allied armies. Once Napoleon had identified the Prussian concentration area and deployed his main force to fight it, Blücher had little option but to fight a defensive battle and hope that Wellington would be able to support him with a proportion of his army.

Blücher's army, less Bülow's IV Corps, numbered about 84,000. His deployment reflected a critical dilemma. According to the rules of war of those days, it was vital to cover his lines of communication which ran east and northeast down which Bülow would be marching, but he also needed to cover the road down which he hoped Wellington would aim to join him. However, to do this effectively required a kink in his line which gave it a rather odd orientation and which would make it very difficult for his left wing to have any influence over the fighting in the centre or on the right. He therefore chose a position for I and II Corps between the villages of Saint-Amand and Sombreffe to cover Wellington's arrival, and III Corps was ordered to occupy the area between Sombreffe and Balâtre which would cover Bülow's advance from Gembloux.

Zieten's I Corps formed the front line between Saint-Amand and Sombreffe, with Pirch I's II Corps in reserve behind, protected by the heights above the Ligne brook, from which the village of Ligny took its name. Thielemann's III Corps covered the line from Sombreffe to Balâtre. This was an unusual deployment, with I Corps spread thinly across a wide frontage and reliant on a different corps, II Corps, with a different chain-of-command for its key reserves. Even the troops within I Corps seemed oddly mixed up: Brye was occupied by three battalions of the 1st Brigade, whilst the other six of that brigade stood behind Saint-Amand.

Meanwhile, the 3rd Brigade had three battalions in Saint-Amand while the other six formed the rearmost reserve. Ligny was occupied by four battalions of the 4th Brigade, with its remaining two battalions in second line between Brye and Ligny. The remaining eight battalions of the 2nd Brigade were in the second line, along with the two battalions of the 4th Brigade. Finally, the six remaining battalions of the 3rd Brigade were in a third line just behind the 2nd and 4th. The I Corps reserve cavalry was in reserve just in front of 3rd Brigade. Pirch I's II Corps stood along the Namur to Nivelle road as the main reserve with the brigades deployed next to each other; each brigade in three lines in column.

Thielemann's III Corps deployed its 9th Brigade to defend the small villages that ran across its front from Sombreffe to Balâtre. The 11th Brigade defended the main road from Point-du-jour towards Namur, with the 10th defending the ridge of Tongrinne and Tongrenelle; the 12th Brigade and cavalry reserve stood behind them. 9th Brigade only occupied the village of Mont-Potriaux with a single battalion to begin with, whilst the other eight remained in reserve behind the village. 11th Brigade occupied the valley of the Ligne brook with one battalion and kept the other four back in reserve. The 10th Brigade occupied the Ligne valley with two battalions and kept the other four back on top of the ridge. Thielemann's chief of staff was Colonel von Clausewitz, who was to become one of history's most celebrated military theorists. The Prussian artillery was spread along the heights with particularly strong batteries overlooking the villages of Saint-Amand and Ligny.

Blücher was not one to sit idly in a defensive position and let his enemy attack him. He planned an aggressive defence; his intent was to hold the strong line of the Ligne brook and the villages which lay on it with a thick skirmish line to hold the French for as long as possible and cause heavy casualties, and then, when the French attempted to deploy beyond the river line and through the villages, to smash them with heavy artillery fire and attack them in force with his reserves. The single weak point of this position was its right flank. However, this could be anchored on the village of Wagneleé, although could easily be outflanked across the open ground to the west. However, Blücher expected Wellington to arrive on this flank and close it to the French; indeed, the open ground here offered the opportunity to counterattack the French on this side and threaten their communications back through Charleroi.

The French Deployment

Vandamme's III Corps took position facing the village of Saint-Amand. Interestingly, Vandamme's corps artillery did not arrive before the battle started; it was held up passing through a congested Fleurus. Lefol's and Bertezène's divisions were in the first line (Lefol left and Berthezène right), with Habert's division in reserve. About a kilometre to its left was Girard's division (which was detached from II Corps). Domon's cavalry division (eight squadrons) of III Corps was placed in observation on the extreme left of the line.

Gérard's IV Corps provided the centre of the French army, deployed opposite the village of Ligny. As it was placed in the centre and would fight almost exclusively in the village, General Maurin's light cavalry division was attached to General Exelmans' dragoons further to the right. However, not all of IV Corps were to fight for Ligny; General Hulot, who now commanded the division from which Bourmont had deserted, was given a new task:

> During this march I received the order from the corps commander to provide a battalion to move quickly to a clump of trees towards Tongrinne, an officer from the headquarters was to lead it there. The 50th Regiment was closest to me when I received this order and Colonel Lavigne was detached to the area indicated with his first battalion which he commanded himself throughout the day.
>
> From in front of Fleurus, I received the order to attack the villages of Sombreffe and Tongrinne with the 3rd Division. The two churches of these places were used for direction, whilst the two other divisions moved on Ligny. When you are close, you realise that they are about a quarter of a league apart. These points of attack were garrisoned by numerous infantry, advantageously posted in the gardens which connected these two villages and behind the very deep Ligny brook which they crossed. The high ground in the rear of these villages, wrapped around them and dominated them, were covered with a numerous artillery, strong columns and lines of infantry and cavalry, which extended to our right as far as opposite and beyond the clump of trees where the 1st Battalion of the 50th Regiment had been posted.
>
> Thus the 3rd Division, with the cavalry that was under the orders of Marshal Grouchy, whose squadrons were formed opposite and behind Tongrinne and Sombreffe, formed the extreme right of the army.[8]

Hulot's division was therefore to operate largely in support of Grouchy, providing a vital infantry force capable of fighting in the close country of the Ligne brook and the villages that lay along it on this flank, but depriving Gérard of one of his divisions, leaving him only two divisions (Vichery and Pêcheux) with which to attack the centre of the Prussian line; his own cavalry (Maurin's division) was covering the right of the corps, linking in with Grouchy's cavalry. There was a gap of two kilometres between Gérard's and Vandamme's troops; quite unusual in a major battle of this sort, but it was covered in large part by the obstacle of the Ligne.

After having swept the plain of Prussian skirmishers, Grouchy, with the cavalry corps of Generals Pajol and Exelmans, went to take position on the extreme right and *en potence* to the main line, facing Thielemann's III Corps. Exelmans' corps of dragoons (two divisions; twenty-four squadrons and two batteries each of six guns) were the left covering between Tongrenelle and Boignée, whilst General Pajol's light cavalry (fifteen squadrons and two batteries; the 1st Hussars had not rejoined the corps at this point) covered from Boignée across the front of Balâtre, with detachments, as far as the minor road to Namur. This was certainly not cavalry country and so troops from Hulot's division were an essential addition to Grouchy's command.

All the Imperial Guard formed up near the Naveau mill where Napoleon observed the Prussian position. Mauduit tells us of their deployment.

> We went to be placed in the second line on the right flank of Fleurus and in the following order:
>
> The foot *chasseurs* in front of the Fleurus [Naveau] mill which was about 800 *toises* from the last houses; the four regiments of this division (eight battalions) were placed in columns by regiment deployed at half distance of battalion. Their battery was with them.
>
> This division had to its left, a little beyond the main road which went from Fleurus to Sombreffe, the two brigades of the Young Guard (eight battalions) also in columns by regiment at a half distance of battalion. They were thus in the second line behind the III Corps. Each brigade of Young Guard also had its battery.
>
> The division of foot grenadiers (4th, 3rd, 2nd and 1st Regiments, or eight battalions) also deployed in columns by regiment at half distance by battalions, supported its left on the Fleurus mill, with its battery behind it.
>
> These three columns were established by echelons so that they could form, firmly, three large squares in case the 102 Prussian squadrons threw their attention on us, had they wanted to attempt a general hurrah into the plain and fall on us there like an avalanche.
>
> ...
>
> The *Grenadiers-à-Cheval*, the Dragoons of the Guard and the *Gendarmes d'Élite* (1,700 men), formed in two columns by deployed squadrons, were placed twenty-five *toises* behind us; having their left level with our right.
>
> The guard artillery, having its guns limbered were placed behind us by only a few *toises*. It was surrounded by the infantry and heavy cavalry of the Guard and by Milhaud's [4th Reserve Cavalry Corps] 3,000 cuirassiers which were placed in columns by squadron close to Fleurus.[9]

As we have seen, Lobau's VI Corps had been ordered forward from the south bank of the Sambre where it had spent the night, but it was kept well back from the battlefield, midway between Charleroi and Fleurus. Although Napoleon could have called on it in an emergency, it is quite clear that he had no intention of using it so that he retained a force that was fresh for future operations.

Such was the position of the army at 2.30pm. The whole of the force under

Napoleon's command in front of the Prussians was about 55,000 infantry, 12,000 cavalry and 232 guns; but this includes Lobau's VI Corps of about 9,000 men and 32 guns that was not involved in the fighting and in fact spent most of the day out of view of the battlefield. Thus it can be fairly said that Napoleon had only a total of about 58,000 men and 200 guns with which to face Blücher's 84,000 men and 217 guns, a significant disadvantage given that Napoleon would be attacking a strong defensive position.

Grouchy
Grouchy had temporarily taken command of the right wing of the army consisting of two infantry corps (III and IV) and three of cavalry (1st, 2nd and 4th); close to 30,000 infantry, 12,000 cavalry and 112 pieces of artillery. However, now they had deployed onto the battlefield, command had returned to Napoleon, as he had warned in his orders of the morning. Grouchy was now given his new orders by the emperor.

> Towards 1pm, at the moment of the attack on the Prussians in Saint-Amand and Ligny, the emperor said to Grouchy, 'With the cavalry corps of Generals Pajol and Exelmans, you are to throw back all the Prussian cavalry of the Prussian army's left wing onto Sombreffe and prevent the enemy troops which arrive from Namur along the road running from that town to Quatre Bras, to effect their junction with Marshal Blücher.'[10]

As we have heard, on the initial deployment, Napoleon had added an infantry battalion, followed by Hulot's entire division, to Grouchy's command. Grouchy's mission, apparently from Napoleon himself, clearly shows that the emperor still felt other Prussian troops (Bülow's corps?) might approach the battle from the direction of Namur. If this was the case, and given the difficult country on this flank, Napoleon must quickly have realised that Grouchy could not have carried out this mission with cavalry alone. So Grouchy was to command the right wing of the French army, with the specific mission of stopping any new Prussian troops moving up from Namur. Everything was now ready for the battle to begin.

Napoleon was clearly confident. All his manoeuvres appeared to have succeeded; the Prussian army lay before him and there was nothing to fear from Wellington, whose army appeared to still not be concentrated. In his memoirs he wrote:

> Everything pointed to the destruction of the Prussian army. Count Gérard, having come up to me to ask for some instructions about attacking the village of Ligny, I told him, 'It is possible that in three hours the issue of the war will be decided. If Ney carries out my orders well, not a single gun

of the Prussian army will escape; it is caught red-handed.'¹¹

Captain Coignet, the wagon-master of Imperial Headquarters, recalls a slightly different final act before the battle started:

> He [Napoleon] was at a village on the left of the plain [Fleurus], at the foot of a windmill, and the Prussian armies were mostly on his right, concealed by gardens, skirts of woods and farms. 'Their position is concealed, we cannot see them,' said all the officers when they returned. The order was given for a general attack. The Emperor went up into the windmill and, looking through a hole, watched all the movements. The chief of staff said to him, 'There goes the corps of General Gérard.' – 'Send Gérard up here.' He came up to the Emperor. 'Gérard,' said he, 'your Bourmont, for whom you said you would be answerable to me, has gone over to the enemy.' And pointing through a hole in the mill to a steeple on the right, 'You must go toward that steeple and drive the Prussians in as far as you can. I will support you. Grouchy has my orders.'¹²

Chapter 8

The Battle of Ligny

At about 2.30pm,[1] all the French troops were finally in position and Napoleon was able to give the order for Vandamme and Gérard to launch their attacks on the villages that lay before them. General Pajol recalled: 'At 2.30pm, three cannon shots fired at regular intervals by a battery of the Guard positioned close to Napoleon's position at the Fleurus mill, was the signal to begin the battle.'[2]

As the attacks got underway, Napoleon had Soult send a despatch to Marshal Ney informing him of this and confirming the requirement for him to send a force onto the Prussian rear. Now he was committed to battle, Napoleon was confident that with the intervention of Ney, the Prussians before him could be destroyed; if this could be achieved, then he felt the outcome of the campaign could not be in doubt. Soult reflected the importance of Ney's contribution in this order that was carried by Colonel Laurent:

'In front of Fleurus', 16 June, 3.15pm
Marshal, I wrote to you an hour ago that the emperor would attack the enemy at two thirty in the position he has taken between Saint-Amand and Brye. At this moment the engagement is very fierce. His Majesty has directed me to tell you that you must manoeuvre onto the field in such a manner as to envelop the enemy's right and to fall with full force on his rear. The enemy army will be lost if you act vigorously. The fate of France is in your hands. Therefore, do not hesitate an instant to move as the emperor has ordered, and head toward the heights of Brye and Saint-Amand to co-operate in a victory that should be decisive. The enemy has been caught *en flagrant délit* while trying to unite with the English.

Major Général, Maréchal de l'empire, Duc de Dalmatie[3]

The battle of Ligny is a difficult battle to describe within accurate timings; it was not a battle that can be broken down into a number of convenient phases such as Waterloo and the timings given in accounts of participants vary considerably. For example, the start of the battle is given variously between 2.30pm and 3.30pm. The fighting continued without respite along the Ligne brook until darkness so it is unsurprising that the participants had no concept of time; few accounts have any timings at all and many of those were no doubt 'guesstimates'. Attack was followed by counter-attack and the reserves of both sides were gradually fed into the furnace that was the string of villages in which most of the fighting took place. Some divisions, brigades and battalions fought virtually all day without rest. It was to become a battle that would be decided by which side ran out of reserves first. With a considerable advantage in numbers, and in a strong defensive position, Blücher must have felt confident.

The Battle Opens
The first French troops into action were Lefol's 8th Division of Vandamme's III Corps. They were forced to attack without full artillery support as not all of the corps artillery had arrived. One of Lefol's *aides de camp*, his nephew, described the action:

> All the dispositions for battle having been taken, our division had the honour of opening the attack on Saint-Amand which became the scene of desperate fighting. All advised the emperor to direct his principal attack there; by this, avoiding the difficulties of the ground and approaching Marshal Ney who was engaged at Quatre Bras with Wellington's advance guard, he would be able to move to the support, or receive it, separate the Prussians from the English, and force the first to retire on Namur; also seized by the desire to exterminate the Prussian army, he decided to engage in a general battle.
> ... Charged with opening fire against Saint-Amand, General Lefol had his division formed in square to read them the emperor's Proclamation to the Army, which ended with this paragraph,
> 'Soldiers! We have forced marches to make, battles to fight, perils to face; but with constancy, victory will be ours; the rights, the honour and the happiness of *la patrie* will be reclaimed! For all Frenchmen who have a heart, the moment has come to conquer or die!'
> Profiting from this opportunity, the general harangued his soldiers with good heart and energy so that they, full of enthusiasm and excited by Napoleon's presence, who passed across the front of the division at this very moment, demanded by loud shouts to march against the enemy.
> The order to attack Saint-Amand having finally been given, the general sent out a large number of skirmishers and advanced at the head of his division that was formed in three columns. This march against the enemy was made to the sound of cannon, and some of the 23rd *de ligne*'s musicians were wounded. The first ball fired by the Prussian batteries fell in our masses and killed eight men in a company of the 64th *de ligne* commanded by Captain Revest, who has since died as a colonel of infantry. This incident, far from suppressing the ardour of our soldiers, only excited them, and it

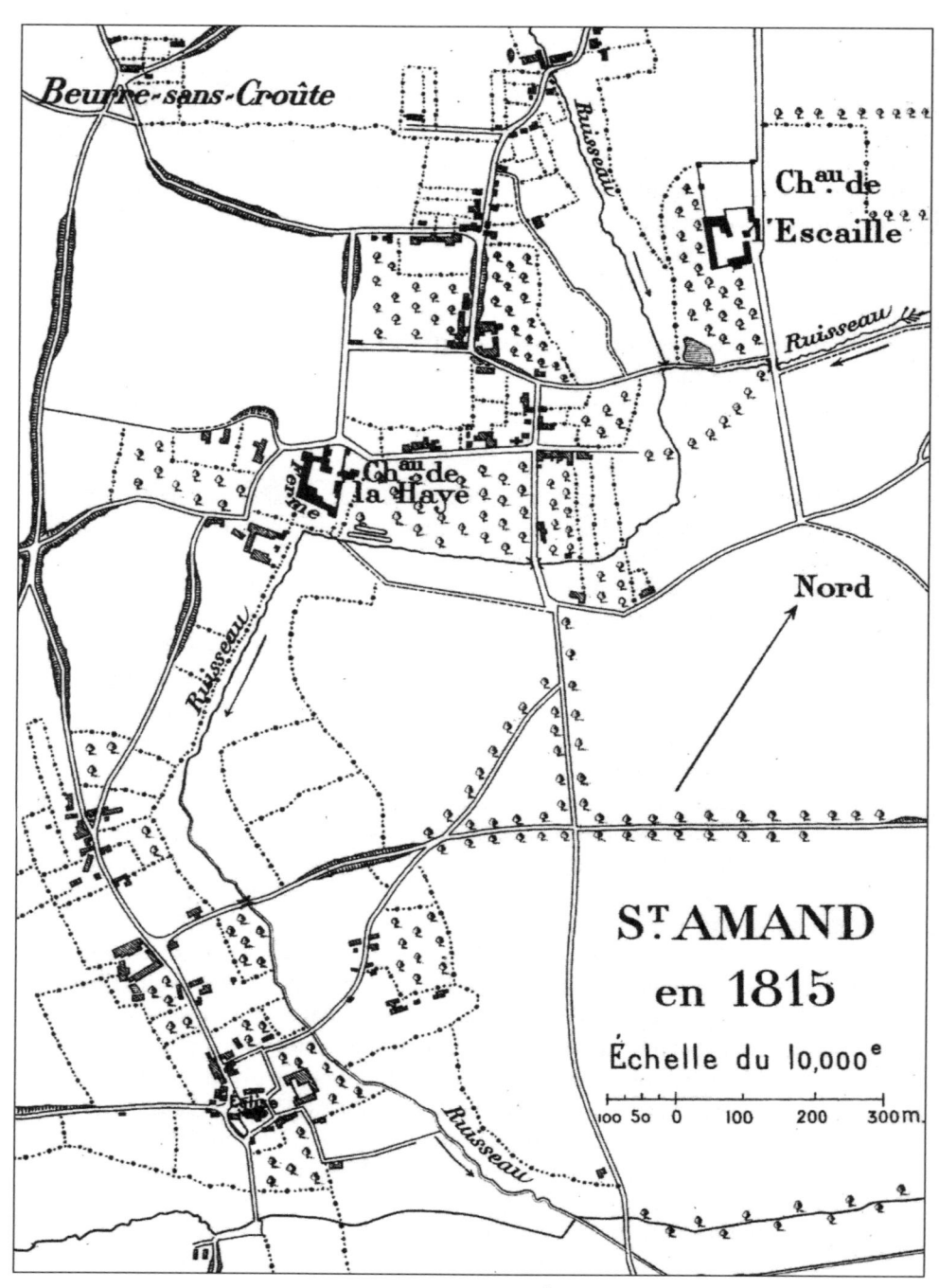

St. Amand

was thus that they arrived at Saint-Amand and cleared it with the bayonet. From this moment, the battle took on a bloody character.[4]

Captain Gerbet was a company commander in the 37th *de ligne*. His regiment was part of *Maréchal de Camp* Corsin's brigade, part of Lefol's division, and he describes this attack:

> . . . we were deployed in closed columns in mass by division [*colonnes serrées en masse par division*].
>
> The emperor ordered us to make a change in front to march to attack the village of Saint-Amand; this position was the key to the battle which was about to begin. The gardens and orchards of this village, situated on a height, was enclosed by hedges and walls, and strongly occupied by the enemy, as well as the solidly constructed houses.
>
> The ground in front of this village offered no advantage to the attackers. After the change of face, General Lefol addressed our division, a warm address which informed us of our important task.
>
> We responded with enthusiastic cries of '*Vive l'empereur!*'
>
> Immediately afterwards, the brave General Lefol led us straight at the enemy. No sooner had we set off than we heard the sound of a rain of case shot falling within our ranks, making terrible ravages.
>
> The enemy balls ploughed through our ranks, carrying off entire files.
>
> At the same time, infantry fire, coming from the gardens, orchards and houses where the enemy was entrenched, decimated our closed columns. However, we continued to march with unshakeable courage, with ordered arms and without firing a shot on this village bristling with fire; leaving in our wake long, bloody and cruel traces.
>
> Reaching the enclosures, we launched ourselves on the Prussians and chased them off with the bayonet. Penetrating into the village despite the balls from doors and windows, we captured it; but we were not able to pursue our success far, for at the point where we reached was found a deep cutting where the Ligny stream ran, lined on both sides by big trees, across which there appeared on the other side of this stream on a ridge opposite and sheltered from our fire, masses of Prussian infantry in reserve.[5]

Lefol's infantry had taken the village without facing determined resistance; although the position was strong, it was only relatively weakly held. As Gerbet describes, beyond the village flowed the Ligne, and although not a particularly difficult obstacle to cross, the formed Prussian masses on the high ground beyond threatened anyone who tried to cross, and the Prussian batteries were well positioned to sweep the approaches. Lefol again:

Each side was supported by a formidable artillery, whose detonations sounded like the crack of lightning, and this terrible bombardment was augmented by the alternate attacks of the two armies ceaselessly returning to the charge . . . General Lefol, entering first into Saint-Amand, had his horse killed underneath him in an orchard and faced being killed or captured, when I had the good fortune to escape the fire and give him my own.[6]

Maréchal de Camp Corsin expands on this last episode in a letter he wrote later:

During one of these attacks, and at a moment when we were repulsed, General Lefol[7] had his horse killed underneath him and was going to be made prisoner when *aide de camp* Lefol, thinking only of his duty, dismounted in the middle of a scene of terrible carnage, to give him his own horse. Both came under fire from musketry and looked as if they would be killed or captured, when the unexpected arrival on the scene of a company of the 64th saved them and gave the general time to mount his nephew's horse and move to join this company with his nephew . . .[8]

General Corsin had three horses killed underneath him at Saint-Amand and an old wound re-opened later in the campaign, forcing him to give up his command.

Although his division was not yet committed, General Berthezène identified and described the Prussian tactics for the defence of the line of the Ligne brook:

Saint-Amand was occupied without effort, the enemy defended it meekly; but when our columns attempted to exit into the open ground, they were stopped by superior forces and struck down by a formidable artillery, which it could not withstand for long on its own because of the difficulties of the ground, they were forced to retreat and obliged to return to the village.[9]

Lefol's men crossed the stream, but beyond, in the open ground they were met by a storm of fire followed by a counter-attack by the Prussian 12th and 24th Regiments. After a fierce hand-to-hand fight the Prussians were again pushed out of the village. Thus the pattern appears to have been established; the weak Prussian forces deployed in the villages themselves were quickly pushed out by weight of numbers. However, as the French attempted to break out of the close terrain they were met by strong Prussian counter-attacks into the village, or a hail of musketry and artillery fire. Having rallied, the Prussians returned to the attack, attempting to seize the cemetery; they failed and were forced back onto the defensive outside the village.

Ligny

The attack on Ligny, in the French centre, started a short time after Lefol attacked Saint-Amand. The village was held by four battalions of Henckel's 4th Brigade (I Corps). The fighting in this village was more determined and more savage than in Saint-Amand and the village, bisected by the Ligne brook, was a far more formidable defensive position. Here there were a number of strongly-built, almost fortified, farms, a château and the church with a sturdy wall around it. Sunken lanes and thick hedges also offered plenty of cover for the defenders. The attack was preceded by a heavy artillery barrage from both sides and this continued over the heads of the columns as the French moved forward, Pêcheux's division in the lead.

First the French had to break into the village through the hedges and sunken lanes, then they had to clear the buildings on the near bank of the Ligne, including the fortified farm of d'En Haut and the church. Once these had been cleared, the stream had to be crossed, the main bridge over which was dominated by the farm of d'En Bas. Whilst hand-to-hand fighting in open areas was quite unusual in this period, the same was not true of fighting in the close terrain of towns and villages, where soldiers who were well protected by buildings, walls and thick hedges were reluctant to give up the cover that protected them and which gave them strong fighting positions. What's more, men were far more likely to come across each other suddenly and without warning; fight or flight were the only options and flight had the disadvantage of presenting your back to an opponent who might only be a few yards away.

Captain Francois was a company commander in the 30th *de ligne* and he describes the attack of Pécheux's division:

> Towards three o'clock, General Pécheux gave the order to General Rome, commander of the 1st Brigade of his division, composed of the 30th and 96th *de ligne*, to form in attack column and to march on the village of Ligny to attack it. We, the 30th, at the head of the brigade, despite the caseshot, march with shouldered arms on this village. Arriving two hundred paces from the hedges behind which were thousands of Prussian skirmishers, the regiment formed line whilst on the march. The charge was beaten and the soldiers crossed the hedges. The half battalion of the 1st, of which I was part, went down a sunken lane, cut by *abates*, carts, harrows and ploughs that we crossed with much difficulty and under the fire of the Prussians hidden behind the hedges which were very thick. Finally we crossed these obstacles and, in open order, we entered the village of Ligny. Arriving before the church, a stream brought us to a halt and the enemy, in the houses, behind walls on the roofs caused us a considerable loss as much by their musketry as their caseshot and the balls that were fired at us from front and flank. In an instant, Major Hervieux, commanding the regiment, the *Chefs*

de Bataillon Richard and Lafolie are killed, *Chef de Bataillon* Blain lightly wounded and his horse killed under him; five captains are killed, three wounded; two *adjutant-majors* killed, nine lieutenants killed, seven wounded and almost seven hundred men killed and wounded. For myself, I had only light bruises to the thighs and right leg.[10]

Gérard's *aide de camp* Rumigny describes the first stages of the attack on the village:

Ligny was attacked by the left, whilst one of the brigades, commanded by General Rommieu [General Rome, who commanded a brigade of Pêcheux's 12th Division consisting of the 30th and 96th *de ligne*], the old colonel of the 7th *léger,* attacked the centre of the village. The Prussians occupied Ligny in great strength and as the artillery fire became heavy, the batteries thundered over the houses of the village, long and hard. Towards 2pm, General Gérard ordered me to go and tell General Rommieu not to commit too far if the resistance was too heavy. I found the 30th *de ligne* in the hollow lanes full of sticky mud. The unfortunate soldiers were shot at by Prussians that occupied the gardens and hedges. The 30th was suffering terribly and General Rommieu was soon gravely wounded [he is not recorded as being wounded at Ligny]. I had the 30th retired, who had suffered so much without being able to strike back at the enemy, and I told the officers to move them behind the stream that ran through the centre of the village. I went to tell General Lavigne [Lavigne was actually the colonel commanding the 50th *de ligne*] of everything that was happening.[11]

Captain Francois described his frustration with the attack:

Not for many a day had I fought with so much daring, I was not harmed except for a few slight bruises on the thighs and right leg. The disorder into which the enemy threw us made me curse my existence. I wanted to get killed, so angry was I to see a battle so badly ordered. There was no commander. We saw neither generals, nor staff officers, nor *aides de camp*. The regiment was two-thirds destroyed, without receiving either supports or orders, and we were obliged to retreat in disorder, leaving our wounded comrades and to try to rally near our batteries, which were pounding those of the enemy.[12]

As the French attack developed, the two remaining battalions of the Prussian 4th Brigade moved into the village and the first attack was repulsed.

The descriptions of the fighting give a good impression of its intensity and savagery. First Mauduit:

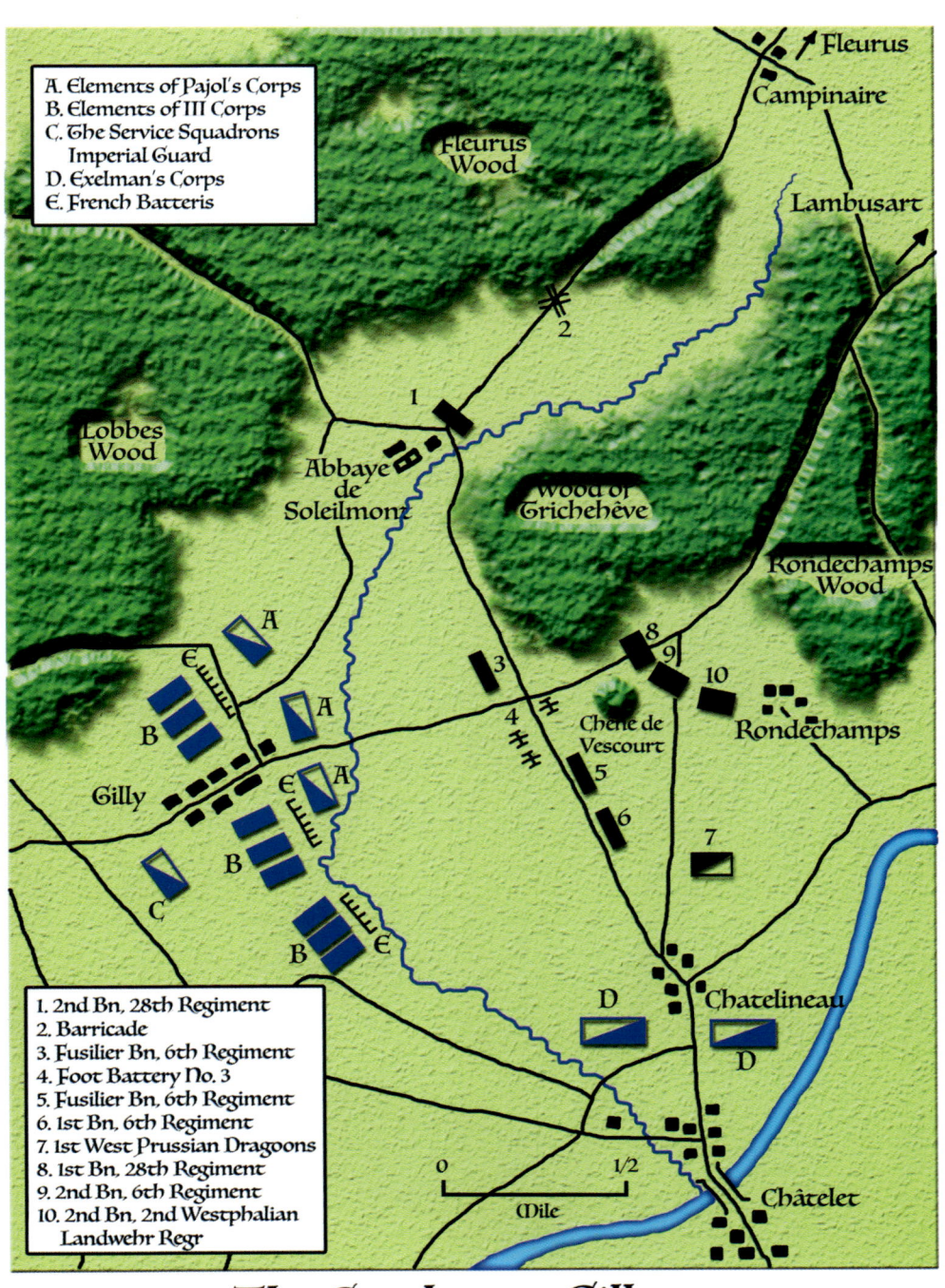

A. Elements of Pajol's Corps
B. Elements of III Corps
C. The Service Squadrons Imperial Guard
D. Exelman's Corps
E. French Batteris

1. 2nd Bn, 28th Regiment
2. Barricade
3. Fusilier Bn, 6th Regiment
4. Foot Battery No. 3
5. Fusilier Bn, 6th Regiment
6. 1st Bn, 6th Regiment
7. 1st West Prussian Dragoons
8. 1st Bn, 28th Regiment
9. 2nd Bn, 6th Regiment
10. 2nd Bn, 2nd Westphalian Landwehr Regr

The Combat at Gilly

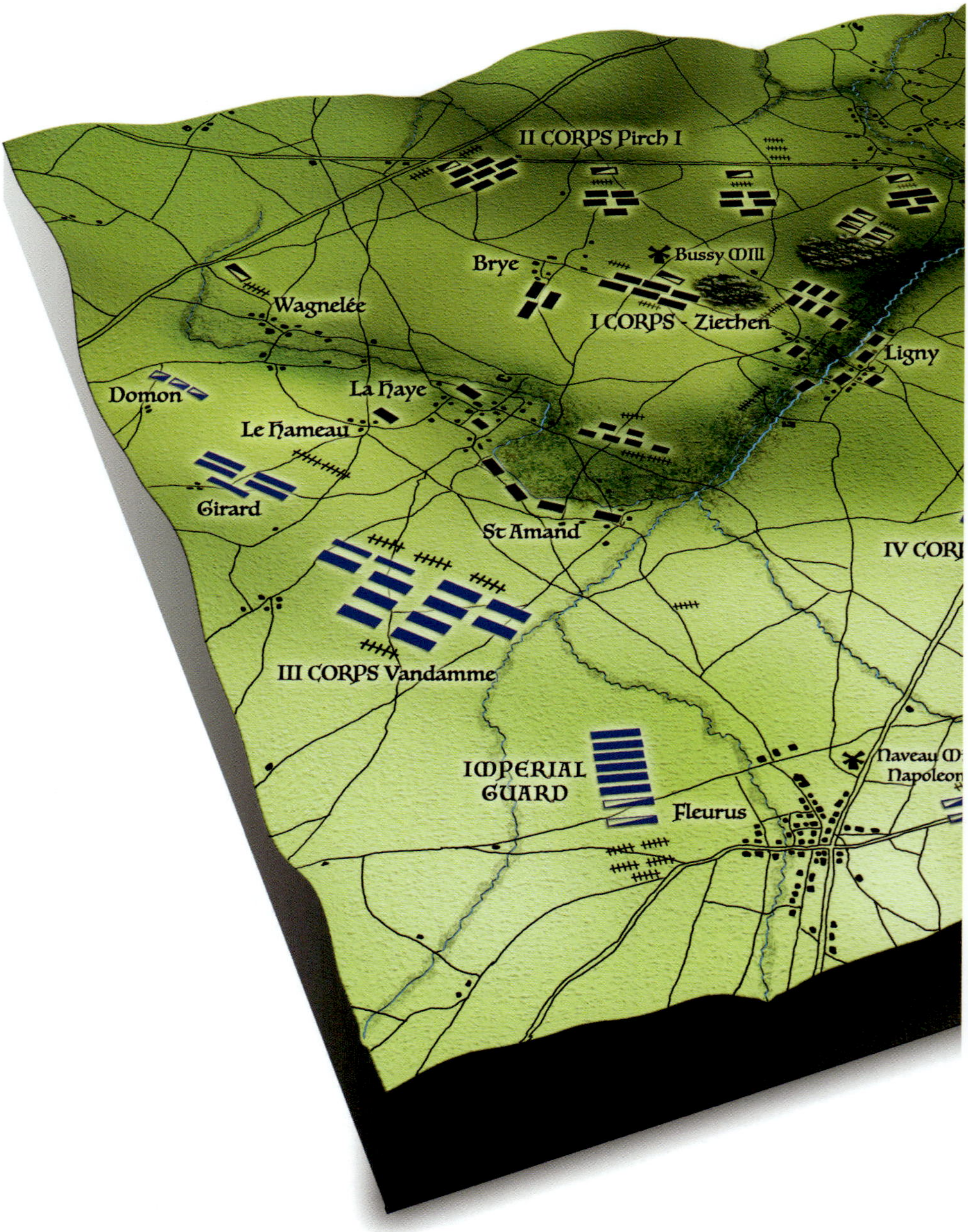

II CORPS Pirch I
Bussy Mill
Brye
Wagnelée
I CORPS - Ziethen
Ligny
Domon
La Haye
Le Hameau
Girard
St Amand
IV CORP
III CORPS Vandamme
IMPERIAL
GUARD
Fleurus
Naveau M
Napoleon

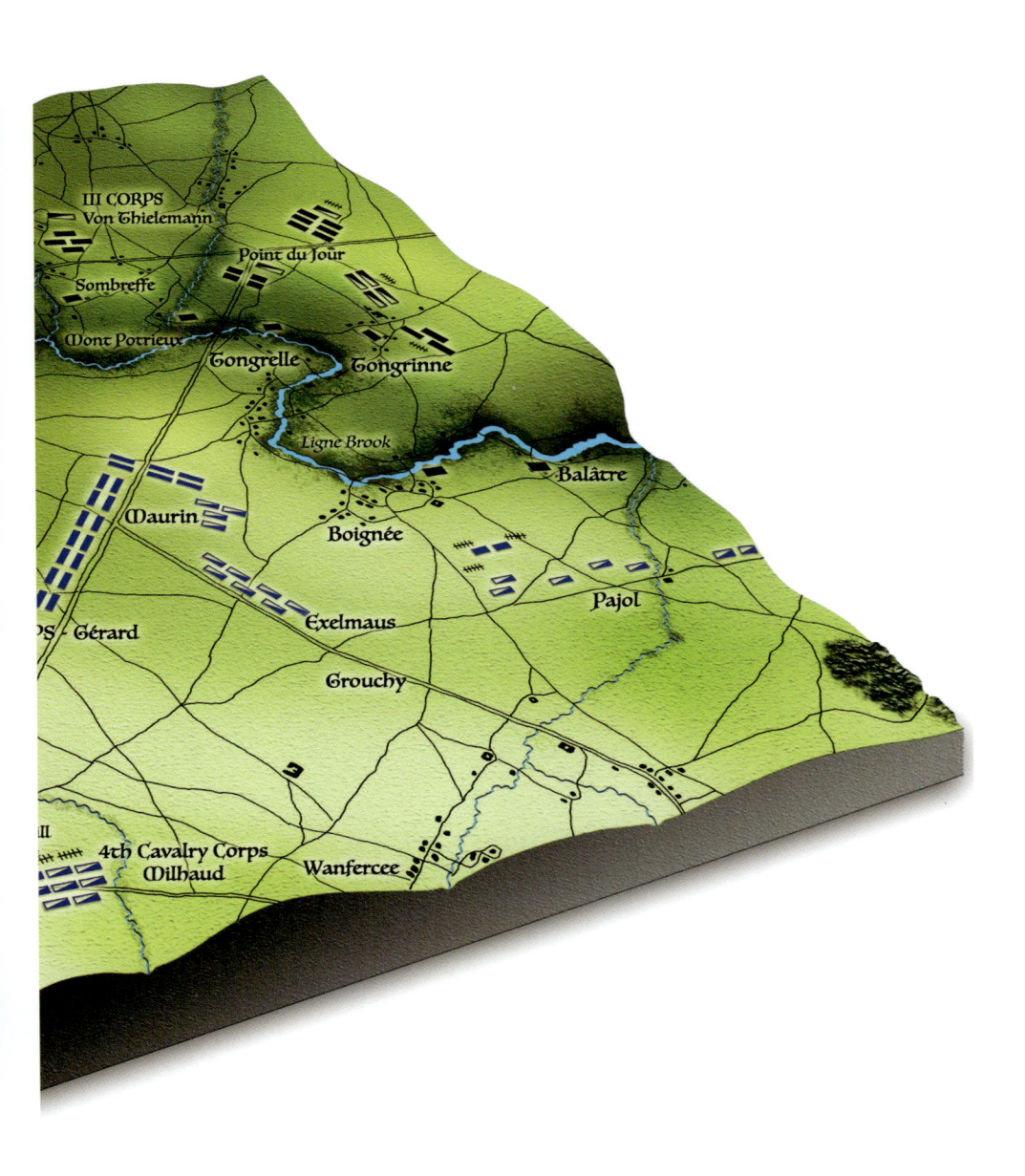

The Battle of Ligny - 16th June 1815
Initial Deployment

The Battle of Ligny
16th June 1815

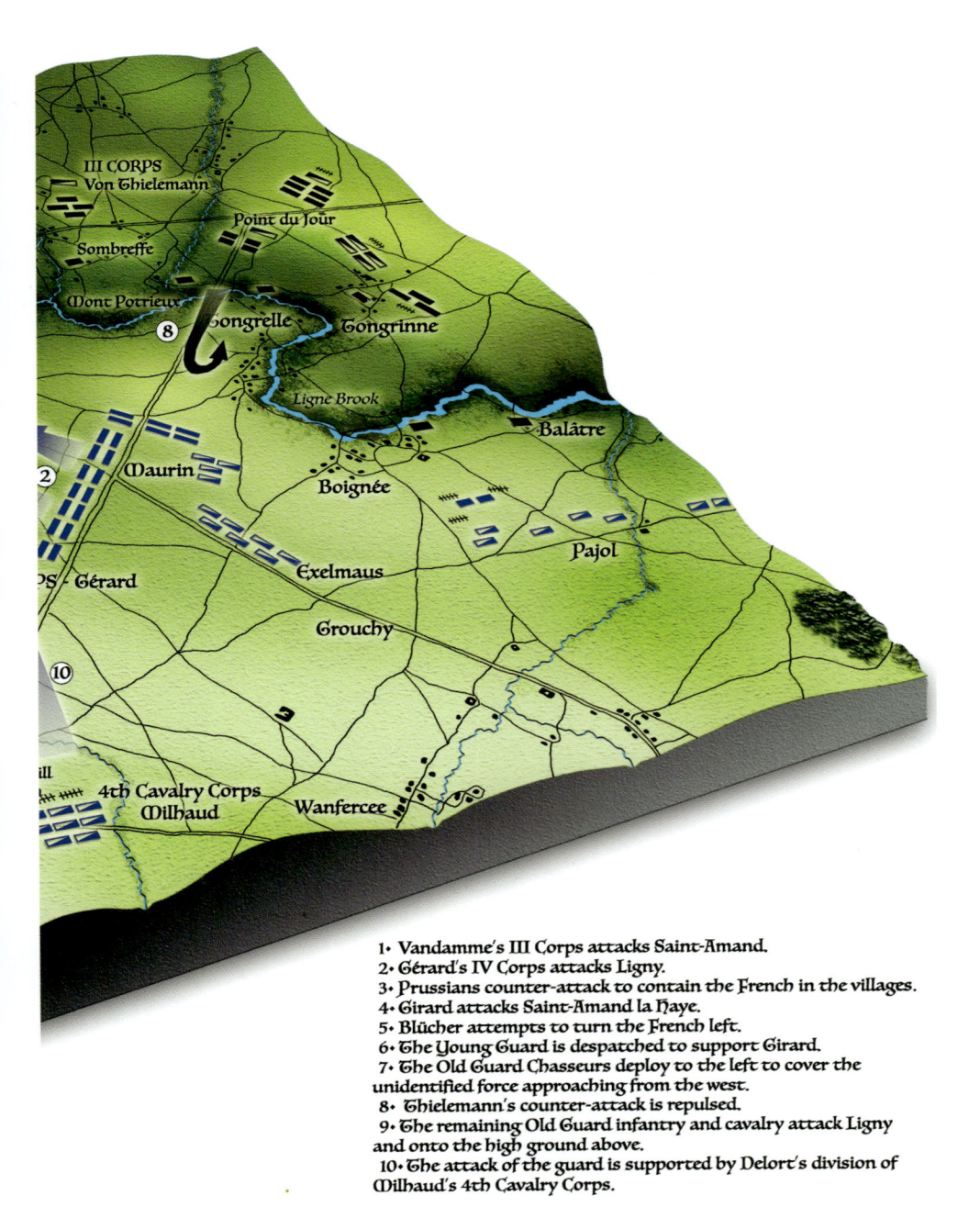

1. Vandamme's III Corps attacks Saint-Amand.
2. Gérard's IV Corps attacks Ligny.
3. Prussians counter-attack to contain the French in the villages.
4. Girard attacks Saint-Amand la Haye.
5. Blücher attempts to turn the French left.
6. The Young Guard is despatched to support Girard.
7. The Old Guard Chasseurs deploy to the left to cover the unidentified force approaching from the west.
8. Thielemann's counter-attack is repulsed.
9. The remaining Old Guard infantry and cavalry attack Ligny and onto the high ground above.
10. The attack of the guard is supported by Delort's division of Milhaud's 4th Cavalry Corps.

The Battle of Wavre
18th and 19th June 1815

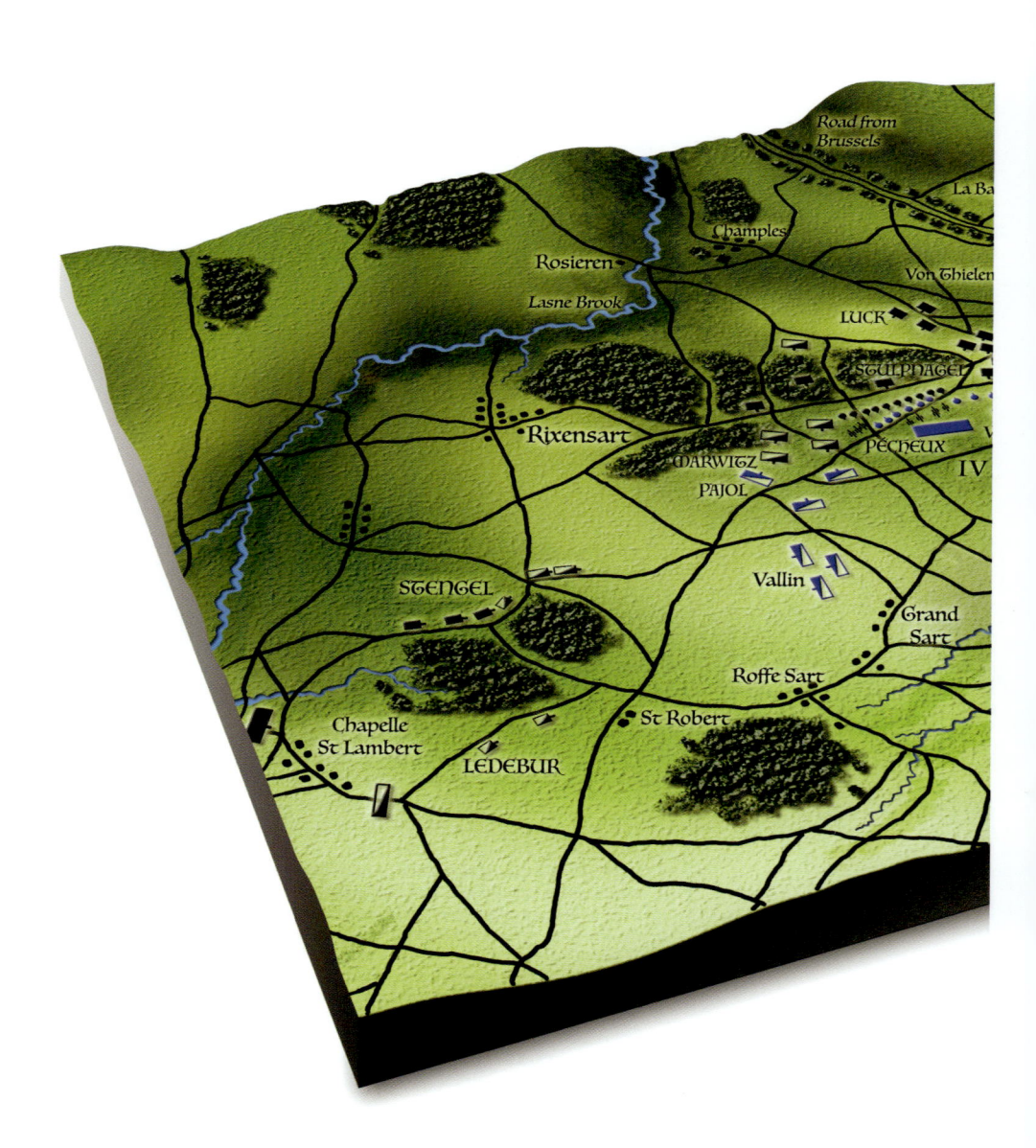

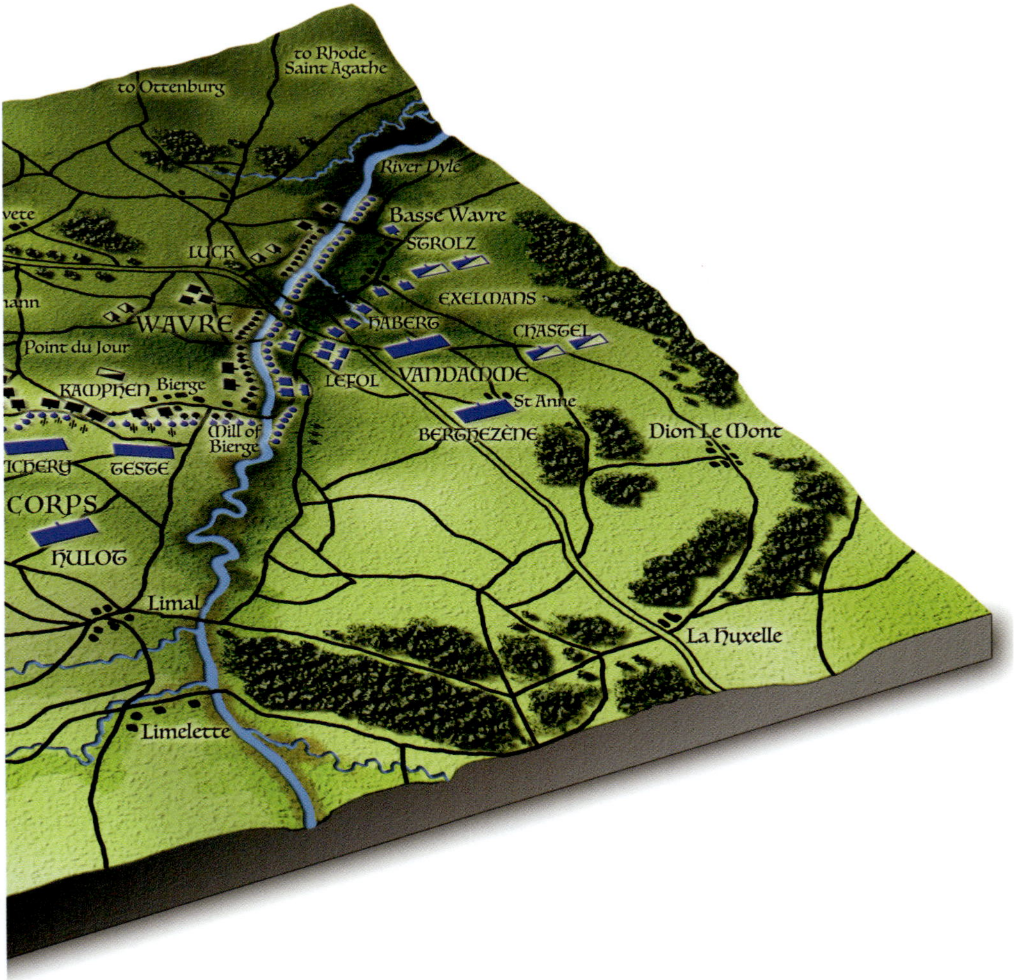

to Rhode - Saint Agathe
to Ottenburg
River Dyle
Basse Wavre
STROLZ
LUCK
EXELMANS
WAVRE
HABERT
CHASTEL
Point du Jour
LEFOL
VANDAMME
KAMPHEN
Bierge
St Anne
Mill of Bierge
BERTHEZÈNE
Dion Le Mont
TESTE
CORPS
HULOT
Limal
La Huxelle
Limelette

The Battle of Wavre
19th June 1815

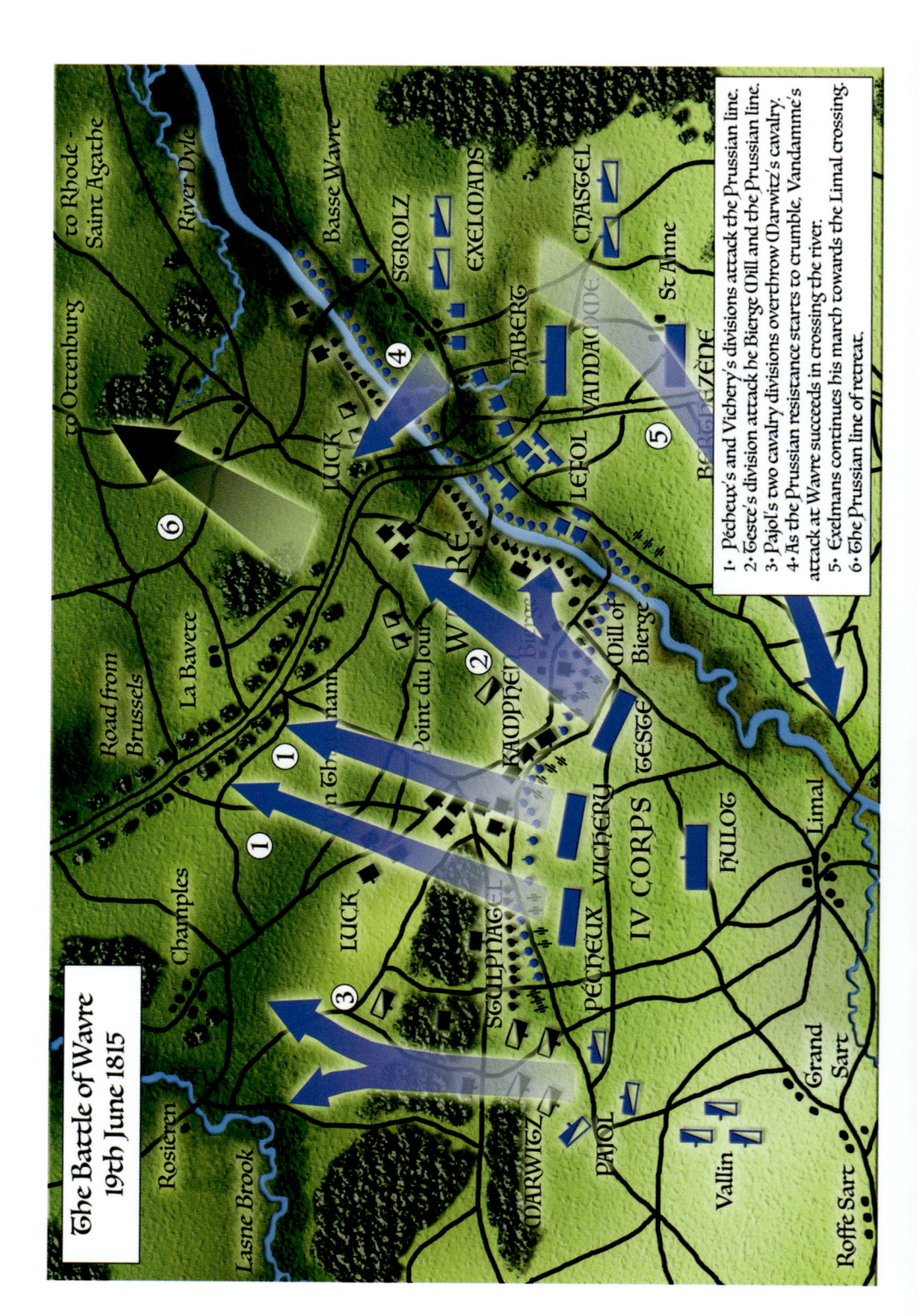

1 - Pêcheux's and Vichery's divisions attack the Prussian line.
2 - Gesete's division attack the Bierge Mill and the Prussian line.
3 - Pajol's two cavalry divisions overthrow Darwitz's cavalry.
4 - As the Prussian resistance starts to crumble, Vandamme's attack at Wavre succeeds in crossing the river.
5 - Exelmans continues his march towards the Limal crossing.
6 - The Prussian line of retreat.

Here [Ligny], the fighting was man to man and ceaseless; it was musket fire at point-blank range, caseshot at fifty paces; not musketry at two or three hundred *toises* and artillery fire at 600 *toises* as is generally the case in modern battles where superior manoeuvre is certain to beat the adversary . . . this fighting was without quarter.[13]

And Bourgeois:

The combat was kept up on both sides with equal obstinacy. It was impossible to form an idea of the fury which animated the soldiers of both sides against each other; it seemed as if each of them had a personal injury to avenge, and had found in his adversary his most implacable enemy. The French would give no quarter; the Prussians they said, had vowed to massacre all the French that should fall into their hands. These menaces were particularly addressed to the Guard against whom they appeared to have an uncommon spite. In fact, on both sides the carnage was awful in the extreme.[14]

Girard's Attack on Saint-Amand-La Haye

Fifteen minutes after Lefol's division moved forward, Girard's division to its left was ordered to attack the small neighbouring hamlet of Saint-Amand-la-Haye. *Chirurgien-major* d'Heralde of the 12th *léger* left an account of the attack.

A quarter of an hour later, we received the order to attack. Never had our soldiers displayed greater enthusiasm. But before we advanced, General Girard sent his *aide de camp* Koffe to the emperor to ask him if he could manoeuvre or enter the wood where the enemy had from 25 to 30,000 men. The emperor responded that he should attack straight ahead and to employ every effort to take the position from the enemy. General Girard, close to whom I was when his *aide de camp* delivered this order, made him repeat it, then said to us with a sign of anger, 'Then my division will be destroyed!'

He called his orderly to help him take off his blue coat that he wore over his embroidered jacket, mounted his horse and appeared at the head of his division in the dress of a full lieutenant general.

He ordered his artillery to move ahead and deployed his masses which he put in two lines. In this attack our soldiers shouted '*Vive l'empereur!*' so loudly that I, who had just been made aware of the great dangers to which they ran, was moved to tears.

At first the enemy fell back before us. The battalion of the 11th *léger* which was in the lead advanced but, arriving at a thicket, a battery of six guns opened fire with canister which broke its formation and forced it to retreat in a little disorder. The general came to move forward our first battalion a little to the right. It was then that we opened a murderous fire on the enemy; in less than five minutes, General Piat, our brigade commander, the adjutant-major and the carabineer captain were all wounded to various degrees.[15]

Girard's division had marched across the exposed plain in closed columns by divisions, Devillier's brigade to the right, Piat's brigade to the left at a brigade's distance. Arriving within range of the Prussian artillery, the first brigade stopped to deploy into its attack formation. *Maréchal de Camp* Devilliers, as well as Colonel Tiburce Sébastiani (colonel of the 11th *léger*), put themselves at the head of the 1st Battalion of the 11th *léger*, dashed at the *pas de charge* on la-Haye and took it. However, no sooner had they occupied the hamlet than the Prussians launched their reserve battalions that stood beyond it in an immediate counter-attack. However, as fresh French forces moved into the hamlet the Prussians were met by a storm of fire and were thrown back.

Part of this Prussian counter-attack tried to turn the left of the hamlet and Devilliers rushed to his brigade to lead it against this force. As they approached, the Prussians opened fire. Encouraging his men forward, Devilliers galloped into the middle of the enemy skirmishers who began to fall back, but he was struck by a ball which broke his arm and obliged him to give up his command.

Whilst the 11th *léger* and the 82nd *de ligne* avenged their brigade commander, the second column, Piat's brigade, led by the 12th *léger*, had also advanced at the *pas de charge* with shouts of '*Vive l'empereur*!' It attacked a Prussian regiment which was coming to meet it and broke it. The Prussians, although with the advantage of advancing downhill, were not able to resist the impact of the 12th *léger* and retreated. However, in this swift attack, General Girard, who marched in the middle of the skirmishers, was struck down and a few moments later, *Maréchal de Camp* Piat, struck by a ball in the thigh, was forced to abandon the battlefield and give up his command. In a very short time, the division had lost all its general officers.

Blücher's Counter-attack
Girard's mortal wound was suffered in throwing back the first of two counter-attacks organised by Blücher. With a large proportion of the French left committed to the attacks on the hamlets of Saint-Amand, Blücher feared he was in danger of having his right flank turned. About 4pm he therefore decided that now was the time to launch a strong counter-attack in order to sweep round the village of Wagneleé and threaten the French lines of communication as he had originally planned. He concentrated a strong force for this attack; one column, consisting of the 2nd Brigade (Pirch II, II Corps), which had stood in reserve near Brye with its eight battalions, was to attack the broad side of Saint-Amand-la-Haye. Meanwhile, General von Jürgass (II Corps cavalry) with the 5th Brigade (Tippelskirch, II

Corps) and seventeen squadrons of cavalry – namely ten from his own brigade and seven from Marwitz's brigade brought over from III Corps – was to advance through and alongside the village of Wagneleé so that he could attack the left flank of Girard's division defending Saint-Amand-la-Haye. In this manner the Prussians hoped to regain possession of this village and subsequently also Saint-Amand itself.

General Pirch II made two attacks on Saint-Amand and committed 12,000 men. The first attack miscarried completely; his second, under Blücher's personal leadership, went right into the village and resulted in the capture of the churchyard and pushed most of Girard's division out.

General Jürgass also made two attacks, but these do not appear to have been well co-ordinated with those of Pirch II. In the first attack, the 25th Regiment, which was leading the advance out of Wagnelée, quickly fell into disorder and the attack was a total failure; attempts to take the château also failed. General Jürgass then renewed it with the same troops after reforming them in the rear and this time he was more successful; he pressed forward into the area around the village of Saint-Amand-le-Hameau, but the fighting became something of a stalemate. By 6pm, Blücher had drawn a large proportion of his reserves into the close fighting without achieving an appreciable advantage.

The French cavalry on this wing faced a considerable force of Prussian cavalry that supported these counter-attacks and Napoleon reinforced Domon's division with that of Subervie drawn from Pajol's corps. However, there was no cavalry action and the two forces sat and faced each other exchanging only artillery fire. Captain Aubry, of the 12th Regiment of *Chasseurs à Cheval*, part of Domon's division, wrote:

> During the height of the fighting we were in reserve behind the infantry and we were struck by several cannon shots which killed three officers, but few others. One of the last balls passed through my horse and broke my stirrup which was driven into my foot. I was lucky that it did not take off my leg. General Vino, who commanded us, was wounded at the same time and I was taken with him to his lodgings in Fleurus.[16]

Attack and Counter-attack at Saint-Amand and Ligny
Saint-Amand
Having captured Saint-Amand, French attempts to break out and advance towards the high ground beyond the Ligne were met by heavy Prussian fire. Beyond the village lay six battalions of the Prussian 1st Brigade (*Generalmajor* von Steinmetz) who, having contained Lefol within the village, then launched a counter-attack to attempt to wrest it from French control whilst they were still somewhat disorganised. Captain Gerbet of the 37th *de ligne* describes the action:

New [Prussian] battalions were detached to re-conquer the village; we fired a rain of balls and canister at them; it was necessary for us to retire back into the village. But helped by reinforcements, we immediately returned to attack the enemy who had entrenched himself in the church and cemetery; making this position the centre of the defence of the village, he made a determined resistance. There, men fought hand-to-hand, only the bayonet was used.

After a bloody mêlée, we finally retook this point of resistance, covered in bodies and the rest of the village of Saint-Amand.

But these dense masses in reserve, moved forward again and numerous assailants tried a second time to retake the position from us. The church and cemetery was now for us what it had been for them, and all their efforts were checked against these fortifications.[17]

Lefol's nephew claims that the village was 'taken and re-taken three times in the middle of scenes of terrible carnage.'[18] During the fight for Saint-Amand one of many small vignettes was played out; *Chef de Bataillon* Darru commanded a battalion of the 23rd *de ligne*:

On the 16th June 1815 at the battle of Fleurus, *Chef de Bataillon* Darru conceived the bold idea of capturing four guns which, deployed on the plateau beyond the village of Saint-Amand in a most advantageous position, blasted our troops for three hours. *Chef de Bataillon* Darru was then with thirty young soldiers to whom he proposed should march with him, but they refused to second him. 'Well!' he said to them, indignant at such a refusal, 'I will go alone, I will succeed and then you will be ashamed that you did not follow me.' So he left and advanced with determination when he encountered a *brigadier* of the 12th *Chasseurs à Cheval*. This man wore the Legion of Honour. Darru suggested he should charge with him; the *brigadier* accepted and a *sous-lieutenant* of the 15th *léger* joined them and these three brave men moved forward together towards the flank of these guns so that they would avoid their fire. Arriving a hundred paces from the battery, the commandant shouted, 'Come on my friends, glory calls us!' They launched themselves forward so quickly, that in less than a minute they had covered the distance which separated them from the enemy. Two gunners had bitten the dust before they had time to react and the others, frightened by the appearance of the French, fled, abandoning one of their guns on the plateau, attached to six horses. The *sous-lieutenant* and the *brigadier* immediately led it to the main headquarters and commander Darru, satisfied in having succeeded in his enterprise, returned to his regiment. If the thirty soldiers had followed the attack of this warrior, there is no doubt that the whole battery would have fallen into their hands.[19]

Lefol's division had been completely committed and was in danger of being overrun by the Prussian counter-attacks and the bitter fighting amongst the houses and orchards. To maintain their increasingly tenuous hold on the village, Vandamme ordered Berthezène's division forward to secure it. In his report on the action, Berthezène gives us a glimpse of how a division was deployed on such a task:

> The General-in-Chief himself gave the order to chase off some skirmishers that were in front of this village and to attack the village immediately after. The first was achieved without much difficulty and the village was attacked at 2.30pm. The 12th [*de ligne*] was chosen for this mission and was supported by the 86th; the 56th turned the village to stop the efforts of the enemy on this point and the 33rd remained in reserve.
> The attack on the village was energetic and succeeded perfectly. An artillery piece of large calibre harnessed to six fine horses was captured; Sergeant Brossière of the 12th *de ligne* and one of my orderly officers contributed most; it was taken back to Fleurus.
> The enemy having attacked and routed some units of foreign troops[20] of the division which threw themselves in disorder onto the 11th Division, and had put . . . [illegible], without the *sang froid* and firmness of the colonel of the 86th (Pelecier); we lost ground, but returned to the charge and soon regained it. Towards 6pm the enemy made a great effort against St-Amand and to the left of this village; they captured part of it but were never able to take it all or exit from any point. Little by little we retook what had been lost and we left for the second time into the open ground.[21]

Captain Putigny of the 33rd *de ligne* of Lagarde's brigade in Berthezène's division took part in this attack and describes it for us:

> The advanced posts, the advanced bastions are swept away. Our bayonets throw the Prussians back onto the far bank [of the Ligne]; we do not hesitate to join them on the other side of Saint-Amand.
> I emerge from the river bank at the head of my company. An artillery salvo hurls its song of death and makes me flatten against the ground. I try to leap up; my shoulder burns, I fall heavily; my arm is bleeding, only a bit, but it will not move. I cannot hold it up. My right hand drops my sabre at my feet; I pick it up and refuse my lieutenant who presses me to go and get it bandaged. One must be mad not to take such a journey! Profiting from a pause, I get the useless arm put in a sling. The village is taken, lost, retaken. The regiment has made a serious slaughter.[22]

The attritional aspect of this fighting is clear. General Berthezène again:

To profit from this partial success, Marshal Blücher sent some of his reserves on Saint-Amand and succeeded in chasing us out. His attacks, lively and repeated, failed, but the fighting was bloody and the moment critical. Each farm became a private battlefield where the enemy lost the elite of his troops.[23]

Finally, with Berthezène's division re-deployed to support Girard's battered division, Vandamme's final reserve, Habert's division, was drawn into Saint-Amand. Colonel Fantin des Odoards commanded the 22nd *de ligne* of this division and he recorded that:

I had cause to be satisfied with the conduct of my new regiment on this brilliant day. After having driven the Prussians out of Saint-Amand, against which they continually launched new attacks, the brigade which it formed with the 70th *de ligne* having had to deploy beyond this village in order to cover it, enemy cavalry came to attack it and we were deployed to receive it in squares by regiment *en échiquier*. The 70th were to my left and the Prussians directed themselves against them first with much determination. However, I did not think they would push the charge home; but, without waiting for them, this unhappy regiment, intimidated, fled and was immediately struck and sabred. If this terrible panic had spread to my 22nd, the brigade would have been lost. But it held firmly, vigorously repelled the charge that quickly fell on it, covering the plain with men and horses struck down by a well-aimed fire and the situation was saved. The fugitives of the 70th were rallied behind my square and they soon retook their place to my left in the same order as before. More encouraged by the lack of solidity of the 70th than put off by my bearing and fire, other bodies of Prussian cavalry tried to launch new charges against us. But this time, the 70th, animated by the voice of their excellent colonel, M. Maury, did their duty and the attackers were always repulsed and badly mauled.[24]

Ligny
The fighting in Ligny seems to have been even more savage than in Saint-Amand, though no doubt Vandamme's troops would have challenged this. Here the balance of success swung one way and then the other. Blücher committed ever more troops into this village as it guarded the very centre of his line. Failure here would see his army split in two.

As Gérard renewed the attack, with Pêcheux's division supported by Vichery's 1st Brigade (Le Capitaine), the Prussian 4th Brigade gradually became too weak to resist and the 3rd Brigade (*Generalmajor* von Jagöw), after leaving two battalions to protect the artillery batteries on the slopes, moved four battalions into the village for support. Von Jagöw wanted to advance with them out of the village to attack the French line, but the fire of their batteries made it impossible to break out. This led to disorder among the troops in the village itself, and another French attack wrestled half the village once more from the Prussians. The fighting around the château to the west of the village was particularly fierce. The château caught fire before the Prussians were forced to give up the defence.

So as not to lose the other half, the remaining four battalions of the 6th Brigade (*Generalmajor* von Krafft) were ordered into Ligny (one battalion had already been used up in Ligny and four others had been employed by General Pirch II in the attack on Saint-Amand). These were later followed by five battalions of the 8th Brigade (*Generalmajor* von Bose), which had previously moved from the area around Sombreffe to the mill of Bussy. Of the remaining four battalions of this brigade, one stayed at the mill and the other three were those that Blücher led into Saint-Amand. Ligny was slowly but surely swallowing up all of Blücher's reserves.

The Prussian artillery also seemed to be suffering. Although Gérard's corps had only twenty-four guns available that covered the village, these were eventually reinforced by batteries from the Imperial Guard and possibly also from Milhaud's cavalry reserve. Prussian infantry moving down the slopes into Ligny had to march through a storm of artillery fire; it appears that the French even dragged some guns into the village itself. Bourgeois commented on the effectiveness of the French artillery fire:

> The cannonade never eased for an instant and our artillery, as far as I could judge, made a most dreadful havoc in the Prussian columns, which, posted in masses on the opposite ridge of hills and upon plateaux were in clear view; all the shots from our numerous batteries struck their target. Our own troops were all hidden in the folds of the ground, and were little exposed to the fire of the Prussian artillery, which however, replied with much perseverance if little effect.[25]

The contest in Ligny now continued in a very confined space and with the most bloody exertions; Gérard was compelled to commit Vichery's second brigade (that of Desprez). Gérard now had no reserves left; but the whole of the brigades of Henckel, Jagow and Krafft had all been fed into the battle. The mass of Prussian infantry employed there amounted to almost twenty battalions, thus about 14,000 men; considerably more than Vichery and Pêcheux were able to muster. Napoleon was determined save his precious imperial Guard for the decisive blow.

The Prussians had temporarily re-occupied the whole of the village, but a French response was not long in coming. Rumigny, Gérard's *aide de camp*, takes up the story:

The 30th and General Rome's brigade were not able to resist such an effort; for the time being the village remained the prize of the Prussians. Their skirmishers appeared at the hedges on the edge of the village from which their musketry was very heavy.

At this moment, General Gérard called me; he ordered me to take two battalions and chase the Prussians from the village.

I took two battalions of the 76th and put myself at their head. We crossed the hedges without firing a shot and the grenadiers reached the cemetery without having fired. There, a Prussian battalion, stuck in a defile, was almost wiped out by our bayonets. Then, placing the second battalion to guard what we had captured in the village, I led the head of the column to the right, and after having followed a wall and passing before an inn, I directed the 76th to the hedges forming the edge of Ligny. This movement put us on the Prussian left flank . . .

I advanced the two battalions. A Prussian *chasseur*, hidden in the last hedge, aimed at us and when I said to the battalion commander, 'Commandant, it's you or me!' My horse collapsed with a ball in the head; I continued on foot at the head of the troops.

It is necessary to have experienced the happy sensation that one feels when, in a battle that is disputed with determination, one seizes the weak point of the enemy and one senses that victory is in your hands, to understand the joy with which we realised, in leaving the hedges, the Prussians opened a fire of hell against the village, but turned their backs on us. They did not understand they were completely turned and only realised when we were three hundred paces from the houses. Our balls, which took them from the rear, caused a complete rout which spread to the centre of the village. Unfortunately, we did not have a single squadron with us; we were only able to grab a few prisoners who surrendered without resistance. They came from the East Prussia Regiment.[26]

Captain Coignet, a very experienced soldier attached to Imperial Headquarters, wrote, 'This was not a battle, it was a butchery. Drums beat the charge on all sides. There was but one shout, "Forward!"'[27] Gérard's men had consolidated their hold on the southern bank of the Ligne brook; the château, the farm of d'En Bas and the church and cemetery were in French hands and a number of Prussian counter-attacks had been beaten off. The brigades of Langen (8th) and Stülpnagel (12th) were spent.

Captain Francois was also involved in the attack and counter-attack into Ligny and although we should take some of his claims with a pinch of salt, his account well illustrates the ebb and flow of the fighting for the village:

Captain Christophe and I rallied the remains of the regiment, and, I can say to my glory, the soldiers were glad to see me again amongst them and asked me to lead them into the fight once more. In spite of the check we had received, we had taken about 500 prisoners. Just as we were trying to get the regiment together, General Rome [their brigade commander] arrived, and ordered us to re-enter the village of Ligny. The soldiers, not at all disturbed by their [previous] failure, nor alarmed at the loss of nearly two thirds of their comrades, cried '*Vive l'empereur!*' and marched forward. Captain Christophe sounded the charge; the battalion entered the village and was repulsed. He rallied the men and tried three times with the like result. Then General Rome ordered Captain Christophe and me to assemble the men behind the batteries of the division, which had not ceased firing; about 200 men assembled. General Rome, seeing their courage, ordered me to take 100 men (they all wanted to follow me) and make a fresh attempt. These 100 soldiers, glad to see me at their head, cried, 'Long live the emperor and Captain Francois!' I was proud of their confidence and General Rome said some very generous things to me on the subject. We arrived at the hollow road that led to the village. The enemy's fire had greatly diminished. I ordered silence. Just as we were about to enter the village, we met a company of Prussians commanded by an officer; we were both surprised at finding ourselves so close to each other. I hit General Rome's horse on the nose with my sword, for he was right in front of my men, and the General squeezed as close to the bank as he could. I stooped down and gave the command, 'Ready, present, fire!' The Prussians did the same and although I was in front I was not hit. But there were dead and wounded on both sides. I was hit by a bullet, but it was stopped by my cloak, which was in a tight roll over one shoulder and across my body. I found the bullet afterwards in my cloak. All it had done was to give me a bruise on the left breast; but that made me spit blood for several days. I ordered my men to charge with the bayonet; the enemy defended himself and for some minutes the carnage was terrible. In parrying the thrusts that were made at me, my sword broke. At last I was knocked down and trampled underfoot by my own men and the enemy. At that moment, General Rome ordered the 96th Regiment [the other regiment in the brigade] to advance. The enemy fled. I was picked up, along with several of my wounded soldiers who had not abandoned me.

I was badly bruised in many places by being trampled underfoot, but I re-joined the regiment which was posted behind our batteries. I had seven men killed and eleven wounded, but most of them slightly. I was only stunned and was able to get back to the regiment, upon which the enemy was still firing.[28]

By evening, the deadlock in Saint-Amand had not been broken, Lieutenant Lefol wrote:

The fight continued without advantage to either side until evening. However, the Prussians were unable to retake either the church or the cemetery, which our division had captured with such *élan* at the beginning of the battle.[29]

Gérard's two divisions that fought in Ligny lost one general (Le Capitaine), a major, two *chefs de bataillon* and twenty three-other officers killed, Colonels Laurède of the 63rd and Laurain of the 59th, *Commandant* Gémeau of the 6th *léger*, another *chef de bataillon* and seventy-four officers wounded (Laurède died of his wounds on the 27th, whilst Laurain was to be wounded again at Wavre two days later).

Twenty-one Prussian battalions had been committed to the brutal fighting in Ligny[30] against the nineteen committed by Gérard. Although these numbers are roughly even, Prussian battalions were generally much stronger than French battalions and the fact that the Prussians were defending a very strong position says much for the courage and resilience of the French soldiers.

Girard
Chirurgien-major d'Heralde was one of the first to reach the prostrate Girard.

> The unfortunate General Girard, who had already suffered two heavy bruises, received a third shot which was essentially mortal and knocked him to the ground, where he lay motionless. The ball had fractured the right arm, passed under the shoulder and stuck in the vertebrae.
>
> The fall of the general and several others inevitably led to some disorder. The young Colonel Sebastiani took command of the brigade which, attacked by overwhelming numbers was forced to retire for a moment and to abandon some wounded of which several were killed by the Prussians.
>
> Running to give some aid to the general, I saw the severity of his wound. As the enemy were pushing hard, the general said, 'Kill me, but do not abandon me alive!'[31]

Girard, one of Napoleon's most promising divisional commanders was to die in Paris on 27 June, having been awarded the title of *Duc de Ligny* by Napoleon. Mauduit described the continued fighting on this flank:

> This first shock had cost us dear; the three generals, a great number of officers of all ranks and seven to eight hundred NCOs and soldiers had been killed or wounded, resulting in a moment of hesitation, soon followed by a disordered retreat, provoked by a panic in the 4th *de ligne* for which we have searched in vain for the true cause.
>
> In the middle of these annoying circumstances, Colonel Mouttet of the

12th *léger* was, in his turn, knocked from his horse by a projectile that struck him and although he had only a shock, this colonel was too shaken to return to the head of his soldiers and handed the honour to *Commandant* de Chaunac, who was now the senior of the three battalion commanders, *Chef de Bataillon* Berlier having become *hors de combat*.

Seconded by the energetic conduct of *Chef de Bataillon* Vissec de Latude and of the officers of this brave regiment, *Commandant* de Chaunac, an officer of high distinction and great courage, managed to re-establish order and retook the offensive. He re-conquered the ground that had been lost and was able to hold it this time until the moment [7.30pm] when the division of the Young Guard of General Barrois came to support him against the determined efforts of the Prussian brigades.

Helped by this reinforcement, Girard's division, although deprived of its generals, successfully repulsed the enemy's efforts and finally remained masters of a battlefield bought at the price of 2,000 of its bravest soldiers, and the next day it was able to see the ravages that it had inflicted on the ranks of the Prussian army. During this relentless struggle, Colonel Tiburce Sébastiani was noticeable at the head of his brave regiment, by his courage, his *sang froid* and his presence. Always in the middle of the mêlée, he had his horse killed and his clothing riddled with balls and was able to take, for part of the battle, the command of the division following the loss of the three generals.[32]

With all three general officers of the division now casualties, Colonel Matis of the 82nd *de ligne* took command of the division. Mauduit describes how the rout of the division started in the 4th *de ligne*. The history of this regiment seems to accept responsibility for this rout, although unaware of the cause:

By an inexplicable event, the 4th, seized by a sudden panic, retreated and dragged along the rest of the division. The Prussians re-entered la Haye. Rallied by Colonel Sebastiani of the 11th *léger*, the division returned to the charge, and, reinforced by the Young Guard, we then maintained ourselves in the position for the rest of the battle.[33]

It seems that the rout coincided with a strong Prussian counter-attack, the mortal wounding of Colonel Dubalen of the 64th *de ligne* (who died on the 20th) and the appearance of an unexpected column in their rear. Girard's division was rallied by officers sent by Napoleon himself:

Saint-Amand and Ligny above all were disputed with an incredible stubbornness. General Girard was mortally wounded and his division was instantly repulsed in the greatest disorder. Napoleon directed Labédoyère and I to rally and concentrate the brigades. General Labédoyère said passionately, 'Soldiers! Are you not ashamed to retreat before the same men that you have defeated so often, who have thrown down their arms at your feet and asked for clemency at Austerlitz, Jena, Friedland? Advance and you will see them flee again and once more be seen as their conquerors.' The noble voice of this brave young man was heard and the soldiers rallied, managed to get themselves into the cemetery of Saint-Amand and maintained themselves there despite the repeated efforts of the Prussians to chase them out.[34]

D'Heralde claims that officers within the division also took a hand in rallying the disordered regiments:

Finally, the efforts of Colonel Sebastiani and the brave *Commandant* de Chonac, who had taken command of the 12th *léger*, rallied the division which, supported by a movement in the centre, advanced briskly and made the enemy pay dearly for the damage they had caused.[35]

In his post-action report, General Berthezène claimed that after his deployment into Saint-Amand, the problems that Girard's division were experiencing in Saint-Amand-la-Haye led to much of his division being re-deployed there: '. . . A second very lively attack on Girard's division required the greater part of the 11th to go to its support, although we did not abandon the village at any point.'[36]

The whole of Vandamme's corps and Girard's division were now committed, but the Prussian pressure on the villages did not decrease. Blücher still hoped to win back the villages and advance to cut Napoleon's communications back to Charleroi. In order to ensure Vandamme and Girard held the line, Napoleon was forced to commit the Young Guard division to this flank.

Napoleon
Once Napoleon had committed himself to battle, he next sent the order to draw Lobau's VI Corps closer to the battlefield in case of need. He had Soult write as follows:

In front of Fleurus, 16th June at 3.30pm.
To M. *le comte* Lobau. Carried by M. Poireau
M. *le comte*, the Emperor orders that you are to order your corps to march to take position mid-way between Charleroi and Fleurus and that you are to guard Charleroi, where you are to provisionally nominate a commandant. I have ordered that all the prisoners, as well as all the enemy and French wounded, are to be sent to Avesnes. I request you to execute this order.[37]

Napoleon's moves during the battle are reasonably well documented. His personal servant, Mameluke Ali, wrote in his own memoirs:

> During the whole afternoon, the emperor remained close to a mill situated on a mound from where he could see the whole of the enemy's right.
>
> Just forward of the emperor at the mill, a short distance away, there was group of young officers of the headquarters, amongst which there were some orderly officers. This group laughed out loud, joking noisily at the different scenes taking place just a short distance in front between Prussians and Frenchmen. The emperor, who heard the noise these officers were making, shot them looks from time to time that displayed his irritation and boredom with their behaviour. Finally, impatient and bothered by their gaiety he said, looking severely at the one who laughed and chattered the most, 'Monsieur! You should not laugh and joke when brave men are cutting each other's throats under your eyes!'[38]

Sergeant Mauduit of the Guard, which remained close to the Naveau windmill, was also in a position to observe Napoleon and some of the events that took place around him:

> After his inspection of the battlefield, having closely examined the Prussian position and having covered the whole line of our advance posts, the emperor came to a position about 150 paces from our battalion. It was here that his headquarters spent almost the whole battle and until the moment when it became our turn to take a part in this relentless struggle which had no other decisive results than to heap up thousands of bodies from both sides.
>
> We soon noticed a group of about fifty men on horses coming towards us. They came from the direction of Saint-Amand. We went to intercept them. It was a trophy that was being brought to be presented to the emperor by a young *maréchal de logis* of the *chasseurs-à-cheval*. This trophy was an artillery piece which this intrepid young man had captured after having sabred the crew. He even used the Prussian train drivers to bring it and to pay tribute to his sovereign. He also made some of the crew march before him as prisoners.
>
> Nothing can take away the noble expression, proud and satisfied of this twenty year old hero as he presented himself to Napoleon and his brilliant entourage . . . The emperor approached an officer, asked for his cross and himself fixed it on this *maréchal de logis*, adding these words which will never be forgotten; 'Here, *mon brave*, is your reward! Return to your regiment, you are now a *sous-lieutenant*.' We do not know what became of him and we regret we did not note his name. Perhaps he died on this day,

throwing himself in a frenzy of heroism and happiness, into the middle of some Prussian battery or column, for such is nearly always the result of these intoxicating rewards given by the emperor during the fight![39]

Although differing in minor details, this story appears to support the account of *Chef de Bataillon* Darru's capture of a Prussian gun and limber.

Movements of the Guard
Napoleon had always attempted to keep his Guard intact throughout an action in order to have it available as a final reserve to either deliver the final and decisive blow, or to cover a disaster. However, as his reign continued, he became more prepared to commit them to the fight earlier in a battle. He was also prepared to allocate them to different parts of the battlefield if there was a need, using them almost as a fire brigade, deploying them in cases of emergency, to stabilise an area of the battle whilst always ensuring his troops with the most battlefield impact, the senior regiments of infantry and cavalry of the Old Guard and the cuirassiers of the cavalry reserve, remained uncommitted.

So it was at Ligny. Napoleon was quite prepared to exhaust his line troops in the fierce battles for the villages along the Ligne in order to draw in the Prussian reserves, but he was also ready to send his junior Guard regiments to critical areas of the battlefield. This may be to take a decisive part in the fighting, or to provide moral support and an ultimate reserve where the fighting was fiercest. The moral impact on both friendly and enemy troops at the appearance of the famous bearskins of the Old Guard must not be underestimated.

The first Guard troops to be deployed were Duhesme's division of the Young Guard. As the troops of Vandamme and Girard were used up in the fierce battles for the hamlets of Saint-Amand, there was a danger that the frequent Prussian counter-attacks might overwhelm them. As we have seen, after the fall of their commander, several French regiments of Girard's division were beginning to waver, and a Prussian success here could not be tolerated, even if they were stripping out their own reserves from the centre in a way Napoleon no doubt welcomed.

The *voltigeurs* and *tirailleurs* of the Young Guard were the first Guard troops that would be committed to the fight. Their deployment into Saint-Amand-la-Haye, turned the fight here back into the favour of the French. Shortly after their deployment, Napoleon also sent the junior *chasseur* regiments of the Old Guard, to prop up this wing and to reassure them after the near panic caused by d'Erlon's appearance on their rear. General Petit, who commanded the *chasseurs* of the Guard later wrote:

During the battle, several units were successively engaged; the last three regiments of *chasseurs* (4th, 3rd and 2nd) marched in the direction of Saint-

Amand in reserve to the corps of the line who were engaged there and even obliged to make a retrograde move. They supported them to advantage.[40]

The Old Guard *chasseur* regiments that were sent to the left flank were not engaged in any fighting, as Adjutant Prax of the 3rd *Chasseurs* informs us:

> This regiment suffered no loss on the 16th; not having been engaged . . . The 3rd Regiment of *Chasseurs* were not then with the rest of the Guard. It had been detached to go in observation to the extreme left of our line, the side from which it was said that the enemy was coming; it was the corps of Drouet d'Erlon.[41]

Mauduit also mentions these deployments and the impact that they had.

> It was then about four o'clock when the division of *chasseurs* of the Old Guard left its position in front of us to march in the direction of Saint-Amand with the order to be the reserve to the III Corps and the Young Guard, which was so strongly engaged there would not be able to retake this village, let alone hold it, without the formidable support of this division. Its presence alone sufficed for them to rediscover their initial confidence, such was the prestige attached to the Old Guard!
> . . .
> It was there [Saint-Amand] that General Chartrand, commanding a brigade of the Young Guard, particularly distinguished himself: The Prussians came to retake the advantage over General Vandamme's troops, at the moment when, arriving with this brigade, General Chartrand was advancing to reconnoitre the position, he stopped several companies of the line which were retiring, put himself at their head and soon appeared on the heights occupied by the enemy. But these opposed them with fresh forces and these brave soldiers were forced to give ground.
> At this moment the Young Guard entered the line and fought man-to-man with the Prussians under the protection of the division of *chasseurs*.[42]

Mauduit also tells the story of a most interesting and unusual action involving the mounted gunners of a Guard horse artillery battery that was sent with the Young Guard and *chasseurs*:

> The gunners of this battery, having noticed an isolated 12 pounder battery, fell on it to capture it, but the Prussian artillerymen defended themselves with their tools and the assailants found they were not strong enough to take them away when reinforcements came to free them, even though they were already prisoners of our artillerymen. It had been a brilliant feat of arms to

be included in the annals of the Imperial Guard horse artillery that were already so brilliant!⁴³

Nor were these the only deployments of the Guard. Mauduit also tells us of two grenadier regiments that were deployed to support Gérard's hard-pressed divisions at Ligny:

> Also at about 4pm, the 4th and 3rd Regiments of Grenadiers left us to go and become the reserve behind IV Corps; they took with them eight guns that were attached to our division. This battery passed Ligny with these two regiments and caused heavy casualties to the enemy at the exits of the village. The 3rd and 4th Regiments of Grenadiers were sent to Ligny to replace the 2nd Battalion of the 50th Line of Hulot's division that had been sent towards our extreme right where it contributed powerfully in preventing Prussian III Corps from outflanking our right which Marshal Grouchy was not able to do with his cavalry alone.⁴⁴

Orders to Ney⁴⁵

Unfortunately for the emperor, Ney received the 3.15pm despatch demanding he march on the Prussian rear just as he was facing a deteriorating situation at Quatre Bras. As if this was not bad enough, and before Ney had the time to decide how he should act in the light of this order, General Delcambre, d'Erlon's chief-of-staff, rode up and informed him that the emperor had ordered I Corps to march towards the Ligny battlefield and that the movement had already begun.

A little after four o'clock, d'Erlon had been joined by Colonel Forbin-Janson, a staff officer from Imperial Headquarters. He carried an order from Napoleon to Marshal Ney ordering him to send d'Erlon's corps to the east and attack Ligny from the heights of Saint-Amand. The order was written in pencil and was almost illegible. Unfortunately, Forbin-Janson was unable to offer either clarification or elaboration; he had been promoted straight to colonel after the campaign in France the previous year in recognition of his exploits in commanding a band of partisans against the invading allies, but was inexperienced in conventional military manoeuvres. What was more, whilst it was to his credit he had taken a more direct route than Colonel Laurent, the carrier of Soult's 3.15pm order to Ney, and had thus arrived earlier, inevitably much of the context and imperative of Soult's order was lost. Forbin-Janson also informed d'Erlon that in passing his troops on the road he had already, in the name of the emperor, directed them off towards Ligny in line with the emperor's intent.

As has been noted, the order for d'Erlon to march towards Ligny was addressed to Ney, but exhibiting the same lack of experience as his failure to understand Napoleon's overall design, having informed d'Erlon of Napoleon's order, he forgot to continue his mission to deliver it to Marshal Ney! Thus Ney was not only unaware of the order, but also that d'Erlon's troops were already marching east. Forbin-Janson hastily returned to Imperial Headquarters where this error was identified and he was sent back to complete his task with no possible hope of being in time to influence events. D'Erlon had immediately departed to join his troops, but wisely took the precaution of despatching his chief-of-staff, General Delcambre, to inform Marshal Ney of what was happening.

About 5.15pm, Colonel Laurent finally arrived with Soult's despatch. Colonel Heymès, Ney's acting chief of staff, wrote:

> It was at this time that Colonel Laurent, sent from Imperial Headquarters, came to inform the marshal that I Corps, by the emperor's order, which had already been given to General d'Erlon, had left the Brussels road instead of following it, and was moving in the direction of Saint Amand. General d'Elcambre [Delcambre], the chief-of-staff of this corps, arrived soon after to announce the action it was taking.
>
> The enemy now had 50,000 men at Quatre Bras. He was pushing us back; and the marshal, a great captain, now judged success impossible.[46]

By the time this despatch arrived, I Corps had been marching towards Ligny for over an hour. For Ney, whilst the urgency of Napoleon's order was clear, Soult had failed to inform him that the emperor was engaged with the main body of the Prussian army, a significant piece of information in itself and one that should put all other activity into perspective. The message also lacked sufficient information for Ney to clearly understand that the action at Quatre Bras was very much of secondary importance should the Prussian army be destroyed. Napoleon wanted Ney to do enough to hold Wellington's army at Quatre Bras whilst releasing the maximum possible force to intervene at Ligny and contribute to a decisive victory. But Soult's order fails to make this clear. Ney, furious that his own position was being undermined, sent Delcambre back to d'Erlon, insisting that he turn his corps around and march back to Quatre Bras to join him. Colonel Petiet reports:

> Marshal Ney did not want to carry out this order and replied to Colonel Laurent, 'The emperor is in his chair, he cannot see what is happening here; the English are before me and I am going to beat them.'[47]

This response, if accurate, clearly demonstrates that Ney failed to see the bigger picture.

Unfortunately, the message carried by Forbin-Janson has been lost, so we are unable to see for ourselves exactly what direction it contained. However, General Deselles, commander of I Corps artillery, quotes the message in his own account of what happened. He later wrote:

As we slowly closed up on II Corps, a *sous-officier* of the Guard arrived with a letter from the emperor which directed,

> *Monsieur le comte* d'Erlon, the enemy has fallen headlong into the trap that I have set for him. Move immediately with your four infantry divisions, your cavalry division, all your artillery and the two divisions of heavy cavalry that I put under your command and move, as I say, with all these forces to the area of Ligny and fall on Saint-Amand. M. *le comte* d'Erlon, you will save France and cover yourself in glory.

It is well known that the generals of artillery and engineers do not leave their commander-in-chief; I can thus give precise information on these events which had such disastrous consequences for us.

In execution of the imperial order, all the nominated forces directed their march across the plain towards Ligny (or Saint-Amand).

With a weak escort we went ahead of the marching columns, when we suddenly saw General Delcambre, the chief of staff of our corps, sent by Marshal Ney to demand our support.

Count d'Erlon was unsure and hesitated; he needed advice. General of Engineers Garbé and I thought that the emperor's order was the one that was definitely more pressing, that if executed we would later be able to take the English in the flank and thus disengage the marshal. But General Delcambre insisted. The Count d'Erlon took a middle course which upset all the plans of the General-in-Chief. He sent Durutte's division, which was the lead division, Jacquinot's cavalry division and two batteries, to the heights of Ligny. With the rest, he moved to the support of Marshal Ney . . .

In a footnote to this account, Deselles added, 'Not having a map of Belgium in front of me, it is possible that I have got the names of these two villages the wrong way round. I believe it was Saint-Amand to fall on Ligny . . .'.

To make matters worse, Napoleon believed that d'Erlon would be approaching the battlefield down the main road from Quatre Bras onto the right rear of the Prussian army. In fact, because of the slow advance of Ney's wing, d'Erlon's lead division was still some way short of Quatre Bras when the order was received. His corps, therefore, took the shortest route from their present location. The implications of this we shall see in due course.

D'Erlon's dilemma can be well understood; on one side, he had the emperor's order to march to the Ligny battlefield in order to take a potentially decisive role in the destruction of the Prussian army; on the other, he had his immediate superior ordering his return to Quatre Bras where the left wing was in danger of being defeated. The dilemma should have been settled by a simple appreciation of the situation; although he was not approaching the Ligny battlefield from the direction

Napoleon expected, he had a substantial force close enough (three kilometres) to be able to make a significant contribution to the battle taking place there. On the other hand, he was twelve kilometres from Quatre Bras (about a three- to four-hour march for a complete corps) and it was now too late to make a counter-march and arrive in time to have any significant influence on the outcome of the fighting there. Furthermore, he had received a direct order from the emperor himself. The decision should not have been a hard one and yet d'Erlon took a middle course that was to influence neither battle.

General d'Erlon wrote two accounts of the sequence of events; the first was his response to an enquiry from Ney's son which appeared in *Documents inédits sur la campagne de 1815 publiés par le Duc d'Elchingen*, and the second in his own book *Le Maréchal Drouet, Comte d'Erlon. Vie militaire ecrit par luimême*. In the first of these he wrote:

> Towards 11 o'clock or midday, M. *le maréchal* Ney sent me the order for my corps to take up arms and to move on Frasnes and Quatre Bras, where I would receive further orders. Thus my corps started its move immediately. After having given the commander of the head of the column the order to take the necessary precautions, I went ahead to see what was happening at Quatre Bras, where General Reille's corps appeared to be engaged. Beyond Frasnes, I stopped with generals of the Guard [presumably of Lefebvre-Desnouëttes's light cavalry] where I was joined by General Labédoyère [one of Napoleon's ADCs], who showed me a note in crayon which he carried to Marshal Ney, which ordered this marshal to send my corps to Ligny. General Labédoyère warned me that he had already given the order for this movement, having changed the direction of march of my column, and indicated to me where I could re-join it. I immediately took this route and sent my chief-of-staff, General Delcambre, to the marshal, to warn him of my new destination. Marshal Ney sent him back to me with definitive orders to return to Quatre Bras, where he was hard pressed and counting on the co-operation of my corps. I thus decided that I was urgently required there, since the marshal took it upon himself to recall me, despite having received the note of which I spoke above.
>
> I therefore ordered the column to make a counter-march; but, despite all the effort that I put into this movement, my column only arrived at Quatre Bras as it got dark.
>
> Was General Labédoyère authorised to change the direction of my column before having seen the marshal? I do not think so; but in any case, this single circumstance was the cause of all the marches and counter-marches which paralysed my corps throughout the 16th.
>
> D. *comte* d'Erlon
Paris, 9 February 1829[48]

Between these witnesses, it will be noticed that each described a different carrier of the order. However, the direction given in these orders is consistent and we must put this discrepancy down to either a slip of memory or the possibility that more than a single order was sent by different officers and accept that this had no effect on the outcome.

Ney seems to have been so absorbed in his own battle that he was incapable of understanding that Napoleon was trying to achieve an infinitely more important strategic outcome. But the succession of orders from the emperor and Imperial Headquarters should have convinced him that there was now a greater good than the simple seizure of Quatre Bras and that his own battle was now nothing more than a sideshow.

Even later, Napoleon made one last effort to make Ney understand the importance of carrying out his orders. Colonel Baudus, Soult's ADC, explains:

> At the moment when the affair [Ligny] was closely engaged along the whole line, Napoleon called me and said, 'I have sent Count d'Erlon the order to move with his entire corps onto the rear of the Prussian army's right; you go and take a duplicate of this order to Marshal Ney which has to be communicated to him. You are to tell him that, *whatever the situation he is facing, it is absolutely necessary that this direction is executed; that I attach no great importance to what happens on his flank today; that the key is what happens where I am, because I need to finish off the Prussian army. As for him, he should, if he cannot do better, to be content with containing the English army.*' [My emphasis]
>
> When the emperor had finished giving me these instructions, the *major-général* recommended me, in the most energetic terms to insist with equal force that nothing should hinder the execution of the movement prescribed to Count d'Erlon.[49]

Unfortunately, we cannot be sure from Baudus's account exactly what time he was despatched or what time he reached Marshal Ney. If this was indeed the last message sent, it is likely that it was received too late to make any difference. This message would surely have made the situation clear to Ney and one wonders why earlier messages were not posed in similar terms.

The Appearance of d'Erlon

After three hours of close combat, the fighting for the key villages of Saint-Amand and Ligny had become a bloody stalemate. Despite the rolling commitment of reserves it appeared that neither side was any closer to victory; the French had been unable to establish themselves beyond the Ligne and develop an attack on the high ground beyond and the Prussians had equally failed to deny the French a foothold in the villages or managed to turn their left flank. Napoleon had decided that the time for the decisive blow had come; the remaining regiments of the Old Guard infantry, supported by their own artillery and the Guard artillery reserve, would smash through the very centre of the Prussian line, break it in two and then the Guard heavy cavalry of General Guyot and Milhaud's cuirassiers would exploit the breech.

Sergeant Mauduit described the move of this impressive force:

> It was 5pm and our regiment had still not moved from its position. Finally, at 5.30pm, Colonel Gourgaud, whom the emperor had detached to General Gérard to follow his attacks closely, came quickly to announce that the reserves of the IV Corps were all engaged or were going to be, without the possession of the village being finally decided.
>
> It was then that we took up our arms and formed into columns by division to move on Ligny. We marched, left ahead, having in front of us the 2nd Regiment of Grenadiers; our four battalions formed a column at half distance and the 1st Regiment of *Chasseurs* with the Guard *sapeurs* and *marins*, a second column parallel to ours and about one hundred *toises* on our left.
>
> To our right, and only a few *toises* away, the terrible reserve of artillery of the Old Guard formed a third column of eight guns frontage.
>
> Behind us came two other superb columns; that of the right was composed of the *Grenadiers à Cheval*, Guard Dragoons and *Gendarmes d'Élite*; that of the left, 1,500 cuirassiers of General Delort. Each of these two columns had a frontage of a squadron of sixty-four files.
>
> Arriving at a cannon's range from the enemy, suddenly our head of column stopped without us knowing the cause.[50]

This unexpected halt coincided with the panic which struck some of Vandamme's troops that has already been mentioned. Lieutenant Lefol reported:

> It was, as far as I can remember, towards 6 o'clock when the soldiers of one of the regiments were suddenly seized by panic, which was happily unknown in the army and which could have led to dire consequences if it had not been for the energy of General Lefol, and without the quick reactions of several officers who were able to suppress this kind of panic occasioned by the widespread false news that an enemy column came unexpectedly on the left of our division, and by the painful impression made on the 64th Line by the death of Colonel Dubalen whom it loved and respected [he was actually severely wounded and did not die until the 20th]. Several soldiers left the ranks, threw away their muskets and might have been able to upset, perhaps even disband, the whole army corps, when several officers, amongst which was General Corsin, commander of one of

the brigades of the division, ran after them, stopped the fugitives, reassembled them and brought them back to the fight, which they then supported until evening with the same fearlessness with which they had entered it.

General Lefol, judging with his experienced eye, that this panic in our soldiers could bring about very serious results, did not hesitate. He sent me to direct the artillery officer to turn his guns against the fugitives who then, seeing themselves taken between two fires, that is between our guns and the division they thought was the enemy, returned to their ranks and their enthusiasm to the fight repaired the shame they had covered themselves with an instant before.[51]

In the second paragraph, Lefol alludes to the fact that the panic was caused by the appearance of a column of what were suspected to be enemy troops in the rear of Vandamme's corps. Whilst Napoleon might have quickly deduced that it was d'Erlon's troops approaching the battlefield, albeit from an unexpected direction, Vandamme, and certainly his troops, would not naturally have come to this conclusion. The psychological impact of having enemy in your rear is great, and in the uncertainty of the moment the French troops clearly feared it was a column of Wellington's army marching in support of the Prussians. A passage in Vandamme's published correspondence explains the situation:

Vandamme himself led his troops to the charge to support General Girard's division of which half its troops were laid on the ground. With his habitual bravery, he repulsed Blücher's right at all points, when suddenly, he saw a deep column on his left. Not knowing if this column was friendly or enemy, he suspended his offensive movement and warned the emperor, who sent a reconnaissance to these troops whose bayonets could be seen on the left flank. It was one of the divisions of Drouet d'Erlon's corps which was heading for Ligny in accordance with an order carried by one of Napoleon's *aides de camp*.[52]

Despite the orders he had sent to Ney and d'Erlon to march on the rear of the Prussian army, it seems that Napoleon too was unsure of who the troops were and immediately suspended his planned attack on the Prussian centre. In his memoirs he wrote, 'I halted the march of the Guard and sent my *aide-de-camp*, General Dejean,[53] a reliable officer, in all haste to reconnoitre the number, the strength and the intentions of this column.'[54]

The column was approaching from an unexpected direction; even now it seems that Napoleon believed Ney would have seized the Quatre Bras crossroads and marched his troops from there down the Namur road. This would have placed them immediately in the rear of the Prussian right flank. We have already seen how d'Erlon came to approach from a different direction and the fact that this caused some anxiety in Napoleon's mind is not entirely surprising. However, even if Napoleon was reasonably confident the troops were French, he could not countenance launching his decisive attack until it was confirmed. The delay in the final attack was to have serious implications on the outcome of the day.

General d'Erlon had resigned himself to the need to restart his march towards Quatre Bras. Given the conflicting advice he had received from his key staff officers, he decided on the compromise outlined by General Deselles: the 4th Division (commanded by General Durutte), three of the four regiments of cavalry from the corps cavalry division (commanded by General Jacquinot) and two batteries were to continue towards Wagnelée, whilst the remaining three infantry divisions and cavalry regiment would turn and march on Quatre Bras. Clausewitz claims that the time was now 8pm; like Ney, d'Erlon seems not to have calculated that his arrival there would be too late to have any significant impact.

The French Right Wing – Sombreffe and Tongrines

Many histories of the battle make little reference to the French right flank where Marshal Grouchy commanded, painting a picture of a largely cavalry force tying down the whole of the Prussian III Corps commanded by General Thielemann. It appears as if there was no fighting here at all, just rather desultory skirmishing. Both sides took troops from this flank to help in other areas of the battle.

It will be remembered that Grouchy was ordered to 'throw back all the Prussian cavalry of the Prussian army's left wing onto Sombreffe and prevent the enemy troops which arrive from Namur along the road running from that town to Quatre Bras, to affect their junction with Marshal Blücher'. On the extreme French right was General Pajol's 1st Cavalry Corps, an exclusively light cavalry formation, ideal for securing the right flank by sending patrols out in all directions and identifying any Prussian troops approaching the battlefield from the direction of Namur. Although he had two divisions under his command, one of his regiments, the 1st Hussars, had still not re-joined the corps having followed the Prussians out of Charleroi towards Brussels. Pajol's deployment is described in his memoirs:

> On the right wing, Grouchy skirmished with the Prussian *tirailleurs* who were deployed in front of Boignée and Balâtre, and was seconded by Hulot's division (from Gérard's corps, which threatened Tongrenelle and the Potriaux mill). Pajol completed Grouchy's demonstrations by sending strong patrols towards Onoz and into the Orneau valley, to make the enemy think that he wanted to get onto the Namur/Mazy road. Thielemann, worried by these manoeuvres, did not dare, throughout the battle, to thin out his left and was not able to support Zieten and Pirch who were exhausting themselves bit by bit at Ligny and Saint-Amand.
>
> . . .

Unable, without infantry, to approach Boignée or Batâtre, Pajol nevertheless accomplished his mission; Hulot's division in front of Tongrenelle and Exelmans' dragoons on the Fleurus to Boignée road obliged Thieleman to commit his forces. But the demonstrations threw the Prussian general into uncertainty which paralysed his actions.

These manoeuvres were to be Pajol's role throughout the battle. His corps, indeed, was placed at the north-east extremity of the Fleurus plateau, where the steep slopes finished, on this side, at the Ligny valley and on that of the Grand-Vau stream. Kept in the area of the Onoz road, and in the rear of the line that separated the two valleys, by the enemy skirmishers sent from Boigné and Balâtre as far as the 'tree of Charlemagne', the 1st Cavalry Corps had only to move in the direction of Onoz, turning the heights of Tongrinne where were massed Kemphen's division and the cavalry of Thielemann's corps. Not wanting, without infantry, to go into Boigné and Balâtre, Pajol accomplished his mission within the limits of the orders he had received. Hulot's division in front of Tongrenelle and Exelmans' dragoons on the road from Fleurus to Boignée, obliged Thielemann, by effective attacks, to actually disengage; but the demonstrations of Pajol's cavalry threw the Prussian general into an anxiety that paralysed his actions.[55]

It is certainly true that as well as the obstacle offered by the numerous villages and hamlets along the Ligne, the slopes on the far side of this brook were much steeper here than further upstream, making the far bank unsuitable for cavalry action. The Prussian infantry garrisons of the villages were unlikely to be ejected by cavalry alone. Although Hulot's division fought on this flank as we shall soon see, only the single battalion of the 50th *de ligne* could be considered as fighting in direct support of Grouchy's cavalry. As Mauduit describes:

This battalion, the 2nd Battalion of the 50th *de ligne* of Hulot's division, commanded by the intrepid Choppard, covered itself in glory there. This battalion of the 50th had been detached in haste in the fear that the enemy had seized a small clump of trees on a small conical height between Tongrenelle and Tongrinne, beyond the Ligny brook, in support of Exelmans' dragoons, who were to prevent the Prussians from deploying by Tongrenelle at any cost . . .

The battalion of the 50th, having first seized Tongrinne, worried the enemy on this side. These retook the village and advanced the left of his infantry as far as Vilzet, to oppose, said the Prussian report, a large body of troops that were present at this point. Indeed, this battalion conducted itself here throughout the day with such intelligence and courage, that it appeared much stronger than it actually was.[56]

Whilst his patrols roamed the surrounding area and the battalion of the 50th kept the Prussian infantry occupied, there was little more Pajol could do. His *aide de camp*, Biot, describes how they passed the time:

> Whilst we were in position before the Prussians, only separated from them by the ravine ending at Sombreffe, and the artillery on the two sides were the only ones with a role in the fighting, I procured a few chairs and the general and I sat between our batteries. Behind us, the cavalry stood in line, covered by the high crops that were still standing.[57]

The main fighting on this wing was conducted by Hulot's division; the division from which General Bourmont had deserted. The extent to which their moral had been effected by this treason was about to be tested. Hulot's report to General Gérard outlined their part of the battle:

> Hardly had we arrived at the two points we had been directed to when the corps commander in person ordered the attack. The two battalions of the 9th *léger* were sent forward, one on Sombreffe, the other on Tongrinne. A battalion of the 50th and two of the 44th covered and supported these attacks. The greater part of the division's artillery was placed on a plateau between these two villages and two guns on the same narrow pass of Sombreffe, a small distance to the rear. I put the 111th Regiment into reserve where it could move in whichever direction it was necessary according to circumstances.
>
> The two battalions of the 9th *léger*, having quickly driven back the enemy's advance posts, attacked Sombreffe and Tongrinne; the entry to the first of these was barricaded and stubbornly defended. It was soon taken, but fresh troops quickly took it back. Tongrinne, easier to access, was first taken, but then lost again. Throughout the day, at each success obtained by our troops, enemy columns descended from their positions or made strong detachments to regain the ground they had lost and were able to maintain themselves on these two points of attack and it was in this way that the whole action passed on the right wing.
>
> The division's artillery could see the Prussian lines and masses perfectly and continued a well-nourished fire on them which caused many losses. It was also forced into a counter-battery fire with the enemy batteries which, favoured by the ground, took ours in enfilade from the right. It required all the courage and devotion of our gunners to maintain their position on this Sombreffe plateau whose occupation was absolutely necessary for the whole of the army's right wing and against which the enemy continually made offensive movements, but which were always repulsed.
>
> This essential point particularly occupied my attention. Also towards

my left where I sent several detachments along the stream in order to scout towards the village of Ligny against which the corps commander directed the attacks of his two other divisions. That of Tongrinne was observed by General Toussaint [commander of the 2nd Brigade]. Marshal Grouchy himself co-ordinated the movements of his cavalry with those of the battalion of infantry which fought on this ground.

Thus the division's infantry was deployed on the ground in the following manner; from Tongrinne as far as the clump of trees and beyond had been placed the 1st Battalion of the 50th under the orders of Colonel Lavigne: this battalion, two of the 44th and one of the 9th *léger*. Opposite Sombreffe, to the right and left, I deployed one battalion of the 9th *léger* and one of the 50th, two of the 111th and all the artillery. I estimate that the frontage of ground from my right to my left was from 1,000 to 1,200 *toises*.

Towards 7 o'clock, the corps commander sent me a reinforcement of a battalion of the 30th *de ligne* from the III Corps [he means IV Corps]; much weakened from its participation in the actions at Ligny. At this very moment, the enemy reserves were taking the offensive. These reserves were the whole of III Prussian Corps which had just arrived on the battlefield [not true, the Prussian III Corps had been present all day]. From then on the regiments that had provided the detachments on the various points of attack had to be employed as skirmishers, they first repulsed the enemy battalions and the position opposite Sombreffe was maintained until nightfall.

In this situation, the troops of the division that were on the extreme right also made the best efforts to maintain their positions and to protect the movements of the cavalry which made several successful charges. Also, despite the last lively attacks of the enemy, all the right wing remained masters of the battlefield. The battalion of the 30th, although exhausted, also took a very active part in the fighting. Towards 9.30pm, a division of the VI Corps came to reinforce us, but the firing had ceased.

. . .

My division that started with a strength of 5,000 men, suffered 1,200 casualties. Three distinguished *chefs de battalion* were killed opposite Sombreffe; one of the 9th *léger* whose name I forget [it was Billon], M. Mondon of the 50th and M. Danjoie of the 111th. We also suffered a loss in officers out of all proportion; nearly all the mounted officers of the units and of the headquarters lost their horses and most of us had our jackets pierced by balls. [In a footnote he continued: 'General Hulot, to better direct his troops and observe Prussian movements, placed himself on an open vantage point and thus offered himself as a target to the enemy. He forbade his officers, coming to receive orders, to approach him, fearing they would be killed. *Adjutant-Major* Aupick, later a divisional general, not having complied with this warning, was seriously wounded in this very area. This information was supplied by the son of General Hulot, who heard it from General Aupick.']

. . .

I confirm on my honour, that I had never seen troops fight with more fervour, more steadiness and more devotion, and if a reproach is necessary, it is that they threw themselves on the enemy with too much abandon and fury. More calm, in fact, would have been more favourable to the success and have spared many brave men.[58]

Hulot's men had therefore carried most of the burden of fighting on the French right, consistent with the difficulty of the ground for the employment of cavalry. Across the wide frontage that Hulot describes, both commanders-in-chief could see that the fighting here would not be decisive and both were prepared to take troops from this flank to reinforce other areas of their line. Pajol was to lose one of his two light cavalry divisions:

It was 5pm . . . Despite the heroics of his soldiers, Vandamme was not able to get across onto the left bank of the Ligny stream. Blücher tried to turn him by the side of Wagnelée, with a strong cavalry attack which Domon's division was not strong enough to counter alone. Napoleon ordered Pajol to send Subervie's division to the left flank to support Domon and the arrival of this division stopped the enemy's turning movement. But this left Pajol with only Soult's two regiments, the 4th and 5th Hussars, in his corps, as the 1st Hussars were still deployed on the left flank between Ney's and Napoleon's forces and had not returned. Despite this considerable reduction in his command, Pajol continued, with these 800 cavalry, to try and fulfil the orders he had received.[59]

Despite Pajol's claims that Grouchy's relatively weak force tied down the entire Prussian III Corps, from early in the battle Blücher took troops from his left to reinforce his centre. As early as 3pm, Blücher ordered General Thielemann to detach a brigade of his reserve cavalry; Colonel Marwitz's brigade was placed under command of General Jürgass (the commander of the II Corps cavalry) who was preparing the major attack against the French left. Then, around 4pm, Thielemann received orders to send a brigade of infantry; whereupon the 12th Brigade (*Oberst* [Colonel] Stülpnagel) marched off to Ligny. It was placed in reserve between Sombreffe and Ligny in place of the 8th (*Oberst* Langen) which was sent to take part in the attack on Wagnelée.

From the Prussian perspective, two of their infantry brigades (the 10th and 11th Brigades, a total of eleven battalions) and the 2nd Brigade of reserve cavalry (six squadrons) were fixed in place by the French right wing. The infantry action took place almost entirely on the terrain occupied by the 10th Brigade (*Oberst*

Kemphen) between Tongrenelle and Boignée. Thus, although Grouchy's wing tied down two infantry brigades with Hulot's single equivalent, Exelmans' cavalry alone significantly outnumbered their opposite numbers.

However, it is clear that Thielemann was aware of his apparent inactivity and was looking, despite the unpromising ground, to strike a blow. As the afternoon wore on, he felt that the French cavalry opposing him was dwindling in number (presumably after Subervie's division had been sent to the French left) and concluded that the French were retiring; when he saw the skirmishers of his 12th Brigade, which was between Sombreffe and Ligny, crossing the stream about 7pm, he felt an opportunity was presenting itself. He decided to advance across the Ligne and down the road which led to Fleurus with his remaining brigade of cavalry. At 7.30pm *Generalmajor* Hobe, commander of the III Corps cavalry, was ordered to advance down this road to Fleurus with all the remaining III Corps cavalry (seven squadrons of *Oberstleutnant* von Lottum's brigade and one of *Oberst* von Marwitz; about 700 men) and a battery of horse artillery. The horse battery initially deployed to prepare the advance, but quickly lost a gun to French counter-battery fire. Leaving two guns behind to cover the advance, the remaining five limbered up and followed the advance. Across the Ligne, these five guns again unlimbered and opened fire on Exelmans' two batteries; the Prussian cavalry continued their advance, with two squadrons leading, leaving the battery without cover.

Soon after this force crossed the narrow bridge over the Ligne, Exelmans, his cavalry hidden from the Prussians by a fold in the ground, seized his opportunity. He ordered Bonnemains' brigade (4th and 12th Dragoons) to charge the head of the column whilst Stroltz's 9th Dragoon Division, led by Burthe's brigade (5th and 13th Dragoons) charged it in the flank. The history of the 4th Dragoons includes the following report from *Maréchal de camp* Bonnemains:

> The brigade was in the front line on the extreme right opposite Sombreffe and was, throughout the whole action, exposed to a murderous artillery and musket fire. Twice the Prussians attempted to attack it, and although outnumbered, Bonnemains' brigade succeeded in throwing them back beyond the Sombreffe defile and caused them a considerable loss. In a third attempt, towards the end of the day, the enemy cavalry again advanced with even stronger forces than on the previous occasions and was supported by an artillery battery. Its head was attacked by *Maréchal de Camp* Bonnemains and its flank by a brigade of Stroltz's division. These charges had, like the two previous attempts, the happy result of throwing the enemy back beyond the stream and to capture his artillery.
>
> The brigade has lost about 200 men killed or wounded. Amongst the number of the latter is Colonel Bouquerot des Essarts of the 4th Dragoons and Lieutenant Tilly, the general's *aide de camp*. [The 4th lost a total of twelve officers on this day.][60]

Mauduit, who we must remember corresponded with many officers who took part in this campaign, gives more detail:

> The 5th Dragoons, commanded by Colonel Saint-Amand, occupied the right of the first line of this corps (Exelmans'), protecting, at the same time, a battery which was causing heavy losses to the enemy. On his left he had the 13th [Dragoon] Regiment commanded by Colonel Saviot, when suddenly, a mass of Prussian cavalry was seen preparing to charge. This movement not having escaped the vigilant eye of *Comte* Exelmans, he crossed the ground between himself and the threatened point at the gallop and at the head of these two regiments moved to meet the Prussian squadrons. At the same moment, the two enemy columns sounded the charge and they fell on each other with equal boldness. The shock was most violent and the mêlée was one of the most confused which has been recorded in the annals of cavalry combat, for each engaged with a sort of rage.
>
> The Prussian cavalry was forced, despite its bravery, to give ground after having lost a good number of men and horses and to rally in the rear under protection of its guns.
>
> The 5th and 13th Dragoons pursued them so impetuously that they passed through several thick hedges which hid some Prussian battalions, falling in the middle of them like an avalanche and overthrowing all those that offered any resistance. Not content with these exploits, our dragoons launched themselves at the battery which they cut down and captured five guns. *Maréchal des Logis* Frémillot of the élite company of the 5th Dragoons, having been thrown under one of the guns at the moment it fired was hit by the box of caseshot and was horribly mutilated . . .
>
> Grenadier Brazé, of the same company, achieved even more; he passed through the enemy's first line, pursuing a superior officer who he wanted to take prisoner, but found himself immediately surrounded by thirty cavalry who hacked at him and his horse. But supernatural courage triumphs over all obstacles. Brazé was of this type; he killed or wounded all those that faced him, managed to break clear, pass for a second time through the Prussian line and re-join his company to the applause of the whole of his regiment that had obeyed the rally and which from its position had witnessed this herculean struggle. But Brazé's face no longer looked human [presumably from his wounds], although he wanted to retake his place in the ranks so as not to miss another opportunity of taking revenge . . . In this charge, the 5th Dragoons suffered almost one hundred men *hors de combat*, but with what brilliant results![61]

One account states that a single squadron of Burthe's brigade, under *Commandant* Letellier, pursued the Prussians as far as the windmill at Potriaux where it was stopped and turned back by Prussian infantry.[62]

Wanting to follow up his success, Grouchy requested reinforcements and permission to take the heights of Tongrinne and Point-du-Jour, from which the Prussian artillery was bringing down effective fire on Grouchy's troops; particularly his cavalry. Grouchy successively sent several officers, notably his son Victor and his senior *aide de camp*, Blocqueville, to ask for infantry to complete the rout of the enemy that he had pushed back beyond Sombreffe, but it is reported that the emperor replied to Bloqueville, 'I have only the Guard as you can see; tell Grouchy to hold with his cavalry; I am going to attack the centre of the enemy's army with Milhaud's cuirassiers and the day will be ours.'[63] Pajol reports that towards the end of the day his men occupied Boignée and Bâlatre, although given his small force of light cavalry, this could only have been when the Prussians evacuated them during their withdrawal.[64]

The Final Attack
We have seen that Napoleon had planned to launch his final, decisive attack at about 6pm. However, the appearance of d'Erlon's column had disordered Vandamme's troops and forced the emperor to delay the attack, reinforce Vandamme with troops of the Guard and to send a staff officer off the discover the identity of the approaching column. This whole process took a considerable amount of time; accounts vary between an hour and an hour and a half. It was probably not until about 8pm that the attack was ordered forward once more. Mauduit, in his own inimitable style, describes the renewed advance:

> We thus lost more than an hour [due to d'Erlon's appearance]. This fateful time stationary, made Blücher think that we had given up our general attack; perhaps even that we were preparing to retreat. It also hastened him to attempt a last spurt in directing, always on Saint-Amand, the object of his constant desires, all that remained disposable to him, in order to retake this post and to cut off our retreat. But he did not get the chance to realise his design, for at 7.30pm, we continued our movement and this time nothing presented an obstacle; everything had to give way before us!
> . . .
>
> There was something solemn and religious about this immense military procession marching to death with a firm pace and heads held high . . .
> Our infantry columns, black and deep, were silent, but a calm and manly courage was marked on all those noble faces. The drummers did not beat, they held their drumsticks crossed, only awaiting the signal for the charge.
> . . .
>
> Sixty guns, ready to vomit death to open us up a passage through the masses that they went to demolish, marched to our right and to the front the dipping ground led like us towards this fateful valley!

Coming finally to complete our patriotic work, were thirty-two élite squadrons, dazzling in the last rays of the sun, which disappeared towards the high hedges serving as the limit and support of our extreme left.

The Prussian army could observe our warlike march and calculate, watch in hand, the moment of the shock that it would have to meet. All its twelve-pounder batteries were directed against us for we were in their range.

The ground was so regular that one would have thought we manoeuvred on the Champs du Mars, so well aligned were our divisions.

Thus we marched for twenty minutes, to the continuous rolling musketry, to the relentless roar of more than two hundred guns! All the ridge, from Ligny as far as Saint-Amand, was enveloped in cannon smoke, resembling the thick fog which, in the morning, covered white and undulating, the valley of the Alps and cutting in two the hills from the mountains. Such indeed it seemed to us, the heights that we went to tackle. From time to time, thick masses of smoke rose suddenly to the sky and shortly after the flames escaped! There were several parts of the village which had been burning for three or four hours!

This spectacle was without doubt dreadful and heart rendering to think of, but what horror in such a moment.

From time to time, the balls struck true and knocked down several files.

We came, finally, to the steep banks of the gullies of Ligny. The balls, the canister, the cannonballs, all were aimed at us, for the enemy knew our mission!

There, we close up in mass, even under Prussian fire; there only, we load our muskets and receive our final instructions. It was there also that General Count Roguet, our *colonel-en-second*, having brought all the officers and NCOs into a circle around him, addressed the following memorable words which provoked such cruel reprisals at Planchenoit and during the retreat from Waterloo, 'Messieurs, warn the grenadiers that the first one of them that brings me a prisoner, I will have shot.'[65]

Interestingly, a Dutch account[66] declares that Roguet's threat could not have been real as General Friant who was the commander of all the foot grenadier regiments was a man of such unblemished character that he would not have countenanced such an action!

A number of officers of the Guard wrote about this attack and we shall look at several of them. Let us start with Major Duuring, who commanded the 1st Battalion of the 1st Regiment of *Chasseurs* of the Guard:

These three regiments [the 1st Regiment of *Chasseurs*, and the 1st and 2nd of Grenadiers] received the order to follow the emperor who moved towards the right one hour before dusk. We marched in column by division under fire which wounded two men. Then, the three regiments passed through the village after the heavy cavalry.[67]

In contrast to this account, a number of histories have the 2nd, 3rd and 4th Grenadiers going around the position of Ligny to the west, whilst the 1st *Chasseurs* and Grenadiers went by the east. It would certainly have been tactically sound for the Guard to by-pass the village; not only would it have avoided the congestion and disorder this would inevitably have caused by passing through, but it would also have forced the Prussians out without a fight as they saw themselves being outflanked to east and west. We must also not forget that Gérard's troops were also still fighting in the village and that they would have made a telling contribution. Sergeant Mauduit certainly credits some of Gérard's men with taking part in this attack:

> Everything was ready. General Pécheux's division of the IV Corps only awaited the signal to fall, heads lowered, on the enemy masses and leave the village. This signal came! A volley of sixty cannon shoots from our right! It was the artillery of the Guard saluting the Prussian army![68]

The advance of the supporting heavy cavalry seemed to have made quite an impression on those who watched its advance. Napoleon's servant, Mameluke Ali, wrote:

> As night fell, the emperor approached the village of Ligny. The artillery of the Guard fired volley after volley at the slope the other side of the valley which was occupied by the Prussian army, whilst the head of a column of cuirassiers appeared. At this moment, this brave troop rushed up the road that passed through the village, crossed the valley and went to fall on the enemy. It passed the emperor at the gallop. These brave soldiers, whose squadrons quickly passed one after the other, were so full of enthusiasm that they shouted '*Vive l'empereur!*' at the tops of their voices, and which could be heard from afar. But the cuirassiers, taking no notice of what they were told, although Marshal Soult had it repeated, did the same as those preceding them. The sight of this parade in such light and to the sound of the cannons was a magnificent spectacle. Brave cuirassiers! I can still see you now, swords raised and rushing to the fight! What a sight![69]

The commander of the 2nd Grenadiers, General Christiani, notes that the Prussians, exhausted by their previous determined resistance and perhaps somewhat intimidated by the sight of the bearskins of the Old Guard, did not dispute the advance, but apparently fell back before it: 'The four regiments of grenadiers received the order to flush them out [of Ligny]. This movement was made without any enemy resistance.'[70] Christiani claims that the 2nd Grenadiers lost no men in this advance. Other officers also speak of the lack of resistance as the regiments by-passed, or passed through, Ligny; General Petit:

> In the evening all the units of grenadiers with the 1st of *Chasseurs*, concentrated on the heights in the rear of this village which had been quickly forced and taken from the enemy, who had defended it with vigour against the different corps of the line since the beginning of the affair.[71]

However, finding themselves beyond Ligny and not having met any organised resistance, the Guard were faced by the open slopes on top of which Blücher's final reserves were waiting. Whilst the French had so far found that the Prussians had counter-attacked as soon as they showed any attempt to form up for an attack on the heights beyond all the villages, perhaps showing the tiredness of the Prussians by this stage of the battle, the Guard were soon prepared to meet the Prussian response. Duuring again:

> In exiting, we formed up to the right of the village and then we formed battalion squares. The grenadiers went forward and to the left; our cavalry was pushed back and the grenadiers faced several charges from the enemy cavalry, who suffered a considerable loss because they thought they were the National Guard in their chapeaux.
>
> The balls of our batteries which were on the heights the other side of the village, passed along the 1st Battalion each moment, but did us no harm, 'but did to our heavy cavalry. Several enemy skirmishers also fired on us, but we did not lose a man.[72]

Almost devoid of infantry reserves, Blücher relied on his cavalry to attempt to drive the Guard back. Although we know some Prussian infantry were involved in this fighting, the Guard officers speak almost exclusively of cavalry action. General Petit wrote:

> The 4th and 3rd Regiments of Grenadiers formed the head of the column; the 2nd marched behind. It was these three regiments which, after having chased the enemy infantry from its position on the other side of the village, received a brilliant cavalry charge which was repulsed by them with a great loss of men and horses.
>
> The 1st Regiment of *Chasseurs* and the 1st Regiment of Grenadiers, having also deployed out of Ligny, formed up on the right of this village, facing and observing the enemy forces which still occupied the heights and the route leading to Wavre until the arrival of Count de Lobau's corps which arrived as night fell. This army corps formed up in front of these two regiments.
>
> Several Guard batteries had been advantageously employed against Saint-Amand and Ligny. A battery from the Grenadiers passed through the village with the last two regiments (4th and 3rd) and caused the enemy great damage.[73]

General Christiani also spoke of these cavalry charges and, interestingly, notes how the squares were not fully formed as the Prussian cavalry struck:

> Whilst they were forming into battalion squares having passed to the far side of the village, we were surprised by a charge of Prussian lancers which passed through the intervals of the squares without us being able to use our muskets; the squares not having had the time to place themselves in echelon. The enemy would have been better received if he had attempted a second charge, but he did not return.[74]

We have already heard that it was the 4th Grenadiers that headed the advance. Consisting of only a single battalion and the junior of the grenadier regiments, its men had famously not all received all the iconic bearskins for which the Old Guard was famous. Duuring has already mentioned how the Prussians mistook their motley appearance for troops of the National Guard. Let us now hear from a junior officer of that regiment:

> The 4th Foot Grenadier Regiment commanded by the intrepid General Harlet, was first to pass through the village of Ligny under a terrible fire, and was first to rush against the Prussian reserve. At the entrance of the village, the emperor alone, amid the bullets and shells, stopped this regiment, 'Grenadiers', he said,' go through the village with the bayonet, fall on the Prussian reserve and only stop when you are on the heights'. The brave 4th who only counted 600 men, did not hesitate; the village is crossed, the enemy pushed back, and alone for half an hour, the 4th struggled against 15,000 men and repelled two cavalry charges.[75]

Almost as a summary of this attack, let's return to the eloquent, if somewhat emotional and romantic, pen of Sergeant Mauduit:

> The emperor was close to us, on a mound next to a sunken lane that we went to cross under his eyes, saluting him with a '*Vivat!*'
> At this moment, the charge was beaten, our heads of column launched into the valley by sections and half-sections, following the ground and ways through, each regiment following the movement at the *pas de course* and soon were beyond Ligny that more than five hours of relentless combat had not completely put into our control. But, this time, it is finally taken *à la bayonette*. Everything is knocked over and trodden on, like weak shrubs by the rush of a hurtling torrent!
> What human strength would be able to resist a combined attack on such a scale, executed by such troops!!!
> Despite ourselves, several times in fact, we stumbled on the heaps of

bodies that lay in the streets of Ligny! . . . but thanks to the light, several minutes had sufficed for us to have crossed this kind of valley of Josaphat [a biblical place where God was going to judge the people of all nations], where the dead and living are mixed together!

Our heads of column reform, by divisions, at the base of the high ground, for we have still to assault the masses that await us, to strike us down on our appearance on the hills that they occupy in force.

Hardly are we two thirds of the way up the Brye heights than we are struck by a volley of canister and soon after cavalry charges are announced. A regiment of lancers approaches the square of grenadiers, taking it for national guard because of the peculiarity of its uniforms . . .

The service squadrons which on this day were a squadron of *Grenadiers à Cheval*, a squadron of dragoons and a company of *Gendarmes d'Élite*, having come up at almost the same time as the foot grenadiers, set off in pursuit of this cavalry. An infantry square attempted to stop them, but were immediately broken and sabred. This attack allowed the Prussian lancers that were being pursued to rally and return to the charge against our three squadrons who, too few in number to sustain the shock, came to reform behind our grenadiers who had continued their advance.

The Prussian lancers, received by them as before, turned about. The service squadrons retook the charge with vigour and the enemy cavalry was not seen again.

It was again the 6th Uhlans, this brave regiment, commanded by Lieutenant Colonel Lützow, who gloriously ended his day here; he fell before our grenadiers with thirteen of his officers and seventy lancers [Lützow was captured].

During this curious episode, which cost this regiment of Prussian lancers so dear . . . our regiment was half way up the first hill, reforming its divisions, whilst the *Grenadiers à Cheval*, the Guard Dragoons as well as Delort's cuirassiers, leaving the defile and reforming at the 'grand trot' by squadron, went to complete the victory . . .

This general huzzah of three thousand heavy cavalry on a single point had a prodigious and frightening effect; there were several very violent encounters on the Brye heights.[76]

Having thrown back the initial desperate Prussian cavalry counter-attacks, the Guard infantry now effectively handed over the fighting to their own heavy cavalry that were now coming forward:

The service squadrons and the squadron of *Gendarmerie d'Élite* [that is to say the squadron of lancers and grenadiers and a company of the *Gendarmerie d'Élite*], deployed from Ligny almost at the same time as the 4th, 3rd and 2nd Regiments of Grenadiers, pursued the enemy cavalry and forced back an infantry square which retired in good order. During this time, the enemy cavalry rallied and charged the service squadrons in their turn and, when the enemy were stopped by the fire of the three last regiments of grenadiers (who were formed in battalion squares) they retook the charge with the greatest vigour, although inferior in number.[77]

The service squadrons would normally have also included squadrons of Guard *chasseurs* and dragoons,[78] although Petit does not mention these. However, Sergeant-Major Chevalier of the Guard *Chasseurs* wrote:

> At 8pm, Napoleon, at the head of the Imperial Guard finally takes the village [Ligny] once and for all. It is then that we broke through the centre, overthrew everything that we found before us, infantry, cavalry and artillery. We made a horrible carnage and, the Prussians suffered twice as much as we did; we took 40 guns, eight flags and a great number of prisoners, this affair was extremely murderous. Never had I seen the French fight with such fury; it was not a fight, it was a horrible butchery and it is said that the enemy had more than 25,000 men *hors de combat.*[79]

Putting aside what are clear exaggerations in Chevalier's account, the intensity of the fighting is clear. It appears that it was actually Delort's division of cuirassiers that did most of the fighting after the initial repulse of the Prussian cavalry. Blücher threw every available squadron into the attack and even at aged seventy-three led them forward himself until famously his horse was killed and he was pinned beneath it until rescued by his men. Delort wrote his own account of this fight:

> This decisive attack was only launched towards 4pm [?] and then the village of Ligny had to be retaken for the third or fourth time. Delort's division of cuirassiers was *alone* [his emphasis] sent in pursuit of the enemy. This division broke all the Prussian battalions deployed in square on the heights which dominated this village, charged and overthrew ten times all their cavalry, knocked Blücher from his horse, but received no reinforcements. It was only able to maintain itself there by an extraordinary vigour on ground where it is true to say it was surrounded by Prussian infantry, cavalry and artillery. During this fighting, the second cuirassier division of General Milhaud's corps remained in reserve and this is not explained in the coverage entitled, *Memoire pour server à l'histoire de France en 1815*. All the details which are entered into otherwise on the day of Fleurus are otherwise perfectly exact and conform to the truth . . . The official reports of Lieutenant Generals Milhaud and Delort on the beautiful charges of the 14th Cavalry Division make known how the 5th, 10th, 6th and 9th Cuirassier Regiments had contributed to the success of the battle.[80]

Here we see Delort's complaint that he had to maintain this fight alone, without the support of Milhaud's second division, that of Watier Saint-Alphonse. This position is taken by most other historians, but Colonel Ordener, who commanded the 1st Cuirassiers in this division, wrote:

> On the morning of the 16th, conforming to the dispositions adopted by the emperor, our corps formed the reserve, placed in the second line, two or three hundred metres in front of Fleurus, not far from the village of Saint-Amand.
>
> For a long time we remained immobile; the false marches of d'Erlon prevented Napoleon from employing us . . . Finally, at the moment when the sun began to touch the horizon, we received the order to stir ourselves. We left together; eight regiments of cuirassiers. We crossed part of the battlefield at the trot and passing the village of Ligny, we charged the debris of the Prussian infantry in mass, who were overthrown in a moment and filled the stream with their bodies. However, Blücher reformed them in squares, put himself at the head of his last cavalry reserve and threw himself in desperation on our squadrons. His efforts were broken there. Broken and a prey to the most terrible disorder, his cavalry found their salvation in flight, we pursued them closely. Blücher fell under the feet of our horses, but the night was already dark and to the misfortune of France he escaped our notice . . . The loss of this division during the day of Ligny was about 200 cavalrymen.[81]

In fact, Watier's division did follow up that of Delort, but, having passed round Ligny, were directed east towards Sombreffe and, with the remains of Vichery's division, pushed back *Generalmajor* von Steinmetz's brigade (1st Brigade of I Corps). The casualties they suffered certainly suggests that they were involved in some fighting at the end of the day. More Prussian cavalry were committed to this fight as they were drawn from the Prussian right, but being brought up rather piece meal, they were charged and thrown back one after the other; The Dutch historian Winard Aerts describes these desperate Prussian charges as a '*Todenritt*' or 'death ride'.

As has already been suggested, the Guard were not the only troops to be involved as night approached. Apart from Gérard's final efforts in Ligny, elsewhere on the battlefield, the troops were called on to make one last effort. Colonel Fantin des Odoards, commander of the 22nd *de ligne* of Habert's brigade, recalls the last actions of the day near Saint-Amand-la-Haye:

> Seeing the uselessness of their efforts, the Prussians, favoured by a fold in the ground, brought up two guns which fired case shot just at the very moment when the final attack, in which the reserve, that is the Imperial

Guard, took part, finally swept across the battlefield and gave us victory. All this had happened without losing too many men. The 70th, harshly sabred, saw its ranks badly thinned; my 22nd had twenty six dead, of which one was an officer, and 194 wounded, including eight officers.[82]

General Berthezène, whose division had suffered much in Saint-Amand, wrote in his official report on the action:

> Towards 8pm, the division was relieved in its position by four battalions of the Young Guard, then it all advanced out of the village and advanced against the mill of St-Amand on the heights of Brye and took position there.[83]

Interestingly, in his memoirs, referring to the final attack, he wrote:

> To second the principal attack, which was made in the centre, a division of III Corps had deployed out of Saint-Amand and moved against the Bussy mill where it established itself; but night not permitting an attack on the village of Brye, Zieten profited from this to extract himself from the difficult position he found himself in. This movement had been agreed between General Barrois [a brigade commander in the Young Guard] and General Berthezène and therefore was only a partial movement. If Vandamme, commander of III Corps had ordered it, it would have been made by the whole of the III Corps and its results could have been more important.[84]

It may be remembered that Colonel Rumigny had been sent to lead an attack by the 76th *de ligne* into Ligny village by his commander General Gérard. Having passed through the village, he left them at the boundary to try and get reinforcements. His task having been overtaken by the attack of the Guard, he returned to the two battalions and takes up the story again:

> When I noticed the charge of the cuirassiers, which I was not far from, I put my two battalions into square and moved them to the right of the heights. Then I left them to return to General Gérard, feeling my mission was complete.
>
> At the moment that I left the battalion commanded by M. de Moucarville, I heard a cry of distress, and turning round, I saw disorder in the battalion. I went back into the square, where an officer rolled dying on the ground. I learnt that when the enemy showed himself, the soldiers shouted '*Vive l'empereur!*' and this officer, perhaps inadvertently, shouted '*Vive le roi!*' An NCO, incensed, had bayoneted him. The desertion of

General Bourmont had raised the cry of 'Treason!' and this unfortunate officer fell victim to this fear.

In the middle of the heat of battle, this passed unremarked; if the NCO escaped the punishment he deserved, this was due to the events which caused it, for General Gérard was very severe, but just, in his vigour and application of military law. No corps was more disciplined than his. He displayed, the next day, the 17th, with what strict discipline he expected of the men he led. On my return to the headquarters, I found our victory was complete as we owned the battlefield, but few prisoners and trophies. The dead and dying covered all the routes to the centre of Ligny. The fight had been desperate, the village disputed, taken and retaken; and both sides had very heavy losses.[85]

Durutte
It is now time to see what effect General Durutte was to have on the battle. In his own account of events, Durutte wrote:

Before General d'Erlon left, General Durutte asked clearly if he was to march on Brye. General d'Erlon replied that, in view of the circumstances, he could not lay down exactly what he should do and that he should rely on his experience and caution. General Durutte sent his cavalry towards the road that went from Sombreffe to Quatre Bras, leaving Wagnelée and Brye to his right, but bearing towards these two villages; his infantry followed this movement.

General d'Erlon had told him to be cautious because as affairs were going badly at Quatre Bras, General Durutte would do well to observe the Delhutte wood in case Marshal Ney made a retrograde movement, the enemy would be behind him.[86]

We should note that Durutte was advised to act with caution by d'Erlon and this thought clearly dominated Durutte's decision-making. However, there was still the time and opportunity for him to strike a telling blow at Ligny; his force may not have been strong, but he was hovering on the Prussian flank and a bold and aggressive manoeuvre could have achieved telling results. Unfortunately, apart from the advice to act with caution from his corps commander, key officers of his staff had deserted during the march, including Colonel Gordon, his chief-of-staff, and *Chef de Bataillon* Gaugler, his senior *aide de camp*, and a combination of these things no doubt goes a long way in explaining Durutte's less-than-impressive intervention. In an effort to justify his actions that day, Durutte later described his contribution:

Whilst General Jacquinot moved to within artillery range of the road between Somebreffe and Quatre Bras, he encountered a body of enemy with which he exchanged artillery fire for three quarters of an hour. General Durutte advanced his infantry to support him; there was still heavy fighting towards St-Amand.[87]

This action could hardly be described as determined or decisive and probably reflects the advice he had been given. His contribution to the French victory at Ligny was negligible at best.

Durutte's caution, which may well have been endorsed by d'Erlon, was witnessed with growing frustration by his own troops. These could see the battle raging before them and burned to get into action. Captain Chapuis, who commanded a grenadier company in the 85th *de ligne*, which led the 4th Division's column, was a witness to what happened:

> Located at a short distance from the hamlet of Wagnelée, which lies close to the village of Saint-Amand, and awaiting the order that would have us march on Wagnelée, we were all convinced that I Corps had been called on to play a great role in the struggle that was engaged.
>
> ... Our situation behind Wagnelée gave us the absolute assurance that a few minutes would suffice to put the whole of the Prussian right wing between two fires, and there was not one of us, soldier or officer, who could not see that by acting with promptitude and vigour, the salvation of the enemy would be gravely compromised.
>
> This order, on which we expected to obtain such admirable results, arrived, but unfortunately, it was not executed because, on one part, General Drouet d'Erlon had left to return to join Marshal Ney at Quatre Bras, under the orders of whom was found I and II Corps, and on the other, General Durutte did not dare to take it upon himself to order such a movement; refusing the responsibility as a divisional commander rather than the commanding general of I Corps. Consequently, he sent an officer to Quatre Bras carrying this order and demanding instructions that others, put in his position, would not have hesitated to carry out.
>
> ... This intense struggle [Ligny], that we were able to follow through its various phases by the rising and falling intensity of the firing, electrified our soldiers; they impatiently awaited the moment that they would enter the fray, and they expressed their surprise in loud voices that they remained with downed arms when their assistance would render such great services. This order, carried and given in the presence of the whole of the head of the 4th Division, but ignored, was, shortly after, followed by a second so imperative, that General Durutte finally took the resolution to execute it.
>
> Everything was ready for the attack, which we awaited with the highest enthusiasm; but our hopes were to be dashed. [Chapuis goes on to explain

the prevarication of Durutte and the excuses he used not to launch his division into the fray] . . . During this interval, we watched the Prussian corps quietly executing their retreat, of which not a single man would have escaped us. Also, since the two voltigeur companies of the 85th, supported by the grenadier company that I commanded, penetrated into the hamlet of Wagnelée at the end of the day, these companies only found there a weak rearguard which made little resistance before retiring.

Master of this position, the 4th Division established itself there.

Whilst this position was being taken, an angrier scene was taking place between our divisional commander, Durutte, and our brigade commander, Brue. The latter, frustrated at the hesitation of his superior, criticised him loudly. He shouted, 'It is intolerable that we witness the retreat of a beaten army and do nothing, when everything indicates that if it was attacked it would be destroyed.'

General Durutte could only offer as an excuse in response to General Brue; 'It is lucky for you that you are not responsible!'

'I wish to God that I was' said this last, 'we would already be fighting!'

This altercation was overheard by the senior officers of the 85th that were at the head of the regiment . . . It proved, besides, to those who reflected on it, that an enormous fault had been committed in employing certain chiefs for whom, for many years, the words 'glory' and '*la Patrie*' no longer had the same significance as to their subordinates.[88]

Chapuis's view was endorsed by *Maréchal de Camp* Brue, who later wrote in a letter:

> If General Durutte had attacked the Prussian army at the moment when, beaten at Ligny and retiring, this army would have been annihilated; all those who were not killed would have been forced to lay down their arms and would have been captured.[89]

It is unlikely that an infantry division and three regiments of cavalry could have had this much impact on the outcome of the battle, particularly as it was made by someone who might be accused of promoting his own contribution to events. However, the Prussian right was held by Zieten's I Corps, the corps that had fought throughout the previous day, had borne the brunt of fighting during the current battle and was withdrawing in a state of some disorganisation. Pressed more vigorously by Durutte, there is certainly an argument that this corps may have been so disorganised that it could have been unable to take any further part in the campaign. However, the claim that the whole army would have been destroyed is certainly fanciful.

VI Corps

It will be remembered that at 3.30pm Napoleon had ordered VI Corps to take up position between Charleroi and Fleurus. From this position he could call them to Ligny or send them to support Marshal Ney in case of emergency, but it is clear that he did not want to commit them in order to keep them fresh for future operations. *Adjutant-commandant* Janin, the deputy chief of staff of VI Corps, wrote:

> On the 16th, whilst the centre marched on Fleurus and Marshal Ney was at Frasnes with part of the left wing, VI Corps was left at Charleroi with the order to move in support of this last if it had any need of it. Such was the object of which I was charged. If this necessity had been required, VI Corps would have set off; it had a march of four leagues to reach the marshal's battlefield: during this course, things changed; the left wing had success that rendered this intervention unnecessary, whilst towards the centre the fire continued with a less favourable outcome. What was VI Corps to do? Remain mid-way inactive? Await tardy orders to reach it? No, without doubt, the general who commanded it was too well aware of the ardour which animated his troops; he directed them on the point of action which was most lively, which promised him a glorious part of the victory; he thus marched towards the centre, and by his position, the movement which he conducted took it behind the rear of the left of centre which was occupied by General Vandamme . . .[90]

Janin was to fight at Waterloo where he received three sabre wounds to the head, was captured and subsequently imprisoned in Britain. VI Corps were to take no part in the fighting at Ligny, but sent Teste's division to reinforce Grouchy's wing which was short of infantry at the end of the battle, whilst the two other divisions marched forward to cover the rest of the army through the night from a position on the heights above Ligny and Saint-Amand.

Losses

The Dutch historian Aerts, drawing on contemporary Prussian sources, gives the Prussian losses at Ligny as 372 officers and 11,706 men killed or wounded with another 8,000 to 11,000 prisoners and deserters.[91] Desertion was certainly high in the units recruited in the territories recently acquired by Prussia after the peace of 1814. This gives a total of between 20,000 and 23,000 men, or roughly 25 per cent of their fighting strength.

French losses were also extremely heavy. In the regimental history of the 11th *léger*, it claims that Girard's division suffered casualties of 2,200 out of just over 4,000. These casualties of almost 50 per cent resulted in the division being ordered to remain at Ligny to recuperate and to see to the wounded. Captain Francois gave his own regiment's strength at the end of the battle as 467 out of a starting strength of 1,453,[92] although no doubt some of those missing re-joined the regiment later. Even Pajol's light cavalry that were not involved in any real fighting lost 250 men to artillery fire and skirmishing according to that commander.

Gourgaud puts French casualties at 6,800, but Mauduit raises this to a more realistic 13,800[93] with a breakdown as follows:

Girard's division: 960 dead, 1,178 wounded: Total 2,138.
III Corps: 1,757 dead, 3,515 wounded: Total 5,272.
IV Corps: 1,143 dead, 2,287 wounded: Total 3,430.
1st Cavalry Corps: 100 dead, 200 wounded: Total 300.
2nd Cavalry Corps: 200 dead, 250 wounded: Total 450.
4th Cavalry Corps: 100 dead, 200 wounded: Total 300.
Young Guard: 300 dead, 500 wounded: Total 800.
Guard *Chasseurs*: 70 dead, 200 wounded: Total 270.
Guard Grenadiers: 100 dead, 300 wounded: Total 400.
Guard Cavalry: 200 dead, 300 wounded: Total 500.

Total for the army: 4,930 dead and 8,930 wounded: Total 13,860.

The figures for the Guard, both infantry and cavalry, seem artificially high given the testimony of Guard officers; Mauduit may have exaggerated them to credit the Guard with having fought a more stubborn battle than might have been the case. In contrast, the casualties of Gérard's corps seem low in comparison to those of III Corps, given the ferocity of the fighting in Ligny village.

Senior officers had certainly led from the front; Generals Girard and Le Capitaine were mortally wounded; Generals Habert, Domon, Maurin, Berruyer, Billard, Dufour, Farine, Penne, Piat, Saint-Remy, Devilliers, Bourgeois and Vinot were all wounded more or less seriously.

We have already spoken of the high percentage of casualties in Girard's division and how it was leaderless and effectively *hors de combat*. The infantry casualties in Vandamme's III Corps at just under 30 per cent, and Gérard's IV Corps at 26 per cent also show how the size of force Grouchy commanded thereafter was considerably lower than the strengths generally allocated to it; certainly in infantry who had inevitably taken by far the highest percentage of casualties. Only Teste's division had not fought at Ligny, but this was a weak division from the beginning of the campaign. It is also impossible to know what percentage of those categorised as wounded remained with their units and continued the campaign. Whilst it is fair to say that French eyewitness accounts seem to confirm that the enthusiasm and moral of the troops was not affected by these unusually high casualty rates, the physical battering they had taken was considerable.

Chapter 9

The Night of 16/17 June

The fighting continued past 9 o'clock; Captain Francois of the 30th *de ligne* had been involved almost since the first shot of the battle, but even now was still being called on to make one more effort:

> About 9 o'clock that night, 100 men were asked for to support the cavalry, which was attacking the enemy's sharpshooters in a ravine to the right of Ligny. I volunteered and took the command along with Lieutenant Dodet, in spite of the advice of my comrades. Although we had almost won, I foresaw misfortunes and I almost envied those who had fallen. I said to myself, 'Let the end come!' We skirted the brook and had not gone 200 yards when we received a volley which killed three men and wounded seven. Lieutenant Dodet was wounded by a ball through the leg. Most of my men were seized with panic and wanted to fly. I rushed amongst them and compelled them to face the enemy. We went on and lost four more men, and then were ordered back by Marshal Grouchy.[1]

It appears that the fighting drew to a close because of the gathering darkness, not because French aims had been achieved. No doubt Napoleon would have paid handsomely for just two more hours of daylight to allow his Guard to finish the job of routing the Prussian army and now the full implications of the hour or so lost on the appearance of d'Erlon's troops was fully realised. Bourgeois wrote 'The French army prepared to exploit their success; but the approach of night and the fatigues of the day prevented it . . . at ten o'clock the firing had ceased along the whole line.'[2]

This is the same time given by Captain Gerbet, who wrote,

> Night put an end to this tenacious struggle. It was 10pm.
> All the positions that had been occupied by the enemy remained in our hands. The battle was won, but it had cost us dear; our ranks were much thinned. The enemy retired in good order, only leaving us as trophies the debris of their arms and dismounted cannons.[3]

As the fighting died down because the two sides could no longer see each other, the respite gave the Prussians the opportunity to coordinate strong rearguards which might not have been possible if the Guard and French heavy cavalry had had the time to finally break their resistance. Indeed, as the two sides manoeuvred into their final positions, the Prussians often showed they had not lost the will to resist and there were a number of engagements in the darkness. As VI Corps moved forward to cover the guard, their acting chief of staff reported:

> At night on the 16th, night closed on the armies who were still in each other's presence. The dragoons of the Guard, advancing on our right were received by a heavy fire and towards midnight, the Prussian cavalry attempted a charge on our bivouacs which, as at Lutzen, had no other aim than to hide the movements of the enemy army.[4]

Although the Prussian army was beaten, they had not lost their cohesion. The darkness largely hid the strength of their rearguards and made the French wary of engaging them. On the French right, Thielemann's corps had not been seriously engaged and their withdrawal was conducted in good order. Pajol's *aide de camp* had a brush with the Prussians with some of Exelman's dragoons:

> Despite all . . . the battle of Ligny . . . had no great results . . . The enemy, it is true, suffered heavy losses, but he conducted his retreat in good order.
>
> It was in the evening, looking unsuccessfully for Marshal Grouchy, that I encountered one of our regiments of dragoons. This, commanded by Colonel Labille [actually Labiffe commanded the 17th Dragoons of Berton's brigade, Chastel's division], was moving to the position he had been ordered to occupy. We fell on a brigade of Prussian infantry which was retreating slowly and from which we suffered from some fire. The shadows of night luckily hid us in such a way that we did not suffer badly from this fire.[5]

Grouchy's troops could follow them up, but had no opportunity to turn the withdrawal into anything more disorganised. Pajol's memoirs report that:

> The battle was won and the Prussian right withdrew to the heights above Sombreffe. As night was now falling, it was difficult to reap the fruits of success and the troops were dropping from exhaustion. However, Hulot's division had opened the road to Point-du-Jour by taking the bridge and mill of Potriaux and Exelmans was able to lead his dragoons against the retreating brigades of Kemphen [10th Brigade] and Luck [11th Brigade] who were trying to join the rest of Thielemann's corps which was concentrating between Sombreffe and Point-du-Jour in what appeared to be a rearguard. The strength of the Prussians at this point and the gathering

darkness prevented the dragoons from pressing them hard and they were forced to stop for the night. It was about 9.30pm, but skirmishing with Thielemann's troops continued for several hours and it was only just before midnight that Grouchy felt the situation was secure enough to go to join Napoleon at Fleurus.[6]

Grouchy's memoirs also show that the Prussians had not lost their fighting spirit:

> They [the Prussians] retired in good enough order to be able to cover their retreat as required by new attacks; the proof is that when I launched General Vallin's light cavalry after them, they were so robustly received that their charge had no result and was almost immediately followed by a general *hourra* in their turn.[7]

Grouchy was therefore particularly wary, knowing that he faced a superior force which was perfectly capable of striking back. His chief-of-staff later wrote:

> On the 16th June, towards 10 o'clock in the evening, the emperor sent one of his officers to Marshal Grouchy to tell him to join him at Fleurus, where the emperor had gone. The marshal replied that he could not leave his troops, that the Prussians had effected their retreat slowly and in good order; that they were now and then receiving more troops that were coming from Saint-Amand, and that when he approached them closely they halted and appeared prepared to attack so that they would not be cut off from their right wing.
> Hoping to prevent them, the marshal had General Vallin charge them with his cavalry and this attack had the desired result, accelerating their retreat.[8]

Maréchal de Camp Vallin commanded the 1st Brigade of General Maurin's division of light cavalry that was a part of IV Corps. Maurin was wounded in the battle and Vallin took command of the division for the rest of the campaign.

The Prussian Retreat
Although the French had been successful at breaking into the Prussian main line, they had not broken it. In the centre, where the main blow fell and where the Prussian counter-attacks had failed to push the French back, the Prussians fell back to the line of the Namur to Nivelles road and those units that were still formed covered the retreat of those that had lost their cohesion.

On the flanks, however, the situation was very different. On the Prussian right lay considerable forces which, although their attacks had failed to outflank the French left, retained their order. The French had been unable to push out of the Saint-Amand villages and Durutte's cautious advance against Wagnelée had caused them no concern. The village of Brye was strongly held by the Prussians and this proved to be a substantial bastion to cover the retreat. On the Prussian left, as we have already seen, Thielemann's III Corps, although losing a lot of men who deserted down the road towards Namur as it became apparent that the battle was lost, also maintained their order and fell back towards Gembloux.

The key decision for the Prussians, after Blücher's fall, was that of Gneisenau to direct the retreat on Tilly and Mallery, thus maintaining the option of cooperating with Wellington. In this respect, the organising of the retreat in this direction was excellent, despite the inevitable confusion of defeat and darkness. They also had the consolation that Bülow's fresh 30,000 men stood not far to their rear. As Grouchy acknowledged in his memoirs:

> At the end of the day of the 16th, the battle of Ligny had been won by us, but the Prussian army was not disorganised and it went to be reinforced by the IV Corps (Bülow, arriving from Liège on Hannut, Gembloux and Sombreffe). A rain storm soon flooded the ground. The centre of the enemy army retired in disorder by Brye, on the *chausée* from Nivelles on the Sombreffe wood. The right and left wings retired in order.[9]

It is certainly true that many Prussian soldiers retreated in disorder, but they were well covered by those units who had maintained their cohesion and the darkness and exhaustion of the French troops were to give them time to rally the next morning. As General Berthezène wrote, 'The enemy abandoned a great number of wounded and several guns to us, but few prisoners were taken. The night hid some of their disorder from us . . .'[10]

The view from Imperial Headquarters was similar. Colonel Petiet stated:

> The battle was won, but the trophies of this glorious day were only twenty guns and a few flags. Both sides had fought stubbornly. The French army should have pursued its success, but night and the fatigues of the day prevented it. We contented ourselves with crossing the valley and seizing the enemy's positions. At 10pm the fire had ceased along the whole line and the army occupied its bivouacs . . . The battlefield was covered in Prussian bodies; their loss was immense. We collected up a great number of wounded, but these were the only prisoners that fell into our hands.[11]

The French Situation at Nightfall

There is no doubt that until the final attack was launched, the advantage in the battle had swung backwards and forwards between the two protagonists. The success of the Guard's attack clearly came as a great relief for those at Imperial Headquarters; Colonel Gourgaud, Napoleon's senior *officier d'ordonnance*, wrote, 'For some time I feared we would lose the battle, so determined had been the Prussian resistance, their superior numbers and their superb position'.[12] General

Guyot, commander of the Guard heavy cavalry was clearly more optimistic, as he wrote, 'The outcome of the battle was never in doubt, but it was only when this village [Ligny] was taken at the point of the bayonet towards 5.30pm that victory was assured'.[13]

In many ways, it had indeed been a victory against the odds and so hard fought that most of the French army was exhausted, despite the fact that the battle had started relatively late. This is borne out by virtually all the eyewitness accounts. Sergeant Mauduit again captured the mood: 'All the troops were exhausted and fell from fatigue and the need of everything; rest, so dearly bought, was a necessity for everyone.'[14]

The French Left Wing
As the fighting ended Vandamme's and Girard's men established themselves in the villages from Saint-Amand on the right to Wagnelée on the left. Lieutenant Lefol wrote:

> The III Corps, the Young Guard and Girard's division bivouacked on the battlefield where they had so gloriously fought non-stop for six hours and our headquarters was established in Saint-Amand's cemetery . . .
>
> Sentries were placed around the village and we were able to rest on the fresh straw that had been spread in the cemetery, preferring those that showed that the dead had been buried there recently in order to use as pillows the small mounds that are always found above these graves.[15]

Vandamme was covered by the light cavalry divisions of Domon and Subervie who had advanced on the traces of the Prussians until the rearguards brought them to a halt.

Vandamme's left was secured by Durutte's division and Jacquinot's three regiments of cavalry. In his report, Durutte wrote:

> The enemy troops that exchanged artillery fire with General Jacquinot having withdrawn, General Durutte, receiving no more bad news from the left, decided to march on Brye.
>
> By the movement of our troops, he presumed that we were victorious at Saint-Amand. His skirmishers clashed with Prussian light troops who were still at Wagnelée; he took this village as the day ended and being convinced that the enemy were in full retreat, he sent two battalions into Brye who found only a few Prussian stragglers there.
>
> During the night, General Durutte received the order to return to Villars-Perwin on the 17th . . .[16]

The French Centre
In the centre there was a much greater concentration of French troops. Lobau's VI Corps had been called forward to provide the front line on the plateau of the Bussy mill facing the Prussian rearguards to the left of the Ligny axis, whilst Gérard's exhausted troops lay to their right. The Guard and the 4th Cavalry Corps (Milhaud) were in the second line.

Although the Guard were to lie in the second line, VI Corps would need some time to move up in the dark and take over their position in the front line; a tricky manoeuvre even in daylight. General Teste, one of the VI Corps divisional commanders recalls:

> On the 15th, it [the division] occupied a bivouac in the rear of Charleroi and on the 16th it moved off following the army corps at 5.15pm heading for the Ligny battlefield where it arrived towards 9pm in the midst of great obscurity, close to Imperial Headquarters. A lively fusillade could be heard to our right.[17]

In the meantime, the Guard had to provide their own security; first Major Duuring: 'We bivouacked in squares in this position during the night without fires. We heard an attack after midnight; we took up arms, but it did not reach us.'[18] Mauduit gives us a bit more detail:

> Two ranks of each face of the squares stayed awake, arms grounded, whilst the third rank rested or descended into the village to look for some bundles of straw in order to protect us from the rain which had started to fall, for the sky also came to help the big battalions of the enemy and to add its temperamental bad weather to the fatalities which already haunted us.[19]

Christiani, commander of the 2nd Foot Grenadier Regiment of the Imperial Guard, recalls spending the night on the Brye plateau, to the north of Ligny in the area called Bosquet-Mahaux.

The move forward of VI Corps did not go without incident. The corps moved forward to the high ground beyond the village of Ligny where the Guard were waiting for them; Mauduit picks up the story in which he was personally involved:

> From time to time the moon, which appeared between the clouds, changed the atmosphere; we started to disperse to fall into a sweet sleep, when suddenly, towards midnight, we are galvanised by cries of 'To arms! To arms!' Random shots are fired and soon there is a rolling fire without knowing either why or against whom; there is a general alert![20]

After a quick reconnaissance it was learnt that it was a friendly-fire incident; the 75th *de ligne* of Teste's division moving forward to take over the vedettes ran into the 11th *de ligne* (Simmer's division of VI Corps). General Penne, trying to sort out the mess, was wounded in the instep by a bayonet that was lying on the ground! He stopped the firing, but Mauduit says 'This clash also caused the death of several grenadiers, amongst others that of an old sergeant of our battalion named Bucher, who at that moment was fifty paces from our square.'[21]

A regimental history of one of the IV Corps units also recalls the alarm caused by the night move of VI Corps:

> IV Corps bivouacked on the position conquered beyond Ligny. The 76th formed in square in three ranks; two ranks awake on each face whilst the third rested or cooked their rations. Towards midnight, a false alert caused an alarm. It was a division of VI Corps that our sentries had taken for an enemy column. When the error was recognised, calm was re-established and the rest of the night passed quietly.[22]

The French Right Wing
On the French right, Grouchy had followed up the retreating Prussian III Corps until the latter had turned and established a rearguard at the important crossroads at Point-du-Jour. Pajol reported that Hulot's division spent the night at the Potriaux mill, Pavé and Tongrinne and both his and Exelmans' cavalry only bivouacked at midnight before Point-du-Jour, which the Prussians still occupied, and around the Tongrinne château.[23]

Pajol's *aide de camp*, Biot, gives us more detail:

> The 4th and 5th Hussars rejoined us; but Subervie's division [that had been detached to the left wing] did not return, so that, including the 1st Hussars, only three regiments remained in the hands of General Pajol.
>
> At nightfall, Grouchy sent the order to General Pajol to bivouac in place. We had been in the saddle from daybreak; men and horses were 'on their teeth'. There was no hope of finding forage, the land only offered heather and the few crops had been so trampled that it had become a sort of manure.
>
> General Pajol took it on his own responsibility for each regiment to send him a service squadron so that all the rest could be sent into the closest villages for the night to recover.[24]

Teste's division was detached from VI Corps to support Grouchy on the right. He described the move forward:

> General Monthion, carrying orders from headquarters, halted us and directed us to the points where the musket fire had become livelier. I formed my troops in columns by section and, at the moment General Bernard came

to replace Count Monthion, this new guide knew the ground better, having criss-crossed it throughout the 16th, was more sure of our direction.

This movement was made as quickly as possible in a march across ground cut with ditches. We encountered men of various corps who were lost. We rallied them to the left of our column. Our arrival released Morin's [Maurin's] cavalry division and their divisional artillery that was threatened by a night alert of the enemy. This was the cause: in their retreat that they were forced into having lost the battle of Ligny, the Prussians had abandoned ten artillery pieces in a valley which they tried to recover during the night. To our right rear we had General Exelmans' cavalry. I occupied an important position, close to a wood situated beyond the main road which joined that from Namur to Sombreffe and which covered the right wing of the cavalry.

We remained in this position throughout the night, keeping a close watch on all the accessible points. Our artillery was placed in a good position to the left.[25]

Night

Despite their exhaustion, the night was not an easy one. For many, it was passed in the middle of the battlefield, surrounded by the dead and dying of both sides. As Captain Gerbet described it, 'the night was passed in blood!'[26] Others had similar experiences, but also put their minds to finding something to eat:

> During this night, our sleep was often disturbed, sometimes by the groans of the wounded that were being treated around us, sometimes by patrols, but above all by an unusual cause that excited the whole camp. Close to our bivouac was a small hut that we had not noticed and which held a pig, whose presence was betrayed by a snorting that the sentry, who was close by, heard. This soldier, having informed his comrades of his post, these immediately arrived, broke down the door of the hut and without bothering to kill the poor animal first, in order to share it out later, they dispatched it alive, each of them only bothering to choose the part of it that suited them best. The cries of the victim, heard a long way off, occasioned a veritable alert. The head of this dead pig was the share of our headquarters and the soldiers took the rest, which was for them a supplement to their rations for the day, which they had already received thanks to the energy our good commissary, M. Chuffart, had displayed the day before. Whilst we fought in Saint-Amand, finding on his searches and marches, several cows which were killed during the night and served to comfort our soldiers.[27]

But night was to bring some better fare than a pig's head for General Lefol's headquarters, as his nephew explains:

Returning from having taken different orders, I met the commander of the III Corps in the middle of a group of officers who were congratulating themselves on the results of the day. Vandamme was happy, joking and seeing the future as bright; he seemed to judge the campaign already won. When he saw me, he told me to accompany him back to his bivouac and there, he gave me a gift for my general that was very precious in such circumstances; it was a bottle of good wine and a cooked duck. Never was a present more gratefully received by my uncle.[28]

The Emperor

As the fighting died down, Grouchy's memoirs claim that the emperor left the battlefield without sending out any orders, merely sending a message to Grouchy to join him, and retired to Fleurus (a league to the south-west of Ligny). Receiving the message, Grouchy had replied that he could not leave his troops as the enemy had retired in good order and seemed disposed to return to the attack. When he finally reached Fleurus about 11pm, he was astonished to find that instead of receiving orders, he was only told that he would have to wait until the next day to receive the emperor's instructions. Given that Grouchy's troops had been only lightly engaged during the battle, they would certainly have been in a state to put pressure on the Prussian withdrawal and, at the very least, been able to establish the direction in which they were moving.

Interestingly, an officer from Imperial Headquarters, Captain Coignet, claims that orders were sent out:

> The Emperor retired at a very late hour from the battlefield, and returned to the village near the windmill. Thence he sent out officers in every direction. Count Monthion dictated the despatches by order of the *major-général* and the officers on duty started out at once. We were all on duty that night; no one got any rest.[29]

However, this seems to fly in the face of most other evidence and perhaps Coignet, an ardent and unapologetic Bonapartist, was writing to protect his emperor's reputation on this occasion.

Arriving at Imperial Headquarters that had been set up in the Château de la Paix on the eastern edge of Fleurus, Napoleon had the following letter sent to his brother Joseph in Paris.

> Ahead of Fleurus, or in rear of Ligny, at 8.30pm, the 16th.
> To Prince Joseph. Carried by the courier Bécotte.
> The Emperor has won a complete victory over the united forces of the Prussian and English armies under command of Lord Wellington and Marshal Blücher. At this moment the army is deploying from the village of

Ligny ahead of Fleurus to pursue the enemy. I hurry to announce this happy news to Your Imperial Highness.[30]

Throughout his accounts, Grouchy often refers to Napoleon's health, suggesting that the emperor was suffering greatly from haemorrhoids and implying that on this occasion, this is why he was not prepared to meet Grouchy. Once again backing up his superior's story, Grouchy's chief of staff wrote 'You then moved to join the emperor, who was said to be sick and sleeping and that you would not be able to see him'.[31] However, we have been told that Napoleon went straight to bed on returning from the battlefield and it more likely that the emperor's staff were simply ensuring he got some much-needed rest.

Sometime during the night, a despatch from Ney arrived at Imperial Headquarters; it appears that it was the first information they had received on the action at Quatre Bras.

Frasnes, 16 June, 10pm.

Marshal, I have attacked the English position at Quatre Bras with the greatest vigour; but an error of Count d'Erlon's deprived me of a fine victory, for at the very moment when the 5th and 9th Divisons of General Reille's corps had overthrown everything in front of them, I Corps marched off the St Amand to support His Majesty's left; but the really fatal thing was that this corps, having then counter-marched to rejoin my wing, gave no useful assistance on either field.

Prince Jérôme's division fought with great valour; His Royal Highness has been slightly wounded.

Actually there have been engaged here only three infantry divisions, a brigade of cuirassiers and General Piré's cavalry. The Count of Valmy delivered a fine charge. All have done their duty except I Corps.

The enemy has lost heavily; we have captured some guns and a colour. We have lost only about 2,000 killed and 4,000 wounded. I have called for reports from Generals Reille and d'Erlon and will forward them to Your Excellency.

Maréchal Prince de la Moskowa, Ney[32]

From the time given, this report was clearly written immediately after the battle had finished and his blistering criticism of d'Erlon's corps and, by inference, d'Erlon himself, probably accurately reflects Ney's frustration and anger. However, crucially, it did not give the emperor any of the critical information he needed to help him decide on his next move. The despatch gives no indication on the size of Wellington's force, what the situation was at the end of the day, where Ney's forces were concentrated, what he was doing or what he planned to do first thing next morning. At a crucial time after the incomplete victory over the Prussians,

Napoleon was in dire need of useful information on which to make his plans; Ney had provided him with nothing.

Both Gérard and Vandamme had fought their corps hard and confirmed their leadership qualities. Having not been promoted prior to the campaign, no doubt they both hoped that they would be rewarded for their efforts of that day. Napoleon wrote in his memoirs that 'I was so satisfied with Count Gérard commanding the IV Corps, that I intended to give him the baton of a marshal of the Empire. I regarded him as one of the hopes of France.'[33]

We must assume that the hectic few days that followed denied Napoleon the opportunity of announcing Gérard's promotion. That he does not mention Vandamme is telling; he clearly felt this general still had things to prove. Vandamme however, was clearly hoping for the same recognition as although the account of the campaign in his published correspondence was not written by him, the sentiment is clear.

> No one in the army was in any doubt that the next day, Napoleon would finally award, on the battlefield of Ligny, the baton of marshal to Vandamme, from which he had been frustrated by the unfortunate affair of Külm, for which many others, but not Napoleon, had reproached him. But it did not happen and the general had the disappointment of being put under the orders of the most junior marshal, Count de Grouchy.[34]

French Reconnaissances

Before his plans for the following day could be made, as well as some useful information from Quatre Bras, Napoleon needed as much detail as possible on the true state of the Prussian army and what Blücher's intentions were. Given the darkness and strong Prussian rearguards, it was not inconceivable that they would consolidate their forces, join up with Bülow's corps and launch a counter-attack the next morning. Napoleon's deployment of his last fresh forces, Lobau's VI Corps, into the front line, does not suggest that even the emperor thought this was impossible. Night operations were not common during the Napoleonic Wars; indeed, when they were carried out they were so exceptional that they have tended to generate much comment. The last units that advanced were light cavalry; Domon's and Subervie's divisions on the left and Maurin's division on the right were all met by Prussian rearguards and further attempts to advance were given up to the need for rest of both men and horses.

Whilst Napoleon can be criticised for not giving any orders before he retired, it is perfectly feasible that he was expecting reports to start arriving around midnight that would furnish the information he required. This was not unusual; just as the night before, he no doubt planned to sleep for a few hours before the reports started to arrive, would read them, make his plans, give his orders and then grab a last few hours of sleep before the operations of the day began. Corps and divisional commanders should not really have needed to be told what to do; but it at least appears evident that on this occasion orders were expected. Grouchy was clearly expecting some and his memoirs claim having not received any, he took the initiative himself:

> In the night of the 16th to 17th, having no orders either from the emperor or the *major-général*, Grouchy thought to send one of his officers to the commanders of the light cavalry to direct them to send reconnaissances in different directions and to obtain news of the enemy. Thus, from 2 to 3am, Exelmans moved to the north on Gembloux, Pajol moved to the east on the Namur road with Teste's division that had been attached to his command.[35]

Colonel de Sénécal, Grouchy's chief of staff, backs Grouchy's claim,[36] but Pajol's aide de camp Biot presents a different perspective:

> Before daybreak the next day, the 17th, General Pajol requested orders from the marshal. One, two, three officers were sent in succession, but there was no news. The general finally decided to send out a reconnaissance in order to search Sombreffe and to push forwards towards the Nivelles to Namur road.[37]

However, General Pajol's memoirs claim the initiative for himself; first of all he describes the information brought to him during the night:

> Many of the Prussian fugitives from the battle fled down the Namur road which offered them an open and easy escape, and which, moreover, Pirch I's corps had travelled down even the morning of the battle and so were only familiar with this route. Between Sombreffe and Bothey, these fugitives, added to those of Thielemann's corps that Grouchy's troops had chased from Tongrinne and along the Fleurus road.
>
> Of the 10,000 Prussians who had fled during the evening of the 16th and the morning of the 17th, at least 6,000 to 7,000 headed towards Namur along the main *chausée*, and were able to rejoin the army the next day. These 10,000 fugitives pillaged the villages, mistreated the local inhabitants and spread the news of the defeat at Ligny and the retreat of the Prussian army towards the Meuse and the Rhine. On the Namur road, their flight lasted a whole night of extraordinary chaos, which was made worse by the vehicles of all sorts that were abandoned or taken with them. The inhabitants of the villages and hamlets situated on this *chausée* were understandably convinced that the whole Prussian army was running to Namur.
>
> The Prussian withdrawal freed up the Namur road for use by the French from 2am. Pajol, having learnt this from his reconnaissance patrols, moved there with his two hussar regiments. *This was conforming with the direction*

> given several hours previously by the emperor and Grouchy [my emphasis]. As for the direction to take, Pajol had no other than to take that to Namur. He was in position a little to the north of Tongrinne and on the extreme right of the army. On leaving his bivouacs, he came onto the *chausée* close to Bothey. His attention was naturally drawn towards Namur, where he had always been indicated, throughout the day of the 16th, as the point of replenishment and rallying for the Prussians, from which he was to cut them. It thus appeared probable that on the morning of the 17th, the enemy would go that way in strength which was his natural line of operations. In any case, Pajol did not have to worry about the direction of Gembloux, since Exelmans' dragoons were at Point-du-Jour, further along the Namur road to the west. With only 800 cavalry, Pajol did not feel he had the strength to search the country in every direction. On the morning of the 17th, the circle of his operations was very restricted because of the small numbers of men at his disposal.[38]

Here, Pajol's memoirs explain, contrary to many accounts, that reconnaissance patrols were sent out during the night and also why he sent them purely down the road towards Namur. These patrols seem to have been primarily for security, as he claims that he did not send them towards Gembloux because Exelmans was covering that direction. However, Exelmans' dragoons were not normally used for routinely collecting information on the enemy as this was the role of light cavalry; over the next few days Exelmans was to complain of his dragoons being used for this service as it wore out his heavy horses.

So, based on the reports of his patrols, Pajol decided to send out a much stronger reconnaissance towards Namur and command it himself. His memoirs continue:

> Before setting off, Pajol sent his *aide de camp* Dumoulin to Grouchy to inform the marshal that the enemy had disappeared and that he was going to look for them. At this moment, no formal order to pursue the enemy had been given, either by Grouchy or the emperor, but, following his intuition, Pajol did what he felt the circumstances demanded of him and the instructions given the day before.
>
> Dumoulin, after seeing Grouchy, quickly returned with the clear order to advance towards Namur. Warned of the disappearance of the enemy, the marshal immediately informed Exelmans to prepare to go there also and to support Pajol with one of his brigades. General Berton received this mission. A little after 3am, Pajol left the area of Tongrinne at the head of the 4th and 5th Hussars and went onto the Namur road close to Bothey. He searched this village, collected up some prisoners and hunted stragglers. The first information that he collected being absolutely insignificant, he marched on Mazy, further down the Namur road.[39]

Maréchal de Camp Berton confirms his mission to support Pajol: 'I commanded a brigade of dragoons of Exelmans' corps. I was sent as the head of column behind the light cavalry to support it in case of need.'[40]

Although Pajol was patrolling towards Namur, and Exelmans covered Gembloux no one appears to have been responsible for patrolling in the direction the Prussians had actually taken: north towards Tilly and Mellery. Unsurprisingly perhaps, Napoleon has been much criticised for overlooking this; but in his own memoirs, Napoleon claimed, 'Lieutenant-General Monthion was given the task, during the night, of pursuing the Prussian left.'[41] This claim is dismissed by most historians as a retrospective attempt to clear his name. It is certainly odd that if a reconnaissance towards Namur required a division of light cavalry supported by a brigade of dragoons, a similar task in a different direction could be conducted by a single man (albeit perhaps accompanied by some sort of cavalry escort).

Chapter 10

Morning, 17 June

One of the first to stir on the morning of the 17th was Lieutenant Lefol, who was despatched on what turned out to be a most unpleasant task:

> At 3am on the 17th, I was woken on Vandamme's orders to go to Ligny, a quarter of a league from us, to return to Saint-Amand our artillery battery which had been detached the previous day to help to destroy the Prussians and thus end this terrible struggle. Arriving at Ligny, I was a witness to a terrible sight, and those who have not travelled over this battlefield like me, could not imagine such horror, still less conceive the emotions to which one is exposed in such a situation. The village which had been on fire the day before still burnt, grilling the wounded which had taken refuge in the houses. Pieces of body completed a scene that had perhaps never been seen in the greatest wars, for here 4,000 dead soldiers were crammed into a very small area. The alleyways that led into Ligny were equally covered so that it was impossible to be accused of exaggeration. I swear that my horse found it difficult to avoid treading on the bodies. It became worse when it was necessary to pass there with the cannons and caissons that I had gone to find, to take them to Saint-Amand. I can still hear the sound produced by the passage of the wheels crushing the skulls of the soldiers, whose brains, mixed with the shreds of flesh, spread hideously on the road; perhaps even, amongst these men stretched on the ground and who we trampled underfoot, would their hearts have still been beating?[1]

As the troops began to rise, many of them expected to be on the move early in pursuit of the beaten Prussian army. Perhaps speaking for many, Captain Gerbet wrote:

> After a little rest and before daybreak, we waited to follow the retreat of the vanquished; but no! The troops found themselves still in their bivouacs and had grown restless due to the hours of gloomy shadows of a night which hid the bodies of those brave men who had lost their lives on this memorable day. The victory stayed there. The troops were astonished.

Confined to their bivouacs, not following the vanquished, leaving them free to continue their retreat; all this was incomprehensible for those who felt there was an opportunity.[2]

Whilst many of the Prussian rearguards had slipped away in the night, according to General Teste, who had been attached to Grouchy's wing from VI Corps the previous evening, the Prussians made one last attempt to recover the guns that had been lost on the Fleurus road towards the end of the battle. Teste wrote in his account of the campaign:

> At 5am on the morning of the 17th, we faced an attack directed against the cavalry of General Exelmans and that of General Pajol. Four companies of our *voltigeurs* seized the villages of Sombreffe and Tongrinne. They contributed to the taking of the ten guns which the Prussians had left in the Sombreffe valley.[3]

Whilst he probably got the number of guns wrong, it hard to believe that this action did not take place and shows that the Prussians had not lost their courage. However, most of the activity of the morning centred around Pajol's advance towards Namur as this had been the only use of initiative during the night. His memoirs record his actions:

> The first information that he collected being absolutely insignificant, he marched on Mazy, further down the Namur road where he arrived at 5am. There, he learnt that throughout the whole night, a column of fugitives had passed through, estimated at 6 to 7,000 men. He set off in pursuit and a little distance from this village he fell on a convoy of artillery escorted by cavalry. After sabring them, he took eight guns and several ammunition wagons. He immediately sent the guns and the news to Grouchy at Sombreffe. Retaking his route he soon arrived in the area of Isnes, where he found on the road and in the fields a considerable number of baggage and ration wagons that had been abandoned by their drivers and escorts who had taken the horses. Pajol had arrived at the junction of the road which, by Saint-Denis and Meux, led to Leuze or to Egliezée, which are situated on the road between Namur and Louvain. It was 9am. Now finding himself ten kilometres from Sombreffe, and without news of the army, he did not think it prudent to advance further; all the more because the 1st Hussars, which had finally rejoined him [at 9am], had seen no French troops on the Namur road since Sombreffe. The 4th Hussars stopped at the junction of the road to Saint-Denis, pushing scouts almost as far as Temploux. The 5th Hussars stopped a little to their rear and the 1st almost at the exit of Mazy.[4]

164 *Grouchy's Waterloo*

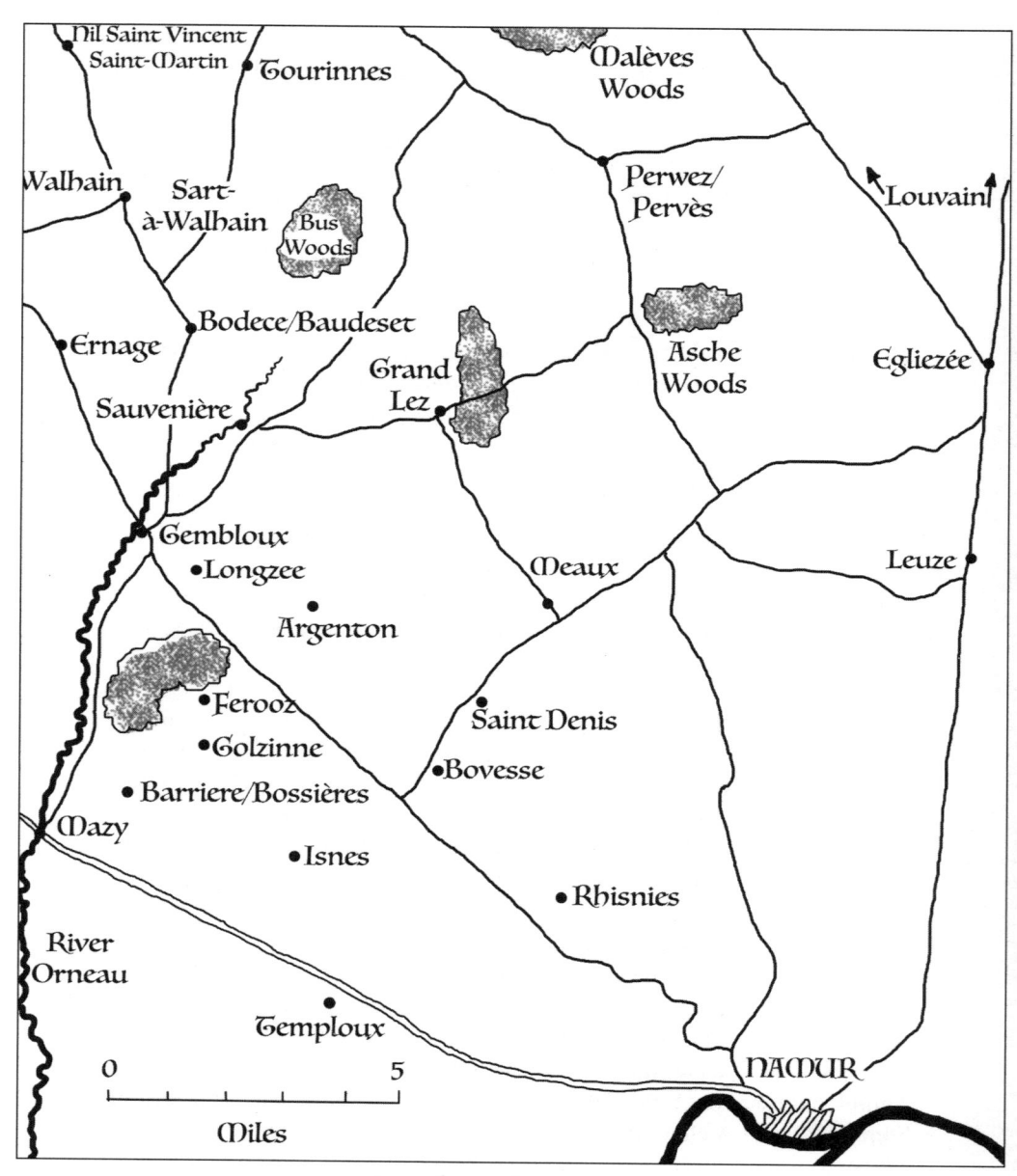

Pajol and Namur

Pajol's actions cannot be criticised and he was quick to send the information he had collected back to Napoleon. Unfortunately, given that the detail contained in Ney's despatch gave little indication of what the situation was around Quatre Bras, and that no one else had moved during the night, we shall see how Pajol's information misled the emperor in deciding what his next move should be.

Pajol's *aide de camp* gives more interesting detail on the actions of Pajol's cavalry:

The general finally decided to send out a reconnaissance in order to search Sombreffe and to push forwards towards the Nivelles to Namur road. It was only by the return of this patrol, it appears, that we learnt the true direction apparently taken by the enemy in his retreat. General Pajol immediately alerted the emperor and also warned him that he was mounting to follow in the tracks of the Prussians. General Ameil with the 5th Hussars formed the advance guard. I received the order to accompany him. We took the road to Namur by which we presumed the enemy had retired. We could see, from afar, parts of the parks that we reached and captured; they consisted of twelve or fourteen guns and several ammunition caissons. We learnt from the reports of the prisoners that the Prussians, after having followed the Namur road for some time were heading off to the left, following a back road which led to Gembloux.

We followed them to the left and, arriving at the ancient wood of the Abbaye d'Argenton, we encountered the Prussian cavalry scouts which covered the wood. From the other side of the wood, the entire enemy park was spread across the plain. It was not wise to pass through the forest without infantry. The 5th Hussars took up a position and I returned to the rear to try and fetch some infantry or artillery. The first was absolutely necessary for us to first assure our passage through the forest and then to protect our retreat in case our charge on the park was not successful. Whilst the artillery would allow us to throw dismay into this mass of cannons and vehicles with its balls and shells. It was, besides, prudent to have a reserve on which we could retire in case we were checked.

Immediately on my arrival, the 4th Hussars, then commanded by the Major (its colonel, Christophe, having been nominated general) came to take position to the left and right of the Namur road, just at the junction of this road with the back road that went to Gembloux. It was all that was available, no one could give me infantry because it had not arrived and I was refused horse artillery, not wanting to risk it, it was said. I thus returned to join General Ameil.

Following the main road, as I passed the bivouac of the 4th Hussars, I noticed they had deployed neither small posts nor vedettes, to either warn them of the general's retreat or the approach of the enemy from some other point, for we would have to be on our guard against this. I approached the major who commanded the regiment to point out that he was unguarded. He replied that he had no orders to do this.

I was reflecting on the means of making him understand the military need to constantly keep guard without having to be ordered when the enemy appeared; observing that the regiment was dismounted and the horses were unbridled. Gazing across the plain, I saw to our right a troop of cavalry arriving very quickly. I pointed them out to the major who sent a patrol towards them.

I continued on my way, but soon, hearing a great commotion behind me, I retraced my steps. I was very surprised to see a troop of cavalry cross the Namur road at great speed, heading across the fields and in groups towards Gembloux. This was two squadrons of Blücher's hussars [it was actually a single squadron of the 7th Uhlans] that had been sent out the day before to operate as partisans on our extreme right. Having become separated, they were attempting to rejoin their own forces. I think it pointless to make the observation that if the 4th Hussars had been properly on guard, the greater part of this cavalry, if not all of it, would have been captured, whereas we actually only took a few prisoners who had been seriously wounded.

The 4th Hussars, who were halfway between the position of the 5th Hussars and the 1st, came to replace them. At this time we were in a position to push ahead as we were supported by a division of dragoons belonging to General Exelmans and then the head of General Teste's infantry division could be seen which had been put under the command of General Pajol.[5]

Biot's account describes how many of the Prussians that had retreated down the Namur road and away from the main army must have been informed of their mistake and, in an effort to rejoin had turned off the Namur road to the north and were attempting to loop round to try and meet up with them in the area of Gembloux. These troops were those who had kept their arms and were keen to rejoin their regiments. Their numbers were augmented by a large number of fugitives who were trying to find the shortest route towards their homes; these were mainly young recruits from areas recently acquired by Prussia, and who therefore had little loyalty to their new masters; but also more experienced soldiers who had once served in the French army and who came from territories that had formally been part of some of the smaller German states. These men made their own contribution in convincing Pajol that a large part of the Prussian army was retreating towards Namur.

Pajol was pleased to have Teste's division attached to him; but this division was not strong. In Pajol's memoirs it is described thus:

At the moment when Pajol wrote this letter to Marshal Grouchy . . . his command was increased by the arrival of Teste's division . . . In the morning, at its departure from Tongrinne, Pajol had only two regiments (the 4th and 5th Hussars); after 9am he had been rejoined by the 1st Hussars, which thus completed Soult's division. But as the emperor had kept Subervie's division and its artillery with him on the road to Brussels, Pajol would have remained at the head of only three regiments of cavalry if Teste's division had not been placed under his orders.

This division, which arrived at Mazy a little before midday, was composed of:

1st Brigade (General Lafitte)
1st and 2nd Battalions of the 8th *léger*, 938 men.
2nd and 4th Battalions of the 40e *de ligne*, 900 men.

2nd Brigade (General Penne)
1st Battalion of the 65th *de ligne*, 503 men.
1st and 2nd Battalions of the 75th *de ligne*, 981 men.

3rd Company of the 8th Regiment of Foot Artillery
3rd Company of the 1st Battalion of the 3rd Engineer Regiment

General Teste's chief of staff was *Adjutant-Commandant* Bernard. His artillery consisted of eight guns.[6]

Pajol now needed to decide what he should do. He could follow the Prussian force that was attempting to rejoin the main Prussian army with his light cavalry, but this would take him further away from his own army and leave him increasingly isolated; or he could retrace his steps, draw closer to Grouchy and having achieved something of value now be available for re-tasking. Whilst he was contemplating his next move, *Maréchal de Camp* Berton, who commanded the dragoon brigade sent to Pajol's support, was also collecting some important information. He wrote:

> I did not pass Barrière, a village on the road close to the Orneau [river] which runs from Gembloux and I learnt there, from the inhabitants, that a large formed body of enemy cavalry had followed this route during the night with vehicles; but that the Prussians had retreated on Wavre and that it had a large force at Gembloux. I was before this town with my brigade at 9am, where, accompanied by informed generals, we saw a body of Prussians that we judged at more than 20,000 men bivouacked in the rear, with a line of vedettes ahead of them on the Orneau. It was evidently a rearguard charged with protecting a retreat of columns which would be in that disorder inevitable after a forced march through the night after a lost battle.[7]

This was significant information and Berton reacted quickly and decisively. We must presume that he informed Pajol of his decision to leave his current task and move on Gembloux. Pajol's memoirs report that:

> Pajol was no longer supported by General Berton's dragoon brigade which had been sent to follow him on the Namur road. Taking position between Bothey and Mazy, Berton had learnt that a considerable body of Prussians were in the area of Gembloux. He had warned General Exelmans who had ordered him to move in that direction. Thus the dragoon brigade left the Namur road and followed the Orneau. Close to Gembloux, Berton was convinced of the presence of Thielemann's and Bülow's corps in position between Baudeset and Sauvenière. He sent a report of this, dated 9am, to Exelmans who soon arrived at Gembloux with the whole of his corps.[8]

Finally, the French had eyes on a significant portion of the retreating Prussian army.

Napoleon's Situation
We should now consider the situation that faced Napoleon when he woke on the morning of the 17th. It was vital after his victory of the day before, incomplete as it might have been, that he exploit the situation to maximum advantage. Many critics and historians, and even some of his own officers and men, condemn him for his lack of activity during this morning. But Napoleon was still in a critical situation; the Prussian army had not been destroyed and whatever his later statements, he must have known that it was not out of the game and would soon be reinforced by Bülow's large corps; he was unsure of its whereabouts and exact condition; he still sat between two armies, which, if co-ordinated, had the combined strength to crush him; he had no information on the situation at Quatre Bras on which he could base an informed decision; his army was tired and out of ammunition; they needed time to rest, clean their weapons, fill their cartridge boxes or caissons and eat. In a nutshell, he lacked the information on which he could formulate an appropriate plan and until that information was available he had an opportunity for his army to get itself back into fighting order both physically and psychologically.

Adjutant Commandant Janin, acting chief of staff of VI Corps, reflected the views of many later critics when he wrote, 'It is said that Napoleon was determined on the preliminary destruction of the Prussian army. It was thus necessary to complete his victory; if he thought he had accomplished this on the 16th, he was blinded by an excess of presumption that I would not expect in him . . .'[9]

But despite some of his declarations, it is hard to believe that such an experienced and successful commander as Napoleon was really so naïve or complacent. For him perhaps, disappointed by the results of the 16th, on the morning of the 17th he could not change the outcome; the need was to make the most of the situation, attempt to keep the morale of his troops high and see what could be done to seize back the initiative. Grouchy's later statement that, 'After midday on the 17th, the battle of the 18th was lost to France',[10] was guided by the knowledge of what followed; there was still much that might happen to swing fortune back to Napoleon's benefit. First, he needed information.

It must have been very frustrating for Napoleon to wake up to find there was no despatch from Marshal Ney on the situation at Quatre Bras. The emperor had been let down by Soult, who had not thought to write to Ney to inform him of the victory at Ligny and to solicit information from him. However, Napoleon was soon joined by General Flahaut, his *aide de camp*, who had spent the previous day with Ney:

> When night came [on the 16th], each side held its ground. I had supper with Marshal Ney and went off afterwards to join the Emperor. I reached Fleurus between 6 and 7 o'clock in the morning [of the 17th]. Marshal Ney had no time to make a report and ordered me to explain to the Emperor what had occurred. My account was far from giving him satisfaction.[11]

Flahaut told Napoleon that Ney had still not been informed of the result of Ligny and consequently remained unsure of what he should do; until he had been given some orders he was inclined to remain on the defensive. This alarmed Napoleon who had presumed that Ney had retaken the offensive to fix Wellington in place so that the emperor could march along the Namur road and attack Wellington's flank whilst he was engaged to his front with Ney. Napoleon immediately had Soult write to Ney to inform him of the victory at Ligny and to press the commander of the left wing to immediately attack the forces in front of him.

Fleurus, 17 June 1815

M. le Maréchal,
General Flahaut, who has just arrived, has informed us that you are still unsure on the results of yesterday. I thought you had been warned of the victory that the emperor has won. The Prussian army has been routed; General Pajol is in pursuit on the roads to Namur and Liège. We have already taken several thousand prisoners and 30 cannon. Our troops were well led: a charge of six battalions of the Guard, the service squadrons and Delort's cavalry division broke the enemy line, throwing their ranks into disorder and capturing the position.

The emperor is going to the mill at Bry where the main road which goes from Namur to Quatre Bras passes. It is thus possible that the English army will act in front of you; if this is the case, the emperor will march directly against it by the main road to Quatre Bras, whilst you attack it from the front with your divisions which, currently, should be concentrated, and this army will be destroyed in an instant. Thus, inform His Majesty of the exact location of your divisions, and all that happens to your front.

The emperor is disappointed that you did not concentrate your divisions yesterday; they acted individually and so you suffered casualties.

If the corps of Counts d'Erlon and Reille had been together, not an Englishman of the corps that attacked you would have escaped. If the Count d'Erlon had executed the movement on Saint-Amand that the emperor had ordered, the Prussian army would have been totally destroyed and we would have made perhaps 30,000 prisoners.

The corps of Generals Gérard, Vandamme and the Imperial Guard were always concentrated; one exposes themselves to a reverse when detachments are made.

The emperor hopes and desires that your seven infantry divisions and the cavalry are well concentrated and formed and that together they do not occupy more than a league of ground in order to have them well in hand and available to use in case of need.

The intention of His Majesty is that you take position at Quatre Bras, as soon as the order is given; but if this is not possible, send details immediately and the emperor will move there as I have already told you. If, to the contrary, there is only a rearguard, attack it and take position there.

It is necessary to finish this operation today and to resupply ammunition, rally isolated troops and call in detachments. Give the necessary orders to assure yourself that all the wounded have be tended to and transported to the rear; there are complaints that the ambulances have not done their duty.

The famous partisan Lützow, who has been captured, said that the Prussian army is lost and that Blücher has exposed the Prussian monarch for the second time.

Le Maréchal d'empire, major général, Duc de Dalmatie[12]

Although this letter does not have a time on it, various French writers have estimated that it was written between seven and eight o'clock, after Flahaut had returned to Imperial Headquarters. Heymès says that it arrived with Ney 'towards 9am'.[13]

In the interests of this study, there are three important elements to this letter. Firstly, Napoleon informs Ney that he will march to support him if Wellington attacks him; this would give Napoleon the opportunity to strike a blow against Wellington before the Prussians were in a position to support him. Even a partial success, in light of his failure to destroy the Prussians the day before, would swing the initiative back in his favour. Secondly, it asks for detailed information on the situation on the left wing; Napoleon would then be able to make a more informed decision. Thirdly, it makes clear that time must be put aside to prepare the force for the next action.

Napoleon Moves to the Ligny Battlefield

Once the letter had been despatched to Marshal Ney, Napoleon set off for the battlefield of the previous day. Grouchy recalls, 'At 8 o'clock, Napoleon had Grouchy informed that he was going to ride to visit the Ligny battlefield; he was to follow him there.'[14] In a footnote to this reference, Grouchy explains that because Napoleon was suffering badly from haemorrhoids, he found it difficult to remain mounted and took a carriage as far as Ligny before mounting his horse.

Napoleon clearly planned this as a morale-raising trip after the horrors and casualties of the day before. Lieutenant Lefol saw him at Saint-Amand:

> Towards 10 o'clock, being still laid out half asleep, I noticed the emperor come out from a small road, which was so covered in bodies that he had to stop in order to give time for a passage to be cleared for him through this human butchery. When the route was clear, he continued his way and he went into an alleyway level with the point where I was when, getting up quickly, I ran to him to warn him that he was going down a dead end. He retraced his steps and stopped for a moment to chat to my general who, having seen him, had run up to him to give him details of the battle . . .[15]

The Guard regiments which had spent the night on the high ground above Ligny, now moved back down onto the plain to parade for Napoleon and be prepared for their next move. Their march took them back across the battlefield of the previous day and gave them the opportunity to describe its grisly scenes. Sergeant Mauduit was a witness to these sights:

> It was 6am when we started this sad inspection. Already the sun had risen above the side of Sombreffe and sent its pale rays into the valley of Ligny and Saint-Amand. The white fog of saltpetre had disappeared to be replaced by that which follows a rainy night; but this in its turn soon disappeared because of the sun, like raising a shroud over the ground of this scene of desolation!
>
> In passing through Ligny at the *pas de charge*, we moved along the main road, covered with bodies, which were run over and crushed by the artillery that followed us at the gallop and that made them bounce like rubber. We saw part of this picture, but we turned our heads; it was too hideous . . .
>
> We took the road parallel to the Ligny brook which gave its name to the village. Here, the scene changed at each step; everywhere a multitude of small bivouacs, around which were ranged eight or ten officers, NCOs or soldiers, for on the day after a battle, there is no hierarchy until the drummer beats 'to the colours'. There, the living, like the dead, are equal and often mixed together.
>
> All these figures are still black with powder and distorted by the fatigue

and the emotions of the previous day! Here, soldiers sorted out their uniforms, cleaned their weapons, washed the blood from their bayonets, if it is possible for those new to combat and without hope.

Some local people risked leaving their homes, others returned, and all contemplated with an air of being lost, the disasters we had brought upon them . . . These unfortunates, surprised by this terrible human tide, had generally retreated into their cellars, or huddled into the more remote corners of their homes, and there more than one ball and more than one shell had struck them in the middle of their farms, their fathers, their wives or children . . .

We found ourselves in front of the famous cemetery, where the struggle of the living had been so stubborn, but where peace now reigned amongst the dead.

The artillery fire had made terrible ravages. The bodies were piled one upon another, and all such that death had touched. A French grenadier, surprised by death at the moment he tried to assault a house, still held in his left hand one of the cross bars by which he had hoped to climb. His head remained leaning against the interior edge of the window, due to a shot which had broken his jaw and taken away part of his skull; his empty musket lay at his feet.

Further on we saw a dead *voltigeur* between two branches of a tree which he had climbed in order to make his fire more effective.

The old château of Ligny was the prey of flames, as well as some nearby houses; they still smouldered.

The French and Prussian wounded had taken refuge in the houses that were still intact, as well as the church and the presbytery. All the buildings were full. One could hear complaints and heart-rending cries . . .

Following the paths which led to Saint-Amand, the picture that was presented to us was no less terrible; there again, the cemetery was too small to offer everyone a grave as it needed to give sanctuary to close to 4,000 braves . . .

One of our regiments, the 82nd Line, was almost all there, mixed up with the Prussians, killed in the merciless fighting that had lasted four entire hours.

A great number of officers and all ranks of both armies also lay in the middle of their soldiers and proved how each had done their duty on this glorious day; for the victors as well as the beaten we are happy to admit the bravery was equal on both sides, though victory was ours. During the whole day, now famous, the Prussian army was the equal of the French! It is the best homage that we can pay them!

One can hardly imagine the fury with which they fell on each other; we can do no better than recall what was written in an Austrian military journal in 1819; 'We fought in the roads of the village with blows of our bayonets and musket butts; we fought man to man with all the fury of personal hatred. It seems that each had encountered in his adversary, a mortal enemy and rejoiced to find the moment of vengeance; no one asked for quarter!'

We re-joined our regiment, crossing the slopes on which the masses of the Prussian army and the artillery had been exposed during five hours of fire from our own artillery. A multitude of bodies of men and horse were scattered here and there, horribly mutilated by shells and balls. This scene was different to what we had seen in the valley where almost all the dead had at least maintained a human look; canister, musket balls and bayonets having been the main origin of destruction. Here however, limbs and bodies were separated, heads were detached, entrails torn out, horses disembowelled. Further on, on the plateau, several *toises* from our regiment, entire ranks were laid out on the ground over which the cuirassiers, *grenadiers-à-cheval* and dragoons of the Guard, as well as the *gendarmes d'élite*, had passed over and re-passed perhaps twenty times in their nighttime charges of the day before.[16]

In these modern times it is hard to appreciate the impact that an individual such as Napoleon was able to have on his soldiers, but the awe and reverence is well documented by those who were there. Napoleon often used reviews to gauge the state and moral of his troops, and after the bloodletting of the day before, and whilst awaiting news, this was a good opportunity to do so again. Gourgaud reported:

On the morning of the 17th, His Majesty visited the various corps on the battlefield, was informed of their losses, praised or questioned the regiments according to what they had achieved. Everywhere the enthusiasm was extreme. He had the wounded cared for, French and Prussian, and gave care and *eau de vie* as well as condolences to all those he saw.[17]

As a member of the Guard, Sergeant Mauduit probably saw Napoleon more than many. He too was on parade on this morning:

However, all the guard was under arms and ready to be reviewed by the emperor. The morning had been allocated for the cleaning of arms, whitening of belts; in a word, to repair our appearance and readiness in case of need as if the inspection had been conducted in garrison.

At the entrance of Saint-Amand and for a distance of several *toises*, the bodies were lying so thick that the emperor had to stop for more than a quarter of an hour to give time to open a passage for him through this human butchery.

Everywhere he was saluted by the loudest exclamations. Napoleon was surrounded by a numerous headquarters; his face was serious, although showing satisfaction.[18]

For a real feel for what these reviews were like, especially after a battle, we must turn to Colonel Fantin des Odoards, commander of the 22nd *de ligne*:

> The next day, the 17th, the III Corps, informed that it would have the honour of being passed in review by the emperor, was, at dawn, formed in a line of regiments in mass. Arriving at the left of this line, His Majesty dismounted and went slowly from one unit to the next, stopping to speak to each colonel and to ask him the usual questions. I had not met the emperor since the day he made me a colonel, two years before, and what had passed since that time! Also, when I saw him, my heart beat with more force than was usual in his presence. Advancing to the edge of my column, on the side on which the 70th Regiment was formed, I listened and heard,
>
> 'How many men present?'
>
> 'So many Sire.'
>
> 'Your regiment did not hold yesterday before the Prussian cavalry.'
>
> 'Sire, I have many young soldiers who had never seen the enemy and who were intimidated; but the disorder was soon repaired.'
>
> 'Yes, but without the 22nd who were to your right and who did their duty, what would you have done? Goodbye Colonel Maury [Maury was actually killed at Ligny and was succeeded in command by Colonel Uny!], repair this fault.'
>
> And the poor colonel, red with embarrassment, did not know what to say.
>
> Leaving the 70th, the emperor looked serious. He started smiling as he approached me with small steps, his hands behind his back, and when I had saluted him with my sword, I found him friendly. After having looked at me with his eagle eye;
>
> 'I know you, you used to be in my guard?'
>
> 'Yes Sire, I had the honour to be part of it and I owe you all my ranks.'
>
> 'Good. How many men present?'
>
> '1,830 Sire.'
>
> 'How many did you lose yesterday?'
>
> '220.'
>
> 'I saw your bearing before the enemy from the mill; you bravely repulsed his charges. It is good, we will meet again. The Prussians have abandoned many muskets on the battlefield; what have you done with them?'
>
> 'Sire, we have made them into hams [broken off the stocks] in the usual way.'

'You have done wrong, great wrong. I gave the order for them to be carefully gathered up to arm our National Guard in the interior, and the artillery has been ordered to pay the soldiers who have collected them three francs for each one.'

'Sire, this order has not been sent to me.'

Then turning to the gilded troop that followed him,

'Did you hear this? Such an important order is still not known; remedy this as quickly as possible. Goodbye Colonel, I am content with you and your regiment.'

This said, the emperor passed to another regiment to my right and little by little he disappeared. I did not see him again after this short appearance and god knows if those words of kindness and hope that he said to me will ever be realised: 'We will meet again!'[19]

For those not involved in the review, the first duty was obvious: 'At daybreak on the 17th, the corps commander ordered that the 3rd Division should be rallied in the rear and to the right of the line. The morning was employed in cleaning weapons which were almost useless.'[20]

Whilst these reviews were being conducted there can be no doubt that Imperial Headquarters were frantically trying to collect the information that Napoleon required. The arrival of the captured Prussian guns at Imperial Headquarters and the reports of Pajol had convinced the emperor that the main Prussian army was heading for Namur, from where it could follow its line of communications back towards Prussia. No information to challenge this assumption had yet been received, although we have identified the failure of the French to patrol to the north; the very direction in which the majority of the Prussian army was heading. Now Napoleon needed information on the situation at Quatre Bras before he could give his orders for the next move.

Whilst awaiting this information, the emperor apparently spent his time discussing the political situation in Paris; derided by many as a waste of time and a failure by Napoleon to grasp the full implications of the situation the French found themselves in, this criticism seems hardly fair, suggesting that Napoleon, one of history's great captains, was amateurish, complacent and over-confident.

Grouchy
We should now return to Marshal Grouchy; but it is important to remind the reader that his many writings were written to justify his own actions during this campaign and with the considerable benefit of hindsight. This is not to say what he writes is necessarily inaccurate, just that he had a considerable axe to grind. His account of the morning is ripe with his apparent frustration:

At daybreak, Grouchy mounted his horse and moved to the emperor's headquarters where he still slept and was suffering a lot. The *major-général*, despite the pleading of the commander of the right wing, refused to disturb Napoleon's sleep and declared that he would not use his own authority to issue orders. Grouchy waited until eight o'clock in the anti-chamber.

In the morning, a battery of eight guns was brought into the courtyard of the house occupied by the emperor that had been captured by Pajol's cavalry on the Namur road. This incident, whilst appearing unimportant, was not without significance, for it contributed to convincing the emperor that the Prussians, abandoning the English, were retiring on Namur on the Meuse, to rally their reserves.

During the night, sometime before he went to the headquarters, Count Grouchy had received from one of Pajol's *aides de camp*, a verbal report making known that the enemy was retiring by the road to Namur. It was the first news that had been received on the Prussians since the day before. Thus everything seemed to support the erroneous idea that was held at Imperial Headquarters that Blücher was retiring on Namur and Maastricht. It was with this conviction that the Duke of Dalmatia [Soult] wrote to the Minister of War. In his despatch, he says that, 'the Prussians are retiring on Namur and Maastricht and the English on Brussels.[21]

Napoleon Decides on his Next Move
In his memoirs, Grouchy claims that it was only at 1 o'clock that Napoleon finally gave him his orders to pursue the Prussians. It must be remembered that these were actually written by his grandson in 1873–4, long after the time and after the critical writings of Napoleon and Gourgaud had been published. Perhaps the truth lies in Grouchy's first account, written by him personally, relatively soon after the events. In 1818, the marshal wrote:

> Up to half-past noon on the 17th of June the Emperor – who until then had ordered no movement of the army – was waiting a report from Marshal Ney; as soon as he received it, he ordered Marshal Grouchy to take his place at the head of the corps of infantry under Generals Vandamme and Gérard and of the cavalry under Generals Pajol and Exelmans, forming a body of some thirty thousand men, and to follow the Prussian army . . .[22]

It will be noted here that Grouchy clearly points out that Napoleon was waiting for information from Quatre Bras before being in a position to send him off. This early account is the only place he does this; in all later works, he, his son and his grandson, all blame the emperor for not sending him off earlier!

Grouchy's grandson quotes his grandfather extensively in this next important passage:

The visit to the battlefield was long. Only at one o'clock in the afternoon did Napoleon, ready to leave the field, say to Grouchy,

> 'Get off in pursuit of the Prussians, complete their defeat by attacking them wherever you find them and never let them out of your sight. I am going to join with Marshal Ney's forces which I shall take to attack the English if they hold this side of the Soignes Forest. Correspond with me by a paved road.'

This road was that of Namur to Quatre Bras. The emperor indicated it with his hand.

Before executing the order that I had received, I felt it my duty to observe to the emperor that if the Prussians, who had commenced their retreat the day before at about 10pm and had continued it throughout the night, would already have gained fifteen to sixteen hours march on the troops that he had sent in their pursuit; that these, who were spread across the plain, would not be able to organise themselves quickly, not having been warned that they would be required to move that day, they had disassembled their muskets, which would not be of any use until they had been cleaned, and that besides, several corps had not been able to find rations for their soldiers nor forage for their artillery horses in the devastated and partly burned-down villages that were close to their bivouacs; they had been forced to send large detachments considerable distances to try and procure some.

I added that I did not feel I would be in time to hold up Blücher in his retreat, nor strong enough with the 30,000 or 32,000 men that remained under my command, to force him to change the direction of his march, anticipate the result of the dispositions that he may have taken, or to complete the defeat of an army of 90,000 to 100,000 men who, although retiring, were not demoralised nor disorganised, since they had even tried to retake the offensive for some time after their defeat. I even dared, besides, to point out to the Emperor some of the strategic designs that appeared to me to support the idea of not leaving the 'circle of operations' of the army with which he went to fight the English, and I begged him not to detach me as far away as I would be by marching towards Namur and Liège.

Unfortunately, Napoleon, thinking the English were in full retreat on Brussels, and which news he had sent to Prince Joseph in Paris by the *major-général*, was offended that I had dared to give him opinions that were contrary to his own. He severely dismissed my proposals and did it in such terms that I feared he dismissed them in a fit of pique rather than because they were improper. Thus, far from modifying his initial orders, the emperor reinforced them saying, 'Marshal, move towards Namur; for, against all probabilities, it is to the Meuse that the Prussians are retiring; it is in this direction that you will find them and that you are to march.'[23]

Whether Grouchy was brave enough to challenge Napoleon's orders in the way he describes has been questioned by a number of historians, who claim it was presented in this way to absolve Grouchy of the mistakes it points out. However, the essence of the marshal's task and the way in which it was delivered by Napoleon is not under suspicion. Flahaut recollects a rather more succinct order:

> About 10 o'clock we got on our horses, and after riding round the battlefield we came back to the high road. At this point, the Emperor took leave of Marshal Grouchy, using words which I remember as well as if it had been yesterday: 'Now then, Grouchy, follow up those Prussians, give them a touch of cold steel in the hind parts, but be sure to keep in communication with me by your left flank.'[24]

No doubt relieved at having received his orders after a frustratingly long wait, Grouchy quickly departed to try and get his troops assembled and moving.

With the pursuit of the Prussians now taken care of, Napoleon turned his mind back to Ney and Wellington. No doubt hoping that Blücher's beaten army was out of the way, he could march with the guard, Milhaud's 4th Reserve Cavalry Corps and the remains of VI Corps (Teste's division having been sent off with Pajol) towards Quatre Bras, hoping to strike a telling blow against the Anglo-Netherlands army. Having sent Pajol's light cavalry corps with Grouchy, the emperor took with him Domon's light cavalry division, detached from Vandamme's III Corps, and Subervie's division of 1st Cavalry Corps. No doubt that when combined with Ney's wing, Napoleon felt these forces, many of them relatively fresh, should be strong enough to beat Wellington. He had Soult write to Ney as follows:

> In front of Ligny, 17 June, midday
> *Monsieur le Maréchal*, the emperor is going to take position in front of Marbais with an infantry corps and the Imperial Guard. His Majesty directs me to inform you that his intention is that you are to attack the enemy at Quatre Bras, chase them from their position, and that the corps which is at Marbais will second your operations. His Majesty will move to Marbais, and awaits your reports with impatience.
> *Le Maréchal d'empire, major général, Duc de Dalmatie*[25]

With Grouchy sent off in pursuit of the Prussians and Napoleon marching to join Ney against Wellington, the stage was now set for the next significant act of the campaign.

Chapter 11

Afternoon, 17 June

Grouchy's accounts of Napoleon giving him his orders and his reactions to them suggest that he did not relish the mission he had been given. Some historians interpret this as Grouchy showing his unsuitability for independent command, suggesting that Vandamme or Gérard would have enthusiastically embraced the opportunity to show what they could do and to enhance their chances of earning the baton. Whilst this might be true, it might also be another example of Grouchy writing with the benefit of hindsight. His concerns are articulated in his writings: the Prussians had had at least fourteen hours start on him, it was not clear at the time he received the order which direction they had taken and, accepting that they were still in some order and would soon have been reinforced by the 30,000 fresh troops of Bülow, he would be considerably outnumbered. An aggressive opponent like Blücher might well turn on him once it was clear how weak he was.

The strength of Grouchy's pursuing wing has been routinely estimated at between 32,000 and 35,000 men. But this does not fully take into account the heavy casualties that the French had suffered at Ligny and it certainly did not number much more than 27,000 when it set off. Although it had been reinforced by Teste's division from VI Corps, this was a weak division, consisting of only seven battalions for a total of about 2,700 men. Girard's division, which had fought with Vandamme's corps, had suffered so heavily at Ligny that it was left behind to cover the rear and make arrangements for the care of the wounded.

Having felt that he had made his disquiet known to Napoleon when he was given his mission, Grouchy now started to get things moving. His *aide de camp* wrote:

> Immediately after the emperor gave you his last orders, you sent one of your *officiers d'ordonnance* to General Vandamme at Saint-Amand, to have him take up arms with the III Corps and to move to an isolated house called Point-du-Jour on the Namur road where you were also going, and where you would give him further orders.[1]

Pont-du-Jour marked the junction of the roads to Namur and Gembloux from Quatre Bras. Wanting to hasten the move of IV Corps, he personally went to Ligny where Gérard had his headquarters. Grouchy's plan was for both Vandamme and Gérard's corps to use the same road to Gembloux, even though two different roads were available, and for some extraordinary reason, he decided that Vandamme should lead the march. With Vandamme at Saint-Amand and Gérard at Ligny, Vandamme was further from that town than Gérard who would have to wait for all Vandamme's troops and artillery to pass his position before he could start his own march.

Arriving at Gérard's headquarters, Grouchy's memoirs recall this awkward time:

> Seeing that IV Corps was not ready to execute a move that Grouchy considered as being of the utmost importance, he remained there for two hours in order to motivate by his presence the taking up of arms by the divisions of IV Corps. It achieved nothing. Vandamme, although further away from the Namur road than Gérard, since having fought the previous day on the extreme left at villages of Saint-Amand and bivouacked there, Vandamme was already near Pont-du-Jour at 3pm, whilst the IV Corps had not appeared.
>
> Tired of the singular obstinacy of one of his generals, Marshal Grouchy, discussing the circumstance with General Le Sénécal, his chief-of-staff, left to join Vandamme.[2]

Grouchy's *aide de camp* Bella gives some more emphasis to Grouchy's frustration.

> I was not with you when you went to General Gérard's headquarters at Ligny to give him the order to start his march immediately and to go to Point du Jour on the Namur to Brussels road; but you told me that this order appeared to much annoy him and that he had so little respect for your authority in directing that he should not lose an instant in setting off, and that instead of giving orders to his men to bring his horses, he gave them orders in your presence to prepare his dinner. You left him indignant and surprised that he did not seem to sense how important it was to make up for the loss of time of the morning of the 17th, that the emperor had been forced to pass in useless promenades on the Ligny battlefield waiting, having not received any reports from Marshal Ney, he could not settle on a plan for his next operations before having heard from him.[3]

But of course Gérard could not 'start his march immediately' because he had to wait for the whole of Vandamme's corps to reach him and then pass. It seems quite reasonable that having given the order to his corps to prepare to march, that Gérard should have his lunch before moving off; he must have had at least two hours, and probably three, before he could get his corps on the move. In his many writings, Grouchy makes no attempt to explain why he chose to move Vandamme before Gérard. To show that Gérard gave timely orders, General Hulot wrote in his report:

> Towards 1pm, the divisions received the order to immediately follow the III Corps on the road to Gembloux. It was about 3 o'clock when they had cleared the road and the IV Corps was able to march. The 3rd Division was always on the tail of the III Corps which marched with all its artillery, its train and equipages.[4]

To make matters worse, about 2pm heavy rain started to fall that lasted throughout the rest of the day and turned the roads into quagmires. General Berthezène reported in his *Souvenirs* that:

> This same day, the 17th, the army started its movements on Quatre Bras and Gembloux. The weather was terrible; the rain fell in torrents and continued throughout the day and part of the night.[5]

There is no conclusive evidence as to when Exelmans' dragoons started their march to Gembloux or who ordered it, but it was to be news from this general that finally got Grouchy's pursuit back on track. We have already heard how Berton's brigade, originally tasked with supporting Pajol's reconnaissance towards Namur, had learnt of a Prussian concentration at Gembloux and without orders had turned and marched in that direction. Either by luck or good judgement it seems the rest of Exelmans' cavalry were already on their way there. Things were now about to change quickly. It was 3.30pm when Grouchy received the following report from General Pajol,

> Before Mazy, 17 June 1815, midday
>
> Sir,
> I had the honour to send you at 3am this morning, my *aide de camp* Dumoulin, to inform you that the enemy, having evacuated his position at 2.15am; I followed him. Since then, I inform you that having charged the rear of his column, I have captured, in front of this village, eight guns and an immense quantity of vehicles, baggage, fodder, etc, of which the horses had been removed.
> The enemy continues his retreat on Saint-Denis and Leuse, to reach the road from Namur to Louvain, and having been warned that a lot of artillery and munitions have left this first town to retire by the same route, I intend to march with Teste's division, which His Majesty sent to me, to attempt to

Afternoon 17th June

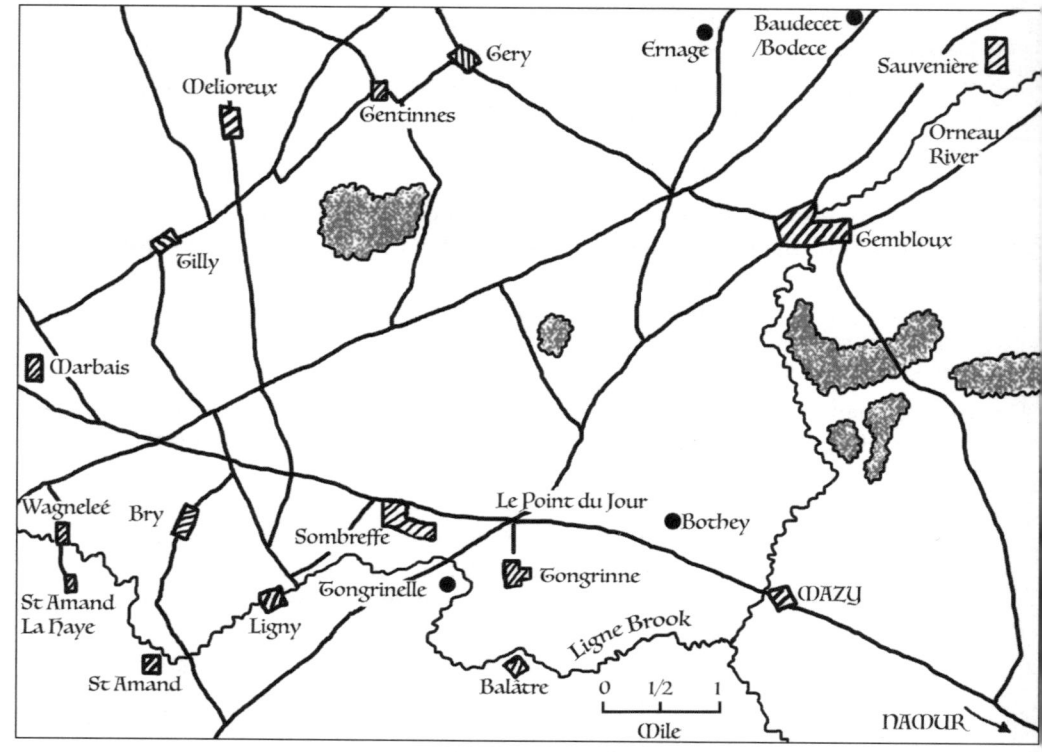

arrive at Leuse this evening, to cut the road from Namur to Louvain and to capture everything that is retreating that way. I request, therefore, that you are good enough to send me your orders by this route.

I am sending Subervie's division its artillery back. I would also request that this division rejoins me, for I have hardly seen it.

Lt Gen Count Pajol[6]

The information contained in this letter had been collected by Pajol's scouts in Temploux and the surrounding villages, and also from the statements made by the prisoners taken by the 4th Hussars from the two enemy squadrons which, arriving from Dinant, were trying to join Thielemann's corps (described by Biot in the previous chapter). In his memoirs Pajol's mistakes were admitted:

In indicating this fact, Pajol should have removed all illusions of the subject of a retreat on Namur. He came closer to the truth in indicating that Louvain was a more certain direction, where the artillery and munitions were going. He made, it is true, another error, in the sense that he spoke of an enemy column, whilst he was only pursuing on the road to Saint-Denis fugitives and convoys, as he had already done on the road to Namur . . .[7]

Very shortly after receiving Pajol's report, Grouchy also received a letter from General Exelmans that was carried by one of Grouchy's own *aides de camp*, Captain Bella. This letter contained important information:

17 June 1815

Monsieur,
I have the honour to inform you of the movement that I have made on Gembloux this morning, following the enemy who has massed there.

I have observed them until now and I have not seen them move. The army is on the left of the Orneau; on the right of this river it has only a single battalion in front of Basse-Bodece. Immediately that it moves off, I will follow it.

I have the honour etc etc
Lt Gen Exelmans

PS. I have informed Your Excellency this morning that my men are exhausted. This tiredness is due to the service that the dragoons were obliged to conduct last night, and one is not able to demand that they do this as well as light cavalry, for they hear almost nothing and they wear out their horses very quickly. This makes me feel that there is a necessity of attaching a few squadrons of light cavalry to a corps of dragoons. I request Your Excellency give some thought to this proposal.[8]

What Exelmans had actually found was Thielemann's III Corps that had retreated through the night and established itself at Gembloux. As it was not pursued by the French, Thielemann was able to give it a rest beyond that town. Even when Exelmans' first dragoons appeared, without infantry they were unable to trouble the resting Prussians.

Captain Bella wrote, 'Myself, having been sent on a mission close to General Exelmans, I only rejoined you at Sombreffe.'[9] This suggests that it was Bella that had carried the order to Exelmans to march on Gembloux. Grouchy now knew that the Prussian main force had not retreated on Namur and that a large body of them was concentrated just beyond Gembloux. His two infantry corps could now be sent in that direction.

Finally, and to ease all remaining doubts as to what he should do next, Grouchy received at about the same time, a letter dictated by Napoleon and written down by General Bertrand, the *Grand-Maréchal du Palais*:

Ligny, 17 June 1815, towards 3 o'clock.

Move to Gembloux with General Pajol's cavalry corps, the light cavalry [division] of the IV Corps [General Maurin's 6th Cavalry Division, which it will be remembered was now commanded by Vallin], General Exelmans' cavalry corps and General Teste's division; the latter of these requires your special attention as it is detached from its own corps [Lobau's VI Corps]; and the III and IV Infantry Corps. You are to reconnoitre in the direction of Namur and Maastrict, and you should pursue the enemy, scout his march and inform me of his intentions. I am moving my headquarters to Quatre-Chemins [Quatre Bras], where the English remained this morning. Our communications should thus be direct by the paved road from Namur. If the enemy has evacuated Namur, write to the General Commandant of the Second Military Division at Charlemont for him to occupy Namur with several battalions of National Guard and several batteries of guns which he is to form up at Charlemont. He is to give the command to a *maréchal de camp*.

It is important to understand what Blücher and Wellington want to do and if they propose to unite their armies to cover Brussels and Liège, risking the outcome of a battle. In any case, keep your two infantry corps constantly within a league of each other, having several lines of retreat. Place detachments of cavalry in between us to be able to communicate with headquarters.

Dictated by the Emperor in the absence of the *major-général*,

Grand-Maréchal Bertrand[10]

This translation comes from Grouchy's memoirs and is noteworthy for the time it is recorded as being written. Napoleon must have known that a strong Prussian force was at Gembloux otherwise he would not have sent Grouchy there. However, most histories have this order written at Ligny, not long after Grouchy had left Napoleon. At 1pm, Napoleon was at Marbais and at 3.30pm, the time Grouchy has this letter written, he was at Quatre Bras; if he was already there when this letter was dictated, there is no doubt he would have said so. It is quite possible that Grouchy changed the time to make his march on Gemboux appear somewhat quicker than it actually was. Although we do not know for sure when the letter was actually written, it seems it must have been around midday as this is supported by Captain Bella who wrote,'This movement on Gembloux was conducted before the emperor endorsed it *when he wrote to you a little time after you had left him* [my emphasis] to march on this small town. This letter was in the hand of General Bertrand to whom he had dictated it.'[11] There are other points of interest: Grouchy is no longer ordered to attack the Prussians wherever he finds them; whilst he was still to conduct a reconnaissance towards Namur, the net is to be spread wider, reflecting a doubt that the Prussians had retreated towards Namur; but most importantly, Grouchy is to 'understand what Blücher and Wellington want to do and if they propose to unite their armies to cover Brussels and Liège, risking the outcome of a battle'. Napoleon finishes by accepting that Grouchy may face being attacked and should keep his force concentrated.

Having left Gérard in anger, Grouchy joined Vandamme near Point du Jour, and directed the III Corps on Gembloux in line with the emperor's letter. This march took place between 3pm and 7pm and he personally went ahead to Gembloux with his headquarters in order to collect what information the locals could provide him with. Meanwhile, Vandamme's corps pushed a league beyond the town, but it was forced to stop and bivouac by the darkness and by the storm. Grouchy was also constrained to stop III Corps since he had been ordered to keep his two corps within a league of each other. He therefore needed Gérard to close up; because of the need to wait for Vandamme's corps to pass, the bad weather and the terrible state of the roads, IV Corps did not reach Gembloux until 11pm. Thus Grouchy's troops had managed only three leagues since midday. The frustrations of many senior officers can be picked up in General Berthezène's memoirs:

> Leaving the battlefield of Ligny towards midday on the 17th, Grouchy's small army went to Gembloux and bivouacked there. The weather had been very poor; the rain fell in torrents and degraded the tracks, which held up our march and made it more tiresome. No one knew which way the enemy had gone for, on the evening of the 16th, their traces had been lost. The darkness had favoured his retreat and the direction he had sent his equipages, which he had sent to Namur, had contributed considerably to throw uncertainty into the spirit of Marshal Grouchy.[12]

Needless to say, Captain Gerbet also had something to say on this:

> Those [Prussians] who had left Ligny after the battle the day before at 10pm therefore had more than a fourteen-hour lead on us. There was reason to think that these fourteen hours would be well employed by the enemy. He rejoined Bülow's corps without a problem, who was 20,000 men strong [actually 30,000!], and who had not been able to arrive to take part in the battle of Ligny. With these reinforcements, Blücher's army found itself more formidable than the day before when he offered battle; from then the vanquished could defy the victor.
>
> Our army corps (that of Vandamme) arrived at Gembloux at 7pm on the same day. A violent storm broke at this moment and we took position in front of this town in a torrential rain which did not cease until 3am. Short of shelter, we suffered much.[13]

The march had been an arduous one, well summed up by Lieutenant Lefol:

> The whole day had been dark and rainy; towards evening the rain fell in torrents, so much that as they marched our infantrymen had water up to mid-leg; the artillery advanced with difficulty and the horses pulled themselves along painfully across the soaked ground.[14]

Exelmans' dragoons had started to follow Thielemann's retreating corps beyond Gembloux, but had not gone far before the weather, exhaustion (especially of their horses) and night stopped them. Bonnemains' brigade that were in the lead reached Sart-à-Walhain, Tourinnes and Nile St. Vincent; the 15th Dragoons were sent to Perwez. At the latter place he encountered some Prussian scouts with whom his dragoons exchanged a few carbine shots and who then made off in the direction of Wavre. However, Bonnemains was informed by the local population that Bülow had joined Blücher and that the whole Prussian army was in position at Wavre. Bonnemains took up a position at Ernage as night began to fall, from where he sent his report to General Exelmans.

Hardly twelve kilometres were covered in this day; everyone was exhausted, and the dragoons and their horses were worn out by the duties they had carried out throughout the whole night and by the battle the day before. In the evening of the 17th, the 5th Dragoons established themselves at Baudeset.

Maréchal de Camp Berton (Chastel's division) summed up the contribution of Exelmans' corps during this afternoon in his examination of the campaign:

> Teste's infantry division had been sent to support General Pajol on the Namur road. It first took position on the heights of Mazy and then followed the light cavalry's march as far as Saint-Denis. This division found itself on the left flank of the Prussians that were at Gembloux, who were quietly conducting their retreat between two and three o'clock by Sart-à-Walhain and Tourinnes in the direction of Wavre, scouting the woods of Bus and Maleves.
>
> General Chastel's dragoon division passed through Gembloux an hour after Bülow's departure [it was actually Thielemann]. It received the order to stop at the windmill a short league beyond the village, where it remained until nightfall. The eight regiments of dragoons were cantoned in the villages and farms ahead of, and to the right of, Gembloux, with the exception of the 1st Brigade of Chastel's division, commanded by *Maréchal de Camp* Bonnemains, that had been sent to Walhain towards the end of the day. This general made known, by double reports, the Prussian march on Wavre. The 15th Dragoons, commanded by Colonel Chaillot, was sent at the same time to Perwez-le-Marché. This officer, who understood war well, also learnt positively from prisoners, that the Prussian columns and the

dispersed men were directed on Wavre, and he immediately reported this.

III and IV Corps remained at Gembloux; Teste's division, with Pajol's cavalry, returned from St-Denis by Bossières to establish themselves at Mazy; Maurin's [now Vallin's] division remained close to Gembloux, on the right bank of the Orneau. The headquarters remained in this town . . .

There was no difficulty in the right wing moving to and establishing itself at Walhain on the 17th, as a cavalry brigade [Bonnemains] had already done this . . .[15]

The last of Gérard's troops to arrive at Gembloux must have been exhausted and miserable. General Hulot reported:

> Half an hour before arriving at Gembloux, an officer from the headquarters came to inform me that the corps commander having decided on where the 3rd Division was to go, he had been ordered to indicate it to me. It was posted to the right of the orchards of the houses that were found a quarter of a league in the rear of the town. I moved beyond a valley, to the right of Gembloux, a battalion of the 9th *léger*, to scout this flank. Everyone belonging to the division arrived at this position during the day and the advance posts were placed out before nightfall.[16]

Pajol

We should now return to General Pajol. Having written to Grouchy at midday, he was finally aware that he was not pursuing the Prussian main body towards Namur, but a park of considerable size and a crowd of fugitives from the battle. Pajol's memoirs take up the story of his afternoon:

> Towards 1pm, having received no instructions to either continue or to suspend the movement he had informed Grouchy of, he started off on the road to Saint-Denis with the 4th and 5th Hussars and all his infantry. He provisionally left the 1st Hussars on the Namur road, between Mazy and Temploux, in order to cover his rear and to assure his communications with Sombreffe.
>
> The hussars occupied Saint-Denis about 2pm. Teste's division, which had, from its position in the rear of Mazy, fourteen kilometres to march, only arrived there at about 3.30pm. Whilst waiting, Pajol had collected information from the inhabitants and even pushed as far as Meaux. He knew then that the previous evening, Bülow's corps, about 30,000 strong, that had come from Hannut, had moved to the north of the Asche woods and Grand-Lez, to go to bivouac close to Gembloux, where it appeared it still was, for his vedettes guarded the hills at Sauvenière and along the Orneau. There was also, it was said, a great movement of artillery and convoys on

Perwez-le-Marché, which were no longer moving on Louvain, between Namur and Egliezée; either that all the materiel was beyond this last location or that fugitives had got a long way towards Liège or Louvain.

In this situation, Pajol thought it necessary to await Teste's arrival, whose march had been a little held up by the violent storm which, accompanied by a violent rain, burst towards 3.30pm at Saint-Denis as well as on the roads to Gembloux and Brussels. He had the wood of Meaux searched and sent patrols off in the direction of Leuze. His riders reported nothing new and he found himself rather embarrassed when towards 4 o'clock, Teste's division arrived. To go to Leuze was to travel further from Sombreffe and to lay himself open to only finding a few stragglers and lost carriages; to move towards Gembloux or Sauvenière could be to encounter forces many times his own strength without knowing if this would be in accordance with Grouchy's own movements or wishes. If Pajol had known of Exelmans' corps presence beyond Gembloux, facing the Prussians, he would not have hesitated to make a demonstration on Sauvenière, since at 4pm he had achieved nothing as Thielemann's corps, who had been in Baudeset, had completely evacuated it at 3 o'clock. It seems Grouchy did not hurry to send orders to Pajol as he was content to be reassured that his rear towards Namur was secured by Pajol's presence. However, that is not to excuse Grouchy for not sending Pajol any word of his intentions or the emperor's plans. In the evening of the 17th Maurin's [now Vallin's] cavalry division of Gérard's corps, was left at Bothey to keep observation on the Namur road. By 6pm, Pajol could have taken position close to Grand-Lez, just a short distance from Exelmans' right flank.[17]

Pajol was clearly frustrated that a lack of orders had resulted in him being much further away from Gembloux than he could have been. His memoirs continue:

While he was at Saint-Denis, and in complete ignorance of the whereabouts of Marshal Grouchy, Pajol felt he had no option but to return to Mazy, where he thought he would be closer to his commander. He recalled his troops to this point passing through Golzinne and Bossière. At nightfall, Teste's division, the 4th and 5th Hussars bivouacked at Mazy. The 1st Hussars, coming from Temploux, established themselves level with Isnes, on the Namur road. The I Cavalry Corps had covered nearly 40 kilometres during this day; Teste's division in particular must have wondered what the point of it all was![18]

Teste certainly must have wondered and no doubt his troops grumbled as only soldiers can. Having marched all morning to catch up with Pajol's light cavalry, he arrived at the moment when Pajol had realised his error; he was ordered to turn around and return up the road he had just marched down! With apparent indifference he wrote:

> Having received the order to march in concert with General Pajol's cavalry, I headed for Mazy (on the main road to Namur), whilst the cavalry moved on Saint-Denis. But the enemy having been seen in very superior strength on our left flank, at Gembloux, which General Bülow occupied with 25 or 30,000 men, we made a retrograde march by Beauvaine. In the evening, we retook position at Mazy, three battalions in front of this village, two battalions and the artillery behind it.[19]

The Prussian Retreat to Wavre
During the night after the battle of Ligny the Prussian staff had gone to considerable efforts to rally the Prussian army at Tilly and Mellery. Unfortunately, Tilly was not marked on many maps and many soldiers had already passed these places. Consequently, Gneisenau changed the rally point to Wavre. Thielemann, due to the French occupation of the main road from Namur to Quatre Bras, was unable to reach these places. He therefore made his way in good order to Gembloux where he had eventually been found by Exelmans' dragoons. He marched north during the afternoon of the 17th where he was able to meet up with Bülow's corps and then move to Wavre. Despite the poor weather and the exhaustion of their own troops after the battle, the whole Prussian army was concentrated around Wavre in the evening of the 17th. In fact, Blücher, tired and bruised as he was, arrived in Wavre at 6am that morning, although he spent the rest of the day in bed whilst his staff re-established control over the army.

Chapter 12

The Night of 17/18 June

The Left Wing
Having heard of the Prussian defeat at Ligny, Wellington left Quatre Bras and marched his army back to a position at Mont Saint Jean. Ney's inactivity on the morning of the 17th and Napoleon's late arrival gave the Anglo-Dutch army the chance for a relatively unhindered withdrawal back to this position. Only the cavalry rearguard had a rather more exciting time and were pushed hard by French cavalry, followed up by Napoleon himself. The torrential rain slowed everything down and as it grew dark, a soaked Napoleon sat on his horse at La Belle Alliance contemplating the line of glowing bivouac fires behind the ridge in front of him. It was clear that a sizeable force stood just out of sight and the number suggested that they may be preparing to stand and face him. A reassured emperor rode back to the small farm of Le Caillou where Imperial Headquarters had been established. It seemed that the next day he would have the opportunity to destroy Wellington's mongrel army. Napoleon had covered twenty kilometres from leaving Ligny; at Gembloux, Grouchy's wing had managed just twelve.

Gembloux
As the crow flies, Mont Saint Jean lies about twenty-two kilometres away from Gembloux where Grouchy's right wing was also experiencing a miserable time. Many of his troops had arrived late and were to find little shelter; Lieutenant Lefol recalled, 'Never had soldiers passed a more terrible night.'[1] As in many other towns and villages they had passed through, the locals seemed genuinely pleased to see them. However, their warm welcome does not seem to have been reciprocated by the wet and hungry French soldiers as Colonel Fantin des Odoards informs us:

> We bivouacked in front of Gembloux, whose population welcomed us to the sound of all its bells and to cries of '*Vive l'empereur*!' which, incidentally, did not prevent our pilferers from committing a thousand disorders there.[2]

Although the small town offered shelter from the rain, most of the troops were forced to remain out in the surrounding countryside; Lieutenant Lefol records, 'Our division however, had to bivouac around the town, without shelter or food.'[3]

But efforts were being made to provide rations for the troops, as Captain Putigny recalled:

> Our 33rd Regiment was used to escort a very important ration and ammunition convoy destined for Marshal Grouchy's army corps. The teams went slowly in the rain and we arrived covered in mud in the night, at the village of Gembloux. On the marshal's orders the bread was distributed immediately to the soldiers.[4]

As we shall see, despite the fatiguing march and the depressing rain, at least the soldiers were to be well fed here; for not only was Putigny's bread available, but the Prussians had also left supplies behind.

Napoleon had chosen Gembloux as the point for Grouchy to march to because not only did the intelligence he had received identify a large Prussian force there, but also because it was a strategically important location. It was well placed from which to march in a number of directions; south towards Namur, north-east towards Liège, which was on the Prussian lines of communication, or north-west towards Wavre and Brussels. Whatever the Prussians chose to do, Grouchy would be able to respond quickly. If Blücher chose to head for Liège, that is away from Wellington, then Grouchy could have remained at Gembloux, able to march in any direction if the Prussian commander turned south to threaten Napoleon's own lines of communication or north to attempt to join Wellington, but also well placed to march and join Napoleon either in Brussels or somewhere on the route to this city.

Before he could send out his orders for the next day, Grouchy needed reliable intelligence on the moves of the Prussians. The most important question that needed answering was whether they were they withdrawing down their lines of communications towards Liège, in which case they had abandoned Wellington, or north in order to maintain their communications with their ally, with the aim of co-ordinating their movements with him or even joining their forces to face Napoleon. To find out their intentions was his specific mission, as Napoleon had written to Grouchy, 'It is important to understand what Blücher and Wellington want to do and if they propose to unite their armies to cover Brussels and Liège, risking the outcome of a battle . . .'

Much information was collected by questioning the inhabitants of Gembloux, no doubt helped by the number of Belgians that still served in the French army. One of Grouchy's *aides de camp*, *Chef d'Escadron* Lafontaine, was Belgian and it is clear that he was employed specifically to collect such information. Locals were also sent off to surrounding villages to bring back on information on recent Prussian activity in the area.

As Exelmans had led the advance to and beyond Gembloux, Grouchy was clearly anxious to receive any information his dragoons had collected. With Pajol's light cavalry still far behind, Exelmans' cavalry had become the eyes and ears of Grouchy's wing, a role for which they were not trained and one they were not entirely comfortable with. On arrival at Gembloux, Grouchy immediately wrote to Exelmans whose men had spread out in a screen from east round to the north-west of the town:

Gembloux, 17 June, 7pm.
My dear general, I have arrived here with the corps of Vandamme and Gérard. Give me your news in all haste so that I can plan our movements after I receive your report, and information on the enemy, who is retiring on various routes and is taking, I am assured, the route to Pervès-le-Marche and Leuse this evening. He is pursued in this direction by General Pajol, who hopes to arrive at Leuse this evening.

Tomorrow, it is necessary that we hound him closely; I will thus get Vandamme on the march very early in the morning and I will link up with you.

Your troubles will be over, since I command the right wing of the army and have as much infantry as I need.

Reply promptly and give me all the details possible so that I can send them on to His Majesty who was going to attack Wellington at Quatre-Chemins [Quatre Bras] if he was still in position there.

This morning Pajol captured eight guns and a great amount of baggage and prisoners.

Agréez etc etc

Marshal Grouchy[5]

Before receiving a response from Exelmans, the marshal received the following letter from *Maréchal de Camp* Bonnemains, a brigade commander in Chastel's division. It was addressed to Grouchy as Bonnemains did not know the location of his divisional commander:

Ernage, 17 June 1815, 10.15pm.
My General,
Until this evening the enemy occupied the village of Tourinnes. He had there, according to the locals, much infantry and some cavalry which was protecting the march of a convoy. I observed them until it got dark and have fallen back on Baudecet, where I have left a regiment with the intention of staying there with a brigade, but I found the 5th Dragoons [who were from Strolz's division] already established there. I then determined to come here and await your orders.

A local man that I sent from Sart-à-Walhain to Tourinnes, assures me that the enemy was leaving the latter last place at 8.15pm.[6]

The location of Tourinnes-lez-Ourdons certainly suggested that the Prussians were retreating north, towards Wavre and Brussels, rather than north-east towards Liège. Other information began to arrive from his other formations and this also included some useful details:

Gembloux, 17 June 1815

M. le maréchal,
I have the honour to inform Your Excellency, that Generals Thielemann and Borstall are part of the army that opposes us. They arrived here this morning about 6am and left towards 10am.

They admitted to my hosts that yesterday the Prussian army had suffered 20,000 casualties. They asked how far it was to Wavre, Pervès and Hannut.

I have the honour . . .

Vandamme[7]

This information is more contradictory as Wavre was north towards Brussels, Pervès was east towards Liège and Hannut was north-east, on the way to Maastricht.

We know from Grouchy's later letter to Napoleon that he collected more information than has been published and was finally able to write the movement orders for his subordinates for the next day. To Gérard he wrote:

Gembloux, 17 June 1815

My dear general, you are to send the order to your cavalry [Vallin's division] which has remained at Bothey, to leave tomorrow at daybreak, to move to Grand-Lez. It is not to pass through Gembloux, which it should pass on its left. The enemy retires on Pervès-le-Marché. Your cavalry is to join us in our movement of tomorrow morning, which will be in this direction, but it is necessary that this cavalry leaves very early tomorrow in order to arrive in time to join us when we are in the area of Grand-Lez.

Do me the honour of sending me an officer of your headquarters who can bring you the movement order for tomorrow; I will send it immediately that I have received Exelmans' report.

Grouchy[8]

First to move the next day would be Vandamme's III Corps and to this general he wrote:

Gembloux, 17 June 1815, evening.

As well as all we have agreed already my dear general, I wish you to start your march tomorrow before 5am and that you move on Sart-à-Walhain. You will be preceded by Exelmans' cavalry and followed by General Gérard's corps.

General Pajol has been ordered to march from Mazy, on the Namur road, to Grand-Lez, where he will receive a new destination according to the one we will take ourselves.

Grouchy[9]

Vandamme's start time is perplexing; having vociferously complained that the Prussians had been given too great a start and that Napoleon's dilatoriness was to blame, it is strange that Grouchy should order Vandamme to start his march at least two hours later than he might. His orders to Gérard prescribed a start time of 8am, with, once again, IV Corps following the same road as Vandamme despite alternatives. Interestingly, Gérard denied he received any movement orders for the 18th! Whilst Grouchy might have considered that his plan for one corps to follow in the footsteps of the other would keep his two infantry corps well in hand as ordered by Napoleon, it was to have damaging consequences. He finishes his letter to Gérard with the advice, 'You would do well to have issued, due to the poor weather, a double ration of *eau-de-vie* to the troops under your command.'[10]

We left General Pajol at Mazy, close to the Ligny battlefield and therefore still six kilometres from Gembloux as the crow flies. Here he received his own orders from Grouchy:

Gembloux, 17 June 1815, 10pm

My dear general, you are to depart from Mazy at daybreak tomorrow morning and to move with your corps and Teste's division, to Grand-Lez, where I will send you new orders.

I am marching on the enemy's tracks who still had 30,000 men here at midday today. I am heading for Sart-à-Walhain, but following information that I have received in the night, along with yours, perhaps I will drive forward to Pervès-le-Marché.

Immediately that you have arrived in Grand-Lez, liaise with me and give me your news.

The emperor ordered me to reconnoitre the road to Namur and to find out what had retired on this town. Push a very strong reconnaissance there that is well commanded, to find out what infantry, cavalry and artillery has passed through there and if it has been evacuated. It should rejoin you at Grand-Lez by the shortest route and without returning to Mazy.

I also desire that you move on Grand-Lez without passing back through Gembloux as you would find it very crowded. Thus, go by the direct route which will be better than the one we followed. Vandamme has ordered Subervie to rejoin you; has he done so?

Send two officers back to me with your news and to acknowledge your receipt of this order.[11]

Having been so close to Namur and no doubt received information about the lack of Prussian presence there, Pajol sensibly decided he was not about to send troops back down the road along which they had so recently ridden.

Having sent out his orders for the next day, Grouchy now wrote a report for the emperor.

> Gembloux, 17 June 1815, 10pm.
>
> Sire,
> I have the honour to inform you that I am occupying Gembloux and that my cavalry is at Sauvenière. The enemy, of about 30,000 men, continues its retreat; we have captured here a park of 400 cattle, magazines and baggage.
> According to several reports it appears that arriving in Sauvenière, the Prussian army divided into two columns: one column has taken the road to Wavre, via Sart-à-Walhain, the other column appears to be going towards Pervès.
> Perhaps one can infer from this that one portion goes to join Wellington, and that the centre, which is Blücher's army, is retiring on Liège and another column, with artillery, having retreated to Namur. General Exelmans has given the order to push ten squadrons on Sart-à-Walhain and three on Pervès this evening.
> After their reports, if the mass of Prussians are retiring on Wavre, I will follow them in this direction to stop them from reaching Brussels and separate them from Wellington.
> If to the contrary my information proves that the principal Prussian force has marched on Pervès, I will go by this town in pursuit of the enemy.
> Generals Thielemann and Borstell are a part of the army that Your Majesty beat yesterday. They were still here this morning at 10am and announced that 20,000 men had been put *hors de combat*. As they left, they requested the distances to Wavre, Pervès and Hannut. Blücher was lightly wounded in the arm on the 16th, but this did not prevent him from continuing in command once it had been bandaged. He did not pass through Gembloux.
> I am etc, etc . . .[12]

To this letter was attached a copy of the various information received from the most senior inhabitants of Gembloux and the surrounding area. We see that late on the night of the 17th, from the information he had received, Grouchy believed that at least part of the Prussian army was marching to join Wellington, but he confidently asserts that in this case 'I will follow them and stop them from reaching Brussels and separate them from Wellington.' Reassuring as this may sound, given the relative positions of the two sides and their current locations, it is difficult to understand just how Grouchy believed he was capable of achieving it; Blücher stood between him and both Brussels and Wellington. Furthermore, other versions of the letter exist, challenging what Grouchy actually wrote in his letter; this is examined in more detail in the last chapter.

Grouchy had two options if he was going to follow the Prussian force towards Wavre: he could either take the main route from Walhain to Wavre which had already been covered by some of the Prussian troops, or he could cross the Dyle at Moustier and march up the left bank of this river. The latter option had the advantage of crossing the Dyle unchallenged and would put his force closer to Napoleon and in a position to intercept any Prussian force marching towards Waterloo, but added considerably to the march. With all the advantages of hindsight, Napoleon's supporters are loud in declaring that this is the option Grouchy should have taken. The first option was to merely follow in the Prussian footsteps, but was attractive to Grouchy as it most closely complied with the orders he had been given by Napoleon.

General Berthezène, astutely but with the benefit of hindsight, wrote, 'It was of the greatest importance to regain the time that was lost. Perhaps we should have made a night march, but we should undoubtedly have approached the enemy from dawn and made it impossible for him to hide his movements . . .'[13]

Napoleon
In his memoirs for the night of the 17th/18th, Napoleon wrote the following:

> At ten o'clock in the evening, I sent an officer to Marshal Grouchy whom I supposed to be at Wavre, in order to let him know that there would be a big battle next day; that the Anglo-Dutch army was in position in front of the forest of Soignes, with its left resting on the village of La Haye; that I ordered him to detach from his camp at Wavre a division of 7,000 men of all arms and sixteen guns, before daylight, to go to Saint-Lambert to join the right of the Grand Army and co-operate with it: that, as soon as he was satisfied that Marshal Blücher had evacuated Wavre, whether to retreat on Brussels or to go in any other direction, he was to march with the bulk of his troops to support the detachment which he had sent to Saint-Lambert.
>
> At eleven o'clock in the evening, an hour after this despatch had been sent off, a report came in from Marshal Grouchy, dated from Gembloux at 5pm. It reported that he was at Gembloux with his army, unaware as to which direction Marshal Blücher had taken, whether he had gone towards Brussels or Liège; that he had accordingly set up two advance guards, one between Gembloux and Wavre, and the other a league from Gembloux in

the direction of Liège. Thus Marshal Blücher had given him the slip and was three leagues from him! Marshal Grouchy had only covered two leagues during the day of the 17th.

A second officer was sent to him at four in the morning to repeat the order which had been sent to him at ten in the evening. An hour later, at five o'clock, a new report came in, dated from Gembloux at 2am; the Marshal reported that he had learnt at 6pm that Blücher had moved with all units on Wavre; that, in view of this, he had wanted to follow him then and there, but that, the troops having already made camp and prepared their meal, he would be starting at daylight, in order to arrive early in front of Wavre, which would come to the same thing, and that the men would be well rested and full of dash.[14]

The dependability of Napoleon's memoirs in respect to the activities of Grouchy has already been questioned in the introduction to this book. His claim to have sent two officers to Grouchy ordering him to send 7,000 men to Saint-Lambert is unsubstantiated by any other dependable evidence and although there is some circumstantial evidence, his claim has been widely discredited and will not be considered further.

Chapter 13

Morning, 18 June

Grouchy could not have got much sleep that night as at 3am he was writing again to the emperor with the latest information that had been gathered:

> Gembloux, 18 June 1815, 3am
>
> Sire,
>
> All my reports and information confirm that the enemy retires on Brussels to concentrate there or to deliver battle having united with Wellington.
>
> General Pajol confirms that Namur has been evacuated.
>
> The I and II Corps of Blücher's army appear to be directed, the first on Corbais and the second on Chaumont. They appear to have left Tourinnes yesterday evening at about 8.30pm and marched throughout the night; happily, the weather has been so bad that they have not got far.
>
> I am departing immediately for Sart-à-Walhain, from where I shall go to Corbais and Wavre. I will have the honour of writing to you from one of these towns.
>
> PS. Conforming to your orders, I wrote to the commander of the 2nd Military Division, at Charlemont, to have Namur occupied by some battalions of the National Guard and some batteries that he is forming at Charlemont. I am leaving twenty-five cavalry here to assure my communications with Your Majesty. The corps of infantry and cavalry that I have with me have only a provision and a half, and that in the event of a major action, it appears to me necessary that Your Majesty would do well to replenish the reserves of ammunition or to let me know the locations where the artillery should go for resupply.[1]

It is interesting that Wavre, which featured heavily in his letter earlier that morning, is not mentioned as a destination for the Prussians, but only as Grouchy's destination. Although Corbais is on the route to Wavre, now only a single Prussian corps appears to be moving there, a force Grouchy should be able face with a confidence that seems to permeate this letter.

This despatch was followed at 3am with another to General Pajol. Grouchy, having fully understood the importance of General Bonnemains's letter sent from Ernage which informed him of a Prussian presence at Tourinnes (a village halfway between Gembloux and Wavre on the left), sent the following order to Pajol:

> Gembloux, 18 June 1815, 3am
> My dear General, you are to leave Grand-Lez on receipt of this order and move to Tourinnes with your cavalry corps and Teste's division, where you will receive new orders.[2]

Grouchy seems to have forgotten that Pajol had only reached Mazy the night before (after all, he had written to him there at 10pm!), which is ten kilometres southwest of Grand-Lez. With the loss of Subervie's division, Pajol was reduced to just 1,100 light cavalry in General Soult's division and Teste's weak infantry division. He had written his own early morning letter to Grouchy from Mazy:

> Mazy, 18th June 1815, 4am.
> I had the honour to report to you yesterday that Namur had been evacuated and that I had pushed my troops into the area of Temploux and Meaux, but learning that a corps of 25 to 30,000 men was concentrated at Gembloux and not being supported, I have felt it necessary to retire to Mazy, which is very unfortunate, for I was already at Grand-Lez where I had gone myself and where I had the honour of seeing you.[3]

Of course, Grouchy had not yet received this letter. However, before leaving Gembloux, the marshal had another letter sent to Pajol, modifying part of his orders:

> Gembloux, 18 June 1815, at first light.
> Some information that does not appear to me as groundless, suggests to me, my dear general, that a large enemy park is at this moment a league and a half from Grand-Lez. Confirm if this is true, and if it is, immediately fall on it with your cavalry and Teste's division. If you are not able to take it because of superior forces escorting this park, I will support you with the troops that I have sent to Sart-à-Walhain, where I am going myself.
> The retreat of Blücher's army appears to me to be on Brussels. Thus, in the case where the information that I give you becomes somewhat lacking in sense, go to Tourinnes as quickly as possible so that we can push ahead to Wavre as promptly as we can.[4]

Grouchy's statement that the Prussian army appeared to be marching on Brussels is interesting; this was his first mention of such a conclusion and he had not included it in his earlier letter to Napoleon. His language suggests it was his own analysis, but if he did believe this, then the obvious route for him to take was directly north to Wavre on the main road to Brussels, rather than north-east towards Sart-à-Walhain!

Ready to leave Gembloux, Grouchy had sent one of his *aides de camp* to Exelmans with the order to provide the advance guard of Vandamme's corps and to move to the north-west; another to Pajol with the orders above; another, Commandant Pont-Bellanger, to find out if Prussians had been seen at the bridge at Moustier (on the Dyle, an equal distance between Gembloux and the forest of Soignes) and his chief of staff to Gérard who occupied the next house to tell him to 'set off without delay and to follow the movement of III Corps'.[5] Grouchy's chief of staff, General Sénécal, gave more detail on Pontbellanger's mission in a letter he wrote to Grouchy in 1830:

> Before daybreak on the 18th, when leaving Gembloux, the marshal sent an officer, his *aide de camp* Pontbellanger, with several men of his escort, to make a reconnaissance to the left and particularly towards the bridge of Moustier, in order to assure himself if the Prussians had crossed there. His report was that the enemy were heading towards Wavre, that none of their troops occupied the bridge nor the banks of the Dyle.[6]

Having concluded his correspondence, Grouchy hastened to the head of Vandamme's column which was already on the march from their bivouacs almost a league beyond Gembloux.

Grouchy appears to have been very active and fully in control during this early morning in Gembloux. Perhaps he would have been more anxious if he had known that as he was beginning his march, Bülow's IV Corps was already starting its own march towards Waterloo and he was to be followed by II and then I Corps with III Corps bringing up the rear. Gembloux was almost twenty kilometres south-east of Wavre from where the bulk of the Prussians were to march and this town was at least an hour's march closer to the battlefield of Waterloo than Gembloux; at this very moment there was almost no possible way that Grouchy could interfere with the Prussian march with any chance of preventing the major part of their army arriving during the battle, even if he wanted to. In fact, Grouchy was thinking only of following the Prussians and his march towards Walhain was actually taking him further from Waterloo!

The heavy rain and the passage of the Prussians the day before had made a mess of the road and Grouchy's memoirs claim that:

> The road was in a terrible state; it was only possible to advance with much pain across ground saturated by the storm of the day before, so that the marshal, seeing how the passage of the first columns had rendered the route

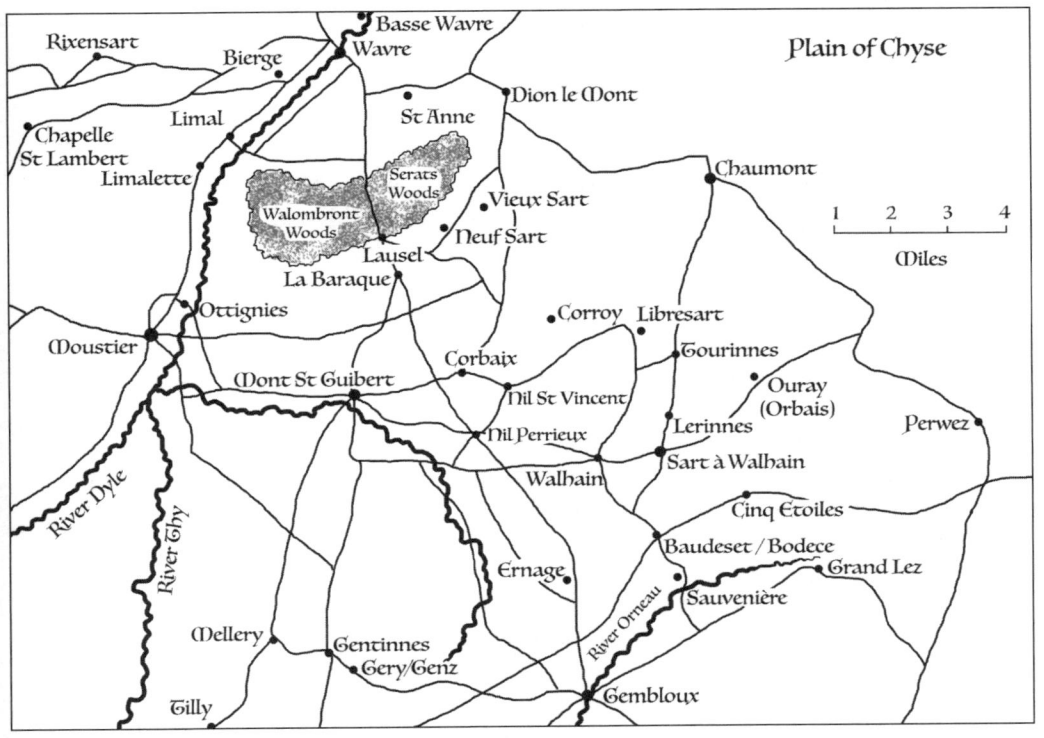

Morning 18th June

even more difficult, had Gérard informed that if there was another way leading from Gembloux to Sart-à-Walhain, to take it so he would not have to follow the abysmal roads left behind by III Corps.[7]

As we have seen, in the absence of Pajol's light cavalry, Exelmans' dragoons became responsible for providing the advance guard. However, their left was extended to the Dyle by Vallin's cavalry division of IV Corps. This was of an unusual organisation, having one brigade of light cavalry and one of dragoons. At 7am, Exelmans had concentrated his regiments at Walhain and then set off along the road towards Wavre. *Maréchal de Camp* Berton's account says they were to scout as far as the Namur to Louvain road.[8] He also reports that 'The scouts of the dragoon corps of the right wing found many [Prussian fugitives] on the slow march of the 18th along the road from Louvain to Namur. They gathered up these detachments; one even having an officer at its head.'[9]

The dragoons reported that even before the long columns of French troops marched on them, 'the tracks were ruined, almost impracticable'.[10] Many others make similar comments; General Berthezène observed:

> On the 18th, the army set off at 7 or 8am. It moved on Wavre via Sart-à-Walhain. Its movement was extremely slow; towards Nil-Saint-Martin, it made a long halt, during which it occupied itself with cutting the hedges and opening the outlets, as if preparing a battlefield.[11]

The latter comment about 'cutting the hedges and opening the outlets' is interesting as this suggests they took measures to facilitate a defence and retreat in case of attack, reflecting Grouchy's concerns that the Prussians might turn on their numerically inferior pursuers.

Given the timings laid down in Grouchy's orders, it is interesting to read the accounts of those who were there and the times they record they set off. III Corps had bivouacked almost a league (four kilometres) north of Gembloux. Lieutenant Lefol wrote of that morning:

> Also, the next day, our soldiers looked as if they had been dug up. Better off than them, the officers of our headquarters lodged in the town, but without being able to take any rest. Thus, for myself, I was sent *en ordonnance* several times during this cruel night.
>
> The movement order was only given towards 10am on the 18th; the day of the battle of Waterloo. We formed the head of Vandamme's column and when we had gone a league beyond Sart-à-Walhain, we waited as long as an hour or two to make our soup as well as I can recall.[12]

Things were not so straightforward for Gérard's corps; despite Grouchy writing that his orders went out during the night, it appears that they were not received until late:

> On the morning of the 18th, the general waited in vain for orders from Marshal Grouchy until 3 o'clock. The troops were ready, waiting to march quickly in pursuit of the Prussians . . . Finally, towards 10 o'clock, after a feverish wait, the orders to march arrived and a league was made in the direction of Wavre.[13]

Gérard's corps also had the difficulty of negotiating their way through Gembloux. *Maréchal de Camp* Hulot wrote in his report:

> Towards 7am on the 18th, I received the corps commander's order which directed all corps troops to start their march at 8am in the same order as the

day before, to move on Sart-à-Walhain following General Vandamme's corps. I immediately had the division take up its arms and set off through the defile of Gembloux whose roads were terrible. Having found the town crowded with troops of all arms who had come to receive rations or were still passing through, it took us more than an hour to arrive at the IV Corps *rendez-vous* a quarter of a league beyond Gembloux. There, all the divisions came together and had to make a long wait whilst the road was cleared.

Immediately that the tail of III Corps had marched off, the corps commander set IV Corps off, directing me to keep close to III Corps, which I did exactly throughout the march.[14]

Once again, Grouchy's decision to use a single route was leading to serious hold-ups. Despite waiting impatiently to move off, it seems that Gérard still had time to hand out some summary punishment to one of his men.

Whilst we were most surprised by the delays that we experienced, the monks of the Gembloux convent came to complain that their community had been pillaged. An officer was sent who seized an NCO of the engineers who, profiting from a hole made by him and the *sapeurs* in the wall of the convent, had gone in and stolen wine and provisions.

The prisoner was brought back and the general, wanting to make an example, ordered that he should be shot. This was carried out without any mercy against the wall of the convent and an order of the day announced that all acts of pillage in Belgium, home of our comrades, would be punished with the utmost severity.[15]

Even before Gérard's corps had set off from Gembloux, at around 9 o'clock, Exelmans found himself in the presence of a Prussian rearguard composed of all arms (at this time the Prussian rearguard included elements of both II and IV Corps as not all corps had yet crossed the Dyle). Although there was some skirmishing as his dragoons scouted the Prussian position, without infantry he would have been unable to push them back and he was forced to draw back and wait for the arrival of Vandamme's corps. III Corps passed through Walhain and continued its march towards Wavre.

Having started his march with Vandamme's leading troops, Grouchy reached the village of Walhain by 11am where he stopped to write to the emperor. Nearly all French accounts speak of Sart-à-Walhain, but as we know exactly which building Grouchy stopped at, we can be sure it was actually the village of Walhain, Sart-à-Walhain being a little under a kilometre to the east. As soon as his letter was finished, he sent it to Imperial Headquarters with one of his *aides de camp*, Major La Fresnaye, 'an officer perfectly capable of giving an account of all I had learnt of the movements of the enemy and to promptly report any orders that might be given to him'.[16]

Sart-à-Walhain, 18 June 1815, 11am

Sire,

I do not lose a minute in sending you the information I have received here; I regard it as certain, and in order that Your Majesty should receive it as promptly as possible, I send it by Major de la Fresnaye, your old page, who is well mounted and a good rider.

I, II and III Corps of Blücher's army are marching in the direction of Brussels. Two of these corps have passed through Sart-à-Walhain or close by on the right; they have marched in three columns, marching more or less level with each other. Their passage has taken six hours without interruption. Those that passed in view of Sart-à-Walhain have been estimated as at least 30,000 men and about fifty to sixty guns.

A corps [Bülow's IV Corps] coming from Liège has joined those that fought at Fleurus (attached is a requisition that proves this). Some of the Prussians that I have in front of me are heading for the plain of Chyse, situated close to the route to Louvain, and at two and a half leagues from this town.

It seems that this is in order to concentrate there in order to turn on their pursuers or to unite with Wellington, which was announced by their officers, who, with their usual haughtiness, pretend that they only left the battlefield on the 16th, in order to affect their union with the English army on Brussels.

This evening, I intend to be concentrated at Wavre, so that I will be between Wellington, whom I presume is retreating before Your Majesty, and the Prussian army [my emphasis].

I need some more instructions on what Your Majesty wants me to do. The country between Wavre and the plain of Chyse is difficult, cut and boggy.

By moving on the road from Wivorde, I will easily arrive at Brussels before all those who will stop at la Chyse, if all the Prussians are going to stop there.

Sire, please send me your orders; I will then receive them before starting my move tomorrow.

The majority of the information that is enclosed in this letter was given me by the owner of the house where I have stopped to write to Your Majesty; this officer served in the French army, is decorated and appears completely devoted to our interests. I include the information with these lines.

First Information
30,000 to 40,000 men have passed through Sart-à-Walhain. The move was made in three columns and lasted from 9am until 3pm. About 60 guns were also seen. The III Corps of Witgenstein [he must mean Bülow's IV Corps] passed through Sart-à-Walhain. We have requisitions from their commissaries. Prince August was with this column. It came from Hannut

and the area around Liège. Their passage was complete, today, the 17th, at 3pm. The back of the column is at Corroy. *Everyone was heading for Wavre* [my emphasis]. The wounded have been sent along the Roman Road to Liège and Maastricht. It is thought that three corps have passed through here, II and III for sure and probably also I [Wrong; it was just III and IV]. I and II Corps took part in the battle of Fleurus. They announced they wished to *give battle close to Brussels* [my emphasis] where they were planning to concentrate. Their artillery had come via Grand-Lez. The best route to Wavre is by Nil-le-Pierreux to the chapel of Corbais, to la Baraque, to Lausel.

Second Information
The wounded are heading for Liège, via Beauwale, Jodoigne and Tirlemont. *Those fit for battle and those that did not take part in the action at Fleurus march on Wavre and some on Tirlemont. The majority are camped on the plain of la Chyse* [my emphasis], close to the road from Namur to Louvain, two and a half leagues from this last town and one and a half leagues from Wavre, on the right, close to Goddechins. This last advice is dependable. It is there that it appears they want to concentrate. They say they want to hold their ground and will only retire to give battle again after the union of the forces of Blücher and Wellington.

Third Information received at Gembloux
The enemy, about 30,000 men, continued their retreat in some disorder. General Exelmans has captured more than 400 cattle. *The enemy is retiring in the direction of Wavre* [my emphasis], and this seems to indicate that *they want to reach the road to Brussels to unite there, if possible, with Wellington* [my emphasis] via Sart-à-Walhain, Tourinnes, etc. They have also passed many men via Hautes-Baudes, following the direction of Sart-à-Walhain. At Sauvenière, they split into two parts; the strongest column headed for Pervès *which perhaps indicates that a portion of the Prussians go to join Wellington* [my emphasis], and the other is heading to join Blücher. All asked for the road to Brussels. Tonight, Exelmans is to detach six squadrons with General Bonnemains to Sart-à-Walhain, three others on Pervès. The Prussians are occupying Sauvenière, Haute et Basse-Baudes, heading for Ouray, going via Grand-Lez. They will follow the Roman Road to head towards Maastricht.[17]

Grouchy summarises his conclusions from this information concisely in the covering letter; the Prussian army is heading for Wavre from where he predicts they will continue to Brussels where they will join Wellington. As the Prussians appear to be concentrating on the la Chyse plain, presumably prior to moving on Brussels, this will allow Grouchy to anticipate that move, occupy Wavre and therefore get between them and Wellington, preventing junction. However, in truth, his interpretation is contradictory as more than once his information says the Prussians are heading for Wavre. Despite this, Grouchy appears to be content that he is achieving his mission and has justified his own march direct to Wavre. He had failed to contemplate a Prussian move from Wavre to Waterloo and thus from this moment he was impotent to prevent the fatal Prussian intervention in that battle.

We now get to one of the most famous incidents of the Waterloo campaign beyond the battle itself and for this reason alone we should examine it in detail. So as not to break up the flow of events up too much, we shall look here purely at what happened and what was said; an objective analysis of what Gérard proposed is considered in detail in the last chapter. Let us start with Gérard's own account:

> It was at Walhain or Sart-à-Walhain, a small village between Gembloux and Wavre, that I joined M. *le comte* de Grouchy, around 11am, a little earlier or later. I found him eating strawberries. Sometime after my arrival, we heard cannon. We immediately went into the garden to better assure ourselves of the direction of the cannonade. The owner of the house, who was French, came with us. He assured us, from his knowledge of the country, that it came from the area of the Soignes forest . . . I offered the opinion that an army corps with some cavalry should manoeuvre towards the emperor's artillery. I do not presume to say that at this moment I calculated the immense results that would have resulted from this manoeuvre if, as events proved, it had been executed. In offering this advice, I was only struck by the idea, for us to simply link up with the troops of the left. M. *le comte* de Grouchy did not share my viewpoint. During the day, I had the occasion to discuss it with many of the generals under my command. We left Walhain and travelled with Marshal de Grouchy for some time. The cannon of the advance guard could be heard distinctly; we each went our own way.[18]

More interesting detail comes from Gérard's *aide de camp* Rumigny, though it is notable how much this varies in detail from other accounts and highlights how even apparent eyewitnesses contradict each other:

> Arriving close to a farm, General Gérard was invited to lunch with Marshal Grouchy. The general, already unhappy with the slowness of our march, went there reluctantly. General Vandamme's corps was approaching Wavre, was in contact with the Prussians and followed them feebly. Concerned that there were senior commanders sitting at table in an isolated farm without any troops to guard them, I left the room and moved into the garden which was surrounded by a wall, with a sort of trellis painted in green at the end. Some distance to the west was a wood. I looked carefully, since the muffled

sound of a cannon firing made me even more attentive. This detonation was followed by several others; I put my ear against the wall to better distinguish the sound. I was alone and I noticed many shots of different calibres. This was not a minor engagement of a rearguard. I re-entered the farm in haste. They were all sitting at table,

'*Monsieur le maréchal*,' I said, 'there is a fierce fight going on to the west.'

'Perhaps it is an advance guard action?'

'I beg *Monsieur le maréchal* to come into the garden to judge for himself.'

I personally led the marshal and General Gérard into the garden, where at first nothing could be heard because of all the other noise. I then put my ear to the ground and distinctly heard a lively cannonade. The marshal was then convinced and he ordered everyone to mount. This done, we set off on the road to Wavre. Leading the march, I heard the start of a lively discussion between Marshal Grouchy and General Gérard. At the moment that we reached General Vandamme's rearguard, our two commanders entered a local's house in which was found an earthenware stove. Everybody was outside, except M. de Pontbelanger, *aide de camp* to Marshal Grouchy and myself. We were both at the entrance door in order to prevent anyone coming in to distract or interrupt them. I was, as I have said, a colonel *aide de camp* to General Gérard, and consequently the most senior of his officers. The general and the marshal had opened a captain's map and the marshal was supporting the map with his right hand, leaning against the stove; the general supported it with his left hand.

The central point of the discussion, which became more and more animated, was the direction in which the army should move.

Gérard wanted to support the emperor, Grouchy, to the contrary, to push the Prussians before him. From where we were, there could be no doubt that the combat was a lively and veritable battle; one could see shells bursting in the air; and more, we could tell by the direction of the fires that we were further to the north than the Prussian left wing and that it could make off without us knowing it. This was as clear as day. But the marshal hesitated, refused, giving reason after reason. Finally, we heard General Gérard say,

'*Monsieur le maréchal*, it is an axiom of war that one should march to the cannon when one hears the cannon.'

'General, you have to execute orders and not interpret them.'

After these words, following a remark that I could not hear, and a few lively words from the marshal, we separated.

Arriving with us, General Gérard was frustrated; he said to us,

'There is nothing to be done; it is awful!'[19]

We must now look at the version of events that appears in Grouchy's memoirs, bearing in mind that these were written by his grandson and are his interpretation of what appears in the marshal's correspondence and other writings:

> Grouchy sent Major La Fresnaye with instructions to ride quickly, since a loud cannonade could be heard to the left. A few minutes later, General Gérard appeared in the room from where Grouchy had written to the emperor. He was followed by several of his generals who, like him, had advanced ahead of their troops. The commander of the IV Corps gave, in a loud fashion that showed little of the respect that is due to a senior officer or of military discipline, the advice that the right wing should move towards the sound of the cannon, in order to effect a junction with the emperor.
>
> Grouchy had no issue with the advice itself, but the way in which it was presented. However, wanting to discuss Gérard's suggestion he replied to him:
>
> That the emperor, in detaching him the day before on the right, had informed him he was to go to attack the English army, if the Duke of Wellington would accept battle; thus he, Grouchy, was not be surprised that there was an engagement taking place to the left.
>
> That if the emperor had wanted him to take part, he would not have sent him to the right at the moment he was moving to Quatre Bras, to the left.
>
> That the cannonade that could be heard appeared to be six or seven leagues from Sart-à-Walhain; and that there was no practicable route to that side, especially for artillery, that would allow them to arrive in time to take part in the action.
>
> That General Baltus, the commander of the artillery of IV Corps, thought it almost impossible to move the materiel that way because of the narrow and muddy lanes.
>
> That finally, the most important consideration of all to take into account, is his orders, which he could not ignore, *formally directed him not to lose the Prussians from view once he had contacted them* [his italics].
>
> That the advance guard were in contact with them, so that he could not execute his demand to move to the left since he would then be letting go of the enemy.
>
> So which general who, in taking account of these considerations and having received such instructions from the emperor as those given to Grouchy, would dare to allege that the place of the marshal was to follow the advice of General Gérard?[20]

Here Grouchy's memoirs claim that General Baltus, commander of the artillery, thought that he would not be able to move his guns along the by-roads that led from Walhain towards Waterloo. However, Grouchy's grandson fails to mention the contribution to the discussion by the commander of Gérard's engineers, General Velazé, who later wrote to his former commander:

> I was in one of the rooms of the château, next to where you were with General Grouchy. Several cannon shots had warned us that the advance guard was engaged with the Prussians, whilst a violent cannonade made us leave quickly. 'That is where the battle is,' we said, seeing smoke on our left. 'Where does the fire come from,' I asked one of my guides who came from the Imperial Guard. 'It is from towards Mont-Saint-Jean,' he replied, 'and in three or four hours we could be where the fighting is.' The proprietor of the château said the same. I saw you immediately engage with General Grouchy in a kiosk raised up in the garden. I approached you, and I remember very well hearing you say loudly that it was necessary to march to the sounds of the cannon; I repeat, it is necessary to march to the cannon. General Grouchy and General Baltus both observed that the tracks were very difficult for artillery. I pointed out that I had three companies of *sapeurs* with which I would sort out any difficulties. You assured him that you would arrive with at least the ready ammunition boxes. It was also noted that the infantry would also suffer much on the back roads because of the rain during the night and the day before. The guide I consulted, who was very excited, claimed that this was not a big problem and I again promised that the *sapeurs* would make many passages.[21]

A number of histories have General Vandamme at this discussion. However, in his published correspondence it says:

> It has been alleged since, that Vandamme had taken part in this discussion and agreed with Gérard. This is impossible, the general was then more than three leagues ahead of the place where Gérard and Grouchy were.[22]

The discussion was cut short by a report from General Exelmans that he was in contact with a Prussian rearguard. In a letter later written to Gérard, Exelmans wrote:

> Whilst my scouts skirmished with the enemy, I sent *Chef d'Escadron* d'Estourmel to Marshal Grouchy to inform him of what was going on and finally, to tell him that the Prussian army had continued its passage through Wavre during the night and the morning in order to approach the English army.[23]

No doubt thankful for the distraction, Grouchy immediately had his headquarters staff mount and moved forward to join his advance guard. It is interesting that

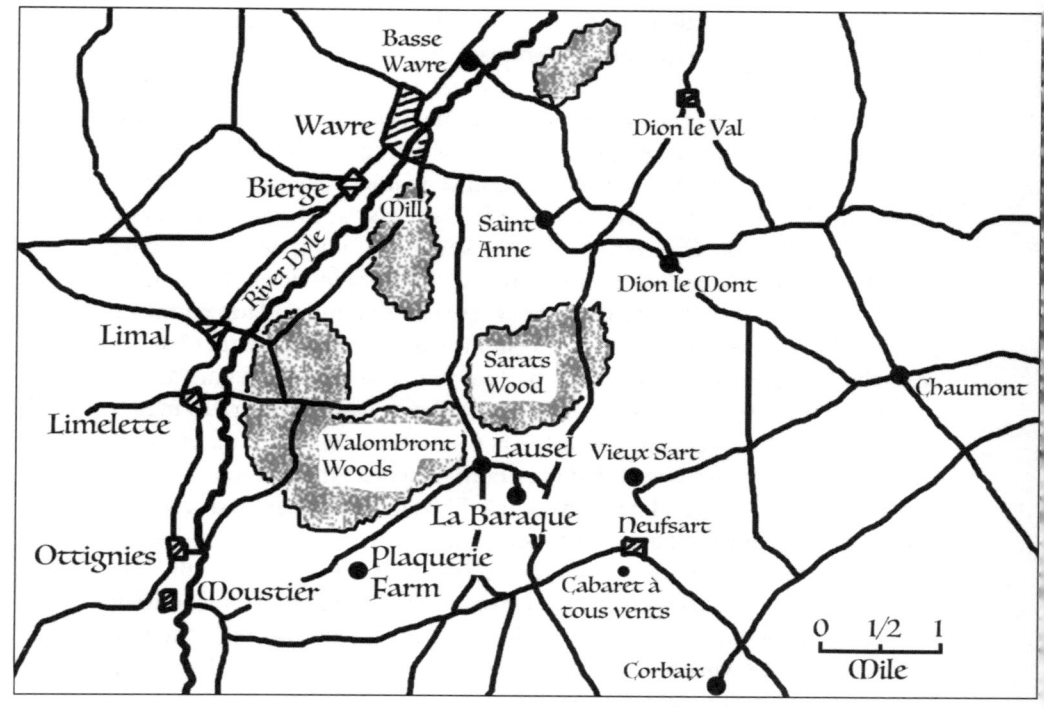

Morning 18th June (2)

Exelmans mentions that the Prussians were moving to join the English; he does not say where he got this information and Grouchy does not mention it. Once again we have to decide if this was another attempt to discredit Grouchy or an example where Grouchy ignored vital information which would have required a reassessment of his plan, the tendency of a weak leader to reject or ignore information which is unpalatable or to avoid having to make difficult decisions.

By this time the whole of III Corps and a single division of IV Corps had passed Walhain. *Maréchal de Camp* Berton reported that they had '. . . encountered a small enemy rearguard at la Baraque, a small village in front of the Serats and Walombront woods. There was a light engagement there, where the enemy offered some light resistance . . .'[24]

In another letter to Gérard, Exelmans describes his position when he encountered the Prussians:

> In your letter of today, you asked me what time my troops set off on the morning of the 18th. It was about 7.30am, but not having light cavalry it

was only towards 9 o'clock that I found the Prussian rearguard on the road to Wavre, level with Moustier and almost at the same time as a convoy escorted by several thousand men near the Cabaret à Tous Vents, which seemed to be heading for Louvain. But I was little distracted in this direction as I concentrated my attention on the Dyle. I formed up my troops, the left at the wooded valley, close to the Plaquerie farm, and the right towards Neufsart.[25]

In fact, what Exelmans did not know was that a body of the Prussian rearguard, which had been centred on Mont Saint-Guibert, had been by-passed by the French march and was scrambling to get back to Wavre before the French arrived there. By this time the battle of Waterloo was well under way and Lieutenant Lefol recalled, '. . . the cannonade of Waterloo was heard with such violence that the earth seemed to shake'.[26]

Grouchy was later to complain that Gérard's corps was too slow in coming forward and later criticised them in several of his accounts. Unsurprisingly, Gérard was quick to challenge him, writing:

As to the slowness so gratuitously attributed to the IV Corps, either on the march of the 17th, or in that of the 18th, it can be seen by the report of General Hulot who marched at the head, that I had several times given him the order to constantly close up to the III Corps, which he did punctually. In the divisions that followed him, only the indispensible distances physically required in a march of a column of 30 to 35,000 men on a single route and above all for the troops that were found on the extreme left. If one had reason to regret the delays, it can only be fairly blamed on who had put such a large body of troops with a numerous artillery, on a single earth track already degraded by the heavy rain of the day before and by the passage of the Prussian columns.[27]

Hulot's report to which Gérard refers describes this march:

The back roads were extremely poor, making the march slow and painful, III Corps obliging us to make frequent halts just as they arrived in a country full of defiles when our column was as long as that preceding us. The head of the 3rd Division arrived at Sart-à-Walhain towards 12.30pm. For close to half an hour we had heard a lively engagement of musketry and artillery to the left.[28]

Whilst the rest of the right wing advanced towards Wavre, Pajol's troops were playing catch-up. After their long diversion down towards Namur, at the end of the 17th they were back at Mazy, close to the Ligny battlefield. They at least understood the need to use all the hours of daylight for their march; Pajol's memoirs tell us:

> At 4.30am on the morning of the 18th, Pajol's troops had begun their march towards Grand-Lez via Bossière, Feeroz and Longsee. The 4th and 5th Hussars marched as the advance guard, Teste's division followed next and the 1st Hussars remained behind on the Namur road as the rearguard. Certain of the evacuation of Namur, of which he had formally assured Grouchy, Pajol did not send the reconnaissance to this town as he had been ordered. It was thus with his entire available force that he moved towards Grand-Lez. His movement, carried out across side roads that were waterlogged and broken by the heavy rain of the day before, was only completed towards 8am . . .
>
> The march of the main body was covered in front by Exelmans' dragoons, who were forced to do the duty normally given to light cavalry. To the left flank was Vallin's division, who had come early from Bothey, and to the right was Pajol's corps which from Grand-Lez had marched to Tourinnes-les-Ourdons.[29]

On his arrival at Grand-Lez, Pajol had found the two letters that Grouchy had written to him in the early hours waiting for him; the first directing him to Tourinnes and the second directing him to try and find and attack a Prussian park near Grand-Lez. To conform with the direction given in the first of these two letters, Pajol immediately sent one of his hussar regiments into the Asche woods to search for the convoy. When all his troops had closed up, Pajol set off for Tourinnes-les-Ourdons. At 9.30am, he was following the route which led there by Cinq-Étoiles and Lorrines. The hussars that had been sent off to Asche and Perwez returned, announcing that they had found nothing and that there were no signs of the Prussian army in that direction. Given the time-lapse between when the order was sent and when it was implemented, the vulnerable Prussian park had had plenty of time to escape. Pajol continued his march towards Tourinnes, which he reached after an arduous march.

Napoleon at Waterloo
Due the poor state of the ground and the fact that all his troops were not yet in their battle positions, Napoleon had been forced to delay the opening of the battle of Waterloo. It was only now, about 10am, that he chose to respond to the reports that Grouchy had written to him from Gembloux the night before and that had arrived at Imperial Headquarters at 11pm and 2am. The fact that Napoleon had sent no orders or information to his lieutenant since midday on the 17th until 10am on the 18th is astonishing and an unforgiveable lapse. Confident that he would be fighting Wellington the next day, the emperor should surely have

informed Grouchy of this the previous night and given him further guidance.

We have already spoken of Napoleon's claim to have ordered Grouchy to send a detachment of 7,000 men to Saint-Lambert and concluded that this was a fabrication. However, what is rather more difficult to refute, is that at 10am he did decide to send orders to Grouchy to march to join him. Colonel Zenowicz, a Pole who had remained in French service after Napoleon's first abdication, published his own account of his activities that day:

> On the 18th June 1815, the day of the battle of Waterloo, I was employed, as a superior officer in Imperial Headquarters, and I was ordered not to leave Napoleon for a moment.
>
> ... he [Napoleon] positioned himself on a small elevation from where he could easily see the various positions of the two armies. After having examined them for some time with his telescope, without changing position, he addressed a few words to the *major-général*; then, as he came down, the emperor signalled me to move close to him; I obeyed. He then made the following speech to me, 'Here is the *comte* d'Erlon, our right,' he said, indicating this general's army corps; then continuing, after making a sweep of his hand towards the right of the line he added, 'Grouchy marches in this direction, go immediately to him, *go by Gembloux* [his emphasis], follow his footsteps; the *major-général* will give you a written order.' I wanted to point out to the emperor that the route he indicated to me was too long, but without giving me the chance he said to me, 'You will surely be taken following the shortest route'; and, then indicating the extreme right flank of the line, he said again, 'You will return this way to rejoin me, when Grouchy moves into line. He must not delay in moving into direct communications with me and in the battle line with us. Go, go.'
>
> Immediately that I received this order, I quickly went to the *major-général*, who at this moment was heading for the farm of Caillou, where the headquarters had passed the night. We arrived at the farm at 10 o'clock; the *major-général* went into his room and had his secretary called. The first thing that is done in beginning to write an order is to put down the date and time; it is easy to see that this hour is not the time the despatch actually departs, but before its departure, for time is required to actually write it. It is also necessary to record it in the *major-général*'s register of orders. All this requires time; in ordinary service, where the hours and minutes have no role to play, this remark is of no importance; but in a particular case, when hours and minutes are important, when the carrier of an order is blamed, he must be allowed to establish the facts as they occurred. I repeat, the time of the order of which I was the carrier was put at 10 o'clock; I then retired to the ante-room. After half an hour of waiting, I rejoined the *major-général*. Still only the date had been written; the *major-général* was looking

at a map and his secretary was cutting a quill. I returned to the ante-room where I found M. Regnault, *ordonnateur-en-chef* of the I Corps, who, knowing that I had been on the move for the last twenty-four hours and had had nothing to eat, sent for some bread and *eau-de-vie* from a wagon. After my meal, I returned again to the *major-général*'s room; he was dictating the order that I was waiting for. I returned once more to the ante-room. After half an hour, I was called for. Marshal Soult repeated to me what the emperor had said as he gave me his written order. I then left.[30]

Zenowicz makes much of the roundabout route that Napoleon sent him, not least because he was later to be much criticised for taking so long to reach Grouchy and wanted to justify the route he took. We will look at the detail of the despatch when we meet Colonel Zenowicz later; when he finally delivers it to Marshal Grouchy. Having delayed so long to respond to Grouchy, and with the hold-up caused by Soult's apparent tardiness in drafting it, the question remained as to whether Grouchy would have sufficient time to execute his new orders.

Chapter 14

Afternoon, 18 June: The Battle of Wavre

We last met Napoleon just before the battle of Waterloo started. However, once all the arrangements were complete, Napoleon took one last look towards the eastern horizon; his memoirs say:

> Before giving it [the signal to open the battle], I wanted to cast a final look over the whole battlefield and perceived in the direction of Saint-Lambert a cloud which looked to me like troops. I said to my chief-of-staff, 'Marshal, what do you see towards Saint-Lambert? I think I can see five to six thousand men there; that is probably a detachment of Grouchy's.'
> All the glasses of the general staff were fixed on this point. The weather was rather misty. Some maintained, as often happens on such occasions, that they were not troops, but trees; others that they were columns in position; some others that they were troops on the march. In this uncertainty, without further deliberations, I sent for Lieutenant General Domon, and ordered him to go with his division of light cavalry and General Subervie's to reconnoitre the right, get in touch with the troops which were arriving at Saint-Lambert, effect a junction with them if they belonged to Marshal Grouchy, hold them if they belonged to the enemy . . .
> A quarter of an hour later, a *chasseur* officer brought in a Prussian Black Hussar who had just been taken prisoner by the despatch riders of a flying column of three hundred *chasseurs*, who were out scouting between Wavre and Planchenoit . . .[1]

From this prisoner Napoleon says he learnt of the approach of the Prussian army. Already in the middle of dictating an order to Soult for Grouchy, this information was added along with directions to march immediately to join them. The exact wording of this letter we shall see later when it is delivered.

This version of Napoleon's is challenged by many modern historians; they claim that Napoleon was not aware of the approaching Prussians until their arrival on the battlefield about 4.30pm and that the despatch he mentions was a fabrication. Whatever the rights and wrongs of this argument, there is enough evidence to convince this author that the letter we shall examine later did exist and therefore when and how Napoleon really learnt of the presence of the Prussians does not directly affect this part of the campaign's narrative.

Back in the east, Grouchy's advance guard of Exelmans' dragoons had encountered the Prussian rearguard in the area of la Baraque, on the high ground south of Wavre. Exelman's dragoons covered the whole of Grouchy's front; Exelmans himself was at Corbais after having detached Berton's brigade to Neuf-Sart, Vincent's to La Plaquerie and having two squadrons at la Baraque.

We know that at about 11.30am, when Grouchy had reached Walhain, that Vandamme's corps had already passed this place and was in or near Nil St Vincent. From Walhain to the tiny hamlet of la Baraque was six kilometres, with another six to Wavre, a total march of about three hours. It was as the two squadrons left la Baraque that Exelmans had found the Prussian rearguard consisting of the 10th Hussars and two battalions of fusiliers commanded by *Oberstleutnant* Ledebur and supported by some troops from the 8th Brigade (von Bose). General Berthezène was apparently the first of Vandamme's divisional commanders to arrive:

> It was only at la Baraque, where we arrived towards 2pm, that we found a rearguard which gave the impression that it wanted to defend itself; but a few musket shots dispersed it . . . We had heard the cannonade and fusillade of Waterloo for a long time and, from la Baraque we could see Prussian columns moving quickly in that direction. It was evident that the emperor was in combat with the English army . . .[2]

Lieutenant Lefol explains how he got caught up in this fighting:

> We followed the marshal, who took the head of his army corps, and I rejoined our division which, at this moment, was engaged with a strong party of Prussians at a place called la Baraque, between Sart-à-Walhain and Wavre.
>
> We did not know which army corps we were engaged with, or what their strength was, when a soldier told us that a man had fallen near us. We immediately went towards the place indicated and we found a young Prussian officer who had been wounded in the thigh. He had become lost in the wheat, which is very tall at this time of the year. General Lefol interrogated him in German to find out the force that was opposed to us and when we had all the necessary information we left this young man without having the time to have him taken to a first aid post; only I remained a little in the rear of our headquarters to throw him my handkerchief which he

Napoleon made many mistakes during the campaign and was quick to blame many of them on Marshals Ney and Grouchy.

Marshal Grouchy was blamed by Napoleon for the loss of Waterloo.

Marshal Soult served as chief-of-staff to the *armée du Nord*. His attachment to Napoleon was questioned by many.

General Vandamme commanded the III Army Corps under Grouchy's command during the pursuit of the Prussians.

General Gérard commanded the IV Army Corps. Like Vandamme, he had a prickly relationship with Grouchy.

General Pajol, commander of the 1st Cavalry Corps under Grouchy's command.

General Exelmans, commander of the 2nd Cavalry Corps under Grouchy.

General d'Erlon commanded the I Army Corps. His appearance on the French flank at Ligny fatally delayed Napoleon's decisive attack.

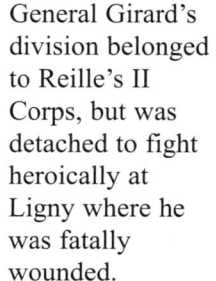

General Girard's division belonged to Reille's II Corps, but was detached to fight heroically at Ligny where he was fatally wounded.

General Letort was a famous commander of the Dragoons of the Imperial Guard and was killed leading them against the Prussians at the combat of Gilly.

General Bourmont was to have commanded the 14th Infantry Division of Gérard's corps, but infamously deserted to the allies during the night of 14/15 June.

General Subervie commanded the 5th Cavalry Division of 1st Cavalry Corps. He fought at Ligny but was detached from Pajol's corps to fight with Napoleon at Waterloo.

General Domon commanded the 3rd Cavalry Division that was part of Gérard's IV Corps. He fought with Gérard at Ligny but, like Subervie, was detached and fought at Waterloo.

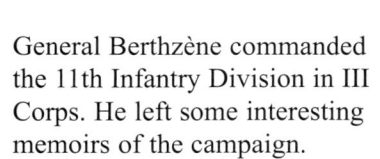

General Habert commanded the 10th Infantry Division in Vandamme's III Corps. His division lost heavily at Ligny and in the attacks on Wavre bridge.

General Berthzène commanded the 11th Infantry Division in III Corps. He left some interesting memoirs of the campaign.

General Vichery commanded the 13th Infantry Division of Gérard's IV Corps. His division led the attack on the village of Ligny and suffered heavy casualties.

Field Marshal Blücher was commander-in-chief of the Prussians during the Waterloo campaign. It was mainly due to his inspirational leadership that they made the decisive intervention at Waterloo.

General von Thielemann commanded the Prussian III Corps. Having made little contribution to the fighting at Ligny, his corps stoutly defended Wavre to allow the rest of the army to intervene at Waterloo.

A modern photo of the Naveau mill. This mill served as Napoleon's command post throughout the battle of Ligny.

The farm d'en Haut today. This farm lay in the village of Ligny on the French side of the Ligne brook. It was the scene of desperate fighting.

The farm of d'en Bas. This lay on the Prussian side of the Ligne brook and dominated one of the bridges. It too saw much fighting.

The farm at Walhain where Marshal Grouchy famously ate his strawberries. The house whose roof can be seen to the right was where Grouchy was confronted by Gérard who demanded they march to the sound of the guns.

A photo of the Dyle river with the modern Bierge mill in the background.

The farm of la Bourse. This lay just behind the French line on the night of 18/19 June. It was here that Grouchy wrote his despatches although he spent the night out with the troops.

A print of the battle of Ligny. Although a victory for Napoleon, he failed to destroy the Prussian army.

An old print of the Bridge of Christ over which Vandamme's corps fought in vain on 18 June.

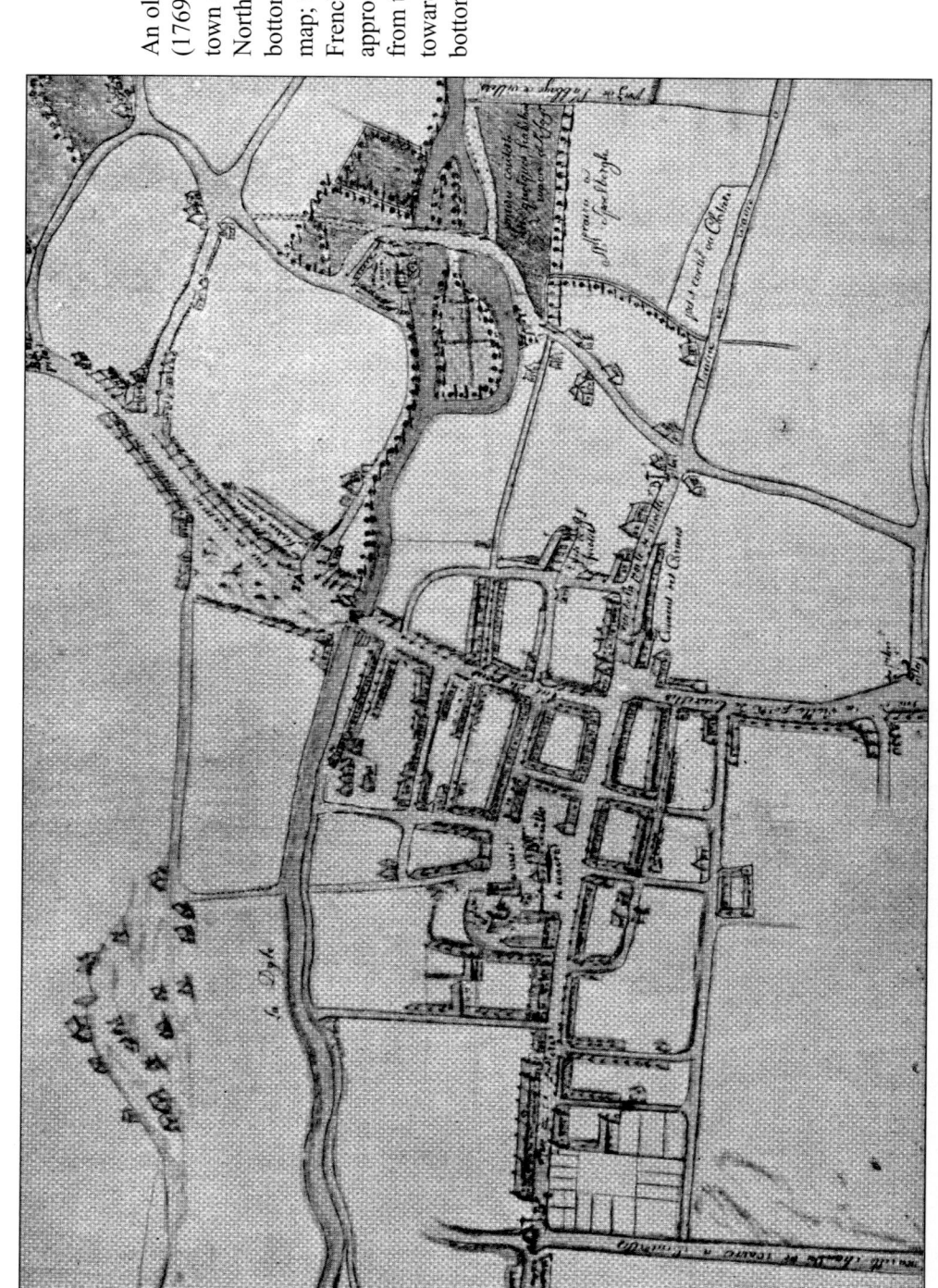

An old map (1769) of the town of Wavre. North is to the bottom of the map; thus the French approached from the top towards the bottom.

appeared to accept with gratitude and which he immediately used to bandage his wound.

... We continued our march ahead in pursuit of the enemy, when my general, noticing that several of our skirmishers had advanced too close to a wood occupied by a party of Prussians, sent me to warn them to turn back onto the road. Hardly had I reached them when a lively fire came from the edge of the wood which killed four men around me and also wounded my horse in the hoof. On the return from this small expedition, I met General Corsin and our chief-of-staff, Colonel Marion, to whom I gave an account of what had happened, when suddenly, I saw the latter fall and caught him in my arms. A ball had seriously wounded him, passing through his body from one side to the other [Marion was actually wounded in the head]. The colonel still had the strength to request that I stay with him. I took with me four *sapeurs* who improvised a stretcher on which he was carried out of range of the enemy's fire.[3]

Grouchy summed up this brief encounter with the Prussian rearguard:

I joined General Exelmans who, since morning, had hounded the extreme rearguard of Prussian cavalry and at 11.30 and a league and a half from Wavre, we finally discovered an infantry rearguard with artillery. Immediately that I realised this, the artillery fire began and General Vandamme arriving with the head of his column we marched on the Prussians who had taken position at the Limelette wood and who were immediately attacked and overthrown. General Exelmans' cavalry turned the wood by the right and moved on Bas-Wavre. We followed the enemy closely and between one and two o'clock we were masters of the part of the town which lay on the left [right] bank of the Dyle.[4]

Berthezène's claim that he could see Prussian columns heading west towards Waterloo is significant as, if true and reported, it would be natural to think that Grouchy should have made a crucial decision: to attack Wavre and be unable to interfere with this movement, or make some special effort to attempt to interdict it. In his various writings, and backed up by those of his key staff officers, Grouchy denies that any such report was made. However, the heavy cannonade from Waterloo had also made Grouchy rather nervous:

Noticing that the cannonade seemed to increase in intensity, Grouchy galloped to get through a wood on the left and was convinced that a general action was taking place in the vicinity of Mont-Saint-Jean. Before reaching this point, he sent one of his *aides de camp*, Bella, to General Vandamme to order him to take position on the heights which dominated Wavre, *not to advance on the part of the town situated on the right bank of the Dyle* [his italics], and to conduct a reconnaissance to determine if the bridge had been destroyed and if there were any crossing points above or below it.⁵

Having pushed back the Prussian rearguard, Exelmans' dragoons pushed on towards Wavre and the smaller Bas-Wavre a little further down the river. The high ground here dominated the river valley, but the heavily wooded slopes were no place for unsupported cavalry and the dragoons sat in observation, once more waiting for Vandamme's footsloggers to catch up. One of these was Captain Gerbet who lets us know what time they arrived:

Having thus arrived at Sart-à-Walhain . . . we continued our move on Wavre and we arrived at 4pm on a plateau which fell in a steep slope, forming with another slope, no less steep and opposite, a deep valley in which the Dyle ran, splitting Wavre into two, joined by a stone bridge.⁶

As Vandamme's divisions came forward they massed on the high ground overlooking Wavre whilst *Maréchal de Camp* Vallin's cavalry division observed the bridges of Limelette and Limal higher up the river to their left rear. Gérard's troops were still struggling along the atrocious roads towards la Baraque; from here they could continue north towards Wavre or turn slightly to the west towards the village of Bierge or Limal.

The Attack on Wavre
The small town of Wavre lay astride the river Dyle and offered an ideal position to hold up an advancing force with one that was smaller. Grouchy's memoirs describe it thus:

This small town, situated on the left bank of the Dyle, has a suburb on the right bank, a suburb connected to the town by two stone bridges, a big one and a little one; this last to the south on the side of Bierge. A good league below, at Limal and Limelette, exist bridges of wood. Finally, at the mill of Bierge, below Wavre, there was also a narrow passage to cross the Dyle. This tributary of the Scheldt is not deep, but on the 17th and 18th June 1815, its waters were swollen by the rains and storms and had flooded. The river valley was formed by wooded slopes. Those of the left [Prussian] bank generally dominated those of the right bank, but these last are steeper, so that the passages to the river are everywhere dominated and that on the whole are favourable to the defence.
    The town is crossed by the main road from Namur to Brussels; several practicable tracks lead to Belgium's capital.⁷

We can get a sense of what the river Dyle was like on that day from an artillery officer tasked with a reconnaissance:

> As far as I can remember, it was about nine metres wide, its banks were elevated which gave it the appearance of a muddy canal. I pushed my horse in, the water came up to my belt (Captain Pellisier and his *voltigeurs* helped me to get my horse out). I gave my report to General Baltus . . .[8]

Due to the slow pursuit of the French, the Prussians had seen few of Grouchy's troops and believed only a weak cavalry force had followed them. Therefore, as Blücher planned his move in support of Wellington, he directed that all his corps should be prepared to march to the west. It was only as the French drew close to Wavre that the Prussians realised their error and Thielemann's III Corps was ordered to defend the crossings over the Dyle centred on Wavre.

Thielemann made the following dispositions; the 9th Brigade was ordered to defend the Wavre bridges; two battalions were deployed into the town and two companies of skirmishers were left to defend the crossing at the village Bas Wavre below Wavre itself (these were later reinforced); the bridge there was destroyed. Unfortunately for Thielemann, due to a misunderstanding, the rest of the brigade marched off after II Corps towards Waterloo! The rest of Thielemann's brigades were deployed as follows:

> 10th Brigade to the rear of Wavre, on the heights north-east of the town.
> 11th Brigade to the rear of Wavre, north of the town astride the Brussels road.
> 12th Brigade with a battery south-west of Wavre on the heights near Bierge.
> The Reserve Cavalry behind the 10th Brigade.
> The artillery was deployed to give covering fire to the brigades and to be able to fire into Wavre.[9]

The main bridge at Wavre was barricaded with twelve large barrels and three wagons; the small bridge was left open. The bridge at Bierge was also barricaded. In total, Thielemann's force consisted of nearly 15,000 infantry, 2,000 cavalry and five batteries. This was inevitably to be an infantry battle and although Thielemann was at a disadvantage in numbers of this arm, the French having about 20,000 infantry, he was occupying a very strong position behind a river across which there were only a few bridging points to defend.

Not long after his own reconnaissance to the west, Grouchy returned to la Baraque where he was joined by an *aide de camp* of General Pajol. This officer warned him that Pajol had found no trace of the Prussian columns that he had followed since they had left the Namur road and that in consequence he required new orders. Without dismounting, Grouchy quickly wrote the following order in crayon:

> On the road from Sart-à-Walhain to Wavre, 18 June 1815
> General, move with all haste with Teste's division and your corps to Limal, cross the Dyle there and attack any enemy that opposes you.[10]

Limal is less than three kilometres upriver from Wavre. Grouchy told this *aide de camp* that he wanted to be promptly and clearly informed of the execution of the movement prescribed and that he was now heading to Wavre where any further correspondence should be sent.

Not long after the departure of this *aide de camp*, Colonel Zenowicz rode up to Marshal Grouchy. The Pole takes up the story from when he left Waterloo:

> Hardly a few minutes after I galloped off, I could hear a fusillade and a cannonade. From this fact, it can be established that I left the *major-général* about midday, the hour at which the battle began. To be precise to the minute is difficult; to occupy yourself with the hour in such a situation requires powerful motives, for on the battlefield a soldier forgets the hours as at a ball, and does not think of the time. The first halt that I made was to ask for the road to Gembloux, and then, at Gembloux, to find out the direction taken by Grouchy's corps. I was not able to get a satisfactory response to this last question from anyone. I therefore followed the emperor's advice and according to the direction that he had indicated to me . . . I finally reached, between three and four o'clock, a division of the rearguard that was part of the army corps I was seeking. A quarter of an hour later I joined the *comte* de Grouchy. He was with General Gérard in a small room of a house where an aid station had been established. I presented the despatches to the marshal and I told him in a lively voice what I had been ordered to do. After having run through the order that I had given him, Marshal Grouchy communicated them to General Gérard who, after having taken them in, angrily shouted at Grouchy, 'As I keep saying, if we are f***ed, it is your fault.' When I saw that the *comte* de Grouchy replied in the same tone, words which it is not appropriate to repeat, I thought it necessary to walk away and, under the pretext of caring for my horse, I retired.
>
> Soon, thinking that the emotion had had time to calm, I returned close to Marshal Grouchy, when he suddenly left his office with General Gérard, and coming right up to me said, 'We will go and see; you will remain with us, ok?' I replied that I had been ordered by His Majesty to only leave when his corps came into the line of battle.
>
> Marshal Grouchy then asked for his *aides de camp*; he gave them orders and then went himself to the banks of the Dyle. Soon the attack on the Bierge mill began . . . [11]

The despatch from Soult read,

> In front of the Caillou farm, 18 June 1815 at 10am
> *Monsieur le maréchal*, the emperor has received your last report dated from Gembloux; you only inform the emperor that two Prussian columns have passed Sauvenières and Sart-à-Walhain; however, reports say that a third column, which was strong, has passed Genz and Gentinnes heading for Wavre.
> The emperor orders me to inform you that at this moment His Majesty is going to attack the English army which has taken position at Waterloo, close to the Soignes forest; also that His Majesty desires that you direct your movements on Wavre in order to approach us, come into our area of operations and tie in your communications, pushing before you the corps of the Prussian army which have taken this direction and which could stop at Wavre, where you are to arrive as soon as possible.
> You are to follow the enemy columns which are on your right with some light troops in order to observe their movements and collect up their stragglers. Inform me immediately of your deployment and your march, as well as any news you have of the enemy and do not hesitate in coming into communications with us. The emperor wants to receive your news often.[12]

Soult can certainly stand accused of being unclear in this letter, directing Grouchy to move on Wavre 'in order to approach us'. This would indeed have been a long route round, whilst the crossings at Limal, Limelette, Moustier and Ottignies to the west offered shorter options and ones less likely to be defended by the Prussians. Interpreting exactly what he means by 'our area of operations' is also problematic. However, arriving at Wavre 'as soon as possible' is unequivocal and Grouchy understandably interpreted this as an endorsement of his decision to march on that town. Seemingly ignoring the reference to a 'new' marching column of Prussians, Grouchy now concentrated on getting his forces to Wavre in order to put pressure on the Prussians. His memoirs take up the story:

> It was 4 o'clock in the afternoon. Grouchy was determined to beat the Prussians that he supposed had concentrated at Wavre and thus to execute the latest order from Napoleon *to move on this town* [his italics] and join III Corps. On arrival, he was angered to find that Vandamme, instead of taking position on the heights above the town as he had been ordered, had rushed his troops into the lower part of the town that lay before the river that had been evacuated by the Prussians, but where they were exposed to the fire of numerous batteries deployed on the far (left) bank of the Dyle and of the infantry entrenched in the fortified houses that lined the river.[13]

In his later writings, Grouchy makes much of Vandamme's failure to obey his order not to attack Wavre. However, in the account Grouchy wrote closest to the event, 1818, he gives a different perspective:

> Towards one o'clock [this timing is manifestly wrong; it could not have been before 4pm] Marshal Grouchy ordered General Vandamme to take by main force the bridge over the Dyle.[14]

So we cannot be sure whether Vandamme was complying with his orders, or whether he had decided to act on his own initiative and capture the town by a *coup de main*. Either way, some time after 4pm, Vandamme launched Habert's division into the suburb of Wavre on the right bank of the Dyle with the aim of capturing the main bridge. To support the attack he deployed two batteries on the right opposite the large bridge to be able to fire into the town; these were later joined by a third. Although Prussian accounts say the fire of these batteries was very effective, it seems to have been a rather unscientific, head-on attack with little attempt at subtlety or manoeuvre; no doubt Vandamme and his men were spurred on by the rolling barrage away to the west.

It seems a solid column of men, inevitably constrained by the width of the road, descended into the town. The Prussians had only deployed skirmishers on the right bank and these quickly fell back in the face of overwhelming numbers. The main Prussian defence was around the main bridge, named the Bridge of Christ because of the iron crucifix that stood above it. The Prussians had used their time well to fortify the buildings that dominated the bridge on the far bank. The French infantry, having suffered from the Prussian artillery during their descent into the town, were then met by a hail of fire as they approached the river. General Berthezène was clearly not impressed by Vandamme's approach to the attack:

> Wavre was occupied by the Prussians; its houses were lined with skirmishers; its bridge was barricaded and beaten by a numerous artillery established on the heights that dominated the left bank of the Dyle. Arriving before this town, General Vandamme had it attacked immediately, without taking any measures to ensure the success of this operation. He simply ordered Habert's division to penetrate into it in column. Despite the enemy's murderous fire, this division reached as far as the bridge. But General Habert having been wounded, it retired in disorder and came to reform at the gates of the town. This crazy attack cost us five or six hundred men; several senior officers were wounded there and Colonel Dubalen, an officer of great potential, was killed [Dubalen was actually mortally wounded at Ligny and died on 20 June]. Yet it would have been easy to have made ourselves masters of this post with little loss. It would have sufficed to have crossed the river below the town or perhaps above it on the bridge at Bierge

and to take the enemy in the rear. Above all, the occupation of Wavre would have had no influence on the outcome of the campaign . . . The local difficulties, the cutting of the Dyle, the Prussian forces concentrated at this point and the crossfire of their batteries rendered the efforts of our soldiers useless.[15]

Colonel Fantin des Odoards, commander of the 22nd *de ligne*, took part in the attack:

Arriving at Wavre, a town on the Dyle, we found them in position and immediately came to grips with them. Instead of crossing the Dyle above or below Wavre, where it is fordable in many places, General Vandamme, charged with crossing it to drive away the enemy, wanted, in the town itself, to seize a well-barricaded bridge which was protected by thousands of skirmishers posted in the houses on the far bank. It was necessary to turn this strong position, but the general persisted to approach it head-on with masses which, committed on a long road running perpendicular to the bridge, were exposed to all the Prussian fire without being able to use its own. We uselessly lost many men there. The 70th regiment, the same that had been broken two days previously [at Ligny], having been ordered to clear the bridge under a hail of balls, was routed. Brought back by its Colonel, it hesitated again when the brave Maury [Maury had been killed at Ligny and command had passed to Colonel Uny], seized its eagle and called out, 'Why you scoundrels, you dishonoured me the day before yesterday and you do it again today! Advance! Follow me!' His eagle in his hand, he rushed onto the bridge, the charge beating, the regiment following him; but hardly had he reached the barricade than this worthy chief fell dead and the 70th fled just the same and so quickly that without the help of the men of my 22nd, the eagle which lay on the ground in the middle of the bridge beside my poor lifeless comrade would have become the prey of the enemy sharpshooters who were already trying to get it.[16]

Captain Putigny of the 33rd adds:

Taking Wavre is all about crossing this river and the marshes on our side. We overturned the carriages which barricade the bridge. Under a heavy fire from all the houses that face us, ten men of my company are *hors de combat* and we regroup in the suburb that the Prussians set fire to in order to check a new attempt by us.[17]

Seeing this first assault fail, Vandamme decided to supplement the continuing attack in Wavre with an attempt to force a crossing at a mill just outside the small village of Bierge, about a kilometre upstream from the town. He sent a battalion of Lefol's division to carry out this task. Although the bridge was essentially only a footbridge, several squadrons of the Prussian rearguard had crossed there earlier in the day. The mill was defended by a company of the 31st Regiment, supported by a battalion of the 6th Kurmark Landwehr and a battery of horse artillery. Despite these relatively meagre forces, the buildings of the mill provided a strong defensive position and the approach was extremely difficult (one officer described the approach route as 'almost impracticable'[18]) and the attack quickly faltered despite the enthusiasm of the troops.

In Wavre, the assaults on the bridge continued. Habert's division included the single battalion of the 2nd Swiss Regiment. This was made up of volunteers from the four Swiss regiments that had served under Louis XVIII; the remainder had returned to Switzerland after Napoleon's return. It was a weak battalion too, just over 400 strong. However, in their distinctive red coats they were to show exceptional courage at Wavre having not been engaged at Ligny. Their commanding officer was Colonel Augustin Eugène Stoffel, the son of a Swiss officer who had served in the Spanish army. His older brother also served during the campaign and took command of the 70th *de ligne* after that regiment's loss of Colonels Maury and Uny. Colonel Stoffel gives this detailed account of the fight for the Wavre bridge:

> . . . We arrive at the entry point of Wavre towards 6pm. The *pas de charge* is beaten. The division is formed in closed columns by division.
>
> I march at the rear of the 10th Division [Habert's]. Entering by the main road at the *pas de charge* there is a terrible fire from all sides. The units in front of me are wavering and their head is stopped at the bridge (Dyle) which is blocked by a wagon. The fire is so murderous that it causes hesitation. From second to second, the converging fire from enemy batteries knock down entire ranks, leading to disorder. The soldiers automatically get into the buildings. This leaves me a passage. By a happy inspiration I command, 'Advance, march!' and I advance at the head of my troops through this opening.
>
> All in the 10th Division bear witness to this *élan*. Arriving on the square, the canister, the shells and the musketry seem like hail: we are under a canopy of fire. The brave Captain Huber is mortally wounded passing the corner in the same place that sergeant of grenadiers Mayer is killed. The danger is so great at this place that I decide to cross the bridge which is obstructed and cluttered by dead and wounded. We cross one by one. I manage to form a platoon in line on the other side of the bridge, but the enemy see the slowness with which this passage is made and detach a body of men which advance with the bayonet. The platoon is broken, pushed back with bayonets in their backs and destroyed. The nimbleness with which I

cross all the obstacles, leaping over the dead, the wounded, the wagon and the bayonets, takes me to the edge of the bridge. Several soldiers float in the river like packets of dirty laundry.

General Vandamme is a witness to my enthusiasm and the bravery of my regiment. He attempts (although uselessly) to prevent anyone firing, being in mass, and to re-establish good order. He insults the cowardly officers who cannot control their men. I insult the engineer general [Nempde] who instead of clearing the bridge is sheltering under an arch.

My servant took two superb horses, richly saddled, in a stable (they undoubtedly belonged to a Prussian general). He stupidly led them into the square where they were both killed in an instant. The brave Lieutenant Demartin had his arm broken; Ms. Ernst, Varena and Magetty are wounded.

I rally all my men for a second attempt to force the bridge.

I join the first platoons with difficulty and they follow me onto the other side of the bridge; the eagle bearer was one of them. We are supported by some grenadiers commanded by my cousin Captain Stoffel, who captured the first houses to the right and left beyond the bridge. We think we have succeeded. The eagle bearer is struck by a ball, the eagle falls to the ground. I go to pick it up, but Sergeant Dubois beats me to it, takes it just a few steps from the head of the enemy column and brings it back with admirable *sang-froid*. I promise him the *legion d'honneur*. [He never received it.]

My intention was to march against the enemy column immediately that I was able to gather a sufficiently large force and to capture the guns which would have caused the defence to weaken from that which met the first attack. At the moment that I give the command '*En avant*!', with a certainty of success, for as the bridge was clear and I could have been supported, I received the order to retire to the square from *aide de camp* Vincent in order to clear the bridge so that General Vandamme could cross over.

The heads of column of the 70th and 88th, which did not recognise me because of the disorder, fired on us; I was terribly exposed and many men were killed.

I found my horse in the hands of a wounded drummer. I had lost a stirrup before I had dismounted.

The intrepid General Vandamme always gave an example of the most heroic courage. Useless efforts! We were poorly engaged. I received the order from him to rally my regiment behind the town (at 10pm). Two thirds of this brave regiment no longer existed, and a third of the muskets of those that survived were broken by canister fire.

I was content with myself, but I was not content with the day. What was the result of the day to our left, the sound of cannon had finished? Positioned on a height; I ask for cartridges. Grenadier Spalinger, my groom, was wounded in the arm. General Vandamme came to find me at 11 o'clock and ordered me to cut the main road from Namur and to place myself astride this road. When I pointed out that the regiment was very weak, only a hundred men remained to me, for such an important task, he replied, 'I count on this small number of brave men as on a complete regiment.'[19]

The attacks on Wavre were summarised by Colonel Fantin des Odoards: 'They were badly planned, feebly executed and the ground badly studied'.[20]

Vandamme's attacks having achieved nothing other than to suffer heavy casualties, it is easy to see why Grouchy was outraged by Vandamme's apparent disobedience. With Habert's division helplessly entangled in the town and closely engaged with the Prussians, valuable time was wasted in trying to extract the committed troops from the difficult position their commander had put them in.

At 5.30pm, sixteen kilometres to the west, the battle of Waterloo was raging. The first Prussians had come into action against Napoleon's right flank from 4.30pm and were now fighting for possession of the village of Planchenoit on the French right rear. Napoleon, wanting to launch a final attack to break the allied centre, needed to ensure this village, and hence his flank, was secure before he could do so. He also claims he was counting on Grouchy appearing on the battlefield at any moment.

Henry Houssaye, the well-known French historian, says it was at this time that Napoleon's second message was received. Two of Grouchy's staff officers say it was between 4.30 and 5pm. Grouchy himself says it was 7pm, though why he should think it was so late is puzzling. From timings given by other officers, Houssaye's time of about 5.30pm seems the most reliable; if Zenowicz is criticised for taking four hours to get to Grouchy, it is hard to believe that this second despatch took any longer.

We do not know who delivered this letter and its exact wording in one or two key points is disputed. Let us look at the version given by Grouchy in his memoirs.

18 June, 1pm

M. le Maréchal,
You wrote to the emperor at 3am this morning that you were marching on Sart-à-Walhain, that your plan was to move to Corbais and Wavre. This move conforms to the dispositions His Majesty that have been communicated to you. However, the emperor orders me to inform you that you are always to manoeuvre in our direction, in order that you are able to join us before any [enemy] corps can come between us. I will not dictate a direction as it is for you to identify the point where we are for you to adjust accordingly and to establish our communications, as well as to be

always ready to fall on whatever enemy troops that attempt to threaten our right.

At this moment the battle is *won* [my emphasis] on the line of Waterloo, in front of the forest of Soignes. The enemy's centre is at Mont-Saint-Jean; thus manoeuvre to join our right.

Le maréchal duc de Dalmatie

PS. A letter that has been intercepted says that General Bülow is to attack our right flank; we think we can see this corps on the heights of Saint Lambert. Thus do not lose a moment in approaching us and join us, and to destroy Bülow, who you will catch red-handed [*en flagrant délit*].[21]

It will be noted that Grouchy claims that the letter said that the battle at Waterloo had been 'won'. However, his chief of staff, General Sénécal, wrote:

During the attack on Wavre and between 4.30pm and 5pm the marshal received and showed to me, a despatch from the *major-général*. This despatch, written in very fine letters and almost illegible (which made us very uneasy), gave a clear order to the marshal to move on Saint-Lambert and we thought it said that the battle had been 'won' on the line of Waterloo. The marshal closely interrogated the officer who had carried this despatch; but he was so drunk that it was not possible to get a clear answer.[22]

Grouchy claims that because he understood the despatch to say the battle was won, he had no concerns for the emperor and concentrated on obeying the orders within the despatch. Others quote the despatch as saying the battle was 'engaged'; clearly a different interpretation with significantly different implications. The mix-up revolves around the difference in French between '*gagnée*', which translates as 'won', and '*engagnée*', which translates as 'engaged'. Given the time it was written (only just as the battle was beginning) it is natural for us to assume that the letter actually said 'engaged' and it seems almost too convenient that the bearer of the despatch was so drunk that the truth could not be established. This is a rather bizarre story for Grouchy and his acolytes to weave and for what? After all, with the despatch arriving so late, there is no way Grouchy could have manoeuvred to Waterloo in time to have any effect on the result. We can only assume that Grouchy presented it as saying 'won' to better justify his subsequent actions and decisions.

Whether the letter actually said 'won' or 'engaged', the direction it gave was unequivocal and the *post scriptum*, 'Do not lose a moment in approaching us and join us', was clear and positive. Grouchy realised he was no longer to pursue the Prussians on Wavre, but to march to the battlefield by moving to the left by Saint-Lambert and to join Napoleon at Waterloo.

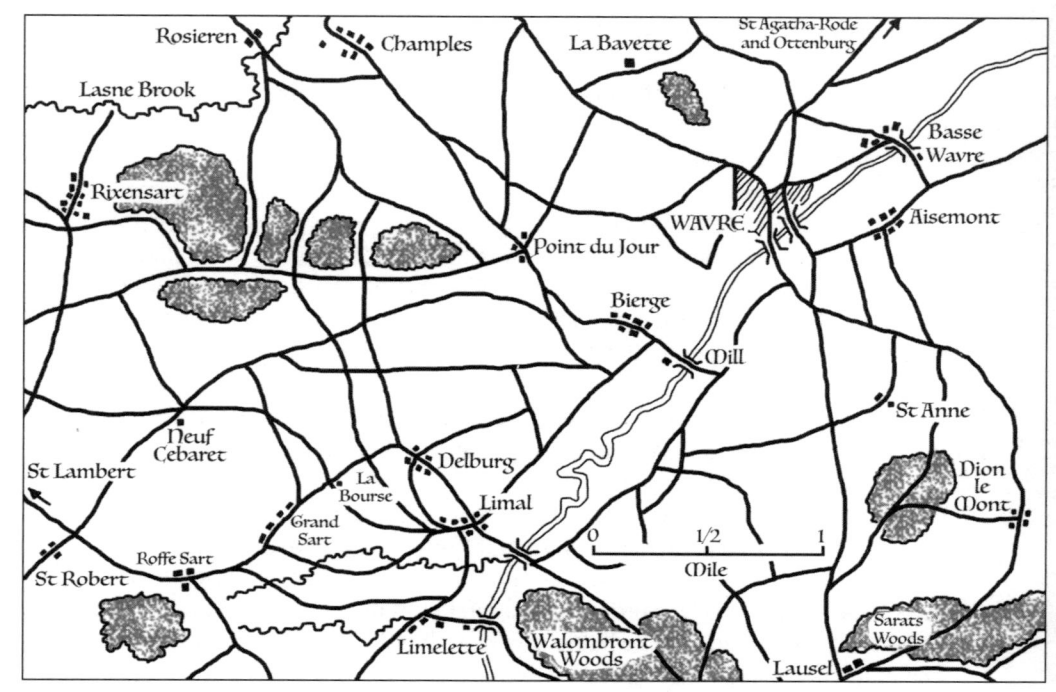

Wavre 18th and 19th June

The Attacks on the Bierge Mill

Unfortunately, Grouchy's troops were not deployed in such a way as to be able to achieve this quickly. Exelmans' dragoons, supported by a single infantry battalion, were deployed downstream from Wavre, observing the bridge at Bas Wavre. Much of Vandamme's corps was compromised in and around Wavre, fighting for the bridge with just a small force of Lefol's division facing the mill of Bierge. Vandamme's artillery had lost the use of its limbers, the riders and horses having been killed, so it was necessary to move the guns by manpower, a slow, difficult and dangerous operation under fire. IV Corps, less Hulot's division that was directly in Vandamme's rear, was still on the road from Walhain. However, Grouchy no doubt congratulated himself on having already sent Pajol towards the bridge at Limal which offered the best route to achieve his mission. Although it was held by the Prussians, he no doubt felt that so far from Wavre, it was unlikely to be held in strength.

In an effort to comply with his new instructions, Grouchy left III Corps and moved to la Baraque in order to meet the main body of IV Corps and direct them to Limal. However, arriving at la Baraque (a league and a half to the south of

Wavre), no troops of IV Corps were to be seen. Wishing to get things moving as quickly as possible, Grouchy sent one of his staff officers down the road to hasten the march of IV Corps. He then returned once more to Wavre hoping that III Corps would now have broken clear and could be re-directed to Limal. Unfortunately, the situation had not changed; Vandamme lacked either the means or the will to disengage and could offer Grouchy no help.

Frustrated by the situation Vandamme was in, Grouchy once more rode to Bierge to oversee a new attack on the mill by Hulot's division; his stated aim was not only to capture this crossing, but also to divert the Prussian attention away from Limal which Pajol would be approaching to try and seize by a *coup de main*. Grouchy wrote:

> But about half of the IV Corps was still in the rear where these troops were on the road from Gembloux to Wavre; they were closer to Saint-Lambert than those concentrated near Wavre. Accompanied by General Gérard, I went towards the rear to meet this part of his corps as far as a house called la Baraque, with the aim of directing it by Limal on Saint-Lambert.[23]

General Hulot, commanding Gérard's lead division, takes up the story:

> From this last place [la Baraque], the head of IV Corps received the order to move to the left of Wavre onto the high escarpment that is opposite the mill of Bierge. This position was occupied by several pieces of artillery belonging to III Corps. The head of IV Corps arrived there at a quarter or half past three [this time must be wrong], at the same moment that the troops of III Corps, engaged in Wavre, retired.
>
> I received the order to halt behind and to the side of this artillery; the other divisions came and massed themselves in the rear between the two woods about half an hour after my arrival.
>
> On this height, the corps commander himself came to order me to attack the Bierge mill with a battalion. An attempt on this post had already been made by a battalion of the III Corps, who I was to relieve.
>
> Immediately, I took a battalion of the 9th [*léger*] Regiment and organised the attack myself. Here, it is necessary to describe the position of this mill on the Dyle above Wavre. From the foot of the heights that I had to descend to the Bierge mill was less than a musket's range. The swamps that filled this area are cut in lines parallel to the river with very deep banks; too wide to be crossed. They were full of four, five or six feet of water. These ditches were found in the whole area between Limal as far as Wavre. The banks of the Dyle are wooded; as well as the Prussian infantry hidden in the mill itself, they lined the left bank of this river. The slopes of the heights which lead down there was manned with troops and the artillery fire, with that of

the mill and the bank, plunged down into this open ground that it was necessary to cross in order to reach the mill's bridge in order to seize it. Such was the lay of the land and the obstacles that I saw that a battalion of the III Corps had already tried to cross.

I thought that by going a little to the left and passing these ditches a little higher up, I would find less water there. I thus went off in this direction about a musket's range and launched my battalion, ordering it to run heads down and to take cover in the ditches if they could not be crossed. The first men that threw themselves in needed the help of their comrades to avoid drowning and to get out. These multiple obstacles stopped the soldiers and prevented them from advancing and I judged that this post could not be attacked in this manner.

As I returned towards the heights to inform the corps commander, I encountered him descending with another battalion. He had seen the failure of my attempt and told me, when I approached him, that he was going to attack again himself and that it was necessary to second him by advancing again with my first battalion. The attack was renewed. The corps commander and the officers of his headquarters took part in this last effort which achieved nothing and had only an unfortunate outcome; it was in this situation that the corps commander was shot in the chest.

General Grouchy arrived at this very moment. Convinced that this mill, if it was to be taken, required him to make other arrangements, he gave the order that these two battalions, the only ones from III Corps [surely he means IV Corps?] that had been engaged, were to remain at the foot of the heights. I was also informed that as General Gérard was no longer able to command, I would now receive my orders from General Vandamme. General Grouchy moved on to Limal with the other two divisions of IV Corps. At least two hours had passed since the arrival of the 3rd Division on the heights, it was thus between 6 and 6.30pm when the final movement of the two divisions began.[24]

Gérard's *aide de camp*, Colonel Rumigny, claims that at this time his commander was still impatient to march towards the sound of the guns, claiming that he could see the Prussian columns already marching in that direction:

Finally, he sent two or three officers in quick succession, to tell the marshal that the Prussians could be seen moving by divisions to their right, moving towards the battle. Battalions followed one after another and a complete corps marched at a good pace before us, to go to attack Napoleon's right flank. The marshal, obstinate, refused to move to the support of the emperor. Time passed and it was getting too late to decide. The general went once more to find the marshal, then, returning to us, said,

'When, after twenty-five years of war, one sees such stupidity, a general officer who has any self-respect should get himself killed.'

Then, despite our representations, he took off his cloak and advanced towards the Prussian skirmishers, who immediately aimed their shots at him. He was wearing a blue frock coat, with the Order of Danebrog [Dannebrog] in diamonds at his throat, several other decorations and the medal of honour.

The balls flew thickly; an officer of the headquarters was wounded, a *sapeur* of the 30th killed; and suddenly a ball or fragment knocked the general to the ground. We seized him and, wrapping him in my hazelnut *carrick*, we carried him to the rear and lay him in a farm. There, we anxiously awaited the prognosis of Doctor Cuttinger, the chief surgeon of his corps.

The ball had struck the third button, taking with it part of the shirt then lodged itself in the left lung.[25]

Captain Gerbet was also a witness to Gérard's wounding:

Our regiment (the 37th) occupied in the evening of the 18th June, the middle of a slope at the bottom of which was a narrow valley in which was found the Bierge mill, in which the enemy had fortified themselves and from which they produced a murderous fire on us, combined with that of their numerous skirmishers who were hidden on the slopes opposite ours.

We returned their fire with our own skirmishers when from 6 to 7pm General Gérard suddenly appeared in our midst. He was on foot and dressed in the colour of dead leaves which concealed his rank. He stopped there and came to say, 'It is necessary to take the mill!' when an enemy ball struck him in the left side. He suddenly moved his right hand to where he had been struck. He did not collapse, but retired. I was only ten or twelve metres away to General Gérard's left and my eyes were constantly fixed on him. It was at this moment, and in this way that General Gérard was wounded by a ball on the evening of the 18th June at the attack on the Bierge mill.[26]

As an interesting aside, after Gérard's wounding and until a more formal arrangement could be made, command should have passed to General Baltus, commander of the corps artillery. However, as one of Grouchy's *aides de camp* later wrote:

Count Gérard was wounded at your side and forced to be transported to the rear. It was then that General-of-Artillery Baltus refused to replace Count Gérard; a refusal which scandalised the army.[27]

Grouchy later described Gérard's attack as 'half-hearted'[28] and felt that that is it why it had failed. In addressing this slight, Gérard gives some more details:

> The first attack on the Bierge mill had been made by the troops of the III Corps. It was only towards 4.30 or 5pm that *M. le comte de* Grouchy gave me the order to replace General Vandamme's troops with one of my battalions at the Bierge mill . . . I ordered General Hulot, an officer as intelligent as he is brave, to go with a battalion of the 9th *léger* to renew the attack that had already been attempted without success by the troops of III Corps. This attack, and another, that was made in the presence of the *comte de* Grouchy, had no more success than the first. The troops cannot be blamed for the failure; they displayed much courage and tried several times, but the nature of the ground offered insurmountable difficulties. At the foot of the heights that dominated the valley, there was just a musket's range to the Dyle; it was very swampy across this space which was cut, in lines parallel to the river, by very deep ditches which were too wide to cross. They were full of four, five and six *pieds* of water. These ditches stretched all the way from Limal to Wavre. The banks of the Dyle are wooded, and the Prussian infantry were hidden in the mill, and lined the left bank of this river as well as the slopes of the hills which led down to it. The fire of a numerous artillery, joined to that of the mill and left bank, reached across this flat ground that had to be crossed to arrive at the bridge. I repeat that it is only with injustice that one tries to find fault with the troops; those of III or IV Corps.[29]

Limal
Whilst III Corps fought in Wavre and IV Corps at Bierge, General Pajol led his command towards the bridge at Limal as he had been ordered. At 4pm they were in movement on the route which passes through Libresart, Corroy-le-Grand and la Baraque. Limal was defended by troops of the Prussian I Corps; three battalions of the 19th Infantry, two squadrons of the 6th Uhlans and one squadron of the 1st Westphalian Landwehr cavalry, the whole under the command of Colonel Stengel. One battalion occupied the village and covered the crossing with the balance deployed on the high ground above. Pajol's memoirs continue the story:

> Pajol, having accelerated his march, joined the tail of the IV Corps, by 7pm he had left la Baraque, where he found General Vallin who was put under his orders.
> After being briefed on the position of Limal, in front of which Vallin's cavalry had manoeuvred since the morning, Pajol prepared to go there when he was joined by M. Pontbellanger, one of Grouchy's *aides de camp*, who shouted from afar, 'Never has the emperor been so great! The battle is won and only awaits more cavalry to turn it into a rout!' Pontbellanger referred

to the emperor's 1pm despatch that had been read as saying the battle at Waterloo had been 'won' rather than 'engaged'. The despatch was written in such a way that it was barely legible . . .

Pajol immediately made his arrangements for the attack. He placed Vallin's division at the head, then Teste's infantry and left Soult's cavalry in reserve as it was very tired from its various moves since morning. He charged Commandant Biot, his *aide de camp*, to direct the head of the column and to scout the river banks near the Limal bridge.[30]

Biot described this attack:

> We were formed in line on the heath. It was necessary, before arriving in the Dyle valley, to descend a defile which dropped down right to the bridge. At this time I was filling the function as the chief-of-staff, so that it was to me that General Pajol addressed himself to provide a guide. I did not have one.
>
> Having seen a local man, I ran to him; the man showed me the route. But when I asked him to march with us he said that he presumed the French were at his house and that he wanted to return there to offer them what he had, fearing that in his absence they would commit some damage . . .
>
> I thus returned without a guide. On my confirmation that I knew the country and the route to take, the general ordered me to march ahead of the column to direct it. Maurin's old division was in the lead. Hardly had we done 200 paces in this defile when the challenge of '*Qui vive*?!' came to me. At my response, 'France', someone replied, 'Do not pass!' At the same time, two balls saluted our arrival.
>
> I went forward alone and I found myself in the presence of a *voltigeur* sergeant from Gérard's IV Corps. He informed me that Prussian infantry, posted in the mill and the houses that were to the left and right of the bridge, defended the river crossing and that they were, besides, supported by batteries installed on the heights on the far bank of the Dyle.
>
> The rout of the enemy announced by Pontbellinger, the report of the *voltigeur* sergeant, the balls that had been fired at us, all seemed to me such a contradiction that, without listening to the sergeant, I pushed my horse onto the bridge. But a volley was immediately fired from the houses which stopped my march. However, I noted the width of the bridge, which would allow us to cross in column of fours; I saw that at the exit, the road made a bend to the left round the houses and there was a junction fifty paces further on. The turn to the right went towards Wavre, the other, to the left, passed through the village which just lined the road.
>
> I left to inform the general of the obstacle that I had encountered and the positions I had looked at. I had already been in a similar situation at the battle of Montereau [in 1814 when Pajol's command charged down a steep

slope into the town and over the bridges]. I knew that as the bridge was not barricaded I could take it by a vigorous charge; that being supported by other cavalry and followed by infantry, we could take the whole village, the enemy not having sufficient forces to throw us back across the bridge and thus put the column coming down the defile in disorder.

When I explained all this, the general reflected for a moment. Then, after one of those inspirations that seemed so natural in him at war, 'It is necessary to cross' he said to me, 'Tell General Vallin to give us the first squadron of the 9th Hussars [this must have been the 6th] and you take the bridge. But do not stop; immediately take the road to the right of which you have spoken and exit onto the plain. I will support you in case of need.'

I ran to pass the order to General Vallin. The Prince of Carignan [Joseph Marie de Savoie Carignan, Colonel of the 6th Hussars], a brave and excellent officer, who was close to him, asked to charge with his squadron. We left at the gallop; the rest of the column followed us at the trot. We took the bridge after having suffered a fire that did us no harm.

Then, taking the road to the right and exiting onto the plain, we found ourselves facing a Prussian battalion. The charge was successful and we entered the square which lay down its arms. We lost an officer and two hussars killed.

As we then passed along the road towards Wavre, between the left bank of the Dyle and the hills, we saw Gérard's corps which had taken position between Wavre and Limal.

The banks of the Dyle are marshy out to a great distance on each bank and, what's more, the river has very steep banks.

We had already made about three-quarters of a league, when an officer came to us to tell us to pull back to take the road that passes through the village. Whilst waiting for us to return, the second brigade, composed of dragoons, had followed this new direction.

It was only a very poor track, very narrow, that offered us a climb up the escarpment on the left of the Dyle valley. The enemy, on the edge of the plateau where he appeared, fired at us. The dragoons followed this route. The 14th Line marched on the flanks, climbing as best they could. A young drummer of this regiment, who was beating his drum, was shot in the hand. He nevertheless continued to beat his drum with just his good one.[31]

Grouchy had successfully captured a crossing-point over the Dyle; now it was important to flood troops across in order to secure the bridgehead before he could consider sending troops on towards Saint-Lambert as ordered by the emperor. A bridgehead is vulnerable to a quick counter-attack and Grouchy could be sure that General Thielemann, his flank threatened, would be making the necessary arrangements.

Chapter 15

The Night of 18/19 June

With the bridge of Limal in French hands, Pajol was quick to follow up this success:

> Pajol then called forward Vallin's second brigade, composed of dragoons, and entered Limal with it. It was a little later than 8pm. He went to chase the Prussian posts from the part of the village that faced Grand-Sart, which had initially run off, but then returned when they saw Vallin's first brigade take the Wavre road.
> All these enemy detachments and posts belonged to a column commanded by Colonel Stengel [he was actually a major], who had been ordered to observe Limal and Limelette. Surprised by this sudden attack, Stengel quickly reassembled his battalions on the heights which dominated the two roads from Limal to Grand-Sart and to Rosieren. From there, by a well-nourished and well-directed fire, he prevented the dragoons from leaving the village. Pajol immediately sent to find Teste's infantry and gave the order to Vallin's first brigade to leave the Bierge road, which it had followed for about half a league, and for it to return to Limal. Teste soon arrived with one of his regiments which he launched towards Grand-Sart. The struggle became lively and murderous; our soldiers climbed the steep slopes on the flanks of the heights with difficulty, from where the enemy shot at them. However, they surmounted all obstacles and arrived on the plateau, where Pajol had them followed and supported by cavalry. The Prussians, outflanked, retired in the direction of Bierge. Limal was ours; Pajol's audacious movement had opened the passage of the Dyle.[1]

During this action, Lieutenant Libert of the 6th Hussars (Vallin's division) was conspicuous by his courage and daring:

> On the 18th June, he was in advance of the bridge over the Dyle at Limal when the Prussians, who had been beaten back several times, returned in

superior numbers. Despite being covered in wounds that he had already received during the day, Libert, with some hussars, fell on the enemy battalions, opening a bloody passage through their ranks and he forced himself into the mêlée where he was struck by several balls. But the pain was insufficient to dent his enthusiasm and he continued to strike the most terrible blows. Soon, enveloped by smoke, he disappeared. The return of his mount with its harness covered in blood was enough to be sure that *la patrie* had lost one of its most unselfish defenders.[2]

In Martinien's list of French officer casualties during the wars, Libert is listed as wounded, presumed dead.

Teste's assault on the heights which the enemy occupied took up more precious time and it was only towards nine o'clock that Pajol was able, by Grand-Sart and Neuf-Cabaret, to each of which he immediately sent off his scouts, to march towards Saint-Lambert.

Grouchy was well placed to observe Pajol's success and was quick to support him. In his memoirs he is quoted as follows:

We arrived from the valley in which the Dyle flows onto the plateau which dominates the villages of Limal and Limelette, only by a steep and craggy track; the darkness of night rendered this climb slow and difficult; the congestion was extreme, there was insufficient ground to deploy properly and the proximity of the enemy was such that their balls struck the head of the defile. I sensed all the dangers of such a position and I remained on this point until close to midnight, occupied by watching arrive the soldiers and putting them into position myself so that they occupied the part of the plateau of which we were masters. General Pajol's cavalry was on the left, having the Dyle behind it; its position was hardly better than that of the infantry and artillery that I had on this side of the river. The Prussians continued to occupy half of Wavre, the mill and village of Bierge and lined their right and the woods with the troops that I had in front of me. It was probable that, if we were vigorously counter-attacked, we would have been thrown back with loss onto the other side of the Dyle.

It was as urgent to push the enemy back at this point as a success was desirable since it would have allowed me to cut off the Prussian troops opposed to General Vandamme and to make a junction with Napoleon, of whom however, there was no need to be anxious as the letter of the *major-général* had informed me that we had won the battle at Waterloo. I was surprised not to have received any news, despite sending several officers and patrols.[3]

Little did Grouchy know as he speculated about his junction with Napoleon, that the emperor's army, far from being victorious, had been catastrophically defeated at Waterloo.

When he had left Vandamme, Grouchy had ordered all Gérard's divisions to follow him to Limal; Hulot was also to join them from his abortive attempts to capture the Bierge mill. As they came forward they were pushed across the river to consolidate the French bridgehead. The plateau above the Limal crossing was described as '. . . covered in heather and wooded in places'.[4] As they came onto the high ground, Gérard's divisions were put into line and kept on the alert. Exelmans, who Grouchy had also ordered to Limal, stopped for the night at Saint-Anne, three kilometres south of Wavre.

General Pajol's deployment is described in his memoirs:

> Pajol, who had been joined by the whole of Teste's division, found himself to the west of Delbourg, with some of his cavalry as far as Neuf-Cabaret. Fortuitously, he was reinforced by Hulot's division of IV Corps that General Vichery (who had replaced Gérard in command of this corps) had placed close to the road to Roserien, a little to the rear and east of Delbourg.[5]

As could have been expected, the Prussians were quick to try and push the French back off the high ground before they had time to organise a defence. Hearing that the French had crossed the Dyle, *Oberst* von Stülpnagel, commander of the 12th Brigade of Thielemann's corps marched against Grouchy's line. Stülpnagel commanded nine strong battalions in three regiments, and two squadrons, and had originally been ordered to defend the Bierge crossing. He left two battalions to defend Bierge and a third to cover between that place and Wavre. He marched with his other six battalions and the support of the corps reserve cavalry (*Generalmajor* von Hobe) that Thielemann sent to him. As he advanced he met Stengel's force retiring. Placing them in reserve he advanced with two battalions of the 31st Regiment in column preceded by a skirmish screen.

By now it was dark and soon the skirmish screens of both forces became engaged in a chaotic close-range firefight in the darkness. Eventually, the Prussian skirmishers fell back on the following columns that advanced to the assault with lowered bayonets. However, they suddenly found themselves confronted by a sunken lane behind which the French were waiting for them. Stopped in their tracks by this obstacle, the Prussian columns were forced back by a devastating series of French volleys. Stülpnagel was forced to give up the attempt and withdrew his men to the edge of the Rixensart woods. He tied his left flank in with the troops he had left at Bierge.

Pajol's memoirs describe the encounter:

> The Prussian columns coming from Bierge collided with Hulot's division, which decimated them in the gullies where they were caught and forced

them into a precipitous retreat. Pajol, on his side, stopped the enemy's right wing and repulsed Hobe's cavalry. Night did not allow him to pursue his success. However, the lines of Vichery and Pajol advanced a little towards Bierge and the Rixensart wood, edging a little closer to the Bierge to Neuf-Cabaret road.

The Prussians, who were retiring slowly and still skirmishing, stopped. Stengal was in the Rixensart wood; Hobe's cavalry were behind this wood; Stulpnagel at Bierge joined Stengal; Kemphen was between Bierge and Wavre; but their scouts had remained at musket range from those of Vichery and Pajol, who were still skirmishing at 11pm.[6]

All the French battalions spent the night in square; it was a dark night and the Prussians remained so close that the sentries often exchanged shots; indeed, several men of Grouchy's escort were hit. Grouchy, after retiring to the farm of la Bourse to send out orders, spent the night within one of the regimental squares of Vichery's division. Hulot's division, that had been engaged at Bierge, was the last division of IV Corps to cross the Dyle at Limal. Hulot wrote:

At 3am on the 19th, I received the order to move to Limal with the 3rd Division; a movement that I executed immediately. I rejoined the other two divisions of the IV Corps on the heights ahead of this place and the 3rd was placed in the second line.[7]

Grouchy's first order was to General Vandamme:

The heights of Limal, 18 June 1815, 11.30pm
My dear General, we have managed to get through Limal, but night has not allowed us to follow up, so we are face to face with the enemy. Since you have not been able to cross the Dyle, will you at once move to Limal with your corps, leaving only sufficient troops behind that can remain to hold that part of Wavre that you currently occupy. First thing in the morning we will attack the troops that are facing me and I hope we will succeed in joining the emperor as he has ordered. It is said he is fighting the English; but I have no more news and am hindered in giving him ours.

It is in the name of *la patrie* that I pray you, my dear comrade, to execute this order at once. I only see this option of getting out of the difficult situation that we are in, and the salvation of the army depends on it.

I put General Gérard's corps under your command. I await you.
Le maréchal Grouchy[8]

Though rather pleading, the order is explicit and offered the wing the opportunity to concentrate and march towards Napoleon the next day. Sadly and perhaps unsurprisingly, Grouchy's *aide de camp* Bella wrote, 'This order was not executed by General Vandamme; like most of those that you gave him during the campaign.'[9]

Grouchy claims that Vandamme made thirteen useless attacks on Wavre.[10] The fighting died out due to the exhaustion of both sides. The 15th *léger* of Lefol's division, commanded by Colonel Brice, lost fifteen officers at Wavre, having already lost one on the 15th and fourteen on the 16th at Ligny. Under cover of the darkness, Vandamme had the opportunity to extract his troops and march down to join Grouchy. We can only speculate why he chose not to do so. Vandamme's subordinates were not impressed; Colonel Fantin des Odoards wrote:

> These feeble and foolish attacks on Wavre and the long exchange of fire which followed, cost us dear. My 22nd lost 146 men; other regiments lost more . . . Unhappy with ourselves, and very anxious as to the results of the long cannonade that could be heard throughout the day from towards Mont Saint Jean, which only ceased towards evening, we passed the following night in bivouac at the gates of the unhappy town of Wavre, which was devoured by the fire that was started during the fighting.[11]

Grouchy had now concentrated four infantry divisions (Pécheux, Vichery, Hulot and Teste) above Limal as well as Pajol's single cavalry division and that of Vallin. During the remainder of the night he made the preparations for an attack the next morning.

In the seizing of the bridge at Limal and the repulse of the Prussian counter-attack, the day had ended with something of a success, but not everyone was impressed; as a summary of the day, *Maréchal de Camp* Berton had this to say:

> Instead of attempting a flanking manoeuvre in order to cross the Dyle we all marched on Wavre, without even looking at the Moustier bridge. We remained for part of the day firing balls up against a formidable position beyond a river which in any other case we would have already crossed without firing a shot. Instead, we launched successive infantry attacks against the bridge at Wavre and the Bierge mill where we uselessly lost many men on the two points where the enemy could defend with advantage. Four-fifths of our infantry could not be engaged in front of Wavre and eighteen regiments of cavalry had nothing to do; deployed partly in the rear and partly to the right where there was no enemy.[12]

Chapter 16

Morning, 19 June

Grouchy now had four infantry divisions and two light cavalry divisions across the Dyle; a force that outnumbered Thielemann's stretched units. Vichery, Pêcheux and Teste were in the first line with Hulot in the second. Grouchy was now strong enough to launch an attack at first light and as it approached he had the divisions form up in three columns with Teste on the right and Pajol's cavalry on the left. Hulot remained in reserve. Each division had its battery deployed to its front. Exelmans was ordered to continue his march and cross the Dyle at Limal.

After the failed night attack, Stüpnagel's infantry and Hobe's cavalry reserve were still deployed before the French, but unfortunately for Thielemann, after their repulse, Stengel had marched his force off to the west to rejoin his own corps, and the majority of Borke's 9th Brigade, that had mistakenly marched off towards Waterloo the day before, had not returned. What remained of Thielemann's corps was insufficient to stop what he realised would be coming the next morning. However, he used the night to reinforce his right flank and form a continuous line at right-angles to the Dyle; six battalions of the 12th Brigade lined the forward edge of the Rixensart woods; three weak battalions lined the road to the west of Point du Jour; five battalions of the 10th Brigade linked these to Bierge supported by the two cavalry squadrons of 12th brigade and Hobe's reserve cavalry was deployed on the right of the line, behind the Rixensart wood, supported by a single infantry battalion; four battalions under *Oberst* von Zeppelin along with three further battalions of the 10th and 11th Brigades remained in Wavre facing Vandamme. The Prussians had only two batteries on this side of the battlefield, the others remained sited to cover the river crossings. The whole Prussian force was considerably outnumbered by Grouchy's six divisions and seven batteries.

Sometime in the early morning, Thielemann learnt from an officer of von Hobe's cavalry, who had been sent in reconnaissance towards Waterloo, the first intimation of Napoleon's defeat the day before. Presuming that Grouchy would have received the same news and would be contemplating retreat, Thielemann resolved to attack at first light in an attempt to disrupt the move.

As 3am approached both sides were standing to, ready to attack. Grouchy wrote, 'The enemy freed me from the need to go to look for him by advancing against me.'¹ Thielemann's attack was led by Hobe's cavalry that moved through the Rixensart wood and formed up in the open ground opposite Pajol. Thielemann's two batteries also deployed in front of the wood and opened fire. Pajol's *aide de camp* described the combat:

> At dawn the next day, the 19th, the bivouac of the 1st Hussars was saluted by a hail of balls. It was Tauentzin's [Thielemann's] Prussian corps that formed Blücher's rearguard that had been left to defend the bridges at Wavre and Limal . . .
> At the first cannon shot, I went towards the area attacked and returned to warn General Pajol of what was going on; he went to the area himself.
> Our troops were already formed up, but not facing up. It was feared that, if pushed back hard into the defile that was behind them, they would break into Gérard's divisions and drag them along in their retrograde movement . . .
> I received the order to accompany General Ameil who had been ordered to pursue the enemy and accelerate their retreat with the 4th and 5th Hussars. Beyond the Rixensart wood, which was in front of us, we could see the Prussians clearly. General Ameil, who possessed a good *coup d'oeil*, said to me, 'These men have not been routed, but are retiring in good order. As we cannot turn the wood in front of us, it would not be wise to go in there without infantry. Go and ask for some.'
> We halted and I went to request a battalion from Marshal Grouchy. As I led this battalion towards the enemy, I encountered General Pajol. He sent me back to the marshal to find out if he was to pursue the enemy in the direction of Rosieren, or to the left towards the village of Waterloo.
> The cannon had been heard all the previous day, but since the evening they had been silent. The battle was over and we remained convinced that it had been to our advantage.²

Pajol also described this action:

> The Prussians were ready first; at first light, between 2 and 2.30am, they threw themselves on the outposts of Pajol and Vichery. The French troops were on their guard however, and successfully repulsed the Prussian attack. A little later, Thielemann executed his main attack on the French left, attempting to get twelve squadrons out of the Rixensart wood, preceding eight guns and supported by the battalions of Stülpnagel's first line. Soult's division had to support the full weight of this attack, and the bivouac of the 1st Hussars was riddled with musket shot. Pajol hastened there, got his artillery into battery and deployed the rest of Soult's regiments as well as those of Vallin.³

The infantry columns also came under the Prussian fire; General Teste wrote:

> At 3am on the 19th, the enemy attacked. His skirmish fire was well maintained. He at once showed three guns in battery which threatened our infantry squares. They found some cover by retiring just a few paces. Our divisional artillery opened fire and was so effective that it forced that of the enemy to change position several times; it dismounted two of his guns.[4]

The French artillery very quickly overwhelmed that of the Prussians and started to cause heavy casualties amongst von Hobe's cavalry. In fact five Prussian guns were put out of action and the 1st Brigade of Hobe's cavalry (12th Hussars, 7th and 8th Uhlans) were forced to withdraw back through the wood. Seeing the Prussians withdrawing, Grouchy released his three columns which attacked the wood. The edge was held by a thick line of skirmishers, but as Grouchy's *tirailleurs* advanced, the Prussians fed ever more troops into the firing line from their columns in the rear. In danger of being overwhelmed, the Prussian infantry fell back and formed a new line behind the wood; their cavalry reformed at Champles. The French occupied the Rixensart wood and prepared to advance again. On the right of the French line, Teste's division attacked the village of Bierge; here the Prussian resistance was much more determined and Teste was held up by a strong skirmish line.

It was at this time, about 8am, that Thielemann received confirmation of the allied victory at Waterloo. Spreading the news throughout his force he organised a counter-attack on the Rixensart wood with much cheering, hoping that the French would understand the significance of it. The counter-attack succeeded in temporarily re-taking the wood, but soon French numbers overwhelmed them and they were quickly forced out again. However, it seems some French troops realised what had happened, as Captain Francois relates:

> General Pêcheux sent us forward and we surprised a Prussian guard of about 300 men, some of whom we bayoneted and the rest we took prisoners. I was the last to cut and slash in the enemy's ranks; being enraged and wanting to avenge myself, I did not know on whom, whilst cursing most of our generals whom I considered traitors. This affair being over, we advanced noiselessly and, when daylight came, formed a line of skirmishers. Then we fired on *messieurs* the Prussians who retired without making great resistance towards Wavre and the woods to draw us on. These boasters seemed to know of the disaster of Waterloo. Many of them, after having fired, retired crying in German, 'Come along with us brave Frenchmen. You have no army left; Napoleon is dead.' I and several of my comrades who understood German did not know what to think of these rumours.[5]

Penne's brigade (65th and 75th *de ligne*) of Teste's division was sent against Bierge. Teste reported that:

The enemy manoeuvred to our right, the marshal sent forces to repulse them and they were pursued as far as the bottom of the valley from where they had departed. A large number of skirmishers from the 1st brigade of the division chased them further and soon captured the first houses of the village of Bierge, which was on a steep height and cut by several sunken roads.

Following this advantage, our skirmishers captured the church, which dominated the village, and moved to attack the mill. They were ordered to stop. Marshal Grouchy awaited General Vandamme's corps which was on our right. It was at this moment that General Penne, pressing his horse to follow the movements of our brave *voltigeurs*, had his head taken off by a cannonball. This general officer, full of daring and merit, was regretted by all. Captain le Roux, his *aide de camp*, became mine for the rest of the campaign.

The masses of the III Corps were soon seen on the left of Bierge, our skirmishers, supported by the 1st Brigade pursued their success against General Thielemann's troops which retired in the greatest disorder.[6]

It appears Lefol's division of III Corps, seeing Penne's brigade attacking Bierge from the far bank, also moved forward. Captain Gerbet of this division wrote:

Returning to the attack like the day before, the enemy did not put up the same determined defence of Wavre or Bierge.

In the morning of the 19th June, I found myself attacking the Bierge mill that we took without much resistance. The enemy retired, knowing that we still did not realise the fatal result of the cannonade of the previous day. A little time later this fatal news was brought to us.[7]

After the Bierge mill had been occupied by Lefol's division, Berthezène's division crossed and joined Grouchy on the left bank. After their robust defence of the day before and the renewed fighting in the morning, Thielemann's troops were beginning to run short of ammunition. This, the news of the allied victory and Grouchy's aggression resolved Thielemann to withdraw. As the Prussians did so, Vandamme was quick to throw Habert's battered division across the bridge in Wavre. Menaced on his left, and almost outflanked on his right by Pajol, Thielemann ordered a retreat on Louvain. The impact of this sudden withdrawal after such a stubborn defence was striking; Colonel Fantin des Odoards wrote:

On the morning of the 19th we again came to blows with them; but soon he suddenly disappeared and a sinister silence settled on the countryside which had trembled the previous day to the sound of artillery fire . . .[8]

Vandamme reacted quickly and passed through Wavre on the Brussels road, pursuing the Prussians as far as La Bavete and then taking his place in line to the right of IV Corps; he captured a number of wounded Prussians and five guns. With the Prussians now withdrawing more quickly, Pajol occupied Rosieren with the 4th and 5th Hussars led by General Ameil. The Prussians were already about two and a half leagues from Wavre. Coming close to this point, Pajol sent Commandant Biot to Grouchy to seek direction as to whether he should pursue the Prussians down the Brussels road or move to the left towards Waterloo.

Thielemann's troops retained their order, but were now retreating fast to try and break contact with the French. With the road to Brussels cut by Pajol's cavalry, Thielemann ordered a move back to Saint-Agatha-Rode, two hours march from Wavre on the road towards Louvain; his rearguard took position at Ottenburg. With Thielemann beaten, Grouchy was now poised to re-direct his troops back towards Saint-Lambert as ordered by the emperor; he had lost about 2,400 men in the fighting of the last two days.

Colonel Zenowicz, who had been ordered to remain with Grouchy until he had rejoined Napoleon, was clearly pleased with what had happened so far that morning. His optimism was to be misplaced:

Finally, at dawn on the 19th, the mill was taken and General Thielemann's corps retreated. We were all overjoyed in the hope that there were no more obstacles to joining the emperor and his army. After having paid my final respects to my friend General Penne who had been killed, I advanced along the left bank of the Dyle with some *chasseurs* that General Pajol had given me. I encountered no one; the enemy was retreating hastily along the road to Brussels.

I quickly returned to take Marshal Grouchy's orders; I met him in a field where he was writing. On approaching him I said, 'Marshal, this is a good day for you!' He received me with his usual pleasantness, but I soon noticed with surprise that he was preoccupied, which was unusual given his recent success. He noticed my surprise and asked me if I knew the officer from general headquarters who had arrived. On my response that I had not seen him, he pointed him out in the middle of a group of officers. Now anxious myself, I hurried over to him. I then learnt the distressing news of the battle of Waterloo![9]

The arrival of the shocking news from Waterloo was witnessed by a number of officers who later wrote of their experiences; let's start with *Commandant* Biot:

I was on my way to the marshal with the general's request, when an *aide de camp*, covered in dust and whose horse appeared literally broken from being ridden too hard, passed close by me, desiring to see the marshal on behalf of the emperor. I pointed him out.

He approached and the conversation took place with lowered voices.

From this alone, I felt it did not bode well; it seemed to me that if this officer had brought good news, he would have hurried to announce it loudly.

As I have said, the cannonade had ceased the day before; the battle had thus finished. But in whose favour had it been decided? It is there that the enigma was to be found.

After a short time, the marshal asked his *aides de camp* to carry the order for all the generals to assemble . . . Then, with a distressed look, the marshal turned, asking for General Pajol's *aide de camp*. I advanced; 'Go at the gallop,' he ordered me, 'and tell your general to come and talk to me!' I left, but, reflecting that I had not received a response to my first question, I retraced my steps. 'And the movement?' I said to the marshal, 'Remain in place, and hurry.' All this hardly reassured me, and this is why. My thoughts led me to imagine some disaster, but I did not know what sort. I even thought that perhaps the emperor had been killed. I was soon back with General Pajol and I gave him the orders I had received. It was at least the eighth or tenth time since the morning that the marshal had asked for my general; but this last had a sense of urgency that demanded a response. I told him a little of what I had heard and did not hide from him my secret apprehension. He went straight off and I followed him.[10]

General Hulot was also a witness:

The offensive movement that the enemy had made in the morning, their stubborn resistance, then their sudden retreat and the absence of any news of Napoleon gave rise to contradicting conjectures on the battle of the day before. The generals attempted to exchange their ideas and General Grouchy having appeared, was soon surrounded. It was nearly 10 o'clock. He confirmed that he still had no news of the emperor. It was at this very moment that calling those generals that were not too far from the group to join him, he declared that his honour demanded that he should explain his military arrangements of the day before, that he wanted to make it clear that instructions had not given him the latitude to manoeuvre on any other point than Wavre, that he acknowledged the talents and brilliant courage of General Gérard who, at this point, did not agree with General Vandamme and himself, but that whatever had happened to the rest of the army, he could only act as prescribed in his orders. Without doubt, other generals than I recall these clear words of General Grouchy.[11]

Grouchy's memoirs give the details from his perspective:

Thielemann, not seeing Pirch coming and not being strong enough on his own, continued to fight as best he could whilst retiring. Grouchy pushed him towards Brussels without knowing the events of the previous day. Finally, towards 10.30am, an officer of the general headquarters of the *Duc de Dalmatie*, joined him before Rosieren and gave him the fatal news. The officer from the *major-général* carried no despatch and it was only verbally that he informed Marshal Grouchy of the fatal outcome of the previous day. He was overcome by fatigue, and was unable to be precise about the direction taken by the emperor in retiring. He replied to the questions put to him so incoherently, that the marshal at first thought that he was drunk or had lost his head. But the details into which he entered concerning the disorganisation of the corps and our losses in men, horses and materiel, finally convinced the marshal of the sad state of affairs.[12]

The officer who carried the news was Captain Dumonceau, an *aide de camp* of General Gressot, the *sous-chef de l'état-major general*.

Grouchy felt that if the emperor was in such a critical position as Dumonceau claimed, he would have ensured Grouchy knew the direction in which he was retiring and would have ordered him to join him as quickly as possible. The arrival of Grouchy's corps with the emperor's army would have doubtlessly have eased the situation and have provided a rearguard behind which the army might have rallied. But this would have required Napoleon nominating a point on which Grouchy should move; clearly, Grouchy did not get this.

Grouchy claims that at first he considered trying to hold up the allied pursuit by moving rapidly onto their rear. This seems somewhat daring for Grouchy and it is unsurprising that in the account of the campaign that appears in Vandamme's published correspondence it claims this daring idea belonged to Vandamme:

> A sort of council of war was held. Vandamme wanted to march on Brussels, throwing themselves on the rear of the enemy to make a diversion in favour of the beaten army. This advice was that of an enthusiastic man, audacious to the point of temerity, and for a moment, Grouchy appeared to take this advice. However, on reflection, he renounced it, considering it wiser to retreat to Paris with a small army of 30,000 brave soldiers that was not disorganised or demoralised on which to provide the nucleus for a defence of the country.[13]

Having sent for all the senior officers to join him, Grouchy claims to have written the following despatch to Napoleon:

Rosieren, 19 June 1815

Sire, yesterday, at the moment I was attacking Wavre, I received Your Majesty's letter which directed me to move on Saint-Lambert and to attack Bülow. Your Majesty's cannon made me hasten my movement, but I had the whole of Vandamme's corps closely engaged. I suffered great difficulties crossing the Dyle. However, I went to affect a crossing at Limal, but it was night and I was not able to make great progress, especially as at the passage of Wavre and that at Bierge, there was no success. In trying the latter, General Gérard received a ball in the chest, although it is not thought to be mortal. No longer hearing the cannon this morning, and thinking Blücher and Bülow before me, I thought I would attack them; they avoided me at all points.[14]

This letter is clearly an attempt to explain why he was unable to comply with the orders that the emperor had sent him. What seems strange is that given his surprise at not being given any orders by the emperor, he seeks no information on the positions Napoleon and his army were in, nor asks what he should do or where he should direct his march. Whatever condition Napoleon's army was in, a reinforcement of 25,000 men would inevitably have offered a number of options.

Biot accompanied General Pajol back to Grouchy:

When he arrived, the other commanding generals were already formed in a circle around Marshal Grouchy. On my side, I succeeded in getting close to the officer who had come on this mission. It did not take much begging from me for him to describe the disaster of Waterloo and the disorganisation that this fatal day had thrown into the ranks of the survivors.

I was appalled. I sensed how important it would be to keep this bad news secret for as long as possible in order to avoid the demoralisation that it would produce. I thus bound the officer to maintain a profound silence above all.

I left him to reflect on our position which was certainly not good. A few moments later, the commanding officer of the service battalion close to the marshal called me and told me that he had already learnt. I was incredulous. Then, to convince me, he confirmed all the details from the mouth of the officer sent by the emperor. It was clear that my advice had not been followed.[15]

If the content of Grouchy's letter seems strange, then given the critical situation he suddenly found himself in, his next act was stranger still; as his own memoirs put it, he, 'thought it his duty to inform the officers that surrounded him the motives that had determined his movements since he had been despatched by the emperor.'[16] When he had all his senior commanders around him, he gave the following speech justifying his actions since the battle of Ligny:

'They had been based,' he told them, 'on the successive orders that he [Napoleon] gave me. On the 17th, at 1pm, he ordered me to pursue the

Prussians, to fight them as soon as I encountered them and not to lose sight of them,' and added, 'it is on the Meuse and in the direction of Maastricht, that Marshal Blücher retires, thus it is towards Namur that you are to march. I am going to Quatre Bras where I will attack the English if they take position this side of the Soignes forest.' Several hours later, the emperor modified these initial orders and wrote to me by the *Grand Maréchal du Palais*, General Bertrand, for me to go to Gembloux and to restrict myself to sending a reconnaissance towards Namur.

'It is important, he added in this letter, to discover what the Prussians plan to do; will they separate from the English, or do they intend to risk the outcome of another battle. In any case, always keep your two infantry corps within a league of ground, occupy a good military position every evening, with several lines of retreat, and move on Gembloux.

'During the night of the 17th and at dawn on the 18th, I wrote three letters to the emperor from Gembloux, to pass to him the information I had received relative to the movements of the Prussians and to warn him that the tardy arrival of the IV Corps at Gembloux, where it still had not arrived by 11pm, and the storm of the day before had not allowed me to move the III Corps further than a league beyond Gembloux; but on learning that several Prussian columns had appeared towards Sart-à-Walhain, moving towards Wavre, I proposed to start off very early in the morning and to head first on Sart-à-Walhain from where I would address a new despatch to him.

'Towards 12.30pm, a letter from the *major-général*, dated from the farm of la Caillou, 18 June, 10am [as we have seen this letter was actually received at about 4pm], announced to me that the emperor was going to attack the English army which was in position on the edge of the Soignes forest. In this letter, my movement on Sart-à-Walhain was approved as conforming with the instructions that had been sent to me. Finally, it ended with this observation, that in informing the emperor of what I had learnt of the march of the Prussian army, I had said nothing of an enemy column of considerable strength which, when leaving the battlefield of Fleurus in the evening of the 16th, that was moving on Géry and Gentines, but which then moved on Wavre where I was to arrive as soon as possible.

'From this letter, it appeared evident to me that the emperor did not judge that he had need of my co-operation to beat the English army, since the moment when he was attacking them, he directed me not to go to join him, but to move rapidly on Wavre, the direction that took us no further apart.

'It still remains to me, *messieurs*, to briefly let you know for what reasons I did not accept the advice that Count Gérard thought he should rightly give me, when the sounds of a cannonade could be heard at Sart-à-Walhain towards 11.30am. It should not, I said to him, surprise us, since when leaving the emperor the day before, he warned me that he was going to Quatre Bras to attack the English army if it was not retreating on Brussels. This cannonade was, besides, not of sufficient intensity to allow us to judge if it was a rearguard engagement or a general engagement. I stopped at Sart-à-Walhain to write to the emperor and was about to send off my letter with Major de la Fresnaye, one of my *officiers d'ordonnance*, when General Exelmans warned me by one of his *aides de camp*, that he was facing a Prussian rearguard barring the route to Wavre.

'I immediately mounted my horse to go to have it attacked, but I was held up by Count Gérard who pressed me again, as he had already done, to march to the sound of the cannon, or to allow him to march there with the IV Corps if I did not think it right to do this with all my troops.

'You would, like me, be surprised that he did not feel it was inappropriate for a general officer to ignore orders received from the emperor, and that were given to a marshal of France under whose orders he was serving, ventured to publicly tell him what he should do, and undermine, by a disapproval displayed before a number of subordinates, the confidence that is desirable that the officer and soldier display for their commander-in-chief, confidence which is one of the most necessary elements to lighten the burden of an obedience that difficult circumstances render painful and often from a position of ignorance.

'In any event, from one part of the emperor's letters that I have made known to you, the advanced hour of the day, the distance from where the cannon were heard, the state of the roads which were entirely broken up by the storm during the night, made it impossible to arrive in enough time to take part in the affair which was taking place.

'Besides, there was then only a single one of the divisions of the IV Corps that had reached Sart-à-Walhain; the rest were still a league and a half in the rear.

'The III Corps was in the presence of the Prussian army that I was pursuing, of which the strength was triple that of mine, and all the reports announced that they were concentrated at Wavre.

'Should I, in such circumstances, ignore the intention of the emperor and the first rules of strategy, which permit neither the division of my forces [remember Napoleon had told him to keep his corps 'within a league'], nor to abandon to its own resources the III Corps at the moment that it was engaged with the enemy and to separate it from the IV by an un-fordable river, separating them by several leagues.

'All this thus made it my duty to ignore this absurd advice and to act as I have.

'The difficult position in which the disasters of Waterloo placed us, did not permit me to give in this moment to the motives of my determinations; but I am convinced that they will finish with you agreeing and I take the engagement of the subject in all their details to the understanding not only of men of merit, but also to the whole of France.'[17]

With the dangers that Grouchy's forces were now in and with time being of the essence, this is a rather odd time to deliver a speech of self-justification in front of his most senior generals, suggesting both indecision and a lack of self-confidence. It is possible that this speech was a much later work which was added to his memoirs to put forward his position to the readers. However, it is mentioned by Hulot is his report of 1818. Pajol, who was present, wrote:

> The marshal, appalled, called together all his senior generals: Vandamme, Exelmans, Vichery and Pajol. Weeping, he announced the immense misfortune then consulted with them on the action to be taken. After a short deliberation, it was decided that in the absence of precise directions from the emperor on where to go, they should retire as quickly as possible to Namur, in order to get the Sambre river between them and the pursuit of the victorious enemy.[18]

Thus we hear of the catastrophic news being passed on to his commanders and a collective agreement on what should happen next. Vandamme suggested continuing the march on Brussels and acting on the allied rear, forcing at least some of their forces to turn against them and easing the pressure on Napoleon's army. Grouchy claims to have considered this suggestion seriously at first, but then decided that such an action would most probably result in their destruction. It was agreed that they should retreat, keeping to the east in an effort to avoid any attempt to cut him off from France and use his own small army for the core of a new one that could protect Paris, justifying his decision thus:

> I marched on Namur. Going in this direction I was covered by the Sambre and Meuse and, masked by these two rivers, I would also be able to fall on the flank of the Anglo-Prussians if they made a false move or the nature of the ground offered me an opportunity to strike with advantage.[19]

General Pajol gives the outline plan:

> Exelmans' dragoons were immediately directed towards Namur with the wounded and the reserve parks, III and IV Corps were to stop on the line of la Bavette, which they currently occupied, then go in two columns towards Namur; IV Corps would lead by Limal and Gembloux, followed by III Corps by Wavre, Tourinnes-les-Ourdons and Grand-Lez. Vallin's cavalry would cover IV Corps, whilst Pajol, with Soult's and Teste's divisions, remained last on the current positions and to continue to pursue the enemy

so that he did not consider turning about. Meanwhile, Vandamme was to occupy Wavre long enough to help Pajol contain Thielemann if he reappeared before IV Corps had crossed the defiles of Limal and revealed his march on Gembloux.

These arrangements agreed, Pajol immediately rejoined Soult's division at Rosieren and led it along the heights on the right bank of the Lasne in the direction of Rhode-Sainte-Agathe. The hussars charged the enemy rearguards several times, accelerating their retreat and thus effectively masking the retrograde movements of the rest of Grouchy's army. As a precautionary measure, Pajol had supported Soult with Teste's infantry which marched towards Ottenburg, but before arriving at that village, Soult and Teste were stopped and only some scouts were sent to continue to follow the Prussians for a little longer. Thielemann had not turned about; he established his bivouacs at Rhode-Sainte-Agathe, where he passed the night.[20]

Grouchy or Exelmans ordered the pursuit of Thielemann to be halted, although as Pajol wrote, light cavalry continued to advance to cover the retreat and to convince Thielemann that the French were continuing to advance. Exelmans was ordered to move with his dragoons to Namur and ensure he got there and held the place before the enemy could. General Strolz would take his division down one road, whilst General Chastel would take his down the other. Dragoons were ideal for such a mission; they could reach the town quickly and then dismount to use their muskets to defend its strong walls if necessary.

Despite the devastating news, the retreat appears to have been well organised and conducted in good order. Grouchy left behind Exelmans with IV Corps, leaving III Corps to travel down the other route once IV Corps was clear. Berthezène does not appear to have been very happy with the role his corps was given:

> Grouchy . . . left the III Corps before Wavre throughout the 19th without thinking that this corps, abandoned, could be attacked and beaten and himself exposed to being compromised between very superior forces . . .[21]

In fact, Vandamme's corps was in no immediate danger; Thielemann was in no position to interfere and there was still time to reach Namur before other Prussian troops could interfere. Captain Gerbet, whose regiment was part of Lefol's division, obviously formed the rearguard:

> Grouchy immediately took the necessary measures to ensure the retreat of our two corps. He did this with the left leading, thus our division, which was the first of the III Corps, that had formed the head of the column in the advance, found itself the last in the retreat.[22]

With the two infantry corps taking different routes and a sense of urgency instilled in the troops, the move contrasted starkly and tellingly with the advance across much of the same ground as the day before. Colonel Fantin des Odoards wrote:

> This retrograde march, although quick, was made in order, in two columns, in the direction of Namur. The enemy did not appear during the day and, at night, we were a quarter of a league from Gembloux, where we halted for a few hours, without fires and with the same order that we had moved in.[23]

General Hulot states, 'Our movement was only followed by a few parties of cavalry.'[24] In the combats of the last twenty four hours, French casualties had been relatively light, but Prussian casualties were put at seventy nine officers and 2,400 other ranks *hors de combat*.[25]

The Prussian Pursuit
After their decisive intervention at Waterloo he previous day, Blücher's headquarters now put its mind to trying to cut Grouchy's force off from Paris with the hope of capturing or destroying it. Therefore, on the morning of the 19th, plans were drawn up to continue the pursuit of the main French army whilst trying to cut Grouchy's direct route towards Paris and then to beat him to Namur. Pirch I's II Corps was allocated the latter task. However, it was only at 11am that his troops had concentrated at Mellery. After their exertions of the previous few days it is hardly surprising that the seventeen kilometres they had marched had taken nine hours; they were clearly exhausted. Grouchy, by taking a more easterly route, had passed through Gembloux before Pirch I had been able to reach it

The race was now on to be the first to the strategically-important town of Namur. If Grouchy could reach it first, he had a good chance of saving his command; if the Prussians arrived first, then Grouchy faced almost inevitable capture or destruction. Grouchy's retreat and the fate of his small army will be covered in detail in the final book of this series, *Retreat from Waterloo*.

Chapter 17

Analysis and Conclusion

Everyone can think and write of war, few men understand it well, many can only judge the results on which they raise the reputations of a few men and destroy those of others![1]

For many years after their humiliating defeat, the French inevitably sought to examine why the campaign had ended in catastrophe. As we have already heard, Napoleon himself, ever careful to try and maintain his own military reputation, was quick to blame his two principal lieutenants, Marshals Ney and Grouchy. To this end he had inferred their guilt in a number of accounts and reports even as the campaign collapsed and consolidated his criticism in the accounts that he dictated on Saint Helena. It was these accounts and others that were based on them that sparked almost two centuries of debate and argument. Having given as thorough and accurate an account of Grouchy's campaign as possible, it may now be useful to look at each of the areas of controversy in detail.

Grouchy's Orders from Napoleon
Speculating about what Grouchy should have done, without careful consideration of what he was ordered to do by Napoleon is unhelpful at best, and very poor military analysis at worst. Let us therefore look at each of the four sets of orders Grouchy received from Napoleon.

First Order
Napoleon's first order to Grouchy was the verbal order given at about 11.30am on the morning of the 17th, the day after the battle of Ligny:

> Get off in pursuit of the Prussians, complete their defeat by attacking them wherever you find them and never let them out of your sight. I am going to join with Marshal Ney's forces which I shall take to attack the English if they hold this side of the Soignes Forest. Correspond with me by a paved road.[2]

In this order Napoleon gives the minimum of detail, doubtlessly trying to get

Grouchy off after the Prussians as soon as possible after the delays of the morning. Napoleon wanted him to locate the Prussians and then keep the pressure on them so that they could not restore order after Ligny and be left free to intervene in Napoleon's planned battle with Wellington, although this latter part is at best only inferred. Once Grouchy's troops had started their march, the emperor could then refine and expand on those orders as the situation developed. He informs Grouchy that he plans to attack the 'English'.

Second Order
Napoleon's written order to Grouchy, dictated to General Bertrand about three hours after the verbal order, changed things considerably,

> Ligny, 17 June 1815, towards 3 o'clock
> *Move to Gembloux* [my emphasis] with General Pajol's cavalry corps, the light cavalry [division] of the IV Corps [General Maurin's 6th Cavalry Division, which it will be remembered was now commanded by Vallin], General Exelmans' cavalry corps and General Teste's division; the latter of these requires your special attention as it is detached from its own corps [Lobau's VI Corps]; and III and IV Infantry Corps. *You are to reconnoitre in the direction of Namur and Maastricht, and you should pursue the enemy, scout his march and inform me of his intentions* [my emphasis]. I am moving my headquarters to Quatre-Chemins [Quatre Bras], where the English remained this morning. Our communications should thus be direct by the paved road from Namur. If the enemy has evacuated Namur, write to the General Commandant of the Second Military Division at Charlemont for him to occupy Namur with several battalions of national guards and several batteries of guns which he is to form up at Charlemont. He is to give the command to a *maréchal de camp*.
> *It is important to understand what Blücher and Wellington want to do and if they propose to unite their armies to cover Brussels and Liège, risking the outcome of a battle* [my emphasis]. In any case, keep your two infantry corps constantly within a league of each other, having several lines of retreat. Place detachments of cavalry in between us to be able to communicate with headquarters.
> Dictated by the Emperor in the absence of the *major-général*,
> Grand-Maréchal Bertrand[3]

This order is far more thorough and prescriptive. Grouchy is clearly told where to go and what to do. Any mention of attacking or harassing the enemy has disappeared and the mission now is to be purely one of reconnaissance; to find the Prussians and to try and divine their intentions. This latter part of the mission is of particular importance; Napoleon raises the possibility of a Prussian intervention at the battle he was planning against Wellington. He thus needed to know whether the Prussians were manoeuvring in a direction that would make this possible. It is perhaps no coincidence that he repeats the importance of understanding Blücher's intentions. Significantly however, the emperor does not give Grouchy any direction as to what to do if the Prussians look as if they are attempting to join Wellington. Napoleon acknowledges the possibility that Blücher could turn on Grouchy by recommending he keeps his troops within supporting distance of each other.

To illustrate how orders can be variously interpreted, this is what Major Becke wrote of this order in his analysis of the campaign in 1936, 'It clearly implied that Grouchy was to act as a shield to the right flank of the *Armée du Nord*.'[4] Is this really true and, given Napoleon's command style, can Grouchy really be expected to act according to what might or might not be implied?

Grouchy long and repeatedly denied that this order existed.

Third Order
On the evening of the 17th, Napoleon concluded that Wellington was preparing to fight the next day. Surely, this was the time to inform his marshal of the likelihood of a battle and to solicit the latest information from Grouchy about the direction of march of the Prussians. Amazingly, it was not until 10am the next morning that Napoleon had Soult write to Grouchy, and as we have seen, this letter was not sent off until 11.30am at the earliest and was not received until about 4pm; too late for Grouchy to have any chance of influencing events at Waterloo.

> In front of the Caillou farm, 18 June 1815 at 10am
> *Monsieur le maréchal*, the emperor has received your last report dated from Gembloux; you only inform the emperor that two Prussian columns have passed Sauvenières and Sart-à-Walhain; however, reports say that a third column, which was strong, has passed Genz and Gentinnes heading for Wavre.
>
> The emperor orders me to inform you that at this moment His Majesty is going to attack the English army which has taken position at Waterloo, close to the Soignes forest; also that His Majesty desires that you *direct your movements on Wavre in order to approach us, come into our area of operations and tie in your communications, pushing before you the corps of the Prussian army which have taken this direction and which could stop at Wavre, where you are to arrive as soon as possible* [my emphasis].
>
> You are to follow the enemy columns which are on your right with some light troops in order to observe their movements and collect up their stragglers. Inform me immediately of your deployment and your march, as well as any news you have of the enemy and do not hesitate in coming into communications with us. The emperor wants to receive your news often.[5]

Only now does Napoleon order Grouchy to approach Waterloo and to 'push' the Prussians before him, giving the impression that Napoleon presumed the pushing would be north towards Brussels. But more significantly, he twice directs him to move on Wavre and to arrive there 'as soon as possible'. The mention of a third Prussian column heading for Wavre is presented almost in passing, without any reference to its possible significance and therefore leaving Grouchy to decide how he was to react to this piece of information. Finally, there is no indication that Grouchy may have a significant part to play in the coming battle. It is perhaps, little wonder that Grouchy felt that his march on Wavre had been vindicated.

Fourth Order
Napoleon's final despatch, timed at 1pm, just after the battle had started, was also composed by Soult:

18 June, 1pm

M. le Maréchal,
You wrote to the emperor at 3am this morning that you were marching on Sart-à-Walhain, that your plan was to move to Corbais and Wavre. *This move conforms to the dispositions of His Majesty that have been communicated to you* [my emphasis]. However, the emperor orders me to inform you that *you are always to manoeuvre in our direction, in order that you are able to join us before any [enemy] corps can come between us. I will not dictate a direction, it is for you to identify the point where we are for you to adjust accordingly and to establish our communications, as well as to be always ready to fall on whatever enemy troops that attempt to threaten our right* [my emphasis].
    At this moment the battle is *engaged* [my emphasis] on the line of Waterloo, in front of the forest of Soignes. The enemy's centre is at Mont-Saint-Jean; thus manoeuvre to join our right.
Le maréchal duc de Dalmatie

PS. A letter that has been intercepted says that General Bülow is to attack our right flank; we think we can see this corps on the heights of Saint Lambert. *Thus do not lose a moment in approaching us and join us, and to destroy Bülow* [my emphasis], who you will catch red-handed [*en flagrant délit*].[6]

In this letter, Soult confirms that Grouchy's march on Wavre is in line with Napoleon's wishes; then he orders him to march towards them before the Prussians can arrive; and finally he is to be ready to fall on any Prussians that do appear. The postscript adds the due sense of urgency. We have already examined the confusion between 'engaged' and 'won'. The main body of this despatch was written before the appearance of the Prussians and can only have been written with a complete misunderstanding of the relative positions of both Grouchy and the Prussians to the battlefield and with little appreciation or consideration of the time it would take to carry out. The postscript overrides the main body of the text and gives clear, unambiguous direction; as we have seen, it arrived far too late for Grouchy to comply with it.

Late Pursuit on the Morning of the 17th
No one wrote more critically of Napoleon's performance on the morning of the 17th, following the hard-won victory of Ligny, than Marshal Grouchy. He accuses the emperor of unpardonable tardiness in ordering him off in pursuit of the Prussians and returns to this charge in all of his many writings on the campaign. Subsequent military authors and critics have also spent much time and ink pursuing this charge against Napoleon and it may be of interest to look at the extent to which this criticism is merited.

The charges are clear; let us quickly read a couple of them. The first is from Grouard, a French military historian who wrote in 1907: 'In the situation in which he found himself [on the morning of the 17th], Napoleon's inertia is hardly credible.'[7] Grouchy's memoirs give us this judgement: '. . . Napoleon's inaction on the 17th, from dawn until half past midday, the army having beaten the enemy at Fleurus on the 16th, seems inexcusable to us.'[8]

My own interpretation of why Napoleon delayed his decision on despatching Grouchy's pursuit has been covered in the appropriate chapter and there should be no need to repeat it. In their judgements above, Grouard and Grouchy roundly criticise Napoleon's inertia, but offer no suggestions why Napoleon should have hesitated. Not considering the overall strategic situation at the end of the 16th is rather odd in experienced military critics. They and other commentators seem content to put this delay down to a number of failings in Napoleon; prevarication, over-confidence, illness and a loss of energy and decisiveness due to old age. That Napoleon may well have suffered from some, or even all of these, is incontestable. However, what is astonishing is that none of his critics seem to address what for me are the critical issues that may have caused him to delay: what was the strategic situation that each of the three armies faced at the end of the 16th, what were their strategic or tactical aims and what did their commanders actually know, or even more importantly, not know and needed to find out before making their next decision.

For Blücher, the problem was relatively straightforward; having been defeated, but not destroyed, should he retreat down his lines of communication towards reinforcements and supplies, or should he retreat north, endeavour to join Wellington, and then attempt to overwhelm Napoleon's inferior forces.

For Wellington, the situation was a bit trickier. He did not know the final result of Ligny; the last news he received was that Blücher hoped to be able to hang on until darkness. Before Wellington could act decisively, he had to know where Blücher was and the condition of his army. If Blücher had held on until nightfall, he might well be planning a decisive counter-attack against Napoleon, perhaps even reinforced by Bülow; in this case, Wellington could offer his allies considerable support. If Blücher was beaten, in which direction was he retreating; would he go back down his lines of communication or attempt to join him? The answers to these questions would determine whether he attacked Ney in the morning, or withdrew towards Brussels. No one criticised Wellington for remaining in position at Quatre Bras until he learnt of Blücher's defeat and retreat. For Napoleon, there was still more to learn before he could decide on his next move.

The battle of Ligny finished at about 10pm. Knowing what he knew then, could Napoleon, returning to Fleurus towards 11pm, be clear on his line of operations for the next day? Of course not, and until he had the intelligence he needed on which to make informed decisions, he would not be in a position to write any orders. He could not afford to make a false movement, after all, he always had to bear in mind that he now had only about 105,000 men whilst the two allied armies had together nearly 200,000 and he sat between them. He had manoeuvred on interior lines against forces almost double his own – any error could lead to a disaster.

We must, at all costs, avoid judging Napoleon on subsequent events, that is, with the benefit of hindsight. For Napoleon, the situation was extremely complex. A hasty or ill-conceived decision/movement could have been catastrophic. Although an audacious commander, and Napoleon was certainly that, would wish to seize the initiative by acting before his adversaries and force them to react to his manoeuvres, his actions still needed to be based on some, if incomplete, information.

It appears that Napoleon, no doubt exhausted after another demanding day, slept through the night of the 15th/16th. Whether he was suffering as badly from haemorrhoids as some claim is probably irrelevant as no significant new information came in during the night. As he awoke in the morning therefore, he still knew only the situation of the main body of his own army and that in itself was insufficient to determine his next steps. There is no doubt that the co-ordination and tasking of French reconnaissance immediately after the battle was woeful; he no doubt had the means to collect the information quicker than he did, but we will explore this later.

Although he should have received Ney's report of events at Quatre Bras timed at 10pm during the early hours, this did not give any idea of the current situation on the left. In his report, Ney merely complained that d'Erlon's march and counter-march had deprived him 'of a great victory'. He neglected to inform the emperor of his assessment of the strength or deployment of Wellington's army or what he anticipated its actions might be. He also gave no indication on what he planned to do himself the following morning. Napoleon could only assume that d'Erlon's I Corps had rejoined Ney and therefore, at worst, he could hold his own if Wellington felt strong enough to attack him; if Wellington did attack early the next day, it is reasonable to suggest that Ney would have informed Napoleon at the first indication that it might happen.

Although General Flahaut, Napoleon's *aide de camp*, returned from Ney at about 7am, it seems he was unable to give Napoleon any real indication as to the situation around Quatre Bras; certainly not the level of information that Napoleon required. Having had Soult write to Ney informing him of the victory at Ligny and demanding information, Napoleon sent patrols towards his left wing to get the detail he required. By the time they returned, about 11am, Napoleon had still not received the information from Exelmans' troops that pointed towards the Prussians having withdrawn north-east on Gembloux, so he still did not know if they were moving back down their lines of communications or north to link up with Wellington. Despite Napoleon's demands for information, it appears Ney sent no further report to the emperor.

It could not have been until about 8am that Napoleon received any information on the Prussian forces on the Namur road (from Pajol) and this did not inform him of the location of Bülow's corps which, by this time, Napoleon must almost certainly have realised had not fought the day before. From which direction was he advancing? Perhaps he was coming from Namur, as Thielemann had done? In this case, sending Pajol in that direction was not pointless, even if the main Prussian army had not retreated in that direction. Exelmans was covering Bülow's other possible approach from Gembloux. It was not until Napoleon had received the report from Pajol, whose 1st Cavalry Corps, although only consisting of one of his two divisions, had eventually been despatched down the main road towards Namur, in, as we have already seen, what was the entirely opposite direction taken by the bulk of the Prussian army. Of course, this report only reinforced Napoleon's presumption that the Prussians were heading east.

In this vacuum of reliable information, Napoleon found himself in a precarious position. His intuition (others might say wishful thinking) was probably telling him that the defeated Prussian army was in full retreat down their lines of communication, away from their allies. By acting as if this was actually the case, many have accused him of complacency, but Chesney,[9] no admirer of the emperor, argues strongly that it was natural for Napoleon to expect the Prussians to secure their own direct retreat; that is towards the east, as the Austrians had done after their own defeat at Fleurus in 1794. He also emphasises the difficulties the Prussians faced in opening a new line of operations if they retreated north. Writing to Joseph in 1808, Napoleon wrote, 'The art of war is an art which has principles that should never be violated. To change a line of operations is an operation of genius; the loss is an operation so serious that it renders the general criminal that was responsible. Those who dare to advise such a measure are the first to lose their heads immediately that the folly of their operation becomes clear . . . According to the laws of war, any general who loses his line of communications merits death.' The option taken by the Prussians was not one to be taken lightly.

Furthermore, Napoleon no doubt noted that at Ligny, Blücher had deployed a third of his force, Thielemann's III Corps, with the sole purpose of protecting his communications to Namur. It is inconceivable that Blücher would have deployed such a force there if he had absolutely no intention of using it. It may ultimately have been just an option, but it was a large force to tie down there and could well have served to deceive Napoleon.

It was only after Napoleon finally received news on what the situation was at Quatre Bras that he felt he could finally despatch Grouchy after the Prussians whilst he marched north-west to join Ney. Grouchy wrote:

> Up to half-past midday on the 17th of June the Emperor – who until then had ordered no movement of the army – was waiting a report from Marshal Ney; as soon as he received it, he ordered Marshal Grouchy to take his place at the head of the corps of infantry under Generals Vandamme and Gérard and of the cavalry under Generals Pajol and Exelmans, forming a body of some thirty thousand men, and to follow the Prussian army . . .[10]

It should be noted that in this privately-published account, Grouchy undermines his own argument that Napoleon was slow in acting, by presenting the specific reason for the delay.

The troops Napoleon was to take with him to join Ney had already been pre-positioned; he had not been entirely idle that morning. Indeed, it is fair to say that in waiting for the critical information he needed, a visit to his exhausted troops on the battlefield, the reviews that were described, and his conversations with many of his senior commanders whilst the troops rested, resupplied their ammunition and cleaned their weapons was an ideal opportunity to raise moral in a way Napoleon's presence inevitably did.

As we have heard, it was soon after despatching Grouchy with verbal orders that Napoleon received the first indications that the Prussians were in strength near Gembloux. The emperor immediately dictated different orders to Grouchy, directing him to this latter place, and, content that things were now in order on this flank, left to join his troops marching on Quatre Bras. It was only much later that Pajol finally reported that it was only stragglers that were heading for Namur.

Of course, first thing in the morning of the 17th Napoleon could have set Grouchy off after the Prussians and then marched himself with the reserve against Wellington. However, he would have done so in complete ignorance of the situation at Quatre Bras and the locations, intentions and state of the Prussian army. What's more, Grouchy's infantry would have set off just a few hours after a bloody battle; exhausted, lacking ammunition, with weapons almost beyond use and with insufficient time for regiments to reorganise following the heavy casualties of the day before. To believe this was possible shows a wilful desire to ignore these important issues or a lack of understanding of the realities of campaigning. As General Flahaut, one of Napoleon's *aides de camp*, wrote:

> After a pitched battle, and marches such as we had made on the previous day, our army could not be expected to start off again at dawn. What is truly marvellous is that the Emperor should have been able to do as much as he did with the forces which he had at his disposal on this sad occasion.[11]

In conclusion, although almost all accounts of the campaign accuse Napoleon of a criminal lack of activity on the morning of the 17th, this criticism appears harsh given the lack of useful intelligence he had on the situations and intentions of his two protagonists. Whilst he must accept some of the blame for not ensuring some thorough reconnaissance was not carried out to collect this for him, it is clear that when the key piece of the jigsaw arrived, the situation at Quatre Bras, he acted promptly and decisively, confirming that this was the reason for the delay.

The Failure to Coordinate Reconnaissance
If there is one area of this controversy on which no one on the French side comes out with any credit, it is the failure of the French to coordinate a comprehensive reconnaissance plan after their victory at Ligny. The blame for this failure lies at the feet of each of the key French senior commanders:

Napoleon. As the commander-in-chief, Napoleon must take some of the blame. Whether or not it is fair to describe him as suffering physically and mentally during this campaign is no excuse. Even if he deserved his full night's sleep after the demands of the run-up to the campaign and two days of intense activity and mental stress, giving the necessary order to properly coordinate the follow-up of the Prussian forces would have been the act of two minutes. If he chose to rest his cavalry overnight before setting them off, this would be a legitimate decision, but the order for the need to send out patrols in all directions needed to be distributed in time for the regiments to implement them. He just needed to order this done.

Soult. Marshal Soult seems to have been of no assistance to the emperor on this morning (the 17th). If he had been a competent and efficient chief of staff he would assuredly have had all necessary information ready for the emperor when the latter made his appearance in the morning. As the army chief of staff, and fully alive to the exhaustion of his commander, Soult should clearly have identified the need to coordinate a follow-up without direction from Napoleon. It seems that Soult showed as little mental agility over this night as the emperor, and yet it is quite clearly the chief of staff's job to anticipate his commander's requirements and then to direct and coordinate them. Napoleon might have argued that this was not his direct responsibility; Soult has no such excuse.

Grouchy. As commander of the right wing, Grouchy had a light cavalry corps (Pajol's) whose primary responsibility was reconnaissance and as an experienced cavalry commander he should not have needed orders to send them out on such a task; that was their *raison d'être*. That he sent no orders to his corps commanders is somewhat more than surprising, even if he had received none from Napoleon or Soult. He claims that it was him that finally sent Pajol off down the road to Namur, but Pajol's memoirs suggest that it was on his own initiative and in the light of not having received any orders from either Napoleon or Grouchy that he moved with the single division that was left to him towards Namur.

In his letter to Grouchy outlining his strategy on the morning of the 16th, Napoleon had written, 'My intention is that all these generals [Vandamme, Gérard, Exelmans and Pajol] are directly under your command; they will only take orders directly from me when I am present.' Grouchy may have felt that as Napoleon was present, that he would have given orders for reconnaissances to be sent out if that is what he had wanted. However, if this was Grouchy's defence, he did not articulate it in his many writings on the campaign.

Although the light cavalry divisions of III and IV Corps had been engaged at Ligny, it was but lightly and they were surely still in a state to provide the necessary patrols to the north. The 1st and 2nd Cavalry Corps were on the 'wrong' side of the battlefield for this, but this would not totally exclude them from such a role. All in all, this was an inexcusable neglect. There was plenty of cavalry with the army. Exelmans could have sent patrols towards Tilly and Wavre as easily as he did towards Gembloux and Pajol did towards Namur; all these routes were open to the Prussians. It was certainly not impossible that Blücher should, in spite of his defeat, endeavour to keep up his communications with Wellington.

In his memoirs Napoleon claimed that he personally sent General Monthion, a close and highly trusted staff officer (he was *chef d'etat-major-général*) to reconnoitre to the north. This is unconvincing and smacks of trying to cover up what proved to be a serious error. Unconvincing because this is not mentioned by any other first-hand account, it seems strange to send a single officer, even if he did have an escort rather than a unit that could cover a much wider frontage, and because if Monthion did go, he failed to identify anything significant along a route which had been used by the Prussians' most disorganised formations.

We know that on the morning of the 17th, most of Exelmans' dragoons marched on Gembloux, but no convincing evidence seems to have appeared on who actually ordered them there; Exelmans himself, Grouchy, Soult or Napoleon. The failure to identify the direction taken by the bulk of the Prussian forces was a major failing of the campaign. It is useless to speculate what might have happened if this had been properly coordinated, but it is difficult not to conclude that it had a significant impact on the outcome of the campaign.

Napoleon failed to even order the necessary reconnaissances to be sent out before he retired, but Soult, Ney and Grouchy should all have sparked early in the morning even as Napoleon still slept: all three marshals had the power and authority to have directed the necessary preparations for an early move. They could have established intercommunication between the two battlefields, reconnoitred widely to their fronts and flanks and thus provided the information Napoleon required when he woke up on the morning of the 17th. None of them rose to the occasion, none of them made any arrangements to prepare for the forthcoming operations which in modern times would be considered the worst kind of incompetence. Whereas up to nightfall on the 16th the hours had been precious, on the morning of the 17th the very minutes were golden. Many commentators believe that in the twenty-four hours from 5pm on the 16th to 5pm on the 17th the campaign was lost to Napoleon.

A Pursuit?
Whilst Napoleon had achieved a great victory against the odds at Ligny, all eyewitnesses acknowledge, and particularly Grouchy, that the Prussian army had not been destroyed nor even pushed into a disorderly and uncoordinated retreat. Although some Prussian units had certainly suffered very heavy casualties and some chaos was inevitable in a retreat carried out in darkness, they maintained strong rearguards during the night and even attempted to recapture some of their lost guns. No one really believed that they would be incapable of defending themselves robustly the following day.

A pursuit is an aggressive follow-up after a successful battle in which the enemy have suffered a heavy defeat or even a rout, with the aim of preventing them from rallying and reforming in order to be able to continue the campaign with a hope still of victory. In 1796, the Russian Field Marshal Prince Alexander Suvorov wrote:

> Defeat the enemy with cold steel, bayonets, swords and pikes . . . don't slow down during the attack. When the enemy is broken, shattered, then pursue him at once and don't give him time either to collect or reform . . . Spare nothing, don't think of your labours; pursue the enemy night and day, so long as anything is left to be destroyed.

Perhaps a more reasoned description was left by *Maréchal de Camp* Berton who commanded a brigade of dragoons during the Waterloo campaign. He wrote:

> All those who know the first principles of war, know well that it is important to pursue a beaten army relentlessly; whilst it is still suffering from its defeat; whilst it has lost his cohesion and whilst its central control has ceased to be in harmony with the force which consists in the combination of all its parts; whilst it does not have good communications between it nor the will which makes it do its duty.[12]

But had the Prussians lost their cohesion and had central control ceased? Was the Prussian army in such disarray that a proper pursuit could be launched; and was Napoleon's army in a fit state to launch such an operation after a hard-fought battle? Although Napoleon had fresh troops available, VI Corps and the Imperial Guard, he had another, undefeated enemy army still to fight. Napoleon was a recognised exponent of a devastating pursuit as he had shown after defeating the Prussian army at the double battles at Jena/Auerstadt in 1806, but the situation after Ligny was completely different.

Two points need to be borne in mind. Firstly, any casualties that the Prussians had suffered at Ligny were immediately compensated for by the arrival of Bülow's un-blooded IV Corps. These 30,000 fresh troops ensured the Prussians would significantly outnumber Grouchy's pursuing force. Secondly, the French troops that had fought at Ligny were exhausted; not just from that day of battle, but from their marches and skirmishes of the previous days. Rest, re-organisation after high levels of casualties and resupply of ammunition would be required if the force was to be capable of further action. Grouchy's memoirs admit, '. . . the obscurity of the night rendered it about impossible to distinguish their [Prussian] movements and the extreme fatigue of the [French] troops, who, after forced marches had fought on the 15th and 16th, were hardly capable of pursuing the enemy.'[13]

A true pursuit was therefore both inappropriate and almost impossible in the circumstances. This could not be a pursuit of the kind that followed Napoleon's victories in 1806, but rather an armed reconnaissance. Although he ordered Grouchy to attack the Prussians wherever he found them, Napoleon's written order to Grouchy directed him to ensure he maintained a number of lines of retreat, suggesting the emperor was fully alive to the possibility of the Prussians turning and falling on their pursuers with overwhelming force. Grouchy's writings show that he harboured a similar concern and strongly imply the threat of this happening made him cautious.

Before making any movement with his part of the army, therefore, Napoleon needed to know the direction in which the Prussians were moving, and the only credible thing in the circumstances, was not a pursuit, but to follow them with cavalry in order to find out, whilst waiting for news from Ney. But Napoleon also needed to give his tired squadrons a little rest before launching them in pursuit. The Prussians were withdrawing in some (more or less) disorder, in the dark and had therefore not gone either very quickly or very far before daylight. A light cavalry force could surely pick up their trail soon after.

Grouchy's task, therefore, was clear: his mission was not the aggressive pursuit of a defeated and disorganised Prussian army, but to identify their line of retreat, harass them and to keep Napoleon informed as to their location and likely intentions; a reconnaissance in force. This mission is clearly articulated in Napoleon's written orders to the marshal:

You are to reconnoitre in the direction of Namur and Maastrict, and you should pursue the enemy, scout his march and inform me of his intentions ... It is important to understand what Blücher and Wellington want to do and if they propose to unite their armies to cover Brussels and Liège, risking the outcome of a battle.

The final confirmation of what Napoleon could have expected from his subordinate is evident in the force that he gave him to carry out this mission.

The Size and Composition of Grouchy's Force
Given that we have accepted that Grouchy was not conducting a conventional pursuit of a routed and demoralised Prussian army, the next question is what size of force should he have been given to conduct his mission. Grouchy himself accepted the dilemma that Napoleon faced:

> The extraordinary energy in Bonaparte's pursuits that brought such brilliant results in preceding campaigns, simply consisted of pushing hard from behind *with very superior forces, an enemy completely beaten* [my emphasis]. But now it was necessary for him, with his principal masses and principally with his freshest forces, to throw himself against a new enemy [Wellington], against whom to gain another victory. III and IV Corps, which were to pursue, were precisely the two which, until 10 o'clock at night, had found themselves in the most bloody fighting, and who now, indispensably, had need of time to re-establish order, strengthen themselves and resupply ammunition. The cavalry corps had certainly not suffered and could thus have been capable of pressing the Prussian rearguard early; that they did not might be considered a fault, but cavalry alone cannot produce such results as those achieved in their general pursuits after their previous victories, for the terrain was too broken to allow cavalry on their own to achieve much.[14]

So what size of force did Grouchy require to achieve this mission? Inevitably, there are conflicting views. *Adjutant Commandant* Janin, who became the acting chief-of-staff of VI Corps after *Maréchal de Camp* Durrieu was wounded during the early stages of Waterloo, wrote in his critical analysis of the campaign:

> The detachment of General Grouchy would be nothing more than punishing and offered no favourable outcome. It is absurd to suppose that it was only supposed to scout the movements of the Prussian army; it was too strong; if it was to fight it, to complete its destruction, it was far too weak ...[15]

Soult certainly believed the force given to Grouchy was too strong. His *aide de camp* Colonel Baudus wrote:

The Marshal *major-général*, persistent in his opinion that Napoleon was wrong to give two infantry corps to Marshal Grouchy, thought it was his duty to advise that most should be recalled immediately for the battle of the next day; but his observations on this subject were not listened to during the evening any more than they had been in the morning.[16]

Here, Soult is reflecting a well-established principle of war, articulated by Clausewitz in his renowned classic, *On War*, 'There is no higher and simpler law of strategy than that of keeping one's forces concentrated.'[17]

But could Napoleon really have just screened the whole Prussian army with a relatively weak cavalry force? This would surely have left Blücher free to operate either against Napoleon's line of communications or unopposed against his flank and rear. This option is not credible in these circumstances; the general principle of keeping your forces concentrated is for their employment against a single force, not two separate armies, each about the same strength as his own. Grouchy therefore needed to be sufficiently strong to harass the Prussian rearguard in order to keep the whole force on its toes (this would require a combined-arms force), and to delay their advance should the Prussians turn on him. Ultimately, Grouchy's force needed to be sufficiently strong to give Napoleon two or three days freedom to dispose of Wellington and/or to occupy Brussels.

Colonel Edward Hamley, in his book *Operations of War*, gives us a useful insight into how strong a force needed to be to be able to harass a rearguard:

> As a rearguard is seldom more than a fifth or a sixth of the total force, especially if it be formed entirely of the troops of the reserve, it follows that the pursuing force, in order to press confidently on the rearguard, attacking boldly, and augmenting the disorder, need not be more than a third of the beaten army. Thus two-thirds of the victorious force (supposing it to have been equal to its adversary at first) will be disposable elsewhere.[18]

By this calculation, Grouchy's force, about 21,000 infantry and 6,000 cavalry after the losses of Ligny are taken into account, would appear to be a little weak. However, the Prussian rearguard, Thielemann's III Corps, was only just weaker than Grouchy, which left Grouchy perfectly capable of keeping the pressure on the Prussians, although without being strong enough to fix the whole army; but this was not his mission and his force did indeed leave Napoleon with two-thirds of his force to be 'disposable elsewhere'.

Criticism of the strength of Grouchy's small army, based on the principle of concentration of force, is not appropriate in these circumstances; placed as Napoleon was between two forces each of at least equal strength to his own. Grouchy's force needed to be big enough to give Napoleon sufficient time to defeat Wellington, without it facing certain destruction if it was attacked by the Prussians.

Napoleon's remaining force should have been sufficient to defeat Wellington if he fought without Prussian help.

The Direction of Pursuit
In his verbal orders to Grouchy, Napoleon clearly directs the marshal to organise his pursuit towards Namur, slightly south of east and considerably different from the main axis of the actual Prussian retreat to the north. Napoleon had been fooled by Pajol's reports and the fact that the deployment of Thielemann's III Corps during the battle of Ligny was exclusively to keep the Namur route open. Napoleon has been much criticised for this, but he was acting on the only information he had at that moment combined with military probability. The reality is that Pajol's cavalry were already on that route and although both Vandamme and Gérard had started their march, neither of them had marched a step down this false trail before Napoleon's written order sent them to Gembloux. Therefore, no time had been wasted.

Having committed the unpardonable sin of not having co-ordinated a comprehensive reconnaissance plan to gather information on the direction of the Prussian retreat, Napoleon had naturally, if erroneously, assumed that the Prussians were heading back down their lines of communications. Generally, critics of Napoleon have said that Gembloux was a false direction; however, it was a position of waiting and nothing else until the mystery of what Blücher planned was cleared up. Once this was divined, it would allow Grouchy to react to the full variety of Prussian options.

In his written orders, Napoleon wrote, 'It is important to understand what Blücher and Wellington want to do and if they propose to unite their armies to cover Brussels and Liège, risking the outcome of a battle.' He thus fully appreciated at this early stage the possibility of Blücher marching to join Wellington and posed the question that Grouchy was to answer.

Napoleon had therefore changed the direction of Grouchy's march before his force (less Pajol's single cavalry division and Teste's infantry) was committed on the wrong route. Gembloux was a logical first destination from which Grouchy was to identify Blücher's line of march. Of course, a force should have followed the Prussians through Tilly and Mellery, but given the failings of the French reconnaissance plan, Napoleon was unaware that any Prussians had retreated in that direction. Once the Prussians had been located, Grouchy was free to pursue the route he felt best achieved his mission.

Left or Right Bank of the Dyle?
Grouchy was directed to march on Gembloux by the written orders of Napoleon; there was no scope for him to re-interpret that direction in any way. Once he had reached that place, he had more flexibility in the direction he marched which would be dictated by Prussian movements. The many military critics that argue that the only sensible direction for him to then take was to cross the Dyle at Moustier and Ottignies are clearly influenced by what they knew happened next; i.e., they knew

the outcome of Grouchy's actual manoeuvres and came to their conclusions based on the benefit of hindsight. The real test is whether they would have made that decision if they only knew what Grouchy knew at that time and what Napoleon had ordered. Hindsight makes it easy to re-interpret the information that Grouchy collected and sent on to Napoleon.

Crossing the Dyle would have fundamentally contravened Napoleon's orders if Blücher had continued to march north towards Brussels or north-east towards Maastricht, as Grouchy would have lost touch with the Prussians. He would then have been unable to send Napoleon any information on their whereabouts or intentions. Crossing the Dyle would have been to anticipate Blücher and risked losing contact with him.

The real evidence seems to point to both Napoleon and Grouchy making the same mistake; once Namur had been ruled out as a line of retreat, they both anticipated that Blücher was marching north to join Wellington in front of Brussels and to offer battle there. This is suggested by Napoleon's apparent endorsement of Grouchy's movements until late on the 18th. But neither of them, whilst talking of that possibility, considered that Wellington would hold at Mont-Saint-Jean and that Blücher would march across poor back roads (or more accurately back tracks), in order to meet him there. Napoleon was therefore delighted when Wellington decided to stand at Waterloo because he did not envisage Blücher joining him and because he would not then be fighting a combined force.

It is evident that it was only once Napoleon was aware of the Prussian march onto his flank that he suddenly sent orders to Grouchy to come to his assistance and subsequently blamed him for not doing so. The blame lies squarely with Napoleon rather than Grouchy. If Grouchy had indeed been ordered to act as a flank-guard, then crossing the Dyle early, and not in the face of the Prussians, was entirely sensible. It is true that if Grouchy had been on the left bank of the Dyle instead of the right, he may have been in time to intercept the Prussians or at least keep some of them from reaching Waterloo, but by no interpretation other than with the benefit of hindsight can Grouchy be criticised for not acting as a flank guard for the main army. This was a specific mission and not one he had been given until the 1pm letter (that was received about 5pm) that directed him to, 'always manoeuvre in our direction, in order that you are able to join us before any [enemy] corps can come between us.'

March to the Sound of the Guns
Napoleon's supporters have long condemned Grouchy for not accepting Gérard's advice at Walhain to march to the sound of the guns, desperately wanting to believe that if he had done this he may have saved the battle, either by intercepting the Prussians or arriving on Napoleon's right in order to fight alongside him. Both they and Grouchy's supporters have argued back and forth about whether the Prussians would have overwhelmed him first or at least prevented him from

interfering, and whether he would have been able to arrive in time to take a part. My aim here is not to repeat these arguments, which generally produce no conclusive result, but to examine whether Grouchy was right in not even trying.

Although Grouchy argues that the back roads that his men and guns would have had to have taken were so poor, and the distance so great, that he would not have arrived in time, he justifies not even attempting the move because he had been given specific orders to pursue the Prussians and would have been disobeying those orders if he had chosen to march towards the battle. Indeed, this would have left the Prussians free to act as they chose. There is no need to quote Napoleon's orders again; Grouchy's job was to maintain contact with the Prussians in order to determine what they were intending.

However, the key deduction is, if it was established that they were attempting to join Wellington at Waterloo, should Grouchy attempt to stop them. This is a logical conclusion, but is not expressed in any of Napoleon's orders to Grouchy. That Grouchy understood this might be necessary he describes himself in his letter to Napoleon on the morning of the 18th: '. . . if the mass of Prussians are retiring on Wavre, I will follow them in this direction to stop them from reaching Brussels and to separate them from Wellington.' The question remains how he thought he could achieve that if he was following behind them and they were closer to Wellington than he!

There can be no argument that if Grouchy had given up on pursuing the Prussians north and marched west towards Waterloo, then he would certainly have been disobeying his orders; Napoleon was hoping to fight Wellington and had not ordered Grouchy to march to his support if he did. To turn his troops to march towards Waterloo, Grouchy would therefore have been acting on his own initiative; not something that was encouraged by any senior commander of that time, and certainly not by Napoleon or Wellington. Both were authoritarian leaders and expected their subordinates to obey their orders without question and without necessarily expecting to be told the required outcome. Wellington was notorious for condemning the use of initiative in his army, although conveniently overlooking it when it was successful.[19] Even Gérard subsequently admitted that he would not have dared to carry out the action he had urged on Grouchy!

To march to the sound of the guns was absolutely the right thing to do when a force was an integral part of the army that was fighting; in the book, *Moltke on the Art of War*, the famous Prussian general wrote:

> Leaders of individual parts of the army must remember the old rule always to march in the direction of the cannon thunder. Tasks prescribing another direction must be re-examined to ascertain whether they were issued under conditions that did not foresee the ensuing engagement.[20]

However, Grouchy commanded a detached force with a specific mission and had been briefed by Napoleon that the emperor was going in pursuit of Wellington and hoped to bring him to battle. As Grouchy rightly pointed out, he would have been more surprised if he had not heard the sounds of heavy artillery fire. There can be little doubt that Napoleon fully expected to be able to defeat Wellington with the forces he led against him; if he had wanted the support of Grouchy he would have made this clear in his orders.

From Grouchy's letters to Napoleon, it seems clear that Grouchy expected Blücher to continue his march from Wavre on Brussels and to join Wellington in front of this city strong enough to give battle; he does not appear to have contemplated that the Prussian commander-in-chief would march to join Wellington at Waterloo, for if he had, he would surely have taken a different course.

Napoleon had no expectations that Grouchy would march to Waterloo and only ordered this when he realised that the Prussians were approaching the battlefield. By the time his order reached Grouchy it was too late for the marshal to execute it in time and if Napoleon truly believed Grouchy could arrive in time he was either deluding himself or preparing the ground for Grouchy to take some of the blame for his defeat. Those of Napoleon's acolytes that believe Grouchy should have marched to the sound of the guns are doing so with the benefit of hindsight in an attempt to deflect any blame for the loss of the battle from the emperor. Indeed, Napoleon had had the opportunity to defeat Wellington before the Prussians could have arrived to stop him, but did not take it.

Did Napoleon Really Expect Grouchy to Arrive on the Battlefield in Time to Save Him, or was the Claim Mere Artifice to Deflect the Blame for the Defeat onto Grouchy?

Napoleon's memoirs are clear that he expected Grouchy to make a significant intervention at Waterloo. We have already dismissed his claims that he twice wrote to Grouchy ordering him to send a force of 7,000 men to Saint-Lambert as there is no collaborating evidence to support these claims. However, there are two first-hand accounts that seem to support the idea that Napoleon did expect him.

Colonel Marbot, who commanded the 7th Hussars, a part of Jacquinot's cavalry division of I Corps, wrote the following in a letter written only eight days after the battle, too early to have been influenced by the subsequent debate:

> I was with my regiment on the right flank of the army almost throughout the battle. They assured me that Marshal Grouchy would come up at that point . . . Instead of Grouchy, what arrived was Blücher's corps. You can imagine how we were served. We were driven in and in an instant the enemy were in our rear.[21]

In a letter addressed to Marshal Grouchy in 1830, he gave more detail:

> At the commencement of the action I was detached from the division with

my regiment and an infantry battalion placed under my command. These troops were placed *en potence* on the extreme right, behind Frichermont facing the [River] Dyle.

Detailed orders were given to me, on behalf of the Emperor, by his *aide de camp*, Labédoyère, and an *officier d'ordonnance* whose name I do not remember. They instructed me to always leave the main body of my force in view of the battlefield, to move two hundred infantrymen into the Frichermont wood, a squadron at Lasne, pushing its posts as far as Saint-Lambert; another squadron, half at Couture and half at Beaumont, sending reconnaissances as far as the [River] Dyle, to the bridges of Moustier and Ottignies. The commanders of these various detachments were to maintain small posts a quarter of a league [about a kilometre] apart, forming a continuous chain to the battlefield, in order that, by means of a hussar galloping from post to post, the officers on reconnaissance could quickly warn me of their junction with the advance guard of Marshal Grouchy, who was to arrive from the direction of the Dyle. Finally, I was to send the information gathered on these reconnaissances directly to the Emperor.[22]

Marbot clearly believed that his mission was to establish contact with Grouchy's advance guard and to warn Napoleon of its arrival. These accounts appear incontrovertible, but Marbot is often accused of being rabidly pro-Napoleon and quite capable of embellishing the truth to protect his reputation. However, *Chef d'Escadron* Dupuy of the 7th Hussars also wrote of this mission:

Until towards 4pm we remained peaceful spectators of the battle. At this time, General Domon came to me; the fire of the English had almost ceased. He told me that the battle was won, that the enemy army was in retreat, that we were to make a junction with Marshal Grouchy's corps and that by evening we would be in Brussels. He left.[23]

Despite this evidence, we must remain somewhat sceptical about whether Napoleon truly believed Grouchy would be able to arrive on the battlefield in time to make a telling contribution. None of the four orders we have already examined, given the times they were sent, suggest that Napoleon could have had a realistic expectation of his being able to do so.

Vandamme's and Gérard's Relationship with Grouchy
Many histories of the campaign have highlighted the difficult relationship between Grouchy and two of his key subordinates, Generals Gérard and Vandamme. It is widely accepted that both generals were jealous of Grouchy's recent promotion to the marshalate whilst they had been overlooked. Some critics have speculated that the fallout from these rather fractious relationships contributed to the failure of

Grouchy's operations in 1815 as Grouchy himself states:

> ... the manifest dissatisfaction that had developed in this general officer [Vandamme], as well as in General Gérard, their mutual jealousies of the command that had been entrusted to me, the tardy and incomplete obedience of them both and their pretensions that could give up a constant and boundless patience and forbearance that was so little appreciated by them since it made them weak, overwhelming me with bitterness and disgust and effectively threatening the success of my operations.[24]

In his various writings, Grouchy accused Gérard of the following infractions:

- On the 17th he refused to start his march when directly ordered to do so by Marshal Grouchy.
- The march of his corps was slow and disorganised on the 17th and 18th.
- He was insubordinate at Walhain when demanding they should march to the sound of the guns.

In the main body of this narrative we have already judged in favour of Gérard on the first two points; he could not march on the 17th until the whole of Vandamme's corps had moved past him and his pace of march was dictated by Vandamme's troops that preceded him down the same road which was in a terrible state due to the bad weather and the passage of both the Prussians and Vandamme's corps. On the 'charge' of insubordination, Gérard probably stands guilty of the way he challenged Grouchy despite the well-intentioned advice he offered.

Grouchy's 'charges' against Vandamme are rather more serious and in keeping with his chequered disciplinary record in dealing with superior officers:

- After the action at Gilly he refused to support Grouchy's cavalry in the wooded country towards Fleurus and refused to advance further despite being ordered to do so.
- He attacked Wavre on the afternoon of the 18th despite Grouchy's order not to.
- He refused to join Grouchy at Limal during night of 18th/19th despite a written order to do so.

These failures by Vandamme to obey Grouchy's orders are damning and would no doubt have been laid before Napoleon if the outcome of the campaign had been different. Vandamme is unlikely to have been able to present a credible defence and given his previous reputation, would probably have done his chances of promotion irreparable harm. Whilst writing his father's memoirs, Marshal Grouchy's grandson speculated:

It is most likely that the emperor put Vandamme under Grouchy's orders to ensure that this general officer, of awkward character, hurt by not having been made a marshal and jealous of Grouchy, would not refuse to obey orders as he had done at the beginning of the campaign. By giving Vandamme an immediate commander, Napoleon hoped that he would execute the orders given by this chief. It would have been much better, we think, to place under Marshal Grouchy's orders, corps commanders who were better disposed than Vandamme and Gérard, to obey him.[25]

Vandamme's published correspondence gives an account of his part in this campaign. The author of this account, Albert du Casse, gives this reason for Vandamme's insubordination:

> ... the general had great and true military talents, unequalled bravery and a wholesome character. He detested Grouchy since this last had been made marshal in reward for his political campaign in the Midi against the Duke of Angoulême. Seeing himself again frustrated in receiving the baton, the object of his most ardent desires, and thinking himself a better soldier than Grouchy, he obeyed the orders of the latter with regret and difficulty. It was a fault of the emperor's to put a man such as Vandamme under the command of Grouchy.[26]

Grouchy's frustration and weakness in dealing with Vandamme is evident in his letter pleading with him to march to Limal on the night of the 18th/19th.[27]

In the circumstances of a short and hectic campaign and with the hindsight of modern times, it is hard to dictate what Grouchy could or should have done to bring his subordinates into line. It is too easy to say that he should just have sacked them; these were two of Napoleon's hardest-fighting corps commanders, appointed by the emperor himself and considered by him as possible future marshals. Indeed, in these circumstances, it is hard not to feel a little sympathy for Grouchy, placed as he was in an extremely difficult position. He later wrote:

> Moreover, thinking that he [Gérard] found it painful to serve under my orders, I made a particular effort to leave them [Gérard and Vandamme] as much latitude as possible [in the execution of their orders] and to show deference that their talents and experience truly warranted.[28]

Gérard himself also wrote on his relationship with Grouchy in response to the marshal's criticism:

> M. le maréchal de Grouchy says on page nineteen of his *fragmens historique*, speaking of General Vandamme and myself, that he thought he

noticed that it was painful for us both to serve under his orders . . . Since M. *le maréchal* de Grouchy forces me to explain myself on this point, I say openly that he would not have been the chief of my choice, but, as an officer of duty above all, I obeyed him as punctually as I would have the emperor himself . . .[29]

It seems that Grouchy was unfairly critical of Gérard, although the latter served under Grouchy with reluctance and a lack of respect. However, Vandamme deserves particular censure for his calculated failure to undermine his superior's authority which resulted in considerable loss of life at both Wavre and later in front of Namur, but probably did not have a decisive effect on the campaign.

Grouchy's Performance – an Overview

So what are we to make of Marshal Grouchy during this campaign?

Grouchy's many critics paint him as a man who lacked the strength of character and self-confidence to impose himself on his subordinates; a man who lacked the flexibility and initiative to fully understand what his role in his commander's strategic plan really was or how he should support it; a man shackled to the letter of his orders and in thrall to the icy grip of Napoleon's superior intellect and strength of character; and a man somewhat overawed by his responsibilities on a mission he was never entirely comfortable with.

Nearly all of the officers who wrote their memoirs of this dark time in French military history, wrote in support of Napoleon. Hence, influenced by this devotion and by his criticisms of his key lieutenants that appeared in his memoirs, they heap their criticism on Grouchy and it is no surprise that that marshal felt somewhat victimised. As a typical view, let us see what Gérard's *aide de camp*, Colonel Rumigny, had to say:

Marshal Grouchy has often been accused of treason, it is a terrible slander. He was a man of honour, but alas, little capable of independent command. He was exclusively a cavalry officer and, consequently, little able to command an army composed of different arms. General Gérard judged him the same as me. I can guarantee that Marshal Grouchy, if he had lost his army, he would certainly have been sincere. There was incapacity on this fatal day, nothing more. He was not only one to show this during the days of failure. Ney and others had their part in the sad results of our defeats in 1814 and 1815. In moments of victory, everyone is happy to carry on; but in days of reverses, it is necessary to have hardened souls and capable heads.[30]

When Grouchy's formations did not act in accordance with his wishes, it was almost inevitably due to the lack of co-operation and support from his key subordinates rather than the orders themselves. But his inability to impose his authority over his subordinates or earn their respect does reveal a weakness and lack of confidence in his character that perhaps did manifest itself in his somewhat blind obedience of his orders.

Grouchy fundamentally failed to impose a sense of urgency on his subordinates and this reflects the poor state of the relationship between them and weaknesses in Grouchy's character. A strong and energetic commander instils a sense of urgency into his subordinates by his strength of personality, the respect these subordinates have in his experience and competency, their sense of discipline and their understanding of the need for this urgency. These officers will then instil this same sense of urgency into their own commands until it reaches the lowest ranks. If subordinate commanders lack the respect for their commander and his abilities, through jealousy, envy, contempt for their ability etc, or do not understand the need for a sense of urgency, they will fail to pass this down to their commands. If this is the case, no matter how much the senior commander frets and cajoles his subordinates once the operation begins, he will inevitably fail to generate the sense of urgency he is looking for.

It may also be worth revisiting the quote from Marshal Marmont that was used in the introduction:

> Grouchy is the worst officer to put at the head of an army. He lacks neither bravery nor some talent for the handling of troops, but he lacks resolution and is incapable of seizing an advantage: this is the worst thing in war.

Grouchy was certainly resolute in his determination to stick to the letter of Napoleon's orders, but does this make him a resolute commander, or one who hides behind his orders to avoid making more critical decisions? He finally resolved to follow the Prussians to Wavre, but never appeared to make any deliberate attempt to get between them and Napoleon. Having correctly identified that the main Prussian force was heading for Wavre and possibly Brussels, he seemed content to follow on behind and only attacked when Thielemann made a stand behind the Dyle. Grouchy found it easier to do this than to work out why the Prussian held at Wavre. It never seemed to occur to him that the remainder of the Prussian army might be moving to join Wellington.

Grouchy's thinking and interpretation of orders was certainly muddled and indecisive at times and he may well have hidden behind the precise execution of his orders. But the information that he had to interpret in order to determine his actions was contradictory and incomplete. Once again, perhaps we are guilty of judging him with the benefit of hindsight. As Marmont pointed out, his tactical ability was sound; after Vandamme's failure to take the bridge in Wavre, Grouchy was prepared to attempt to outflank the town at two different locations and was able to drive Thielemann from a strong tactical position.

It seems that many of those who have chosen to criticise Grouchy have done so with a lack of objectivity. It is easy to identify what mistakes have been made when the critic has all the benefit of hindsight; being able to coolly and under no pressure see the repercussions of decisions and actions that have taken place and are well documented. But it less easy to be able to understand not only the pressures that commanders of those times operated under, especially the lack of clarity of the true situation, particularly in regard to the actions and locations of your enemy, but also the particular pressures and restrictions that working within the system of command, the restrictions on the use of initiative and the unique pressures of working for a commander of Napoleon's stature.

The key to objectivity seems to hang on how each person interprets Napoleon's orders. Every effort should be made not to allow this to be coloured by an individual's opinion of Grouchy or Napoleon and judgements should be based on what the commanders actually knew at the time, not with the benefit of hindsight. All this becomes more complicated still if they are interpreted in a modern military context. Here, the key issue is the latitude commanders are given, or would expect, for the use of their initiative. In Napoleonic times, commanders were generally given little latitude and both Wellington and Napoleon were famously strict in this regard. In 1806, Napoleon wrote to Berthier, who had been his chief-of-staff for ten years, 'Keep strictly to the orders that I give you; execute your instructions punctually; I alone know what is required.'[31]

Grouchy's first orders on 17 June sent him on a mission of reconnaissance; of finding the Prussians and most importantly, establishing their intentions. Unfortunately, the slowness with which this was done, where the fault lies collectively with Napoleon, Grouchy and his subordinates, determined that by the time this was achieved it was too late for Napoleon to give the necessary orders that would deny the Prussians the chance to intervene decisively at Waterloo and Soult's rather vague and unclear despatches did nothing to help Napoleon ensure that his intent was clearly transmitted to his subordinates.

We have already judged that it was unreasonable to expect Grouchy to cross to the left bank of the Dyle straight from Gembloux on the morning of the 18th as the Prussian situation and intentions were still unclear and such an action would have meant breaking contact with them before divining their plans in direct contravention of Napoleon's orders. Grouchy was also right not to march to the sound of the guns later that morning as he was expecting Napoleon to be fighting at that time and the emperor was confident of defeating Wellington without support from his lieutenant. In fact, at this point, it was probably too late for Grouchy to have any chance of interfering with the Prussian march, even if he had the force to do so.

But the key is what would have triggered such an action and this is surely the orders he received. To conclude that Grouchy should have used his initiative to take such a decision is almost certainly the failure of someone in the twenty-first century to understand the way of war and Napoleon's system of command 200 years ago. Few commanders of that time would have had the courage and confidence to receive information that convinced them they should completely change their course of action and flagrantly disobey their orders.

In the background, but casting a haunting shadow across Grouchy's mind was the French emperor who was undoubtedly losing his sharpness of vision, intuitive decisiveness and *coup d'oeil*. However, for this author at least, accusations of overconfidence and even complacency are wide of the mark; here was a man who was desperately trying to motivate and infuse with confidence a group of senior commanders who hearts were no longer dedicated to war and who were beginning to lose their faith in Napoleon's star. Whilst the emperor was still capable of conjuring up plans of strategic brilliance, perhaps he no longer had the energy and stamina to maintain the tempo of decision-making and capacity to execute them.

So perhaps the biggest failing might be laid at the feet of Napoleon himself. If he demanded only obedience from his subordinates, without explaining why he gave the orders he did, he cannot have expected them to use their initiative. It was thus beholden to him to give clear direction; at no point did he order Grouchy to keep between him and the Prussians or even to prevent them from joining Wellington. This was only implied, at best, in the two orders Grouchy received before Napoleon had confronted Wellington. If the emperor had written to Grouchy on the evening of the 18th, explaining that the Anglo-Netherlands army looked as if it were going to stand and that Grouchy should manoeuvre to impose himself between the Prussians and their allies, then Grouchy might still have had a chance to have made a telling contribution. By the time the battle started the next day it was too late. This failure is hard to understand. Whilst many French officers and historians have calculated that Grouchy still had the time to march to the battlefield on the 18th, or to intercept the Prussians' march, the truth is that by the time he reached Walhain, he had no orders to do so, nor realistic hope of achieving it; and however painful the result, it is perhaps harsh to blame Marshal Grouchy for the loss of Waterloo.

In neither Napoleon nor Grouchy did there appear to be any sense of the possibility or consequences of a Prussian intervention at that iconic battle. Napoleon's lack of clear and comprehensive orders left an uncomfortable Grouchy, lacking self-confidence, never clearly getting to grips with his mission, finding the blind obedience of orders the easiest course of action. It is easy to criticise Grouchy for this, but the reality is that Napoleon's command style made this inevitable. A far more experienced and confident independent commander such as Soult or Davout was probably required before more might have been expected. Everything considered, Napoleon failed to give clear direction to his newly-appointed subordinate and the lack of clear, unambiguous orders suggests that the blame for the failure of Grouchy to influence the outcome of the battle of Waterloo lies squarely at the feet of Napoleon.

Orders of Battle

The French Army at the Battle of Ligny
(Taken from *La Campagne de 1815 aux Pays-Bas*, Vol. 3, by F. de Bas and de T'Serclaes de Wommersom. Figures will not be exact and do not include HQ staff.)

Commander-in-Chief: The Emperor Napoleon

Aides de camp of the emperor: Generals *Duc de* Plaisance, Count Drouot, Count Corbineau, Count Flahaut, Count Dejean, Baron Bernard, Count de la Bédoyère.

Premier Officier d'ordonnance: Colonel Gourgaud.

Grand Quartier Général

Major Général: Marshal Soult, *duc de Dalmatie*.
Chef d'État-Major Général: Lieutenant General Count Bailly de Monthion.
Adjutants-Commandants: Baron Michal, Baron Stoffel, Babut, d'Hincourt, Petiet.

Commander-in-Chief of Artillery: Lieutenant General Ruty.
Commander-in-Chief of Engineers: Lieutenant General Baron Rogniat.
Commander of Gendarmerie: Lieutenant General Radet.

Imperial Guard
(19,909 all ranks, 76 guns/howitzers)
Aide-major-général de la Garde: Lieutenant General Count Drouot.

Old Guard Infantry
(255+8,189)
General Commandant of Grenadiers: Lieutenant General Count Friant
    1st Regiment of Grenadiers: 2 battalions (32+1,006) General Petit.
    2nd Regiment of Grenadiers: 2 battalions (32+1,063) General Christiani.
    3rd Regiment of Grenadiers: 2 battalions (34+1,146) General Poret de Morvan.
    4th Regiment of Grenadiers: 1 battalion (25+503) General Harlet.
    5th Company, Guard Foot Artillery Regiment.

General Commandant of *Chasseurs*: Lieutenant General Count Morand.
    1st Regiment of *Chasseurs*: 2 battalions (36+1,271) General Cambronne.
    2nd Regiment of *Chasseurs*: 2 battalions (32+1,131) General Pelet.
    3rd Regiment of *Chasseurs*: 2 battalions (34+1,028) General Mallet.
    4th Regiment of *Chasseurs*: 2 battalions (30+1,041) General Henrion.
    6th Company, Guard Foot Artillery Regiment.

Young Guard
(117+4,166)
Commander: Lieutenant General Count Duhesme.
Divisional Commander: Lieutenant General Barrois.
1st Brigade: *Maréchal de Camp* Chartrand
    1st Regiment of *Tirailleurs*: 2 battalions (32+935) Colonel Trappier de Malcolm.
    1st Regiment of *Voltigeurs*: 2 battalions (31+1,188) Colonel Secrétan.
2nd Brigade: *Maréchal de Camp* Guye.
    3rd Regiment of *Tirailleurs*: 2 battalions (28+960) Colonel Pailhès.
    3rd Regiment of *Voltigeurs*: 2 battalions (26+1,083) Colonel Hurel.
7th Company, Auxiliary Foot Artillery.
8th Company, Auxiliary Foot Artillery.

Heavy Cavalry of the Guard
(99+1,617)

Commander: Lieutenant General Count Guyot.

Grenadiers à Cheval: (44+752) General Dubois.
Dragoons: (51+765) General Ornano.
Gendarmerie d'élite: (4+102) General Dautancourt.
3rd Company, Guard Horse Artillery Regiment.
4th Company, Guard Horse Artillery Regiment.

Artillery of the Guard

Commander: Lieutenant General Desvaux de Saint-Maurice.
Commander Horse Artillery: Colonel Duchard.
Commander Foot Artillery: General Lallemand.
Reserve: 1st, 2nd, 3rd and 4th Companies Guard Foot Artillery Regiment.

Guard Engineers (*sapeurs*): 3+109.
Sailors of the Guard (*marins*): 3+104.

III Corps
(748+16,652 and 38 guns/howitzers)
Commander: Lieutenant General Count Vandamme
Chef de l'état-major: *Maréchal de Camp* Revest.
Commander of Artillery: *Maréchal de Camp* Doguereau.
Commander of Engineers: *Maréchal de Camp* Nempde.

8th Infantry Division
(230+5,031 and 8 guns/howitzers)
Commander: Lieutenant General Baron Lefol.
1st Brigade: *Maréchal de Camp* Billiard.
    15th *léger:* 3 battalions (62+1,676) Colonel Brice.
    23rd *de ligne:* 3 battalions (62+1,152) Colonel Baron Vernier.
2nd Brigade: *Maréchal de Camp* Baron Corsin.
    37th *de ligne*: 3 battalions (59+1,117) Colonel Fortier.
    64th *de ligne*: 2 battalions (40+891) Colonel Dubalen.
7th Company, 6th Foot Artillery Regiment, (4+83) Captain Chauveau.
1st Sqn, 1st Company of Train (12).
2nd Company, 2nd Battalion, 2nd Regiment Engineers, (3+100) Captain Carré.
Ambulances (11).

10th Infantry Division
(243+5,602 and 8 guns/howitzers)
Commander: Lieutenant General Baron Habert.
1st Brigade: *Maréchal de Camp* Baron Gengoult.
    34th *de ligne*: 3 battalions (55+1,384) Colonel Mouton.
    88th *de ligne*: 3 battalions (57+1,265) Colonel Baillon.
2nd Brigade: Maréchal de Camp Dupreyroux.
    22nd *de ligne*: 3 battalions (55+1,406) Colonel Fantin des Odoards.
    70th *de ligne*: 2 battalions (45+909) Colonel Baron Maury.
    2nd *Regiment Étranger (Suisse)*: 1 battalion (21+368) Colonel Stoffel.
18th Company, 2nd Foot Artillery Regiment, (4+89) Captain Guérin.
4th Company, 5th Sqn Train (2+92) Captain Lecocq.
2nd Company, 2nd Battalion, 2nd Regiment Engineers, (4+81) Captain Lemaire.
Ambulances (8)

11th Infantry Division
(174+4,617 and 8 guns/howitzers)
Commander: Lieutenant General Baron Berthezène.
1st Brigade: *Maréchal de Camp* Baron Dufour.
    12th *de ligne*: 2 battalions (41+1,171) Colonel Baron Beaudinot.
    56th *de ligne*: 2 battalions (42+1,234) Colonel Delhaye.

2nd Brigade: *Maréchal de Camp* Baron Lagarde.
    33rd *de ligne*: 2 battalions (39+1,097) Colonel Baron Maire.
    86th *de ligne*: 2 battalions (44+870) Colonel Pelecier.
17th Company, 2nd Foot Artillery Regiment, (4+96) Captain Lecorbeiller.
5th Company, 5th Sqn of Train (2+94) Captain Cheanne.
2nd Company, 2nd Battalion, 2nd Regiment Engineers, (2+48) Captain Cotelle.
Ambulances (7).

3rd Light Cavalry Division
(91+1,106 and 6 guns/howitzers)
Commander: Lieutenant General Baron Domon.
1st Brigade: *Maréchal de Camp* Baron Dommanget.
    4th *Chasseurs à Cheval*: 3 squadrons (31+306) Colonel Desmichels.
    9th *Chasseurs à Cheval*: 3 squadrons (25+337) Colonel Dukermont.
2nd Brigade: *Maréchal de Camp* Baron Vinot.
    12th *Chasseurs à Cheval*: 3 squadrons (29+289) Colonel de Grouchy.
4th Company, 2nd Horse Artillery Regiment, (3+74) Captain Dumont.
6th Company, 5th Sqn of Train (3+100).

Reserve Artillery: 1st Company, 2nd Foot Artillery Regiment, (4+95) Captain Vollée.
19th Company, 2nd Foot Artillery Regiment, (4+97) Captain Lachiche.
6th Company, 5th Sqn of Train (2+104) Captain Lestrat.

IV Corps
(664+14,787 and 38 guns/howitzers)
Commander: Lieutenant General Count Gérard.
Chef de l'État-major general: *Adjutant-commandant* Simon Lorière.
Artillery Commander: *Maréchal de Camp* Baron Baltus.
Engineer Commander: *Maréchal de Camp* Valazé.

12th Infantry Division
(183+4,786 and 8 guns/howitzers)
Commander: Lieutenant General Baron Pécheux.
1st Brigade: *Maréchal de Camp* Rome.
    30th *de ligne*: 3 battalions (54+1,399) Colonel Ramand.
    96th *de ligne*: 3 battalions (51+1,387) Colonel Gougeon.
2nd Brigade: *Maréchal de Camp* Schaeffer.
    63rd *de ligne*: 3 battalions (53+1,214) Colonel Laurède.
    6th *léger*: 1 battalion (20+591) *Chef de Bataillon* Gémeau.
2nd Company, 5th Foot Artillery Regiment (3+98) Captain Fenouillat.
6th Company, 5th Sqn of Train (2+97).

13th Infantry Division
(165+3,940 and 8 guns/howitzers)
Commander: Lieutenant General Baron Vichery.
1st Brigade: *Maréchal de Camp* Le Capitaine.
    59th *de ligne*: 2 battalions (42+1,015) Colonel Chevalier Laurain.
    76th *de ligne*: 2 battalions (40+1,014) *Chef de Bataillon* Condamy.
2nd Brigade: *Maréchal de Camp* Desprez.
    48th *de ligne*: 2 battalions (43+834) Colonel Péraldi.
    69th *de ligne*: 2 battalions (40 +1,077) Colonel Hervé.
1st Company, 5th Foot Artillery Regiment, (5+97) Captain Saint-Cyr.
2nd Company, 2nd Sqn of Train (3+92) Captain Thomas.
5th Company, 2nd Battalion, 2nd Engineer Regiment, (58) Captain Brignon.

14th Infantry Division
(169+4,058 and 8 guns/howitzers)
Commander: *Maréchal de Camp* Hulot.
1st Brigade: Colonel Baume.
    9th *léger*: 2 battalions (43+1,215)
    111th *de ligne*: 2 battalions (43+1,035) Colonel Baron Sausset.
2nd Brigade: *Maréchal de Camp* Toussaint.
    44th *de ligne*: 2 battalions (43+934) Colonel Paolini.
    50th *de ligne*: 2 battalions (40+874) Colonel Lavigne.
3rd Company, 3rd Horse Artillery Regiment, (4+80) Captain Tortel.
2nd Company, 2nd Sqn of Train (2+76)
3rd Company, 2nd Battalion, 2nd Regiment Engineers, (3+74) Captain Provence.

7th Light Cavalry Division
(134+1,617 and 6 guns/howitzers)
Commander: Lieutenant General Maurin.
1st Brigade: *Maréchal de Camp* Vallin.
    6th Hussars: 3 squadrons (26+387) Colonel Prince de Savoie-Carignan.
    8th *Chasseurs à Cheval*: 3 squadrons (30+371) Colonel Schneit.
2nd Brigade: *Maréchal de Camp* Berruyer.
    6th Dragoons: 3 squadrons (20+211) Colonel Mugnier.
    11th Dragoons: 2 squadrons (30+134) Colonel Burean de Puly.
1st Company, 2nd Horse Artillery Regiment, (3+75) Captain Leboul.
1st Company, 2nd Sqn of Train (2+79) Captain Nègre.

Corps Reserve Artillery: 3rd, 4th and 5th Companies, 5th Foot Artillery Regiment (13+386).
5th, 7th, 8th and 9th Companies of Train (9+383).
Corps Reserve Engineers: 4th Company, 2nd Regiment, (2+69) Captain Louis.

Corps Bridging Train: 5th, 7th, 8th and 9th Companies, 1st Battalion, (4+63) Captain Moutonnet.

1st Cavalry Corps
(219+2,641 and 12 guns/howitzers)
Commander: Lieutenant General Count Pajol.
Chef de l'État-major: *Adjutant-Commandant* Picard.

4th Light Cavalry Division
(97+1,388 and 6 guns/howitzers)
Commander: Lieutenant General Baron Soult.
1st Brigade: *Maréchal de Camp* Laurent.
    1st Hussars: 4 squadrons (36+489) *Maréchal de Camp* Clary.
    4th Hussars: 4 squadrons (29+346) Colonel Blot.
2nd Brigade: *Maréchal de Camp* Baron Ameil.
    5th Hussars: 4 squadrons (29+399) Colonel Baron Liégeard.
1st Company, 1st Horse Artillery Regiment (2+70) Captain Gotheaux.
3rd Company, 1st Sqn of Train (1+84) Captain Legrand.

5th Light Cavalry Division
(122+1,253 and 6 guns/howitzers)
Lieutenant General Baron Subervie.
1st Brigade: *Maréchal de Camp* Count Colbert.
    1st Lancers: 4 squadrons (40+375) Colonel Jacquinot.
    2nd Lancers: 4 squadrons (41+379) Colonel Sourd.
2nd Brigade: *Maréchal de Camp* Merlin.
    11th *Chasseurs à Cheval*: 4 squadrons (37+336) Colonel Baron Nicolas.
3rd Company, 1st Horse Artillery Regiment (2+74) Captain Walter.
4th Company, 1st Sqn of Train (2+89) Captain Speltens.

2nd Cavalry Corps
(412+4,768 and 12 guns/howitzers)
Commander: Lieutenant General Count Exelmans.
Chef de l'État-major: *Adjutant-Commandant* Feroussat.

9th Cavalry Division
(141+1,551 and 6 guns/howitzers)
Commander: Lieutenant General Strolz.
1st Brigade: *Maréchal de Camp* Baron Burthe.
    5th Dragoons: 4 squadrons (41+465) Colonel Canavas St-Amand.
    13th Dragoons: 4 squadrons (35+389) Colonel Saviot.

2nd Brigade: *Maréchal de Camp* Baron Vincent.
    15th Dragoons: 4 squadrons (34+381) Colonel Chaillot.
    20th Dragoons: 4 squadrons (31+316) Colonel Briqueville.
4th Company, 1st Horse Artillery Regiment (4+55) Captain Cotheraux.
6th Company, 1st Sqn of Train (1+59) Lieutenant Hubert.

10th Cavalry Division
(279+3,217 and 6 guns/howitzers)
Commander: Lieutenant General Baron Chastel.
1st Brigade: *Maréchal de Camp* Baron Bonnemains.
    4th Dragoons: 4 squadrons (35+530) Colonel Bouquerot des Essarts.
    12th Dragoons: 4 squadrons (30+510) Colonel Bureaux de Puzy.
2nd Brigade: *Maréchal de Camp* Berton.
    14th Dragoons: 4 squadrons (34+339) Colonel Sèguier.
    17th Dragoons: 4 squadrons (39+287) Colonel Labiffe.
4th Company, 4th Horse Artillery Regiment, (2+60) Captain Bernard.
1st Company, 2nd Sqn of Train (1+72).

7th Infantry Division
(Detached from II Corps)
(164+3,936 and 8 guns/howitzers)
Commander: Lieutenant General Count Girard.
1st Brigade: *Maréchal de Camp* Baron Devilliers.
    11th *léger*: 2 battalions (42+913) Colonel Sébastiani.
    82nd *de ligne*: 1 battalion (27+550) Colonel Matis.
2nd Brigade: *Maréchal de Camp* Baron Piat.
    12th *léger*: 3 battalions (51+1,141) Colonel Mouttet.
    4th *de ligne*: 2 battalions (44+1,157) Colonel Paulain.
3rd Company, 2nd Foot Artillery Regiment (3+74) Captain Barbaux.
1st Company, 1st Sqn of Train (1+58) Captain Fivel.
2nd Company, 5th Sqn of Train (1+43) Captain Ciren.

4th Reserve Cavalry Corps
(251+2,869 and 12 guns/howitzers)
Commander: Lieutenant General Count Milhaud.
Chef de l'État-major: Adjutant-Commandant Baron Chasseriau.

13th Cavalry Division
(117+1,220 and 6 guns/howitzers)
Commander: Lieutenant General Wathier St-Alphonse.
1st Brigade: *Maréchal de Camp* Dubois.

1st Cuirassiers: 4 squadrons (41+411) Colonel Count Ordener.
4th Cuirassiers: 3 squadrons (28+278) Colonel Habert.
2nd Brigade: *Maréchal de Camp* Baron Travers.
7th Cuirassiers: 2 squadrons (21+151) Colonel Richardot.
12th Cuirassiers: 2 squadrons (22+226) Colonel Thurot.
5th Company, 1st Horse Artillery Regiment (3+75) Captain Duchet.
8th Company 1st Sqn of Train (2+79) Lieutenant Pommier.

14th Cavalry Division
(134+1,649 and 6 guns/howitzers)
Commander: Lieutenant General Baron Delort.
1st Brigade: *Maréchal de Camp* Baron Farine.
5th Cuirassiers: 3 squadrons (34+380) Colonel Gobert.
10th Cuirassiers: 3 squadrons (26+309) Colonel Lahubière.
2nd Brigade: *Maréchal de Camp* Baron Vial.
6th Cuirassiers: 4 squadrons (37+474) Colonel Martin.
9th Cuirassiers: 3 squadrons (32+327) Colonel Bigarne.
4th Company, 3rd Horse Artillery Regiment (3+70) Captain Jacques.
6th Company, 3rd Sqn of Train (2+89) Captain Glautier.

VI Corps
(472+9,991 and 38 guns/howitzers)
(Spent most of the battle in reserve and only arrived on the field at the end of the day)
Commander: Lieutenant General Mouton Count de Lobau.
Chef de l'État-major: *Maréchal de Camp* Durrieu.
Artillery Commander: Lieutenant General Baron Noury.
Engineer Commander: *Maréchal de Camp* Sabatier.

19th Infantry Division
(200+4,035 and 8 guns/howitzers)
Commander: Lieutenant General Baron Simmer.
1st Brigade: *Maréchal de Camp* Baron de Bellair.
5th *de ligne*: 2 battalions (42+910) Colonel Rousille.
11th *de ligne*: 3 battalions (61+1,135) Colonel Aubrée.
2nd Brigade: *Maréchal de Camp* Jamin.
27th *de ligne*: 2 battalions (39+782) Colonel Gaudin.
84th *de ligne*: 2 battalions (45+894) Colonel Chevalier.
1st Company, 8th Foot Artillery Regiment, (3+83) Captain Parisot.
4th Company, 7th and 8th Sqns of Train (4+90) Captain Laude
1st Company, 1st Battalion, 3rd Engineer Regiment, (4+91) Captain Toliot.
3rd Auxiliary Equipages of the Oise (2+50).

20th Infantry Division
(152+3,240 and 8 guns/howitzers)
Commander: Lieutenant General Baron Jeannin.
1st Brigade: *Maréchal de Camp* Bony.
      5th *léger*: 2 battalions (42+834) Colonel Curnier.
      10th *de ligne*: 2 battalions (56+1,375) Colonel Roussel.
2nd Brigade: *Maréchal de Camp* Tromelin.
      107th *de ligne*: 2 battalions (44+692) Colonel Druot.
2nd Company, 8th Foot Artillery Regiment, (3+88) Captain Paquet.
3rd Company, 8th Sqn of Train (2+102) Captain Langlois.
2nd Company 1st Battalion, 3rd Engineer Regiment, (3+87) Captain Euzenate.
1st Company, 3rd Sqn of Equipages (12).
3rd Company of Auxiliary Equipages of the Aisne (2+50).

21st Infantry Division
(115+2,597 and 8 guns/howitzers)
Commander: Lieutenant General Baron Teste.
1st Brigade: *Maréchal de Camp* Lafitte.
      8th *léger*: 2 battalions (42+896) Colonel Ricard.
      (The other regiment of this brigade, the 40th *de ligne*, was still forming at Senlis.)
2nd Brigade: *Maréchal de Camp* Penne.
      65th *de ligne*: 1 battalion (22+481) *Chef de Bataillon* Boumard.
      75th *de ligne*: 2 battalions (42+939) Colonel Mathivet.
3rd Company, 8th Foot Artillery Regiment (3+91) Captain Duvernay.
4th Company, 6th Sqn of Train (2+70) Captain Etienne.
3rd Company, 1st Battery, 3rd Engineer Regiment (3+93) Captain Ferrey.
1st Company, 3rd Sqn of Equipages (14)
4th Company of Auxiliary Equipages of the Aisne (1+13)

VI Corps Artillery Reserve
(5+119 and 14 guns/howitzers)
4th Company, 8th Foot Artillery Regiment (3+92).
3rd, 4th and 5th Companies of the 8th Sqn of Train (2+27).

4th Infantry Division
(165+3,864 and 8 guns/howitzers)
(This division was left by General d'Erlon from I Corps to support Napoleon at Ligny, but was only involved in a little skirmishing towards the end of the battle.)
Commander: Lieutenant General Count Durutte.
1st Brigade: *Maréchal de Camp* Pègot.
      8th *de ligne*: 2 battalions (40+943) Colonel Ruelle.

29th *de ligne*: 2 battalions (40+1,106) Colonel Rousselot.
2nd Brigade: *Maréchal de Camp* Brue.
85th *de ligne*: 2 battalions (40+591) Colonel Masson.
95th *de ligne*: 2 battalions (40+1,060) Colonel Garnier.
9th Company, 6th Foot Artillery Regiment, (3+81) Captain Bourgeois.
3rd Company, 1st Sqn of Train (2+83) Captain Drulin.

Three regiments of the 4th Cavalry Division were also left with Durutte's division, but there is no record of which of the 7th Hussars, 3rd *Chasseurs-à-Cheval* and 3rd and 4th Lancers, these were. No officer casualties are recorded for any of these regiments for the 16th in Martinien's lists.

The Prussian Army at Ligny
Commander-in-Chief: Field Marshal von Blücher, Prince von Walhstatt
Chief-of-Staff: General von Gneisenau

Each infantry regiment consisted of three battalions; two musketeer battalions and a fusilier (light) battalion. Foot and horse batteries consisted of six guns and two howitzers. Cavalry squadrons are shown.

I Corps
Commander: General von Zieten

1st Brigade: General von Steinmetz (8,550).
2 companies Siliesian *Schützen*.
12th Infantry Regiment.
24th Infantry Regiment.
1st Regiment Westphalian Landwehr.
4th Hussars (3 sqns).
6th Uhlans (3 sqns).
Foot Battery No. 7.
Horse Battery No. 7.

2nd Brigade: General von Pirch II (7,700).
6th Infantry Regiment.
28th Infantry Regiment.
2nd Regiment Westphalian Landwehr.
1st Westphalian Landwehr Cavalry Regiment (4 sqns).
Foot Battery No. 3.

3rd Brigade: General von Jagöw (8,050).
    2 companies Siliesian *Schützen*.
    7th Infantry Regiment.
    29th Infantry Regiment.
    3rd Regiment Westphalian Landwehr.
    Foot Battery No. 8.

4th Brigade: General von Henckel (5,000).
    19th Infantry Regiment.
    4th Infantry Regiment.
    Foot Battery No. 5.

Cavalry Reserve: General von Röder.
1st Brigade: General von Treckow (1,370).
    2nd Dragoon Regiment (3 sqns).
    5th Dragoon Regiment (4 sqns).
    3rd Uhlan Regiment (3 sqns).
    Horse Battery No. 2.
2nd Brigade: Lieutenant Colonel von Lützow (1,040).
    1st Kurmark Landwehr Cavalry Regiment (3 sqns).
    2nd Kurmark Landwehr Cavalry Regiment (4 sqns).

Reserve Artillery
Howitzer Battery No. 1.
Foot Batteries Nos. 1, 2, 6 and 9.
Horse Battery No. 10.

II Corps
Commander: General von Pirch I.

5th Brigade: General von Tippelskirch (8,050).
    2nd Infantry Regiment.
    25th Infantry Regiment.
    5th Westphalian Landwehr Regiment.
    Company of volunteer *chasseurs*.
    11th Hussars (2 sqns).
    Foot Battery No. 10.

6th Brigade: General von Krafft (8,115).
    9th Infantry Regiment.
    26th Infantry Regiment.
    1st Elbe Landwehr Regiment.

11th Hussars (2 sqns).
Foot Battery No. 5.

7th Brigade: General von Brause (7,260).
14th Infantry Regiment.
22nd Infantry Regiment.
2nd Elbe Landwehr Regiment.
1st Elbe Landwehr Cavalry Regiment (2 sqns).
Foot Battery No. 34.

8th Brigade: General von Bose (7,000).
21st Infantry Regiment.
23rd Infantry Regiment.
3rd Elbe Landwehr Regiment.
1st Elbe Landwehr Cavalry Regiment (2 sqns).
Foot Battery No. 12.

Reserve Cavalry
Commander: General von Wahlen-Jürgass.
1st Brigade: Colonel von Thümen (1,724).
2nd Uhlans.
6th Dragoons (4 sqns).
1st Dragoons (4 sqns).
Foot Battery No. 6.
2nd Brigade: Lieutenant Colonel von Sohr (1,660).
3rd Hussars (4 sqns).
5th Hussars (4 sqns).
3rd Brigade: Colonel von Schulenburg (1,500).
4th Kurmark Landwehr Cavalry Regiment (6 sqns).
5th Kurmark Landwehr Cavalry Regiment (4 sqns).

Artillery Reserve
Howitzer Battery No. 37.
Foot Batteries No. 4 and 8.
Horse Batteries Nos. 5 and 14.

III Corps
Commander: General von Thielemann.

9th Brigade: General von Borcke (7,600).
8th Infantry Regiment.
30th Infantry Regiment.
1st Kurmark Landwehr Regiment.

3rd Kurmark Landwehr Cavalry Regiment (2 sqns).
Foot Battery No. 18.

10th Brigade: Colonel von Kemphen (4,585).
27th Infantry Regiment.
2nd Elbe Landwehr Regiment.
3rd Kurmark Landwehr Cavalry Regiment (2 sqns).
Foot Battery No. 35.

11th Brigade: Colonel von Luck (4,640).
3rd Elbe Landwehr Regiment.
4th Elbe Landwehr Regiment.
6th Kurmark Landwehr Cavalry Regiment (2 sqns).
Foot Battery No. 36.

12th Brigade: Colonel von Stülpnagel (6,345).
31st Infantry Regiment.
5th Elbe Landwehr Regiment.
6th Elbe Landwehr Regiment.
6th Kurmark Landwehr Cavalry Regiment (2 sqns).
Foot Battery No. 24.

Cavalry Reserve
Commander: General von Hobe.
1st Brigade: Colonel von des Marwitz (1,140).
7th Uhlans (3 sqns).
8th Uhlans (4 sqns).
2nd Brigade: Lieutenant Colonel von Lottum (1,880).
5th Uhlans (3 sqns).
9th Hussars (3 sqns).
7th Dragoons (3 sqns)

Artillery Reserve
Foot Battery No. 7.
Horse Batteries Nos. 18 and 19.

Composition of Grouchy's Right Wing for the Pursuit of the Prussians and the Battle of Wavre

After the heavy losses suffered at the battle of Ligny, it is impossible to give accurate strengths for formations or units; indeed, it is quite likely that weaker regiments amalgamated battalions to make more viable units, so even the number of battalions or squadrons in a regiment may not be accurate.

Commander-in-Chief: Marshal *Comte de* Grouchy
Chef de l'État-major: *Maréchal de Camp* le Sénécal.

III Corps
Commander: Lieutenant General Count Vandamme
Chef de l'État-major: *Maréchal de Camp* Revest.
Commander of Artillery: *Maréchal de Camp* Doguereau.
Commander of Engineers: *Maréchal de Camp* Nempde.

8th Infantry Division
Commander: Lieutenant General Baron Lefol.
1st Brigade: *Maréchal de Camp* Billard.
    15th *léger*: 3 battalions, Colonel Brice.
    23rd *de ligne*: 3 battalions, Colonel Baron Vernier.
2nd Brigade: *Maréchal de Camp* Baron Corsin.
    37th *de ligne*: 3 battalions, Colonel Fortier.
    64th *de ligne*: 2 battalions, Colonel Dubalen.
7th Company, 6th Foot Artillery Regiment, Captain Chauveau.
2nd Company, 2nd Battalion, 2nd Regiment Engineers, Captain Carré.

10th Infantry Division
Commander: Lieutenant General Baron Habert.
1st Brigade: *Maréchal de Camp* Baron Gengoult.
    34th *de ligne*: 3 battalions, Colonel Mouton.
    88th *de ligne*: 3 battalions, Colonel Baillon.
2nd Brigade: *Maréchal de Camp* Dupreyroux.
    22nd *de ligne*: 3 battalions, Colonel Fantin des Odoards.
    70th *de ligne*: 2 battalions, Colonel Baron Maury.
    2nd *Regiment Étranger (Suisse)*: 1 battalion, Colonel Stoffel.
18th Company, 2nd Foot Artillery Regiment, Captain Guérin.
2nd Company, 2nd Battalion, 2nd Regiment Engineers, Captain Lemaire.

11th Infantry Division
Commander: Lieutenant General Baron Berthezène.
1st Brigade: *Maréchal de Camp* Baron Dufour.
    12th *de ligne*: 2 battalions, Colonel Baron Beaudinot.
    56th *de ligne*: 2 battalions, Colonel Delahaye.
2nd Brigade: *Maréchal de Camp* Baron Lagarde.
    33rd *de ligne*: 2 battalions, Colonel Baron Maire.
    86th *de ligne*: 2 battalions, Colonel Pelicier.
17th Company, 2nd Foot Artillery Regiment, Captain Lecorbeiller.
2nd Company, 2nd Battalion, 2nd Regiment Engineers, Captain Cotelle.

Reserve Artillery
1st Company, 2nd Foot Artillery Regiment, Captain Vollée.
19th Company, 2nd Foot Artillery Regiment, Captain Lachiche.

IV Corps
Commander: Lieutenant General Count Gérard.
Chef de l'État-Major general: *Adjutant-Commandant* Simon Lorière.
Artillery Commander: *Maréchal de Camp* Baron Baltus.
Engineer Commander: *Maréchal de Camp* Valazé.

12th Infantry Division
Commander: Lieutenant General Baron Pécheux.
1st Brigade: *Maréchal de Camp* Rome.
    30th *de ligne*: 3 battalions, Colonel Ramand.
    96th *de ligne*: 3 battalions, Colonel Gougeon.
2nd Brigade: *Maréchal de Camp* Schaeffer.
    63rd *de ligne*: 3 battalions, Colonel Laurède.
    6th *léger*: 1 battalion, *Chef de Bataillon* Gemeau.
2nd Company, 5th Foot Artillery Regiment.

13th Infantry Division
Commander: Lieutenant General Baron Vichery.
1st Brigade: *Maréchal de Camp* Le Capitaine.
    59th *de ligne*: 2 battalions, Colonel Chevalier Laurain.
    76th *de ligne*: 2 battalions, *Chef de Bataillon* Condamy.
2nd Brigade: *Maréchal de Camp* Desprez.
    48th *de ligne*: 2 battalions, Colonel Péraldi.
    69th *de ligne*: 2 battalions, Colonel Hervé.
1st Company, 5th Foot Artillery Regiment, Captain Saint-Cyr.
5th Company, 2nd Battalion, 2nd Engineer Regiment, Captain Brignon.

14th Infantry Division
Commander: *Maréchal de Camp* Hulot.
1st Brigade:
    9th *léger*: 2 battalions, Colonel Baume.
    111th *de ligne*: 2 battalions, Colonel Baron Sausset.
2nd Brigade: *Maréchal de Camp* Toussaint.
    44th *de ligne*: 2 battalions, Colonel Paolini.
    50th *de ligne*: 2 battalions, Colonel Lavigne.
3rd Company, 8th Foot Artillery Regiment.
3rd Company, 2nd Regiment Engineers, Captain Provence.

7th Light Cavalry Division
Commander: Lieutenant General Vallin.
1st Brigade
> 6th Hussars: 3 squadrons, Colonel Prince de Savoie-Carignan.
> 8th *Chasseurs à Cheval*: 3 squadrons, Colonel Schneit.

2nd Brigade: *Maréchal de Camp* Berruyer.
> 6th Dragoons: 3 squadrons, Colonel Mugnier.
> 11th Dragoons: 2 squadrons, Colonel Burean de Puly.

1st Company, 2nd Horse Artillery Regiment.

Reserve Artillery: 3rd, 4th and 5th Companies, 5th Foot Artillery Regiment.
Reserve Engineers: 4th Company, 2nd Regiment, Captain Louis.
Bridging Train: 5th, 7th, 8th and 9th Companies, 1st Battalion, Captain Moutonnet.

1st Cavalry Corps
(Subervie's division had been detached with Napoleon leaving only a single division in this corps)
Commander: Lieutenant General Count Pajol.
Chef de l'État-major: *Adjutant-Commandant* Picard.

4th Light Cavalry Division
Commander: Lieutenant General Baron Soult.
1st Brigade: *Maréchal de Camp* Laurent.
> 1st Hussars: 4 squadrons, *Maréchal de Camp* Clary.
> 4th Hussars: 4 squadron, Colonel Blot.

2nd Brigade: *Maréchal de Camp* Baron Ameil.
> 5th Hussars: 4 squadrons, Colonel Baron Liégeard.

1st Company, 1st Horse Artillery Regiment.

21st Infantry Division
(This infantry division was detached from VI Corps and came under command of General Pajol; however, it was not formally part of 1st Cavalry Corps.)
Commander: Lieutenant General Baron Teste.
1st Brigade: *Maréchal de Camp* Lafitte.
> 8th *léger*: 2 battalions, Colonel Ricard.
> (The other regiment of this brigade, the 40th *de ligne*, was still forming at Senlis.)

2nd Brigade: *Maréchal de Camp* Penne.
> 65th *de ligne*: 1 battalion, *Chef de Bataillon* Boumard.
> 75th *de ligne*: 2 battalions, Colonel Mathivet.

3rd Company, 8th Foot Artillery Regiment.

2nd Cavalry Corps
Commander: Lieutenant General Count Exelmans.
Chef de l'État-major: *Adjutant-Commandant* Feroussat.

9th Cavalry Division
Commander: Lieutenant General Strolz.
1st Brigade: *Maréchal de Camp* Baron Burthe.
    5th Dragoons: 4 squadrons, Colonel Canavas St-Amand.
    13th Dragoons: 4 squadrons, Colonel Saviot.
2nd Brigade: *Maréchal de Camp* Baron Vincent.
    15th Dragoons: 4 squadrons, Colonel Chaillot.
    20th Dragoons: 4 squadrons, Colonel Briqueville.
4th Company, 1st Horse Artillery Regiment.

10th Cavalry Division
Commander: Lieutenant General Baron Chastel.
1st Brigade: *Maréchal de Camp* Baron Bonnemains.
    4th Dragoons: 4 squadrons, Colonel Bouquerot des Essarts.
    12th Dragoons: 4 squadrons, Colonel Bureaux de Puzy.
2nd Brigade: *Maréchal de Camp* Berton.
    14th Dragoons: 4 squadrons, Colonel Sèguier.
    17th Dragoons: 4 squadrons, Colonel Labiffe.
4th Company, 1st Horse Artillery Regiment, Captain Bernarde.

Notes

Introduction
1. O'Meara, *Napoleon at St. Helena* (New York: Peter Eckler, n.d.).
2. Charras, *Histoire de la Campagne de 1815, Waterloo* (La Haye: Doorman, 1857), Vol. 2, p. 53.
3. I mean the first by a major player in the campaign. The earliest published account by a Frenchman I have found is *Relation Fidèle et Détaillée de la Dernière Campagne de Buonaparte, Terminée par la Bataille de Mont-Saint-Jean, dite de Waterloo ou de la Belle Alliance, par un Témoin Oculaire*, which was published in 1815. Although noteworthy as being published anonymously, it was subsequently credited to *Chirurgien-major* René Bourgeois of the cuirassiers and takes something of an anti-Bonaparte line.
4. Gourgaud, *The Campaign of 1815 or a Narrative of the Military Operations which took place in France and Belgium during the Hundred Days* (London: James Ridgeway, 1818).
5. Alphonse Grouchy, *Le Maréchal de Grouchy du 16 au 19 Juin 1815* (Paris: Dentu, 1864).
6. Grouchy, *Observations sur la Relation de la campagne publiée par le Général Gourgaud* (Philadelphia: Hurtel, 1818), p. 25.
7. Gérard eventually became a marshal in 1830 under the reign of Louis Philippe.
8. Gourgaud, op. cit.
9. Anon., *Napoleon's Memoirs*, edited by Somerset de Chair (London: Soho, 1986).
10. Bassford, Moran and Pedlow, *On Waterloo, Clausewitz, Wellington and the Campaign of 1815* (published by Clausewitz.com, 2010), p. 123.

Chapter 1
1. Grouchy, *Mémoires du maréchal de Grouchy* (Paris: Dentu, 1874), Vol. III, pp. 211–12.
2. Ibid., p. 220.
3. Ibid., p. 319.
4. Ibid., p. 367.
5. Marmont, *Mémoires du maréchal Marmont duc de Raguse* (Paris: Perrotin, 1857), Vol. 6, p. 16. It should also be noted that Marmont was writing after the campaign, the results of which, and the controversy that followed it, may well have coloured his opinions.
6. Reproduced in Legros, *De Versailles à Waterloo* (Paris: Les Editions de la Bisquine, 2015), p. 361.

7. For a detailed study of the quality and attitudes of the army and the senior officers, see *Waterloo: The French Perspective*, by the same author.
8. Gourgaud, *Campaign of 1815*, pp. 43–4.
9. Houssaye, *1815 Waterloo*, translated from the 31st Edition (London: Adam and Charles Black, 1900), p. 59.
10. Ibid., pp. 428–9.
11. Ibid., p. 429.
12. Grouchy, *Relation Succincte de la Campagne de 1815 en Belgique* (Paris: Delanchy, 1843), Series 3, p. 4.
13. Mortier apparently fell sick with sciatica at Beaumont on 15 June. Many writers have speculated that, despite his previous loyal service and commands in the Imperial Guard, like many other senior officers, Mortier's heart was not in this campaign and that he found a convenient excuse not to serve.
14. Grouchy, *Mémoires*, Vol. III, op. cit., pp. 440–4.

Chapter 2
1. Grouchy, *Relation Succincte . . .,* op. cit., Series 3, p. 6.
2. *Correspondance de Napoléon 1er*, publié par ordre de l'Empereur Napoléon III (1858–70), Vol. 28, p. 325.
3. Register of correspondence of the *major-général*, given in Grouchy, *Relation Succincte . . .,* op. cit., Series 5, p.11.
4. Grouchy, *Memoires*, Vol. III, op. cit., pp. 454–5.
5. Ibid., p. 455.
6. Ibid., pp. 455–6.
7. Ibid., pp. 462–3.
8. Pajol, *Général en Chef* (Paris: Firmin Didot, 1874), pp. 186–7.
9. Ibid., p. 188.
10. Fleury, *Souvenirs, Anecdotes et Militaires du Colonel Biot* (Paris: Vivien, 1901), p. 233.
11. Grouchy, *Memoires*, Vol. III, op. cit., pp. 461–2.
12. Hulot, 'Souvenirs militaries du général Hulot', in *Spectateur Militaire* (1884), pp. 125–6.

Chapter 3
1. *Correspondance de Napoleon 1er*, op. cit., p. 324.
2. Berthezène, *Souvenirs militaries de la République et de l'Empire, par le Baron Berthezène, lieutenant-général, pair de France, grand-croix de la Légion d'Honneur* (Paris: Dumaine, 1855), p. 358.
3. Guyot, *Carnets de Campagnes* (Paris: Teissèdre, 1999), p. 289.
4. Lemonnier-Delafosse, *Souvenirs militaries du Capitaine Jean-Baptiste*

Lemonnier-Delafoss, reprint presented by Christope Bourachot (Saint-Amand-Montrond: Le Livre Chez Vous, 2002), p. 204.
5. Janin, *Campagne de Waterloo, ou remarques critiques et historque sur l'ouvrage du général Gourgaud, par M. E. F. Janin, colonel de l'ancien État major en non-activité* (Paris: Chaument jeune, 1820), pp. 6–7.
6. Berthezène, op. cit., p. 360.
7. Gerbet, *Souvenirs d'un officier sur la campagne de Belgique en 1815* (Arbois: Javel, 1867), p. 5.
8. Lefol, *Souvenirs sur le retour de l'empereur Napoléon de l'Île d'Elbe et sur la campagne de 1815 pendant les Cent Jours* (Versailles: Montalant-Bougleux, 1852), pp. 58–9.
9. Fleury, op. cit., p. 234.
10. Pajol, op. cit., p. 191.
11. Aubry, *Mémoires d'un capitaine de chasseurs à cheval* (Paris-Brussels: Jourdan Editions, 2011), p. 150.
12. Gerbet, op. cit., p. 5.
13. Anonymous, *Relation fidèle et détaillée de la campagne de Buonaparte, terminée par la bataille de Mont-Saint-Jean, dite de Waterloo ou de la Belle Alliance* (Brussels: de Mat, 1816), p. 19. Although published 'by an eye-witness', this account is widely attributed to Bourgeois.
14. Rumigny describes how these two *chasseurs* had escorted Bourmont, unaware of his intentions. Approaching the Prussian outposts, he had invited them to accompany him, but, despite offers of money, they had chosen to return to the French lines.
15. Rumigny, *Souvenirs du Général Comte de Rumigny 1789-1860* (Paris: Émile-Paul Frères, 1921), pp. 93–5.
16. Hulot, op. cit., pp. 126–7.
17. Given in Mauduit, *Histoire des derniers jours de la Grande Armée* (Paris: Dion-Lambert, 1854), pp. 35–6.
18. Ibid., pp. 36–7.
19. Clouet subsequently wrote about this episode, giving details of what happened and his own justification. In it he clearly states that Hulot was fully aware of Bourmont's intention of deserting. See Clouet, *Quelques notes sur la conduit de M. le Cte de Bourmont en 1815* (Paris: Debtu, n.d.).
20. Grouchy, *Observations*, op. cit., p. 13.
21. Gérard, *Quleques Documens sur la Bataille de Waterloo* (Paris: Verdière, 1829), p. 44.
22. Zenowicz, *Waterloo Déposition sur les quatre journées de la campagne de 1815* (Paris: Ledoyen, 1848), p. 18.
23. Janin, op. cit., p. 5.
24. Ibid., pp. 8–9.

Chapter 4
1. Lefol, op. cit., p. 59.
2. Fleurey, op. cit., p. 237.
3. Pajol, op. cit., pp. 193–5.
4. Grouchy, *Relation Succincte* . . ., op. cit., Series 4, pp. 1–2.
5. Biot, op. cit., p. 237.
6. Register of correspondence of the *major-général,* given in Grouchy, *Relation Succincte* . . ., op. cit., Series 5, p. 13.
7. Napoleon, *Napoleon's Memoirs*, edited by Somerset de Chair (London: Soho, 1986), pp. 505–6.
8. Gerbet, op. cit., pp. 8–9.
9. Lefol, op. cit., p. 59.
10. Pajol, op. cit., p. 195.
11. Ibid.
12. Berthezène, op. cit., p. 362.
13. Grouchy, *Relation Succincte* . . ., op. cit., Series 3, p. 15.
14. Figures from Hofschröer, *1815 The Waterloo Campaign, Wellington, his German Allies and the Battles of Ligny and Quatre Bras* (London: Greenhill Books, 1998), p. 184.
15. Biot, op. cit., p. 239.
16. Lefol, op. cit., p. 59.
17. Rumigny, op. cit., p. 95.
18. Hulot, op. cit., p. 127.
19. Grouchy, *Relation Succincte* . . ., op. cit., Series 3, p. 14.
20. Bella in Grouchy, ibid., Series 4, p. 32.
21. In Grouchy, ibid., Series 3, p. 15.
22. Grouchy, *Memoires*, op. cit., Vol. III, p. 460.

Chapter 5
1. Fleury, op. cit., p. 289.
2. Bella, in Grouchy, *Relation Succincte* . . ., op. cit., Series 4, p. 32.
3. Gourgaud, 'Bataille de Waterloo. Relation d'un Officier Général Francais', in *Nouvelle Revue Rétrospective* (1896), Vol. 4, pp. 365–6.
4. Grouchy, *Memoires*, op. cit., Vol. III, p. 463.
5. Grouchy, *Relation Succincte* . . ., op. cit., Series 3, p. 11.
6. Ibid., p. 15.
7. d'Heralde, *Mémoires d'un Chirurgien de la Grande Armée* (reprinted Paris: Teissèdre, 2002), pp. 213–14.
8. Chesney, *Waterloo Lectures*, Fourth Edition (London: Greenhill, 1997), p. 82.
9. For all the detail of the Prussian participation of the campaign see Peter Hofschröer's two-volume, *1815 The Waterloo Campaign* (London: Greenhill Books, 1998 and 1999).

10. Napoleon, op. cit., p. 507.
11. Pajol, op. cit., p. 200.
12. *Correspondance de Napoleon 1er*, op. cit., Volume 31, p. 471.
13. Chaboulon, *Memoires de Fleury de Chaboulon* (Paris: Edouard Rouveyre, 1901), p. 125.
14. Deniau and Moerman, *1815 Napoléon en Campagne* (Waterloo: editions Jourdan, 2008), p. 61.
15. Mauduit, op. cit., pp. 32–3.
16. *Correspondance de Napoleon 1er*, op. cit., 22055.
17. Also known as Jumignon and shown as this on the map. The time is unlikely to be accurate.
18. *Correspondance de Napoleon 1er*, op. cit., 22056.
19. Janin, op. cit., pp. 14–15.
20. Gourgaud, *The Campaign of 1815*, op. cit., pp. 51–2.
21. Radet, *Memoires de Général Radet* (Saint Cloud: Belin Frères, 1892), p. 337.

Chapter 6
1. Pajol, op. cit., p. 200.
2. Gerbet, op. cit., p. 9.
3. Lefol, op. cit., p. 60.
4. d'Heralde, op. cit., pp. 214–15
5. Pajol, op. cit., pp. 200–1.
6. Colonel Grouchy, op. cit., p. 13.
7. Ibid., p. 13.
8. Pajol, op. cit., p.201–2.
9. Grouchy, *Memoires*, op. cit., Vol. IV, p. 10.
10. Mauduit, op. cit., pp. 38–40.
11. Petiet, op. cit., pp. 433–4.
12. Grouchy, *Memoires*, op. cit., Vol. IV, p. 9.
13. Petiet, op. cit., p. 433.
14. Berton, op. cit., p. 22.
15. Gerbet, op. cit., p. 10.
16. Napoleon, *Memoirs*, op. cit., p. 510.
17. Mauduit, op. cit., pp. 46–7.
18. Lefol, op. cit., p. 60.
19. Bella, in Grouchy, *Relation Succincte . . .*, op. cit., Series 4, pp. 34–5.
20. Grouchy, *Observations*, op. cit., p.43.
21. Gérard, *Quelques Documens,* op. cit., pp. 48–9.
22. Hulot in *Le Spectateur Militaire* (1884), pp. 127–8.
23. Rumigny, op. cit., pp. 99–100.
24. Aubry, op. cit., p. 150.
25. Pajol, op. cit., pp. 202–04.

26. Putigny, op. cit., pp. 169.
27. Mauduit, op. cit., p. 41.

Chapter 7
1. Müffling, *The Memoirs of Baron Von Müffling, a Prussian Officer in the Napoleonic Wars* (reprinted London: Greenhill Books, 1997), pp. 230–1.
2. For more detail on this discussion, see this author's book, *Prelude to Waterloo: Quatre Bras, The French Perspective*, and Hofschröer, op. cit., pp. 233–9.
3. A handwritten note from Napoleon dated 'One hour after midday', the original copy was authenticated by Baron Gourgaud, one of Napoleon's ADCs. The note is reproduced in Chandler, *Waterloo, The Hundred Days* (Oxford: Osprey Publishing, 1980), pp. 88–9.
4. Gérard, *Dernières Observations sur les Opérations de l'aile Droite de l'Armée Francaise a la Bataille de Waterloo* (Paris: Verdière, 1830), p. 40.
5. Mauduit, op. cit., pp. 43–6.
6. There is some confusion over the naming of the three villages of Saint-Amand. Here Berthezène refers to La Haie, presumably meaning what is widely called Saint-Amand-le-Haye in many battle accounts, and Longpré. Longpré appears on modern maps, but from its location also seems to be Saint-Amand-le-Haye. Saint-Amand-le-Hameau appears to have been a large farm and perhaps one or two other small buildings and is not named on modern maps. To further confuse things, Ferrari's map, the one used by Napoleon on this campaign, shows, from south to north, Saint-Amand, the chateau of La Haye, albeit it in the middle of a village which we can assume is Saint-Amand-la-Haye, but not named as such on the map, and then Saint-Amand-Longpré! To the immediate north is Wagneleé and to the west a small cluster of buildings which is probably Saint-Amand-le-Hameau, although it is not named.
7. Berthezène, op. cit., pp. 362–3.
8. Hulot, op. cit., pp. 127–8.
9. Mauduit, op. cit., pp. 48–9.
10. Grouchy, *Memoires*, op. cit., Vol. IV, p. 23.
11. Napoleon, op. cit., p. 510.
12. Coignet, *The Note-Books of Captain Coignet, Soldier of the Empire, 1799-1816* (reprinted London: Greenhill Books, 1986), pp. 275–6.

Chapter 8
1. Different accounts and histories have different start times. If three shots from the Imperial Guard artillery was the signal for the attack, it does not mean the troops stepped off immediately. Indeed, few attacks would have gone in without some preliminary artillery barrage, although it appears that Vandamme's corps artillery, having been held up, did not arrive until after his

men had started their attack. However, each division had its own battery, so twenty-four guns should still have been able to support the initial attack.
2. Pajol, op. cit., p. 204.
3. Ney, *Documents inédits*, op. cit., p. 42.
4. Lefol, op. cit., pp. 60–2.
5. Gerbet, op. cit., pp. 10–12.
6. Lefol, op. cit., p. 62.
7. General Lefol and his nephew were not the only Lefols fighting in the campaign; the general's son Louis Lefol, was *chef de bataillon* in the 2nd *léger* who were part Bachelu's division (II Corps) and was in action at Quatre Bras. He was struck by a ball which broke his wrist. Louis was killed at Oran in 1831 as colonel of the 21st *de ligne*.
8. Given in Lefol, op. cit., p. 62.
9. Berthezène, op. cit., Vol. 2, pp. 363–4.
10. Francois, *Journal de Capitaine Francois dit le Dromadaire d'Égypte*, after the original text by Charles Grolleau, presented by Jacques Jourquin (Paris: Tallander, 1984), pp. 879–80.
11. Rumigny, op. cit., p. 100.
12. Francois, op. cit., pp. 291–2.
13. Mauduit, op. cit., p. 71.
14. Bourgeois, op. cit., p. 25.
15. d'Heralde, op. cit., p. 214.
16. Aubry, op. cit., p. 151.
17. Gerbet, op. cit., p. 12.
18. Lefol, op. cit., p. 62.
19. Molières and de Pleineville, *Dictionnaire des Braves de Napoléon* (Paris: Le Livre Chez Vous, 2004), p. 231.
20. Who these troops were is a mystery. The only foreign troops in the army were the squadron of Polish lancers of the Guard and the 2nd Swiss Regiment, and there is no evidence either were deployed near St-Amand.
21. Report from Lt-Gen Berthezène on 16 June (SHD, C15 5), given in Lérault, *De Waterloo à la Légion étrangère* (Paris: Teissedre-Clavreuil, 2008), p. 309.
22. Putigny, *Le Grognard Putigny, Baron d'Empire* (Paris: Copernic, 1980), pp. 169–70. At Napoleon's review the next day, Putigny was promoted to *chef de bataillon* and awarded the Légion d'Honneur.
23. Berthezène, op. cit., p. 363.
24. Fantin des Odoards, *Journal du Général Fantin des Odoards, Etapes d'un officier de la Grande Armée 1800-1830* (Paris: Plon, 1895), pp. 430–1.
25. Bourgeois, op. cit., p. 29.
26. Rumigny, op. cit., pp.100–2.
27. Coignet, op. cit., p. 276.

28. Francois, *From Valmy to Waterloo* (reprint Felling: Worley Publications, 1991), pp. 292–3.
29. Lefol, op. cit., p. 63.
30. Aerts, *Waterloo, Opérations de l'armée Prussienne du Bas-Rhin pendant la champagne de Belgique en 1815* (Brussels: Spineux and Company, 1908), p. 151.
31. D'Heralde, op. cit., pp. 215–16. D'Heralde went back to Charleroi with Girard before rejoining his division in Fleurus. Girard had received twelve wounds by the time he received his last. He was taken back to Paris in one of the emperor's carriages, and cared for by his friend Baron Larrey. Girard died on the day the allies marched into Paris (27 June). He was thirty-nine years old and had been a *général de division* since the battle of Ocana in 1809.
32. Mauduit, op. cit., footnote on pp. 71–2.
33. *Historique du 4e Régiment d'infantrie* (Paris: Charles-Lavauzelle, 1895), p. 86.
34. Petiet, op. cit., p. 435.
35. D'Heralde, op. cit., p. 216.
36. Report from Lt-Gen Berthezène on 16 June (SHD, C15 5), given in Lérault, op. cit., pp. 309–10.
37. From the Register of Orders, given in Grouchy, *Memoires*, op. cit., Vol. IV, p.165.
38. Ali, *Souvenirs sur l'empereur Napoléon*, presented by Christophe Bourachot (Paris: arléa, 2000), pp. 107–8.
39. Mauduit, op. cit., p. 78.
40. Petit, 'General Petit's Account of the Waterloo Campaign' in *English Historical Review*, Vol. 18 (Apr 1903).
41. D'Avout, 'L'infanterie de la Garde à Waterloo', in *Carnet de la Sabretache* (1912), pp. 119–20.
42. Mauduit, op. cit., pp. 66–7.
43. Ibid., pp. 80–1.
44. Ibid., p. 81.
45. Much of the detail of d'Erlon's orders and actions is repeated from the author's book on Quatre Bras, but bears repeating for context. Some further detail and analysis is available in *Prelude to Waterloo: Quatre Bras*.
46. Heymès, *Relation de la campagne de 1815, dite Waterloo, pour server à l'histoire du maréchal Ney* (Paris: Gautier-Laguionie, 1829), p. 14.
47. Petiet, op. cit., p. 436.
48. *Documents inédits*, op. cit., pp. 64–5.
49. Baudus, in *Waterloo, la Campagne de 1815 recontée par les soldats français* (Clamecy: Collections Épopée, 2004), p. 120.
50. Mauduit, op. cit., pp. 82–3.
51. Lefol, op. cit., pp. 63–4.

52. Du Casse, *Le Général Vandamme et sa Correspondance* (Paris: Didier et Cte, 1870), Vol. 2, p. 563.
53. Dejean always denied he was sent on this errand.
54. Napoleon, op. cit., p. 511.
55. Pajol, op. cit., pp. 204–5.
56. Mauduit, op. cit., p. 81.
57. Fleury, op. cit., pp. 240–1.
58. Hulot, op. cit., pp. 128–32.
59. Pajol, op. cit., pp. 205–6.
60. Lemaitre, *Historique du 4e Régiment de Dragons, 1672-1894* (Paris: Charles-Lavauzelle, 1894), pp. 284–5.
61. Mauduit, op. cit., p. 177.
62. Aerts, *Waterloo, Opérations de l'armée Prussienne du Bas-Rhin pendant la campagne de Belgique en 1815, depuis la bataille de Ligny jusqu'a l'entrée en France* (Brussels: Spineux, 1908), pp. 146–7.
63. Chuquet, *Inédits Napoléoniens* (Paris: Fontemoing, 1913), No. 1715.
64. Pajol, op. cit., p. 206.
65. Mauduit, op. cit., pp. 83–6.
66. Aerts, op. cit.
67. Duuring in d'Avout, op. cit., p. 115.
68. Mauduit, op. cit., pp. 86–9.
69. Ali, op. cit., pp. 108–9.
70. Christiani in d'Avout, op. cit., p. 111.
71. Petit, op. cit., p. 323.
72. Duuring in d'Avout, op. cit., p. 115.
73. Petit in d'Avout, op. cit., p. 323.
74. Christiani in ibid.
75. Béraud, *Histoire de Napoléon* (Brussels: de Kock, 1829), pp. 270–1.
76. Mauduit, op. cit., pp. 86–9.
77. Petit in d'Avout, op. cit., p. 323.
78. Petit may well have got mixed up; the Guard lancers and *chasseurs* were with Ney at Quatre Bras and so the service squadrons at Ligny were probably found from the grenadiers, dragoons and gendarmes who were present. Chavalier's account which follows may well have been based on the reports of others rather than him actually being present (his regiment being at Quatre Bras).
79. Chevalier, *Lieutenant Chevalier, Souvenirs des guerres napoléoniennes* (Paris: Hachette, 1970), p. 320.
80. Stouf, *Le lieutenant-général Delort* (Paris/Nancy: Berger-Levrault, 1906), p. 141.
81. Lot, *Les Deux Généraux Ordener* (Paris: Roger and Chernoviz, 1910), p. 90.
82. Fantin des Odoards, op. cit., p. 429.

83. (SHD, C15 5) given in Lérault, op. cit., p. 309.
84. Berthezène, op. cit., p. 366.
85. Rumigny, op. cit., pp. 103-4.
86. Durutte, extract from *La Sentinelle de l'Armée*, 8 March 1838, in *Documents Inédits*, op. cit., pp. 71–2.
87. Ibid., p. 72.
88. Chapuis, op. cit., pp. 26–30.
89. Brue in a letter dated Toulouse, 3 November 1837, published in Chapuis, op. cit., p. 52.
90. Janin, op. cit., pp. 19–20.
91. Aerts, op. cit., p. 163.
92. Francois, op. cit., p. 293.
93. Mauduit, op. cit., p. 124.

Chapter 9
1. Francois, op. cit., pp. 295–6.
2. Bourgeois, op. cit., p. 31.
3. Gerbet, op. cit., p. 12.
4. Janin, op. cit., p. 26.
5. Fleury, op. cit., p. 243.
6. Pajol, op. cit., p. 207.
7. Grouchy, *Observations*, op. cit., pp. 10–11.
8. Sénécal, in Grouchy, *Relation Succincte* . . . , op. cit., Series 4, p. 4.
9. Grouchy, *Memoires*, op. cit., Vol. IV, p. 33.
10. Berthezène, op. cit., p. 366.
11. Petiet, op. cit., pp. 436–7.
12. Gourgaud, *Nouvelle Revue Rétrospective*, op. cit., p. 368.
13. Guyot, *Général Comte Guyot, Carnets de campagne (1792-1815)* (Paris: Teissèdre, 1999), p. 291.
14. Mauduit, op. cit., p. 93.
15. Lefol, op. cit., pp. 66–7.
16. Durutte, op. cit., p. 73.
17. Teste, in *Carnet de la Sabretache* (1912), p. 168.
18. Duuring, in d'Avout, op. cit., p. 115.
19. Mauduit, op. cit., p. 95.
20. Mauduit, op. cit., p. 96.
21. Ibid.
22. Du Fresnel, *Un Régiment à travers l'Histoire* (Paris: Flammarion, 1894), p. 531.
23. Pajol, op. cit., p. 207.
24. Fleury, op. cit., pp. 243–4.
25. Teste, op. cit., p. 168.
26. Gerbet, op. cit., p. 13.

27. Lefol, op. cit., pp. 67–8.
28. Ibid., p. 67.
29. Coignet, op. cit., p. 277.
30. Grouchy, *Memoires*, op. cit., Vol. IV, p. 169.
31. Sénécal in Grouchy, *Relation Succincte* . . ., Series 4, p. 5.
32. Pollio, *Waterloo (1815)* (Paris: Charles-Lavauzelle, n.d.), pp. 247–8.
33. Napoleon, op. cit., p. 512.
34. Vandamme, op. cit., p. 563.
35. Grouchy, *Memoires*, op. cit., Vol. IV, p. 43.
36. Sénécal in Grouchy, *Relation Succincte* . . ., Series 4, p. 4.
37. Fleury, op. cit., p. 244.
38. Pajol, op. cit., p. 210.
39. Ibid.
40. Berton, op. cit., p. 39.
41. Napoleon, op. cit., p. 511.

Chapter 10
1. Lefol, op. cit., pp. 68–9.
2. Gerbet, op. cit., p. 13.
3. Teste, op. cit., p. 241.
4. Pajol, op. cit., pp. 212–13.
5. Fleury, op. cit., pp. 244–7.
6. Pajol, op. cit., pp. 217–19.
7. Berton, op. cit., pp. 39–40.
8. Pajol, op. cit., p. 213.
9. Janin, op. cit., p. 26.
10. Grouchy, *Memoires*, op. cit., p. 38.
11. Flahaut, *The First Napoleon, The Bowood Papers*, edited by the Earl of Kerry (London: Constable and Company, 1925), pp. 116–17.
12. From the Register of Orders and Correspondence of the *major-général*, reproduced in Grouchy, *Relation Succincte* . . ., op. cit., Series 5, pp. 20–1.
13. Heymès, op. cit., p. 17.
14. Grouchy, Memoires, op. cit., p. 43.
15. Lefol, op. cit., p. 69.
16. Mauduit, op. cit., pp. 101–9.
17. Gourgaud, *Nouvelle Revue Rétrospective*, op. cit., p. 368.
18. Mauduit, op. cit., p. 109.
19. Fantin des Odoards, op. cit., pp. 431–3.
20. Hulot, op. cit., p. 133.
21. Grouchy, *Memoires*, op. cit., Vol. IV, p .43.
22. Grouchy, *Grouchy's Own Account of the Battle of Waterloo*, dated 1818 (printed by William K. Bixby, St Louis, 1915), pp. 7–8.

23. Grouchy, *Memoires*, op. cit., pp. 44–7.
24. Flahaut, op. cit., p. 116.
25. *Documents Inédits*, op. cit., p. 44.

Chapter 11
1. Bella in Grouchy, *Relation Succincte* . . ., op. cit., Series 4, pp. 40–1.
2. Grouchy, *Memoires*, op. cit., Vol. IV, pp. 47–8.
3. Bella in Grouchy, *Relation Succincte* . . ., op. cit., Series 4, p. 41.
4. Hulot, op. cit., p. 133.
5. Berthezène, op. cit., p. 375.
6. Grouchy, *Memoires*, op. cit., Vol. IV, pp. 48–9.
7. Pajol, op. cit., pp. 217–18.
8. Ibid., pp. 49–50.
9. Bella in Grouchy, *Relation Succincte* . . ., op. cit., Series 4, pp. 40–1.
10. Grouchy, *Memoires*, Vol. IV, p. 50.
11. Bella in Grouchy, *Relation Succincte* . . ., op. cit., Series 4, p. 41.
12. Berthezène, op. cit., p. 390.
13. Gerbet, op. cit., pp. 13–14.
14. Lefol, op. cit., p. 75.
15. Berton, op. cit., pp. 40–1.
16. Hulot, op. cit., p. 133.
17. Pajol, op. cit., pp. 219–20.
18. Ibid., pp. 220–1.
19. Teste, 'Souvenirs du Général Baron Teste', in *Carnet de la Sabretache* (1912), p. 241.

Chapter 12
1. Lefol, op. cit., p. 75.
2. Fantin des Odoards, op. cit., p. 433.
3. Lefol, op. cit., p. 75.
4. Putigny, op. cit., p. 171.
5. Grouchy, *Memoires*, op. cit., Vol. IV, pp. 53–4.
6. Ibid., pp. 60–1.
7. Ibid., pp. 56–7.
8. Ibid., pp. 54–5.
9. Alphonse de Grouchy, *Le maréchal de Grouchy du 16 au 19 Juin 1815* (Paris: Dentu, 1864), pp. 33–4.
10. Grouchy, *Memoires*, op. cit., Vol. IV, pp. 55–6.
11. Ibid., pp. 57–8.
12. Gérard, op. cit., p. 15.
13. Berthezène, op. cit., pp. 395–6.
14. Napoleon, *Napoleon's Memoirs*, op. cit., pp. 517–18.

Chapter 13
1. Grouchy, *Memoires*, op. cit., Vol. IV, pp. 65–6.
2. Ibid., p. 62.
3. Ibid., pp. 64–5.
4. Ibid., pp. 62–3.
5. Ibid.
6. Sénécal in Grouchy, *Relation Succincte* . . ., Series 4, p. 6.
7. Grouchy, *Memoires,* op. cit., pp. 66–7.
8. Berton, op. cit., p. 45.
9. Ibid., p. 42.
10. De Saint-Just, op. cit., pp. 320–1.
11. Berthezène, op. cit., p. 391.
12. Lefol, op. cit., pp. 75–6.
13. Rumigny, op. cit., p. 104.
14. Hulot, op. cit., pp. 210–11.
15. Rumigny, op. cit., p. 104.
16. Grouchy, *Memoires*, op. cit., Vol. V, p. 120.
17. Ibid., Vol. IV, pp. 71–5.
18. Gérard, op. cit., pp. 7–8.
19. Rumigny, op. cit., pp. 104–6.
20. Grouchy, *Memoires*, op. cit., pp. 75–6.
21. In Gérard, *Dernières Observations* . . ., op. cit., pp. 30–1.
22. Vandamme, op. cit., pp. 565–6.
23. In Gérard, *Dernières Observations* . . ., op. cit., p. 13.
24. Berton, op. cit., p. 46.
25. In Gérard, *Dernières Observations,* op. cit., pp. 24–5.
26. Lefol, op. cit., p. 76.
27. Gérard, *Quelque Documens* . . ., op. cit., pp. 46–8.
28. Hulot, op. cit., p. 211.
29. Pajol, op. cit., pp. 225–6.
30. Zenowicz, op. cit., pp. 28–30.

Chapter 14
1. Napoleon, *Napoleon's Memoirs*, op.cit., pp. 526–7.
2. Berthezène, op. cit., pp. 391–2.
3. Lefol, op. cit., pp. 76–7.
4. Grouchy, *Observations* . . ., op. cit., p. 15.
5. Grouchy, *Memoires*, op. cit., Vol. IV, p. 80.
6. Gerbet, op. cit., p. 18.
7. Grouchy, *Memoires,* op. cit., Vol. IV, pp. 41–2.
8. Thouvenin in Grouchy, *Relation Succincte* . . ., op. cit., Series 4, p. 18.

9. Taken from Hofschröer, *1815, The Waterloo Campaign, The German Victory* (London: Greenhill Books, 1999), p. 159.
10. Grouchy, *Memoires*, op. cit., Vol. IV, p. 81.
11. Zenowicz, op. cit., pp. 30–1.
12. Ibid., p. 68.
13. Grouchy, *Memoires*, op. cit., Vol. IV, p. 81.
14. Grouchy, *Marshal Grouchy's own Account of the Battle of Waterloo,* op. cit. p. 9. Is this another example of Grouchy changing his story to incriminate a subordinate or a genuine mistake?
15. Berthezène, op. cit., pp. 392–3.
16. Fantin des Odoards, op. cit., pp. 433–4.
17. Putigny, op. cit., p. 171.
18. Bella in Grouchy, *Relation Succincte* . . ., Series 4, p. 51.
19. In Lérault, op. cit., pp. 107–10.
20. Fantin des Odoards, op. cit., p. 434.
21. Grouchy, *Memoires*, op. cit., Vol. IV, p. 82.
22. 2nd Declaration of Général Le Sénécal in Grouchy, *Relation Succincte* . . ., op. cit., p. 9.
23. Grouchy, *Observations*, op. cit., p. 13.
24. Hulot, op. cit., pp. 211–13.
25. Rumigny, op. cit., p. 107.
26. Gerbet, op. cit., pp. 19–20.
27. Bella in Grouchy, *Relation Succincte* . . ., Series 4, p. 55.
28. Grouchy, *Observations* . . ., op. cit., p. 17.
29. Gérard, *Quelques Documens* . . ., op. cit., pp. 41–3.
30. Pajol, op. cit., pp. 230–1.
31. Fleury, op. cit., pp. 250–4.

Chapter 15
1. Pajol, op. cit., pp. 232–3.
2. Molières and de Pleineville, op. cit., p. 638.
3. Grouchy, *Memoires*, op. cit., Vol. V, pp. 126–7.
4. Fleury, op. cit., p. 254.
5. Pajol, op. cit., p. 233.
6. Ibid.
7. Hulot, op. cit., p. 214.
8. Grouchy, *Memoires*, op. cit., Vol. IV, p. 85.
9. Bella in Grouchy, *Relation Succincte* . . ., Series 4, p. 56.
10. Grouchy, *Memoires*, op. cit., Vol. IV, p. 287.
11. Fantin des Odoards, op. cit., pp. 435–6.
12. Berton, op. cit., pp. 53–4.

Chapter 16
1. Grouchy, *Memoires*, op. cit., Vol. V, p. 126.
2. Fleury, op. cit., pp. 254–6.
3. Pajol, op. cit., p. 238.
4. Teste, op. cit., p. 242.
5. Francois, op. cit., pp. 300–1.
6. Teste, op. cit., p. 242.
7. Gerbet, op. cit., p. 21.
8. Fantin des Odoards, op. cit., p. 436.
9. Zenowicz, op. cit., p. 31.
10. Fleury, op. cit., pp. 256–7.
11. Hulot, op. cit., pp. 214–15.
12. Grouchy, *Memoires*, op. cit., Vol. IV, pp. 290–2.
13. Vandamme, op. cit., pp. 567–8.
14. Grouchy, *Memoires*, op. cit., Vol. IV, p. 291.
15. Fleury, op. cit., p. 258.
16. Grouchy, *Memoires*, op. cit., Vol. IV, p. 292.
17. Ibid., pp. 292–6.
18. Pajol, op. cit., pp. 239–40.
19. Grouchy, *Memoires*, op. cit., Vol. IV, pp. 299–300.
20. Pajol, op. cit., p. 240.
21. Berthezène, op. cit., p. 398.
22. Gerbet, op. cit., p. 21.
23. Fantin des Odoards, op. cit., p. 436.
24. Hulot, op. cit., p. 215.
25. Aerts, op. cit., p. 291.

Chapter 17
1. Berton, op. cit., p. 67.
2. Supra. p. 177.
3. Supra. p. 184.
4. Becke, *Napoleon and Waterloo*, reprinted by Greenhill Books (Guildford and King's Lynn: Greenhill Books, 1995), p. 145.
5. Supra. p. 221.
6. Supra. pp. 226–7.
7. Grouard, *Le critique de la campagne de 1815: Résponse à M.Houssaye* (1907), p. 25.
8. Grouchy, *Memoires*, op. cit., Vol. 5, p. 98. We must remember that these were written by Grouchy's grandson.
9. Chesney, op. cit., Lecture V.
10. Grouchy, *Marshal Grouchy's own Account of the Battle of Waterloo*, op. cit., pp. 7–8.

11. Flahaut, *The First Napoleon, some Unpublished Documents from the Bowood Papers*, edited by the Earl of Kerry (London: Constable, 1925), p. 120.
12. Berton, op. cit., pp. 42–3.
13. Grouchy, *Memoires*, Vol. V, op. cit., p. 115.
14. Grouchy, *Memoires*, op. cit., Vol. IV, p. 95.
15. Janin, op. cit., p. 28.
16. Baudus, op. cit., p. 224.
17. Clausewitz, *On War* (edited and translated by Michael Howard and Peter Paret for Everyman's Library, London, 1993), p. 240.
18. Hamley, *Operations of War*, Second Edition (London: William Blackwood and Sons, 1864), p. 136.
19. The decision of General Constant-Rebeque to concentrate the 2nd Netherlands Division at Quatre Bras, despite being ordered to march to Nivelles, springs to mind in this campaign. Although not reprimanded, neither was Constant-Rebeque praised for a disobedience of orders whose contribution to the campaign was doubtlessly considerable.
20. Moltke, *Moltke on the Art of War, Selected Writings*, edited by Daniel J. Huges (Navato: Presidio Press, 1993), p. 133.
21. Marbot, *The Memoirs of Baron de Marbot*, translated from the French by Arthur John Butler (London: Longmans, Green and Co, 1892), p. 457.
22. Marbot, reproduced in *Waterloo 1815, les Carnets de la Campagne* (Brussels: Tondeur Diffusion, 2000), Edition 4, p. 37.
23. Dupuy, *Souvenirs Militaires de Victor Dupuy, chef d'escadron de Hussards, 1794-1816* (Paris: 1892), p. 290.
24. Grouchy, *Observations*, op. cit., p. 25.
25. Grouchy, *Memoires*, op. cit., Vol. IV, footnote to p. 6.
26. Vandamme, op. cit., p. 567.
27. Supra p. 238.
28. Grouchy, *Fragments Historique Relatifs à la Campagne de 1815 et à la Bataille de Waterloo*: Lettre à Messieurs Méry et Barthélemy (Paris: Firmin Didot, 1829), pp. 10–11.
29. Gérard, *Dernières Observations . . .*, op. cit., pp. 55–6.
30. Rumigny, op. cit., pp. 109–10.
31. *Correspondance Militaire de Napoléon Ier* (Paris: 1893), Volume IV, No. 739, p. 11.

Select Bibliography

The French Army at Waterloo
Bowden, *Armies at Waterloo* (Arlington: Empire Press, 1982).
Couderc de Saint-Chamant, *Napoléon ses dernières armées* (Paris: Flammarion, n.d.).
Haythornthwaite, *The Waterloo Armies* (Barnsley: Pen and Sword, 2007).
Lachouque, *The Anatomy of Glory* (London: Lund Humpries, 1962).

Campaign Studies
Aerts, *Waterloo, Opérations de l'armée Prussienne du Bas-Rhin pendant la champagne de Belgique en 1815* (Brussels: Spineux and Company, 1908).
Barbero, *The Battle, A History of the Battle of Waterloo* (London: Atlantic Books, 2005).
Bassford, Moran and Pedlow, *On Waterloo, Clausewitz, Wellington and the Campaign of 1815* (published by Clausewitz.com, 2010).
Becke, *Napoleon and Waterloo* (reprinted London: Greenhill, 1995).
Charras, *Histoire de la Campagne de 1815, Waterloo* (Brussels: Meline, Cans et Compagnie, 1858).
Chesney, *Waterloo Lectures*, 4th edition (London: Greenhill, 1997).
Cotton, *A Voice from Waterloo*, revised edition by S. Monick (The Naval and Military Press, 2001).
Grouchy, Alphonse, *Le maréchal de Grouchy du 16 au 19 Juin 1815* (Paris: Dentu, 1864).
Hofschröer, *1815, The Waterloo Campaign, Wellington, his German Allies and the Battles of Ligny and Quatre Bras* (London: Greenhill, 1998).
Houssaye, *1815 Waterloo* (London: Adam & Charles Black, 1900).
Lachouque, *Waterloo*, English edition (London: Arms and Armour Press, 1975).
Logie, *Waterloo, The 1815 Campaign* (Staplehurst: Spellmount, 2006).
Margerit, *Waterloo* (Paris: Éditions Gallimard, 1964).
Pollio, *Waterloo (1815)* (Paris: Charles-Lavauzelle, n.d.).
Ropes, *The Campaign of Waterloo, A Military History* (New York: Charles Scribner's Sons, 1892).
Shaw-Kennedy, *Notes on the Battle of Waterloo* (London: John Murray, 1865).
Siborne, *History of the Waterloo Campaign* (rpr London: Greenhill Books, 1995).
Thiers, *Waterloo* (Paris: Plon, 1892).
Vaulabelle, *1815, Ligny-Waterloo* (Paris: Garnier Frères, n.d.).

French Primary Sources
Anon, 'Rectification de quelques faits relatives à la champagne de 1815, par un

officier general ayant combattu à Waterloo', in *Souvenirs et correspondence sur la bataille de Waterloo* (Paris: Teissèdre, 2000).

Anon, *Relation fidèle et détaillée de la champagne de Buonaparte, terminée par la bataille de Mont-Saint-Jean, dite de Waterloo ou de la Belle Alliance* (Brussels: de Mat, 1816).

Ali, *Souvenirs sur l'empereur Napoléon*, presented by Christophe Bourachot (Paris: arléa, 2000).

Aubry, *Mémoires d'un capitaine de chasseurs à cheval* (Paris-Brussels: Jourdan Editions, 2011).

Baudus, *Études sur Napoleon* (Paris: Debécourt, 1841).

Béraud, *Histoire de Napoléon* (Brussels: de Kock, 1829).

Berthezène, *Souvenirs militaries de la République et de l'Empire, par le Baron Berthezène, lieutenant-général, pair de France, grand-croix de la Légion d'Honneur* (Paris: Dumaine, 1855).

Bro, *Mémoires du Général Bro (1796-1844)* (Paris: Plon, 1914).

Chapuis, *Notice sur le 85e de ligne pendant la champagne de 1815* (Annonay, Ranchon, 1863).

Chevalier, *Lieutenant Chevalier, Souvenirs des guerres napoléoniennes* (Paris: Hachette, 1970).

Clouet, *Quelques notes sur la conduit de M. le Cte de Bourmont en 1815* (Paris: Debtu, n.d.).

Coignet, *The Note-Books of Captain Coignet, Soldier of the Empire, 1799-1816* (reprinted London: Greenhill Books, 1986).

Curély, *Le Général Curély, Itinéraire d'un cavalier léger de la Grande-Armée (1793-1815)* (Paris: Berger-Levrault, 1887).

D'Avout, 'L'infanterie de la Garde à Waterloo', in *Carnet de la Sabretache* (1912).

Drouet, *Le Maréchal Drouet, comte d'Erlon. Vie militaire écrit par lui-même et dédiée à ses amis* (Paris: Gustarve Barba, 1844).

Du Casse, *Le Général Vandamme et sa Correspondance* (Paris: Didier et Cte, 1870).

Dupuy, *Souvenirs militaries de Victor Dupuy, chef d'escadrons de hussards, 1794-1816* (Paris: Calmann-Lévy, 1892).

Fantin des Odoards, *Journal du Général Fantin des Odoards, Etapes d'un officier de la Grande Armée 1800-1830* (Paris: Plon, 1895).

Flahault, *The First Napoleon, some unpublished documents from the Bowood papers* (London: Constable, 1925).

Fleuret, *Description des Passages de Dominic Fleuret* (Paris: Firmin-Didot, 1929).

Fleury de Chaboulon, *Mémoires* (Paris: Edouard Rouveyre, 1901).

Fleury, *Souvenirs, Anecdotes et Militaires du Colonel Biot* (Paris: Vivien, 1901).

Francois, *From Valmy to Waterloo*, reprint of the 1906 edition (Felling: Worley Publications, 1991).

Gérard, *Quleques Documens sur la Bataille de Waterloo* (Paris: Verdière, 1829).

Gérard, *Dernières Observations sur les Opérations de l'aile Droite de l'Armée Francaise a la Bataille de Waterloo* (Paris: Verdière, 1830).
Gerbet, *Souvenirs d'un officier sur la campagne de Belgique en 1815* (Arbois: Javel, 1867).
Gourgaud, *The Campaign of 1815* (London: James Ridgeway, 1818).
Gourgaud, 'Bataille de Waterloo. Relation d'un Officier Général Francais', in *Nouvelle Revue Rétrospective*, Vol. 4 (1896).
Grouchy, *Mémoires du Maréchal de Grouchy* (Paris: Dentu, 1874) Vols 3, 4 and 5.
Grouchy, *Observations sur la Relation de la campagne publiée par le Général Gourgaud* (Philadelphia: Hurtel, 1818).
Grouchy, *Relation Succincte de la Campagne de 1815 en Belgique* (Paris: Delanchy, 1843).
Grouchy, *Grouchy's Own Account of the Battle of Waterloo* (dated 1818, printed by William K. Bixby, St Louis, 1915).
Grouchy, *Fragments Historique Relatifs à la Campagne de 1815 et à la Bataille de Waterloo: Lettre à Messieurs Méry et Barthélemy* (Paris: Firmin Didot, 1829).
Guyot, *Général Comte Guyot, Carnets de campagnes (1792-1815)* (Paris: Teissèdre, 1999).
d'Heralde, *Mémoires d'un Chirurgien de la Grande Armée* (rpr, Paris: Teissèdre, 2002).
Heymès, *Relation de la campagne de 1815, dite Waterloo, pour server à l'histoire du maréchal Ney* (Paris: Gautier-Laguionie, 1829).
Hulot, Souvenirs militaries du général Hulot, in *Spectateur Militaire*, 1884.
Janin, *Campagne de Waterloo ou Remarques Critiques et Historiques sur l'ouvrage du Général Gourgaud* (Paris: Chaumont jeune, 1820).
Jardin Ainé, *With Napoleon at Waterloo and other Unpublished Documents of the Waterloo and Peninsular Campaigns* (London: Francis Griffiths, 1911).
Lefol, *Souvenirs sur le retour de l'empereur Napoléon de l'Île d'Elbe et sur la champagne de 1815 pendant les Cent Jours* (Versailles: Montalant-Bougleux, 1852).
Lemonnier-Delafosse, *Souvenirs militaries du Capitaine Jean-Baptiste Lemonnier-Delafosse*, reprint presented by Christophe Bourachot (Saint-Amand-Montrond: Le Livre Chez Vous, 2002).
Lot, *Les Deux Généraux Ordener* (Paris: Roger and Chernoviz, 1910).
Mameluk Ali, *Souvenirs sur l'empereur Napoléon*, reprint presented by Christophe Bourachot (Paris: arléa, 2000).
Marbot, *The Memoirs of Baron Marbot* (London: Longmans, 1892).
Marchand, *Mémoires de Marchand, premier valet de chamber, exécuteur testamentaire de l'Empereur* (Paris, Plon, 1952–5).
Martin, *Souvenirs d'un ex-officier, 1812-1815* (Paris & Geneva: J. Cherbuliez, 1867).

Mauduit, *Histoire des derniers jours de la Grande Armée* (Paris: Dion-Lambert, 1854).
Napoleon, *Napoleon's Memoirs*, edited by Somerset de Chair (London: Soho Books, 1986).
Ney, *Documents inédits sur la Campagne de 1815, publiés par la Duc d'Elchingen* (Paris: Anselin, 1840).
Noguès, *Mémoires du général Noguès (1777-1853) sur les guerres de l'Empire* (Paris: A. Lemerre, 1922).
Pajol, *Général en Chef* (Paris: Firmin Didot, 1874).
Petiet, *Mémoires du general Auguste Petiet, hussar de l'Empire* (Paris: Éditions S.P.M, 1996).
Petit, in an account given in the *English Historical Review*, Vol 18 (Apr 1903).
Pontécoulant, *Napoléon à Waterloo 1815* (rpr Paris: Librairie des Deux Empires, 2004).
Putigny, *Le Grognard Putigny, Baron d'Empire* (Paris: Copernic, 1980).
Radet, *Memoires de Général Radet* (Saint Cloud: Belin Frères, 1892).
Robinaux, *Journal de Route du Capitaine Robinaux* (Paris: 1908).
Rumigny, *Souvenirs du Général Comte de Rumigny 1789-1860* (Paris: Émile-Paul Frères, 1921).
Stouf, *Le Lieutenant Général Delort* (Paris/Nancy: Berger-Levrault & Cie., 1906).
Teste, 'Souvenirs du Général Baron Teste', in *Carnet de la Sabretache* (1912).
Trefcon, *Carnet de champagne du colonel Trefcon, 1793-1815* (Paris: Edmond Dubois, 1914).
Zenowicz, *Waterloo Déposition sur les quatre journées de la champagne de 1815* (Paris: Ledoyen, 1848).

Magazines and Periodicals
Les Carnets de la Campagne, a series of fourteen editions (at time of writing) (Brussels: Tondeur Diffusion, 1999–2016).

Other Books of Particular Note
Adkin, *The Waterloo Companion* (London: Aurum Press, 2001).
Martinien, *Tableaux par corps et par Batailles des Officiers Tués et Blessés pendant les Guerres de l'Empire (1805-1815)* (Paris: Charles-Lavauzelle, 1899).
Meulenaere, *Bibliographie Analytique des Témoignages Oculaires Imprimés de la Campagne de Waterloo* (Paris: Teissedre, 2004).
Quintin, D. & B., *Dictionnaire des Colonels de Napoleon* (Paris: Kronos, 2013).

Index

Armies:
Anglo-Dutch, actions on the 15th, 60–1; initial deployment, 76–7; withdrawal from Quatre Bras, 190
French: 12;
  I Corps, 12, 19, 22, 23, 25, 35, 47, 65, 73, 120, 121, 144, 157
  II Corps, 12, 18, 19, 21–3, 25, 33, 38, 47, 59, 65, 68, 73
  III Corps, 12, 19, 22–5, 29, 32, 35, 36, 37, 39, 41, 47, 48, 51, 52, 65, 72, 73, 74, 82, 83, 89, 93, 96, 99, 147, 152, 174, 178, 179, 181, 184, 185, 187, 202, 203, 210, 228, 229, 230, 232, 249, 250, 251, 254, 265; ORBAT, 280, 291
  IV Corps, 12, 19, 23, 25, 35, 40, 41, 43, 45, 47, 50, 54, 65, 66, 72–4, 83–4, 86, 89, 94, 96, 147, 180–1, 184–5, 187, 194, 203, 210, 228–30, 232, 249–51, 254, 265; ORBAT, 281, 292
  VI Corps, 10, 12, 19, 20, 22, 24, 25, 35, 37, 44, 47, 66, 67, 71, 83, 95, 96, 146, 149, 153, 154, 178, 184; ORBAT, 285
  1st Cavalry Corps, 17, 19, 21, 25–9, 47, 58, 59, 72, 96, 127, 128, 147, 178, 259, 262, 283, 293
  2nd Cavalry Corps, 19, 26, 40, 47, 59, 72, 79, 96, 147, 262, 283, 294
  3rd Reserve Cavalry Corps, 19, 26, 41, 47, 59, 72, 73
  4th Reserve Cavalry Corps, 19, 23, 25, 26, 47, 59, 72, 95, 96, 147, 153, 178, 284
  Imperial Guard, 12, 18, 19, 22–5, 33, 37, 47, 67, 73, 95, 111, 140, 178, 264, 278
Prussian:
  I Corps, 31, 33, 46, 56, 76, 77, 92, 93, 145, 200, 204, 205; ORBAT, 287
  II Corps, 31, 33, 41, 71, 92, 93, 106, 200, 204, 205; ORBAT, 288
  III Corps, 31, 33, 41, 92, 93, 94, 128, 130, 151, 154, 183, 200, 204, 205, 219, 266, 267; ORBAT, 289
  IV Corps, 31, 33, 61, 76, 87, 92, 200, 204–5

Aulne, abbey, 23, 33
Balâtre, 85–6, 89–90, 92–93, 95, 127–8, 134
Baltus, *Maréchal de Camp*, 208, 209, 219, 231, 281, 292
Barrois, *Maréchal de Camp*, 115, 142, 279
Baudecet, 192
Baudus, Colonel, 124, 265
Beaumont, 12, 18, 19, 20, 25, 36, 39, 65, 66, 271, 296
Berthezène, General, 32, 36, 52, 92–3, 102, 109, 110, 116, 142, 151, 181, 185, 196, 202, 216, 217, 222, 243, 251, 280, 291
Berton, *Maréchal de Camp*, 79, 149, 160, 161, 167, 168, 181, 186, 201, 210, 216, 239, 263, 284, 294
Bierge, 218–20, 222, 224, 228, 229, 231, 232, 235–40, 242–3, 247
Biot, *Commandant/Chef d'Escadron*, 29, 38, 48, 53, 57, 129, 154, 159, 166, 182, 233, 244, 247
Blücher, Field Marshal, meeting with Wellington at Thirlemont, 15; orders concentration of Prussian army, 30–1; concentration on the 16th, 76; meeting with Wellington at Bussy mill, 87–8; deployment at Ligny, 92–3; plan for battle, 93; launches counter-attack, 106–7; commits more troops into Ligny, 110; leads cavalry in final counter-attack and is unhorsed, 140–1; arrives in Wavre, 189; orders move in support of Wellington, 219; tries to cut Grouchy off, 252, 287
Boignée, 85, 90, 95, 127, 128, 132, 134
Bonnemains, *Maréchal de Camp*, 132, 186, 187, 192, 199, 205, 284, 294
Borcke, General, 240
Bose, General, 111, 216, 289
Bourmont, General, 30; desertion, 41–4, 54, 68, 69; Napoleon comments on his desertion, 79, 97, 297
Brussels, 14, 15, 31, 34–5, 40, 46–7, 60, 62, 69, 71, 74–6, 80, 88, 177, 184–5, 191, 193, 195–6, 198, 204–5, 246, 249, 256, 258, 265–6, 268–71
Bry/Brye, 71, 72, 87, 89, 90, 92, 93, 98, 106, 139, 142, 143, 150–3, 169
Bülow, General, 31, 40, 61, 76, 87, 92, 151, 158, 168, 179, 185–7, 189, 200, 204, 227, 246, 247, 256, 258, 259, 264
Bussy Mill, 57, 87, 88, 90–2, 111, 142, 153

Campinaire, 48, 54, 58
casualties at Ligny, 147
Charleroi, 12, 14, 15, 18–27, 31, 33–5, 37, 39–40, 42–3, 46–7, 49–51, 53–5, 57–61, 64,–7, 69, 75–7, 81, 83, 90, 93, 95, 116, 127, 146, 153, 302
Chastel, General, 79, 149, 186, 192, 251, 284, 294
Châtelet, 33–4, 40, 48, 50, 54–5, 61, 66–7, 83
Chatelineau, 48, 52, 54, 55, 73
Chaumont, Treaty of, 11
Clausewitz, 5, 92, 93, 127, 266
Constant-Rebeque, General, 60
Corsin, *Maréchal de Camp*, 101, 102, 125, 217, 280, 291

Delcambre, General, 120–3
Delort, General, 25, 41, 125, 139, 140, 141, 169, 285
D'Erlon, General, 6, 12, 23, 25, 65, 67, 75, 118–19; march towards Ligny, 120–7, 134, 141, 143–4, 148, 157, 170, 213, 258, 259, 286, 302
Deselles, General, 121, 122, 127
Domon, General, 21, 27, 28; composition of his division, 29, 38–40, 53, 54, 65, 71, 83, 93, 107, 131; wounded at Ligny, 147, 152, 157, 178, 215, 271, 281
Duhesme, General, 48, 118, 279
Durutte, General, detached by d'Erlon, 122, 127; at Ligny, 143–5, 150, 152, 286, 287

Ernage, 186, 192, 199
Exelmans, General, 25, 37, 40, 48, 50–4, 57–9, 65, 73, 77, 79, 83, 85, 94, 96, 128, 132, 133, 149, 154, 155, 159–61, 163, 166, 168, 176, 181, 183, 184, 186, 188, 189, 192–5, 200, 201, 203, 205, 209–12, 216–8, 228, 237, 240, 249, 250–1, 254, 259–60, 262, 283, 294

Flahaut, General, 74, 169, 170, 178, 259, 261, 278
Fleurus, 15, 35, 40, 46–60, 62–5, 67–9, 72–5, 77–8, 80–1, 84–5, 87, 89, 91, 93–5, 97–8, 107–9, 116, 128, 132, 140–1, 146, 150, 156–7, 159, 163, 169, 204–5, 248, 257–8, 29, 272, 302
Forbin-Janson, Colonel, 120, 121
Frasnes, 47, 60, 67, 69, 77, 87, 123, 146, 157

Gembloux, 56, 61, 73, 74, 75, 88, 90, 92, 151, 159, 160, 161, 165, 166, 167, 168, 180, 181, 183–203, 205, 206, 212, 213, 220, 221, 229, 248, 250–2, 254, 255, 259, 260, 262, 267, 276
Gérard, General, 3–5, 19, 20, 23, 40, 41, 44, 51, 79, 83, 84, 85, 96, 97; at battle of Ligny, 104, 110–12, 158, 180, 181, 194, 200, 203, 206–8, 211, 220; wounded, 230–2, 248, 249, 269; relationship with Grouchy, 271–4, 295
Gilly, 40, 46; action at, 47–56, 58, 65, 78
Girard, General, 47, 59, 60, 68, 69, 71, 72; attacks at Ligny, 105–6; mortally wounded, 106, 115, 302
Gneisenau, General, 87, 151, 189, 287
Gosselies, 34, 40, 46–8, 65, 67, 71, 72, 87
Grouchy, Marshal, rallies to Napoleon, 7–9; his campaign in the Midi, 9–10; is nominated marshal, 10–11; joins the *armée du Nord*, 16–17; his orders for the 14th, 22, 25–6; to command the right wing of the army, 47; pursues the Prussians to Gilly, 47–51; combat at Gilly, 51–4; Vandamme refuses to obey his orders, 55–6; reports Prussian concentration to Napoleon, 71–2; his orders on the morning of the 16th, 72–4; his advance towards Ligny, 77–9; frustration with the slow march of IV Corps, 83–4; deployment of Grouchy's cavalry at Ligny, 85, 94–5; Grouchy's orders for the battle, 96; Grouchy's right wing during the battle of Ligny, 127–34; refuses to leave his men to receive Napoleon's orders, 150, 156; receives no orders during the night of the 16th/17th, 159; Teste's division attached to Grouchy, 163; joins Napoleon on the battlefield, 171; his frustration in not receiving orders, 75–6; finally receives orders from Napoleon, 176–8; true strength of his wing, 179; problem getting Gérard moving, 180–1; ordered to move to Gembloux, 184; at Gembloux, 192–3; late move-off on the 18th, 194; disagreement with Gérard, 206–9; moves to join the advance guard, 209; orders Pajol to Limal, 219–20; arrival of Napoleon's 10am despatch, 220–1; arrival of Napoleon's 1pm despatch,

226–7; moves to Bierge, 229; orders all troops to cross at Limal, 237, 238; repulses Prussian attack, 237; repulses Prussian attack on the 19th and advances, 240–4; receives news of Waterloo, 244–6; contemplates marching on allied rear, 244; his justification to his generals, 247–50; plans for the retreat to Namur, 250–2; analysis of performance, 253–77
Guyot, General, 33, 125, 152, 279

Habert, General, 93, 110, 141, 147, 222, 224, 226, 243, 280, 291
Hannut, 61, 151, 187, 193, 195, 204
Haxo, General, 24, 39
Henckel, General, 103, 111, 288
Hèymes, Colonel, 121, 170
Hobe, General, 132, 237, 238, 240, 241, 242, 290
Hulot, *Maréchal de Camp*, 30, 42, 44, 54, 84, 94, 95, 96, 120, 127–32, 149, 154, 181, 187, 202, 211, 228, 229, 232, 237, 238–40, 245, 250, 252, 282, 292

Jacquinot, *Maréchal de Camp*, 127, 143, 152, 270, 283
Jumignon, 26, 37, 39, 299
Jürgass, General, 106, 107, 131, 289

Kellerman, General, 21, 41, 59, 67, 74
Kemphen, General, 128, 132, 149, 238, 290

La Baraque, 205, 210, 216, 218, 219, 228, 229, 232
Labédoyère, General, 55, 115, 116, 123, 271
Lambusart, 48, 50, 51, 53, 54, 56, 57, 58, 59, 77, 84
Langen, General, 112, 131
Laurent, Colonel, 98, 120, 121
Lefebvre-Desnouëttes, General, 40, 46, 47, 62, 123
Lefol, General, 36, 47, 51, 93, 99, 101, 102, 103, 105, 107, 109, 125, 126, 155, 216, 224, 228, 239, 243, 251, 280, 291, 301
Lefol, Lieutenant, 36, 47, 51, 54, 68, 101, 102, 108, 113, 125, 126, 152, 162, 171, 186, 190, 191, 202, 211, 216
Liège, 12, 13, 31, 69, 151, 169, 177, 184, 185, 188, 191, 193, 195, 196, 197, 204, 205, 254, 265, 267

Ligny, battle of, 98–147; fighting in the village, 103–5, 110–14; final attack, 134–43
Limal, 218, 220, 221, 228, 229, 230, 232, 233, 234, 235, 236, 237, 238, 239, 240, 241, 247, 250, 251, 272, 273
Lobau, *comte de*, General, 10, 12, 19, 22, 25, 35, 44, 66, 68, 83, 95, 96, 116, 137, 153, 158, 184, 254, 285
Louvain, 163, 181, 182, 188, 201, 204, 205, 211, 243, 244
Luck, General, 149, 290
Lützow, Lieutenant Colonel, 46, 139, 170, 288

Maastrict, 12, 176, 193, 205, 248, 254, 268
Marbais, 73, 75, 88, 89, 90, 178, 184
Marchienne-au-Pont, 22, 23, 25, 33, 34, 35, 38, 40, 61, 65, 67
Marwitz, Colonel, 107, 131, 132, 290
Maurin, General, 94, 147, 150, 155, 158, 184, 187, 188, 282
Mazy, 71, 127, 160, 163, 167, 168, 181, 186, 187, 188, 189, 194, 199, 211
Milhaud, General, 25, 29, 30, 59, 73, 82, 95, 111, 125, 134, 140, 141, 153, 178, 284
Mons, 14, 15, 23, 26, 31, 46, 60
Monthion, General, 154, 155, 156, 161, 262, 278
Mont-Saint-Jean, 209, 217, 227, 256, 268
Morand, General, 279
Moustier, 196, 200, 211, 221, 239, 267, 271

Namur, 14, 15, 19, 23, 40, 41, 46, 48, 63, 64, 65, 69, 70, 71, 73, 75, 77, 80, 84, 89, 90, 93, 95, 96, 99, 126, 127, 150, 151, 155; Pajol's reconnaissance on, 159–69, 175, 176, 177, 179, 180, 181, 182, 183, 184, 185, 186, 187, 188, 189, 191, 194, 195, 198, 199, 201, 205, 211, 212, 218, 219, 226; Grouchy's withdrawal on, 248–52, 254, 259, 260, 262, 265, 267, 268, 274
Napoleon, own accounts of the campaign, 4; return from exile, 7, 9; campaign plans, 13–15, 25; address to the army, 32; reception in Belgium, 39–40; splits his army into two wings and a reserve, 47; at combat at Gilly, 50–3; plans for the 16th, 69–71; his orders to Grouchy on the

morning of the 16th, 73–4; to Ney, 74–5; Ligny reconnaissance 79; plans for the battle of Ligny, 88–9; his plan for Ney's contribution to the battle, 98; during the battle, 116–18; further orders to Ney during the battle, 120, 122, 124; night after Ligny, 156–7; failure to order reconnaissances after the battle, 158–9; his situation on the morning of the 17th, 169; orders to Ney on the 17th, 169–70, 178; visits the Ligny battlefield, 171–5; orders Grouchy in pursuit of the Prussians, 176; written order to Grouchy, 183–4; arrives at Waterloo battlefield, 190; the orders he claims to have sent Grouchy on the night of the 17th/18th, 196–7; finally writes to Grouchy from Waterloo, 212–13; Napoleon observes the Prussian advance on Waterloo, 215; his 10am letter to Grouchy, 221; analysis of his performance and conclusion, 253–77

Naveau Mill, 79, 82, 95, 117

Ney, Marshal, 1, 2, 4, 42, 47, 52, 53, 59, 61, 62, 63, 67, 69, 70, 71, 72, 73, 74, 75, 76, 79, 80, 83, 88, 89, 90, 97, 88, 89, 120, 121, 122, 123, 124, 126, 127, 131, 143, 144, 146, 157, 158, 165, 169, 170, 171, 176, 177, 178, 180, 190, 253, 258, 259, 260, 262, 264

Nivelles, 15, 60, 63, 69, 70, 71, 80, 89, 150, 151, 159, 165, 310

Old Guard, the, 78, 81, 118, 119, 125, 136, 138, 278

Onoz, 85, 127, 128

Ottignies, 221, 267, 271

Pajol, General, composition of his corps, 28–9; provides the army's advance guard, 35; his advance, 37–9; sends 1st Hussars towards Gosselies, 40; ordered towards Gilly by Napoleon, 40; contacts the Prussians at Gilly, 48; action at Gilly, 51–3; pursues Prussians, 53–4; advances on Ligny, 77; deployment at Ligny, 85, 95; role at battle of Ligny, 127–9; Domon's division detached, 131; his casualties at Ligny, 147; sent on reconnaissance towards Namur, 159; his reconnaissance, 159–61, 163–6, 167–8, 181–2; has Teste's division put under command,

166–7; his situation in the afternoon of the 17th, 187–9; his orders for the 19th, 194; attempts to catch up Grouchy, 211–12; ordered to Limal, 219–20; action at Limal, 232–6; deployment on the night of the 18th, 237; repulses Hobe's cavalry, 238; attacked by Hobe's cavalry on the 19th, 241; receives the news of Waterloo, 250; covers Grouchy's withdrawal, 250–1; ORBAT, 283, 293

Pécheux, General, 94, 103, 104, 110, 111, 136, 239, 240, 242, 281, 292

Penne, *Maréchal de Camp*, 147, 154, 167, 242; killed, 243–4, 286, 294

Perponcher-Sedlnitzky, General, 60

Perwez, 186, 188, 212

Philippeville, 12, 19, 23, 26, 27, 30, 41, 65

Pirch I, General, 71, 92, 93, 127, 159, 245, 252, 288

Pirch II, General, 33, 46, 48, 51, 52, 53, 54, 106, 107, 111, 287

Quatre Bras, 47, 60, 61, 62, 63, 66, 67, 70, 73, 74, 75, 76, 77, 80, 87, 88, 89, 90, 96, 99, 120, 121, 122, 123, 124, 126, 127, 143, 144, 157, 158, 165, 168, 169, 170, 175, 176, 177, 178, 180, 181, 184, 189, 190, 192, 208, 248, 249, 254, 258, 259, 260, 261

Regiments:
French:
  Guard Dragoons, 52, 95, 125, 139, 279; Guard *Gendarmerie d'Élite*, 95, 125, 139, 173, 279; Guard *Grenadiers à Cheval*, 95, 125, 139, 173, 279; 1st Cuirassiers, 141, 285; 1st Foot *Chasseurs*, 125, 135, 136, 137, 279; 1st Foot Grenadiers, 64, 95, 135, 136, 137, 278; 1st Hussars, 28, 40, 46, 47, 48, 59, 65, 72, 95, 127, 131, 154, 163, 166, 167, 187, 188, 212, 241, 283, 293; 1st Lancers, 28, 283; 1st *Tirailleurs*, 279; 1st *Voltigeurs*, 279; 2nd Foot *Chasseurs*, 118, 119, 279; 2nd Foot Grenadiers, 95, 125, 135, 136, 137, 139, 153, 278; 2nd Lancers, 28, 283; 2nd *léger*, 46; 2nd Swiss, 224, 280, 291, 301; 3rd Foot *Chasseurs*, 118, 279; 3rd Foot Grenadiers, 95, 120, 136, 137, 139, 278; 3rd *Tirailleurs*, 279; 3rd *Voltigeurs*, 279;

4th *Chasseurs à Cheval*, 29, 38, 281, 292; 4th Cuirassiers, 285; 4th *de ligne*, 114, 115, 284; 4th Dragoons, 132, 284, 294; 4th Foot *Chasseurs*, 118, 120, 279; 4th Foot Grenadiers, 95, 120, 136, 137, 138, 139, 278; 4th Hussars, 28, 131, 154, 160, 163, 165, 166, 167, 182, 187, 188, 212, 241, 244, 283, 293; 5th Cuirassiers, 140, 285; 5th *de ligne*, 285; 5th Dragoons, 132, 133, 186, 192, 283, 294; 5th Hussars, 28, 48, 131, 154, 160, 163, 165, 166, 167, 187, 188, 212, 241, 244, 283, 293; 5th *léger*, 286; 6th Cuirassiers, 140, 285; 6th Dragoons, 282, 293; 6th Hussars, 84, 234, 235, 282, 293; 6th *léger*, 114, 281, 292; 7th Cuirassiers, 285; 7th Hussars, 270, 271; 8th *Chasseurs à Cheval*, 282, 293; 8th *de ligne*, 286; 8th *léger*, 167, 286, 294; 9th *Chasseurs à Cheval*, 29, 38, 281, 292; 9th Cuirassiers, 140, 285; 9th *léger*, 30, 42, 129, 130, 187, 229, 232, 282, 293; 10th Cuirassiers, 140, 285; 10th *de ligne*, 9, 10, 286; 11th *Chasseurs à Cheval*, 28, 283; 11th *léger*, 106, 284; 12th *Chasseurs à Cheval*, 29, 39, 85, 107, 108, 281; 12th Cuirassiers, 285; 12th *de ligne*, 109, 280, 291; 12th Dragoons, 132, 284; 12th *léger*, 68, 105, 106, 115, 116, 284; 13th Dragoons, 132, 283; 14th Dragoons, 284, 294; 15th Dragoons, 186, 284, 294; 15th *léger*, 108, 239, 280, 291; 17th Dragoons, 149, 284, 294; 20th Dragoons, 52, 66, 284, 294; 22nd *de ligne*, 110, 141, 142, 174, 223, 239, 280, 291; 23rd *de ligne*, 99, 108, 280, 291; 27th *de ligne*, 285; 29th *de ligne*, 287; 30th *de ligne*, 103, 104, 112, 130, 148, 231, 281, 292; 33rd *de ligne*, 86, 109, 191, 223, 281, 291; 34th *de ligne*, 280, 291; 37th *de ligne*, 36, 51, 68, 101, 107, 231, 280, 291; 40th *de ligne*, 167, 286, 294; 44th *de ligne*, 129, 130, 282, 293; 48th *de ligne*, 282, 282; 50th *de ligne*, 84, 94, 104, 120, 128, 129, 130, 282, 293; 56th *de ligne*, 109, 280, 291; 59th *de ligne*, 114, 282, 292; 63rd *de ligne*, 114, 281, 292; 64th *de ligne*, 99, 102, 115, 125, 280, 291; 65th *de ligne*, 167, 242, 286, 294; 69th *de ligne*, 282, 292; 70th *de ligne*, 110, 142, 174, 223, 224, 225, 280, 291; 75th *de ligne*, 155, 167, 242, 286, 294; 76th *de ligne*, 112, 154, 282, 292; 82nd *de ligne*, 106, 115, 172, 284; 84th *de ligne*, 285; 85th *de ligne*, 144, 145, 287; 86th *de ligne*, 109, 281, 291; 88th *de ligne*, 225, 281, 291; 95th *de ligne*, 287; 96th *de ligne*, 103, 104, 113, 281, 292; 107th *de ligne*, 286; 111th *de ligne*, 42, 129, 130, 282, 293

Prussian:
1st Westphalian Landwehr Cavalry, 232; 1st West Prussian Dragoons, 34; 2nd Westphalian Landwehr, 51; 6th Infantry Regiment, 35, 51, 53; 6th Kurmark Landwehr, 224; 6th *Uhlans*, 46, 77, 139, 232; 7th *Uhlans*, 166, 242; 8th *Uhlans*, 242; 10th Hussars, 216; 12th Hussars, 242; 12th Infantry Regiment, 102; 19th Infantry Regiment, 232; 24th Infantry Regiment, 102; 25th Infantry Regiment, 107; 26th Infantry Regiment, 65; 27th Infantry Regiment, 65; 28th Infantry Regiment, 37, 51, 53, 65; 31st Infantry Regiment, 224, 237

Reille, General, 12, 22, 23, 24, 25, 33, 34, 35, 38, 46, 47, 59, 65, 67, 75, 123, 157, 170

Rogniat, General, 24, 36, 39, 278

Rome, *Maréchal de Camp*, 103, 104, 112, 113, 281, 292

Saint-Amand, 71, 72, 81, 82, 83, 85, 90, 91, 92, 93, 96, 98; first attack on, 100–2, 103, 106, 107; fighting in, 107–10, 111, 113, 115, 116, 117, 118, 119, 120, 122, 124, 127, 134, 135, 137, 141, 142, 144, 146, 150, 152, 155, 162, 170, 171, 172, 173, 179, 180, 300

Saint-Amand le Hameau, 90, 91, 107, 300

Saint Amand la Haye, 83, 90, 91, 92; Girard's attack on, 105–6, 107, 116, 118, 141, 300

Sart-à-Walhain, 186, 193, 194, 195, 198, 199, 200, 201, 202, 203, 204, 205, 206, 208, 211, 216, 218, 220, 221, 226, 248, 249, 255, 256

Sauvenière, 168, 187–8, 195, 205, 221, 255

Soleilmont Abbey, 48, 51, 52

Solre-sur-Sambre, 19, 65

Sombreffe, 15, 31, 33, 35, 46, 47, 55, 56, 62, 63, 68, 69, 71, 72, 73 74, 75, 76, 80,

81, 88–94, 96, 111, 127, 129–32, 134, 141, 143, 149, 151, 155, 159, 163, 165, 171, 183, 187, 188
Soult, Marshal, 4, 17, 18, 26, 27, 36, 37, 50, 56, 59, 65, 66, 67, 72, 73, 75, 78, 89, 98, 116, 120, 121, 124, 166, 169, 176, 178, 214, 215, 221, 255, 256, 259, 261, 262, 265, 266, 276, 277, 278
Soult, General, 28, 37, 38, 39, 40, 53, 54, 59, 77, 85, 131, 167, 199, 233, 241, 250, 251, 283, 293
Steinmetz, General, 33, 34, 107, 141, 287
Strolz, General, 192, 251, 283, 294
Stülpnagel, Colonel, 112, 122, 237 238, 241, 290
Subervie, General, 28, 38, 39, 40, 53, 54, 71, 77, 85, 108, 131, 132, 152,154, 158, 167, 178, 182, 194, 199, 215, 283, 293

Temploux, 163, 182, 187, 188, 199
Teste, General, 146, 147, 153, 154, 159, 163, 166, 167, 178, 179, 181, 184, 186, 187, 188, 194, 199, 212, 220, 233, 235, 236, 237, 239, 240, 242, 250, 251, 254, 267, 286, 294
Thielemann, General, deployment at Ligny, 92, 93, 94; action at Ligny, 127, 128, 130; attack at Ligny, 132; withdrawal from Ligny, 149, 150, 151, 159; at Gembloux, 183; withdrawal to Wavre, 186, 189; ordered to defend Dyle crossing at Wavre, 219; his force and deployment, 219; attacks Grouchy in the night of the 18th/19th, 237; learns of the outcome of Waterloo and resolves to attack, 240–2; is thrown back in disorder, 243; orders the retreat, 243–4; re-forms at Rhode-Sainte-Agathe, 251
Thuin, 23, 33, 35
Tilly, 151, 161, 189, 262, 267
Tippelskirch, General, 106, 288
Tongrenelle, 85, 90, 93, 95, 127, 128, 132
Tongrinne, 84, 85, 90, 91, 93, 94, 128, 129, 130, 134, 154, 159, 160, 163, 167
Tourinnes, 186, 192, 193, 198, 199, 205, 212, 250

Vallin, *Maréchal de Camp*, 150, 184, 187, 188, 193, 201, 212, 218, 232–35, 239, 241, 250, 254, 282, 293

Vandamme, General, 3, 4, 12, 19; late on the 15th, 35–9, participation at Gilly, 51–2; refuses to advance further, 54–7, 65; formally under Grouchy's command, 73, 82; deployment at Ligny, 93; his corps at Ligny, 99–102, 107–10, 125–6, 131, 134, 142; casualties at Ligny, 147, 158; part of the force to pursue the Prussians, 176; moves off from Ligny, 179; ordered to Gembloux, 185; moves off on the 18th, 193–4; meets Prussian rearguard, 216–17; his corps masses overlooking Wavre, 218; attacks Wavre against his orders, 221–2; his attacks on Wavre, 222–6; ordered to join Grouchy at Limal, 238; fails to do so, 239; captures Wavre, 243; suggests marching on the allied rear, 246, 250; relationship with Grouchy, 271–4; his ORBAT, 280, 291
Vichery, General, 41, 94, 110, 111, 141, 237, 238, 239, 240, 241, 250, 282, 292

Wagnelée, 90, 91, 93, 106, 107, 127, 131, 143, 144, 145, 150, 152, 300
Walcourt, 19, 30
Walhain, 186, 187, 196, 200, 201, 203, 206, 208, 210, 216, 228, 268, 272, 277
Wangenies, 53, 54, 60, 67, 71
Wavre, 63, 114, 137, 167, 186, 187; Prussian retreat to, 189, 191, 193, 195, 196, 197, 198, 199, 200, 201, 202, 203, 204, 205, 206, 207, 209, 211, 214, battle of, 215–34, 240–4
Wellington, Duke of, campaign plans, 15, 16; on the 15th, 60–1; receives news of French offensive, 76–7; meets Blücher at Brye, 77, 87–8; withdrawal from Quatre Bras, 190, 196

Young Guard, 18, 22, 38, 46, 47, 52, 55, 66, 74, 78, 95, 115, 116, 118, 119, 142, 147, 152, 279

Zenowicz, Colonel, 44, 213, 214, 220, 226, 244
Zieten, General, 31, 33, 34, 40, 46, 50, 51, 55, 56, 58, 60, 61, 64, 77, 92, 127, 142, 145, 287